Cinema and the Environment in Eastern Europe

Cinema and the Environment in Eastern Europe
From Communism to Capitalism

Edited by
Masha Shpolberg and Lukas Brasiskis

berghahn
NEW YORK • OXFORD
www.berghahnbooks.com

First published in 2024 by
Berghahn Books
www.berghahnbooks.com

© 2024 Masha Shpolberg and Lukas Brasiskis

All rights reserved. Except for the quotation of short passages
for the purposes of criticism and review, no part of this book
may be reproduced in any form or by any means, electronic or
mechanical, including photocopying, recording, or any information
storage and retrieval system now known or to be invented,
without written permission of the publisher.

Library of Congress Cataloging-in-Publication Data

A C.I.P. cataloging record is available from the Library of Congress

Library of Congress Cataloging in Publication Control Number: 2023017779

British Library Cataloguing in Publication Data

A catalogue record for this book is available from the British Library

ISBN 978-1-80539-105-0 hardback
ISBN 978-1-80539-375-7 epub
ISBN 978-1-80539-106-7 web pdf

https://doi.org/10.3167/9781805391050

Contents

List of Illustrations	vii
Acknowledgments	x
Introduction Masha Shpolberg and Lukas Brasiskis	1

Part I. Industrializing the Bloc: Cinema of the Socialist Period

Chapter 1. Sad and Bitter Landscapes: Ecology and the Built Environment in Czech and East German Photography and Film Katie Trumpener and Alice Lovejoy	21
Chapter 2. From Mastery to Indistinction: Nature in Thaw-Era Cinema Lida Oukaderova	49
Chapter 3. Specters of Ecology in Cold War Soviet Science Fiction Film Natalija Majsova	64

Part II. Environmental Crisis and the Nuclear Imaginary

Chapter 4. Postapocalyptic Landscapes: *The End of August at the Hotel Ozone* (1966) and the Czechoslovak New Wave Barbora Bartunkova	87
Chapter 5. Fallow Fields: Crises of Masculinity and Ecology in Piotr Andrejew's *Tender Spots* (1981) Eliza Rose	107
Chapter 6. Catastrophe, Obliquely: Soviet Documentaries about Chernobyl Masha Shpolberg	124

Part III. Animals between the Natural and the Social

Chapter 7. Is There a Place for the Animal? Shot Scale, Modernity, and the Urban Landscape in Lithuanian Documentary   147
Natalija Arlauskaitė

Chapter 8. Against Interpretation: Animals in Contemporary Hungarian Cinema   158
Raymond De Luca

Part IV. From Communism to Capitalism: Privatization and the Commons

Chapter 9. *Okraina* and "Oil Ontology" in Post-Soviet Russian Cinema   177
José Alaniz

Chapter 10. Upholding the Village, the Beach, the Last Resort: The (Threatened) Idyll in Bulgarian Cinema   196
Dina Iordanova

Part V. Toward an Eastern European Ecocinema

Chapter 11. Coming to the Senses: Environmental Ethics and the Limits of Narrative in Contemporary Slovenian Cinema   217
Meta Mazaj

Chapter 12. Cinema of the Forest People: From Environmental Consciousness Toward Ecocritical Perspectives in Polish (Post)communist Film   238
Kris Van Heuckelom

Chapter 13. Beyond the Utopian Landscape in Post-Soviet Russian Cinema   253
Michael Cramer and Jeremi Szaniawski

Chapter 14. Recycling, Citroën Cars, and Roma Refugees in Boris Mitić's *Pretty Dyana*
Alice Bardan   271

Chapter 15. Foggy Past, Windy Present: Elemental Critique in Recent East Central European Artists' Films
Lukas Brasiskis   288

Index   301

Illustrations

Figures

1.1. *Coal in the Soul* (*Ženy SHR*). Directed by Martin Dušek and Ondřej Provazník. Prague: Česká televize, 2010. Screen capture by Katie Trumpener and Alice Lovejoy.   31

1.2. *Memories of a Landscape—For Manuela* (*Erinnerung an einer Landschaft—für Manuela*). Directed by Kurt Tetzlaff. Berlin: DEFA, 1983. Screen capture by Katie Trumpener and Alice Lovejoy.   40

2.1. *Heat* (*Znoy*). Directed by Larisa Shepitko. Bishkek: Kyrgyzfilm, 1962. Screen capture by Lida Oukaderova.   57

2.2. *The Unsent Letter* (*Nieotpravlennoye pis'mo*). Directed by Mikhail Kalatozov, Moscow: Mosfilm, 1959. Screen capture by Lida Oukaderova.   59

3.1. *Toward a Dream* (*Mechte navstrechu*). Directed by Mikhail Karzhukov and Otar Koberidze. Odesa: Odesa Film Studio, 1963. Screen capture by Natalija Majsova.   69

3.2. *Per Aspera Ad Astra* (*Cherez ternii k zvyozdam*). Directed by Richard Viktorov. Moscow: Gorky Film Studio, 1981. Screen capture by Natalija Majsova.   77

5.1. *Tender Spots* (*Czułe miejsca*). Directed by Piotr Andrejew. Warsaw: Zespół Filmowy Kadr, 1981). Screen capture by Eliza Rose.   113

5.2. *Tender Spots* (*Czułe miejsca*). Directed by Piotr Andrejew. Warsaw: Zespół Filmowy Kadr, 1981). Screen capture by Eliza Rose.   114

6.1. *Chronicle of Difficult Weeks* (*Khronika trudnykh nedel'*). Directed by Vladimir Shevchenko. Kyiv: UkrKinoKhronika, 1986. Screen capture by Masha Shpolberg.   126

6.2. *The Bell of Chernobyl* (*Kolokol Chernobylia*). Directed by Rollan Sergienko and Vladimir Sinelnikov. Moscow: Tsentralnaya Studiya Dokumentalnykh Filmov, 1986. Screen capture by Masha Shpolberg.   131

7.1. *Time Passes through the City* (*Laikas eina per miestą*). Directed by Almantas Grikevičius. Vilnius: Lietuvos kino studija, 1966. Screen capture by Natalija Arlauskaite.   150

7.2. *The Old Man and the Land* (*Senis ir žemė*). Directed by Robertas Verba. Vilnius: Lietuvos kino studija, 1965. Screen capture by Natalija Arlauskaite.   152

8.1. *White God* (*Fehér isten*). Directed by Kornél Mundruczó. Budapest: Proton Cinema, and FilmPartners & Partners Film; Berlin: Pola Pandora Filmproduktions; Mainz: Zweites Deutsches Fernhesen; and Stockholm: The Chimney Pot Sweden, 2014. Screen capture by Raymond De Luca.   162

8.2. *On Body and Soul* (*Testről és lélekről*). Directed by Ildikó Enyedi. Budapest: Inforg-M&M Film, 2017. Screen capture by Raymond De Luca.   166

8.3. *The Turin Horse* (*A Torinói ló*). Directed by Béla Tarr and Ágnes Hranitzky. Budapest: T.T. Filmmuhely; Paris: MPM FILM; Zürich: Vega Film; Berlin: Zero Fiction Film GmbH, 2011. Screen capture by Raymond De Luca.   169

9.1. *The Outskirts* (*Okraina*). Directed by Pyotr Lutsik. Moscow: Goskino, 1998. Screen capture by José Alaniz.   183

9.2. "Death No More" ("Smerti bolshe net"). Directed by IC3PEAK/Nick and Nastya. Moscow, 2018. Screen capture by José Alaniz.   186

10.1. *The Fight with the Untouchable Ahmed Dogan Has Begun*. Directed by Hristo Ivanov, Ivailo Mirchev, and Dimitar Naydenov. Sofia, 2020. Screen capture from YouTube by Dina Iordanova.   197

10.2. *The Last Black Sea Pirates* (*Poslednite Chernomorski pirati*). Directed by Svetoslav Stoyanov. Sofia: Agitprop, 2014. Screen capture by Dina Iordanova.   205

11.1. Maja Smrekar's *ARTE_mis* installation, part of the *K-9 topology* project. Screen capture by Meta Mazaj from the artist's website.   227

11.2. *The Tree* (*Drevo*). Directed by Sonja Prosenc. Ljubljana: Monoo, Nuframe, Staragara Productions, and RTV Slovenia, 2014. Screen capture by Meta Mazaj. 230

12.1. *Spoor* (*Pokot*). Directed by Agnieszka Holland and Kasia Adamik. Warsaw: Studio Filmowe TOR; Köln: Heimatfilm; Prague: nutprodukce; Bratislava: nutprodukcia; Stockholm: The Chimney Pot Sweden, 2017. Screen capture by Kris Van Heuckelom. 248

12.2. *Essential Killing*. Directed by Jerzy Skolimowski. Warsaw: Skopia Film and Syrena Films; Bekkestua: Cylinder Productions; Dublin: Element Pictures; and Budapest: Mythberg Films, 2010. Screen capture by Kris Van Heuckelom. 249

13.1. *Me Too* (*Ya tozhe hochu*). Directed by Aleksei Balabanov. Saint Petersburg: CTB, 2012. Screen capture by Michael Cramer and Jeremi Szaniawski. 263

13.2. *Khrustalyov, My Car!* (*Khrustalyov, mashinu!*). Directed by Aleksei German. Saint Petersburg: Lenfilm, Studiya pervogo i eksperimentalnogo filma, and Petroagropromank; Moscow: RTR; and Paris: La Sept and Canal+, 1998. Screen capture by Michael Cramer and Jeremi Szaniawski. 266

14.1. *Pretty Dyana: A Gypsy Recycling Saga* (*Lijepa Dyana*). Directed by Boris Mitić. Belgrade: Dribbling Pictures, 2003. Screen capture by Alice Bardan. 275

14.2. *The Gendarme and the Gendarmettes* (*Le Gendarme et les gendarmettes*). Directed by Jean Giraud. Neuilly-sur-Seine: SNC, 1982. Screen capture by Alice Bardan. 282

15.1. *The Fog*. Created and directed by Ilona Németh. Bratislava: Slovak Ministry of Culture, 2013. Screen capture by Lukas Brasiskis from the artist's website. 292

15.2. *Almost Nothing*. Directed by Ana Hušman. Zagreb: Studio Pangolin, 2016. Screen capture by Lukas Brasiskis from the artist's website. 295

Table

5.1. Emasculation as the Central Dynamic of Piotr Andrejew's *Tender Spots* (*Czułe miejsca*, 1981). Table created by Eliza Rose. 117

Acknowledgments

Edited volumes are infamous for the length of time they take to come together. We would like to thank our editors at Berghahn—Chris Chappell, Amanda Horn, and Sulaiman Ahmad—for their faith in this project and continual support, as well as our production editor, Keara Hagerty, and copyeditor, Natalie Jones, and indexer Lisa Rivero, for making it a physical reality. for making it a physical reality. Our contributors produced sharp, insightful pieces beyond anything we could have imagined. We thank them for their labor, patience, and commitment. We began dreaming about this project when we were both still doctoral candidates, and we finished work on it having come into our own as scholars and programmers. Our mentors—Jean-Loup Bourget and Françoise Zamour at the Ecole Normale Supérieure, Katerina Clark, Charles Musser, Marci Shore, and Katie Trumpener at Yale University, and Antonia Lant, Allen Weiss, and Toby Lee at New York University—helped us have faith in ourselves through this process. Colleagues Codruța Morari, Tim Palmer, and Maria Sonevytsky provided priceless feedback. Finally, our families were there for us every step of the way. Our mothers, Angela Shpolberg and Beatričė Brašiškienė, have always pushed us to dream bigger than we dared, while Josh Glick drew on seemingly endless reserves of humor, wisdom, and experience to help us resolve various questions and dilemmas. This book is dedicated to them.

Introduction

Masha Shpolberg and Lukas Brasiskis

> He struts proudly across the North Pole
> Changes the rivers' direction
> Moves the high mountains
> The common Soviet man.[1]

Part of the promise of socialism, along with gender and class equality, was the rapid modernization and industrialization of the lands that would eventually become part of the Soviet Union and the socialist bloc. First the Soviet government and, later, that of the satellite states worked to drastically transform the landscape of the region, forcing collectivized farming onto the population and encouraging large-scale infrastructure projects, including the construction of dams, canals, mines, and nuclear power stations, many of which ultimately proved disastrous. The capitalist period that followed the collapse of the Soviet Union saw many of these projects crumble and decay as political elites adopted new, ever more extractive approaches to natural resources.

This rapid transformation and the attendant changes in the way nature was conceptualized, produced, and experienced were inevitably captured on camera. From the earliest days of the Soviet Union, cinema served as a privileged site for the education of the then largely illiterate masses and the promotion of government policy. After Stalin's death in 1953, cinema was able to adopt a more critical stance, at times simply recording the status quo and at others interrogating it and even striving to articulate alternative ways of being in the world. Thaw-era films celebrated the spontaneity of the meteorological, finding in its liveliness an antidote to the set, monumental forms of socialist realism. Andrei Tarkovsky's films blurred the distinction between inner and outer space, luxuriating in the sensorial pleasures of the natural world, and offering it up as an escape from the political and the social into something transcendent that preceded—and was bound to outlast—the Soviet system. In later films by the likes of Alexander Sokurov and Aleksei German, nature seems to densify into something that refuses all signification, that is simply there: a precondition of human existence and, perhaps, a reminder of its finitude.

Moreover, the speed at which this industrialization took place meant that the ranks of the new, Soviet proletariat drew extensively on the former peasantry, as films ranging from *The Radiant Path* (*Svetlyi put'*, 1940) to *Moscow Does Not Believe in Tears* (*Moskva slezam ne verit*, 1979) readily attest. This process was to be repeated in the Central and Eastern European satellite states once they were annexed in the aftermath of World War II. The working-class characters who populated both the silver screen and the theater thus did not resemble the multigenerational proletariat of countries like the United Kingdom or Italy, and the rise of the Village Prose movement in the 1970s spoke to the close ties many city dwellers maintained with the country. Finally, as Michael Cramer and Jeremi Szaniawski demonstrate in this volume, the popular imagination of Russia specifically, if not the entire region, can never be dissociated from its climate, geographic expanse, and vast natural resources.

Yet despite this complex and continuous engagement with the natural world, what we term "Eastern European ecocinema" remains critically understudied. Although rooted in the environmentalism of the 1970s, ecocriticism first coalesced as a methodological approach within the sphere of literary studies in the early to mid-1990s. As Ursula Heise and others have demonstrated, it concerned itself first with Romantic poetry and North American nature writing.[2] The consolidation of postcolonial studies during the same period led the pioneers of ecocriticism to turn their attention next to the literature of the "Global South"—and with good reason: as scientists and humanities scholars grew aware of the dramatic changes taking place in the earth's atmosphere, it became clear that it was the inhabitants of this part of the world who stood to pay the steepest price for the unmitigated activity of those who had colonized and enslaved them. A number of groundbreaking works have sought to reconcile the interest in ecocriticism with "the postcolonial turn," and have gone on to explore how climate justice may, and *ought*, to go hand in hand with social and economic justice.[3]

This shift in attention from what was once known as the First World to the Third World, however, has tended to overlook the Second. The collapse of communist regimes in 1989–91 meant that it was old news at the time these approaches were first taking off in Western academia.

Individual scholars have explored the landscape painting of Isaac Levitan or the exceptional nature writing of canonical literary figures such as Leo Tolstoy, Ivan Turgenev, and Mikhail Prishvin.[4] To our knowledge, however, there has been no attempt thus far to apply a systematically ecocritical approach to the region's art, literature, or cinema. It is our sincere hope that this volume will spark more interest in the subject and that more volumes, monographs, and articles will follow.[5]

The Historical and Geographical Frame

The region's all-too-recent agrarian past as well as the scope and ambition of the Soviet project mean that, once one begins looking at its cultural output ecocritically, one is spoiled for riches. Early Soviet cinema offers remarkably rich material for such an inquiry (one has only to think of the films produced during the first Five Year Plan, such as Sergei Eisenstein's *The Old and the New* [*Staroye i novoye*, 1929], Oleksandr Dovzhenko's *Earth* [*Zemlia*, 1930], or Dziga Vertov's *Enthusiasm: Symphony of the Donbass* [*Entuziazm: simfoniya donbassa*, 1931]). We have decided, however, to focus our attention on the postwar period. First, as Astrid Mignon Kirchhof and J. R. McNeill point out, the rise of environmental movements on both sides of the iron curtain is intimately tied up with the politics and policies of the Cold War.[6] Second, the detonation of the world's first atomic bomb on 16 July 1945 (known as the Trinity Test) is one of the events suggested by scholars as the beginning of the Anthropocene: a new geological period in which humanity—primarily through its mining of natural resources and pollution of the atmosphere—has itself become a geological force.[7]

The roughly two thousand nuclear arms tests carried out since 1945 have contributed to climate change in the most direct of ways.[8] Moreover, their specific effect on the atmosphere has provided one of the least controversial proofs of humanity's ability to influence the environment on a massive scale. While Soviet industrial and civil engineering projects of the 1930s, such as the White Sea–Baltic Canal, often had dire consequences on the local and even the regional level, it took the atomic bomb to make humanity aware of the fragility of the planet as a whole. Consequently, over the course of the Cold War period, atomic power progressively replaced pollution as the environmental movements' chief concern. In the Soviet case one sees this in the progression from a film like Sergei Gerasimov's *By the Lake* (*U ozera*, 1969) to Andrei Tarkovsky's *Stalker* (*Stalker*, 1979) and Konstantin Lopushansky's *Dead Man's Letters* (*Pisma mertvogo cheloveka*, 1986). Likewise, on both sides of the iron curtain, major accidents—Three Mile Island in 1979, Chernobyl in 1986—became turning points in the mainstreaming of environmental consciousness. And while these nuclear power plants responded entirely to civilian energy needs, the image of atomic power could never quite be dissociated from that of nuclear weapons. It is only logical that the beginning of the end for the USSR was marked by Gorbachev and Reagan's 1988 agreement on denuclearization.

Taking 1945 as our starting point thus highlights the importance of attending to the space formerly part of, or dominated by, the Soviet Union, all the while addressing some of the key debates surrounding the usefulness of "the Anthropocene" as a critical framework. In addition to signifying the beginning of the nuclear age, the year 1945, according to environmental historians J. R. McNeill and Peter Engelke, is the moment when "the Great Acceleration" becomes observable.[9] The authors use this term to refer to an exponential rise in human activity, including (among other things) population growth, natural resource use, and the production of greenhouse gasses. Since the idea of the Anthropocene has been introduced, a number of scholars have pushed back against it on the grounds that it transforms all of humanity (the *anthropos*) into a single force bearing equal responsibility, whereas in reality the segment of the population driving the Great Acceleration is not the same as the one that stands to suffer the most from it. This has led scholars Andreas Malm and Jason W. Moore to suggest "the Capitalocene" as an alternative term, one that makes the connection between the degradation of the environment and the capitalist socioeconomic order more explicit.[10]

We hope that this volume will complicate this discourse by providing examples of equally problematic approaches to natural resources by soi-disant communist and socialist states, and glimpses of the way cultural production, untethered from economic demand, might provide something like hope—or at least genuine critique. Thus far, too, scholars interested in the cultural dynamics that have enabled and reflected the Great Acceleration have tended to examine capitalism primarily as lived and experienced in the West. Part of what makes Eastern Europe such rich ground for this kind of analysis is its transition from a planned state economy to a free-market one in the 1990s. Continuing our exploration past the collapse of communism in 1989–91 and into the present day allows us to examine—as José Alaniz's chapter on Russian petro-cinema makes all too clear—the charms that fossil capitalism holds for populations caught somewhere in between the developing and developed worlds.

Narrowing our scope temporally also allows us to broaden it geographically. In addition to marking the start of the Cold War, 1945 saw the progressive instauration of puppet regimes loyal to the Soviet Union across Central and Eastern Europe. In this volume, we make a concerted effort to consider the cinema of the former Soviet Union alongside that of East

Germany, Czechoslovakia, Poland, Hungary, and some of the Baltic and Balkan states. Our initial motivation for doing so was entirely personal and partisan. While it is understandable that Russia, as the largest country in the region, should receive the lion's share of scholarly attention, it continues to overshadow its neighbors. In this way, academic scholarship reproduces Russia's imperialist and colonialist practices. Hailing from Ukraine and Lithuania respectively, we are committed to a truly regional approach that de-centers Soviet and Russian cinema in order to give the cinemas of the former republics and Warsaw Pact countries their due. Since Russia's invasion of Ukraine in February 2022, this has become all the more urgent. At the same time, we genuinely believe such an approach to be more generative. As Kirchhof and McNeill point out, environmental policy varied widely between the republics that constituted the Soviet Union proper and the satellite states.[11] So, too, did models of film production and censorship. Considering Soviet cinema alongside the cinema of these nations helps to check some of our assumptions about the region, allows new patterns to emerge, and sensitizes us to variations in style and form.

A comparative approach is just as productive when we consider the postcommunist period. While East and West Germany merged immediately after the fall of the Berlin Wall in 1989, the other satellite states maintained widely varying ties to the former USSR throughout the tumultuous 1990s. In the 2000s, however, their fates began to differ. In 2004, Poland, Hungary, the Czech Republic, and Slovakia acceded to the European Union along with Lithuania, Latvia, and Estonia. In 2007, they were followed by Bulgaria and Romania. The result has been a fundamental divide between countries that have accepted the environmental policies and standards of Western Europe and those that continue to hold themselves to far less stringent standards. Considering the period from 1945 to the present day allows us to register some of this nuance, all the while providing us with an opportunity to examine cinema produced in the same place under two vastly different political and economic regimes.

That said, this volume represents a first look at the region's ecocinematic output and is not meant to be exhaustive. It is our hope that it opens new avenues for research and inspires other scholars to fill in the gaps present here. In putting the volume together, we were limited by both practical considerations such as length and scholarly ones—namely, the difficulty of securing chapters on some of the more understudied national cinemas, genres, and modes. We are particularly pained by the lack of a chapter that would take into account the robust cinematic tradition of Romania as well as our rather limited engagement with the cinema of both the Baltic states and the former Yugoslavia. Likewise, we are aware of the debates surrounding the proper way to refer to this region, and agree with scholars arguing that Hungary, Poland, and the former East Germany belong to Central, rather than Eastern, Europe. In our discussions with colleagues about this, a consensus emerged that the countries roughly grouped together as "Central Europe" were defined by a shared Austro-Hungarian past. We have decided to adopt "Eastern Europe" for our title not out of any kind of ideological resistance, but rather to signal our desire to think instead across the Soviet Union-satellite state divide.

Wary of not spreading ourselves too thin, we have also chosen not to take on the former USSR as a whole. We were thus not able to give the cinema of the former Caucasian and Central Asian republics the attention they deserve—nor, for that matter, Siberia, a region with an identity stronger than that of many former republics. Both the Caucasian and Central Asian republics have a rich history of poetic cinema and poetic documentary, much of it celebrating the local landscape. Moreover, as Lida Oukaderova's chapter reminds us, many Central Asian republics specifically became the site of disastrous Soviet agrarian and environmental projects: one has only to think of the Virgin Lands campaign or the drying up of the Aral Sea. Finally, Siberia's harsh climate and seemingly endless expanse has attracted countless filmmakers from elsewhere, be it the European part of Russia (Andrei Konchalovsky, once again Sokurov) or Germany (Werner Herzog).[12] It thus raises the question of what counts as "Siberian cinema" and whether there can even be a "Siberian cinema" that is not, essentially, always an ecocinema.

The Siberian case also highlights the advantages of adopting a regional approach, be it on the intra- or inter-national scale. Ursula Heise has shown that ecocritical discourse tends to privilege either the "local" or the "global."[13] In restoring the middle term "regional," we hope to give due consideration to a sense of embeddedness that transcends the familiarity of the local but stops short of the disempowering vagueness of the global. Finally, we recognize that while environmental policy is administered primarily on the level of the nation-state, ecosystems know no borders. As Elena Past points out, "ecocriticism frequently concerns itself with geological formations and material agents (mountains, oceans, winds, mutable riverbeds, dirt, to name a few) that crisscross and complicate national boundaries. Environmental crises ... disregard the limits of the nation state."[14] The same reflection leads Pietari Kääpä, coeditor of the seminal volume *Transnational Ecocinema* (2013), to "challenge the centrality of nations in ecological thinking."[15] Alice Lovejoy and Katie Trumpener's chapter in this volume on photographic and cinematic representations of the Ore Mountains demonstrates just how rich the payoff of such an approach can be. Though it remains an exception in this regard, we hope the regional focus of the volume as a whole will encourage more transnational framings.

Defining "Ecocinema"

Since Scott MacDonald's groundbreaking 2004 article "Toward an Eco-Cinema," scholars have been debating what exactly the term means and how it differs from its older cousin, "environmental cinema."[16] MacDonald introduced the term "ecocinema" initially to describe what he saw as a small but stable trickle of noncommercial films concerned with "preserving 'Nature,' or more precisely," with providing "an evocation of the experience of being immersed in the natural world."[17] Though these films may revel in natural beauty, their tone is decidedly solemn: they operate under a double shadow of annihilation—ours as a species, and nature's as something vast and wild. MacDonald opens his piece by evoking the rapid shrinking of the wilderness and the increasing fragility of ecosystems. As human awareness of the danger has grown, so too have the stakes of these films; no longer content to merely celebrate the natural world or preserve it on film, they now actively seek to "retrain" our senses: "to use spectatorship as a way of expanding our attention span, refining our perceptions of natural process, and making deeper contact with dimensions of existence that have always sustained us."[18] Implicit in MacDonald's article is the hope that if only we might learn to see the world differently, we might act differently as well.

The examples MacDonald provides are all art films, more specifically works of "slow cinema" that privilege observational long takes and little to no narrative. As chance would have it, the first example he offers is an Eastern European one—Andrej Zdravič's film *Riverglass: A River Ballet in Four Seasons* (*V steklu reke*, 1997), discussed by Meta Mazaj in chapter 11. It is easy to imagine how this form encourages a more attentive approach to the natural world—one that teaches us to see it for its own sake, beyond the aesthetic pleasure or utilitarian value it might provide us. In this way, "ecocinema" pursues a very different aim, with a very different set of tools, than narrative-driven "environmental" films like *Erin Brockovich* (2000) or even documentaries like *An Inconvenient Truth* (2006).

MacDonald, in his article, sought to pinpoint a very specific type of film. Since then, however, scholars have tended to broaden the scope of "ecocinema"—in large part due to a radical expansion in the way the concept of ecology has been used and understood. Already in 2005, Pat Brereton remarked that "ecology has become a new, all-inclusive, yet often contradictory meta-narrative."[19] Ten years later, Nadia Bozak would echo this view, explaining that "ecology, by its very definition, is unrestricted; it is impossible to say where nature stops and culture begins, or vice versa."[20] This has led scholars to reexamine everything, from films produced in studio lots to those brought into being entirely on a computer, in terms of their relationship to ecology, and to focus on the content as well as the resources consumed in the very act of production.[21] "It is very difficult to delineate a non-ecological type of cinema," Pietari Kääpä writes, noting that the category has come to include everything "from science fiction to urban crime thrillers, from westerns to fantasy."[22] Jennifer Fay has made the case for a genre as unlikely as film noir, arguing that in its rejection of futurity (of marriages, children), it teaches us the kind of radical pessimism we most need to learn in the age of the Anthropocene.[23] All of this has led scholars like Elena Past to conclude that ecocinema "is an interpretive approach, not a genre"—one that "can be used to describe the aesthetic style or narrative content of films."[24]

This is the inclusive, process-oriented vision of ecocinema that we would like to adopt in this volume. We are far less interested in adjudicating what "counts" as ecocinema than in learning to see films—all films—ecocritically. This volume includes analyses of fiction films and documentaries, works that rely on film stock and digitally produced video art. Following in the footsteps of Elena Past's *Italian Cinema Beyond the Human* (2019), Tommy Gustafsson and Pietari Kääpä's *Transnational Ecocinema* (2013) and Sheldon H. Lu and Jiayan Mi's *Chinese Ecocinema* (2009), we hope to simultaneously expand the canon of global ecocinema and the toolbox of attendant interpretive strategies.

Additionally, we believe that engaging with Eastern European ecocinema will deepen our understanding of each side of that term. The aforementioned rapid industrialization of the region, though genuinely embraced by many at first, increasingly came to be seen in the satellite states as a Soviet imposition. Attending to echoes of this shift in the region's cinema allows us to begin untangling the complex relationship between environmentalism, nationalism, and (anti-)communism. The region has also historically known a great deal of ethnic strife and continues to deal with widespread discrimination on the basis of race and sexual orientation. This has led many scholars in recent years to turn their attention to the reasons why, and the means by which, Eastern Europe constructs its "others." Ecocinema allows us to come at this question from a somewhat unusual angle by exploring these films' articulations of a much more radical otherness, and how we might still find ways of relating to it—or at least respecting it. Thus, while turning to ecocinema breaks new ground in Eastern European area studies, it also allows us to approach some of the discipline's traditional concerns from a new perspective.

At the same time, the region offers a much richer vision of what ecocinema has been and what it can be. As David Ingram has put it, the central problem of ecocinema is that "environmental problems such as global warming, ozone pollution, industrial pollution ... are usually slow to develop, not amenable to fast solutions and are often caused by factors both invisible and complex."[25] This makes them hard to capture on film, particularly given the relatively short time frame of most productions. It also makes them hard to address within "the commercial formulae of Hollywood."[26] While the invisibility and complexity of these forces remained a challenge on both sides of the iron curtain, Eastern European cinema during the communist period was not subject to the same economic constraints—and, consequently, to popular tastes. The state-sponsored system, while censoring any political disaccord, made it possible for filmmakers to occasionally tiptoe away from an anthropocentric model of storytelling in the direction of what Paula Willoquet-Maricondi has termed an "ecocentric" one: a cinema that accords an equally important place to flora, fauna, and the elements as it does to humans.[27] This has led to a greater diversity of approaches. Finally, the sudden shift from a socialist model to a capitalist one in the 1990s allows us to track some of the same processes that have shaped the representation of nature in the West but in far more brutal and condensed form. For all these reasons, we believe that excavating Eastern European ecocinema will transform not only our understanding of the region's cinema and cultural heritage more broadly, but also our understanding of ecocinema as such.

The Structure of the Volume

This volume is structured in roughly chronological order, with slight modifications to allow for thematic clusters. Part I, titled "Industrializing the Bloc: Cinema of the Socialist Period," explores the production and administration of nature in the extended postwar period. Alice Lovejoy and Katie Trumpener's chapter opens the volume with a searing description of Cold War colonialism: the establishment of Wismut, a Soviet uranium mine in East Germany, and filmmakers' attempts to address its legacy on screen. Broadening out to consider the entire mineral-rich region of the Ore Mountains, they show how resource extraction tends to blur borders—particularly in places like Eastern Europe where those borders have been continuously redrawn. Their analysis of the way the region was portrayed—first as a land of opportunity and later as a land of devastation—draws on a wide array of nonfiction media including newsreels, documentaries, and photo essays produced between 1950 and 1993. Comparing representations across time and media, Lovejoy and Trumpener uncover the sedimented layers of the region's geological, political, and cultural history.

Lida Oukaderova's chapter argues that this period represents a watershed moment in the Soviet attitude toward nature—almost literally so, given the ubiquitous rain, puddles, and streams in Thaw-era films. Through close readings of four fiction features, including Mikhail Kalatozov's *The First Echelon* (*Pervyi eshelon*, 1955) and *The Unsent Letter* (*Nieotpravlennoye pis'mo*, 1960), Oleksandr Dovzhenko and Yulia Solntseva's *Poem of the Sea* (*Poema o morye*, 1958), and Larisa Shepitko's *Heat* (*Znoi*, 1962), Oukaderova demonstrates the progressive emancipation of nature from "the state's ends-oriented gaze." Where Oukaderova's chapter focuses on the shifting relationship to nature in films very much focused on the Soviet present, Natalija Majsova examines the u-/dystopian dimension of a genre very much privileged in the USSR: science fiction. Working through a range of examples from the early 1960s until the early 1980s, Majsova outlines what was possible in terms of imagining human/nonhuman relations and points to the correlation, even in this most experimental of genres, between anthropo- and androcentrism. Scholars of ecocinema and science fiction who are not specialists of Eastern Europe will also be delighted by the chapter's analysis of Roger Corman's reedited, American versions of the Soviet *Planet of the Storms* (*Planeta bur'*, 1962). The three chapters in this section thus allow us to trace the major shift that took place in the perception of nature and the relationship between the human and nonhuman worlds from the late 1950s through the 1960s across three major filmmaking modes: nonfiction, realist fiction, and science fiction.

Part II, titled "Environmental Crisis and the Nuclear Imaginary," forms a thematic cluster that extends this analysis into the 1980s. Already in 1965, Susan Sontag pointed out that the "disaster film" had become a staple of American cinema. It is one of the most striking contrasts of the Cold War period that the fallout of nuclear war, and environmental disaster more broadly, could not be addressed directly in the Soviet bloc. As historian Miriam Dobson puts it, "imagining the destructive power of atomic weapons was antithetical to the forward-looking spirit of the communist project."[28] Most of the anxieties generated by the nuclear age were fed into science fiction where, as Majsova's chapter demonstrates, they were conveniently displaced onto other planets, legible as stand-ins for the earth in some hypothetical distant future only to the intellectual elite.

This section examines the rare exceptions to the rule. Barbora Bartunkova's chapter focuses on the Czechoslovak New Wave gem *The End of August at the Hotel Ozone* (*Konec srpna v hotelu Ozon*, 1967)—the earliest Soviet bloc representation of an Earth devastated by nuclear war. Eliza Rose shifts to Poland to analyze another highly unusual film, Piotr Andrejew's

Tender Spots (*Czułe miejsca*, 1981), which takes place after some unnamed event has left water scarce and the air contaminated. As a radio voice-over explains, it is humanity's twilight hour, with enough resources left to support human life only for another ten years.

What these two films share, alongside the Soviet *Stalker* (1979), *Dead Man's Letters* (1986), and, somewhat unexpectedly, the Polish hit comedy *Sexmission* (*Seksmisja*, 1984), is that they all start *after*. The disaster, if invoked at all, is represented as an ellipsis, a cut from the foreboding countdown that opens *Hotel Ozone* to the world many years hence. Where the Hollywood genre serves largely as a hook on which to hang special effects and striking imagery (leading David Ingram to describe these films as "perversely attractive"), its Eastern European counterpart eschews both the spectacle and the attendant melodrama.[29] Its protagonists are not individual survivors, heroes who prove their mettle by rescuing others, but condemned men and women who must adapt or perish. History ends not with a bang but with a drawn-out groan.

In all but the Soviet films, the collapse of civilization results in a return to matriarchy, often with women the sole survivors. Both Bartunkova and Rose attend to these provocative shifts in gender dynamics, interrogating whether they truly are as progressive as they first seem. In this way, they participate in the rich, ongoing conversation between ecocriticism and women's and gender studies.[30] Masha Shpolberg's chapter completes this section by considering what Eastern European cinema had to do when faced not with the threat of nuclear disaster but with the event itself. Olga Briukhovetska and Johanna Lindbladh have written compelling accounts elsewhere of the way the Chernobyl disaster has been narrated in Eastern European fiction film.[31] In her chapter, Shpolberg turns instead to two little-known documentaries produced in the days immediately following the disaster. She examines the way in which these draw on the conventions of the essay film, one of the first filmmaking modes to explicitly tackle "unbearable" or "unrepresentable" subject matter, as well as the unique affordances of analog technology in the face of "an invisible and inaudible enemy," as one of the films puts it.

Part III presents another thematic cluster focusing on animals as creatures caught between the natural realm and the social order. Natalija Arlauskaitė justly remarks that up until recently, stray cats and dogs were a fairly common sight in Eastern European cities. She proposes the term "animals-out-of-place" to describe encounters that take place neither in the sanctioned "wild" nor in domestic settings but rather on city streets. She then traces the meanderings of these figures through a number of Lithuanian documentaries produced from the mid-1960s to the present day, paying particular attention to the philosophical and ethical implications of the camera framing. In his exploration of recent Hungarian films, Raymond De Luca, in turn, tackles one of the central questions posed by Paula Willoquet-Maricondi in her seminal edited volume *Framing the World* (2010): "how can film bring about concern for and identification with the nonhuman without anthropomorphizing it, essentially inviting us to cross species lines in order to connect and empathize?"[32] Reminding us that "celluloid, the very stuff of film, is processed with animal cartilage and bone" and thus "the history of cinema is contingent upon broken animal bodies," De Luca attempts a process of restitution, analyzing the animals' role in the films while refusing to sacrifice them once more—this time to allegory.

The chapters brought together in part IV, "From Communism to Capitalism: Privatization and the Commons," address one of the most painful aspects of the post-1989 transition: the plunder of the region's industrial infrastructure, previously publicly owned lands, and natural resource deposits. The result, especially in countries that did not join the European Union later on, has been unabated resource extraction by powerful elites and flagrant flouting of environmental policy. José Alaniz goes straight to the heart of the matter in a chapter exploring the "oil ontology" of post-Soviet Russian cinema. Alaniz examines how both mainstream representations, such as music videos, and more experimental ones, ranging from art cinema to protest art, try to give audiovisual and narrative form to this traditionally invisible and amorphous yet critical fluid. Dina Iordanova, in turn, considers what remains of the commons—in this particular case, a hard-to-reach part of the Bulgarian Black Sea coast. The first part of her chapter provides an overview of a subgenre of Bulgarian socialist films featuring a romantic escape from urban life to the sea. The second part focuses on *The Last Black Sea Pirates* (*Poslednite Chernomorski pirati*, 2014), a documentary about a ragtag group of eccentrics who choose to live without modern conveniences on this remote beach—and whose future is threatened by plans to erect a luxury resort there.

Finally, part V, "Toward an Eastern European Ecocinema," is dedicated to chapters that make the case for distinctive national traditions of ecocinema within Eastern Europe. Meta Mazaj's chapter begins with an overview of the filmic and photographic experiments carried out by the well-known Slovenian OHO Group during the socialist period. Mazaj goes on to connect these experiments with the more recent work of pioneering ecocinema filmmaker Andrej Zdravič, the performance artist Maja Smrekar, and art cinema director Sonja Prosenc. In this way, Mazaj sketches a history of Slovenian artists' and filmmakers' engagement with the environment from the late 1960s to the present. Kris Van Heuckelom adopts a similarly transhistoric approach, tracing the motif of the forest as a quintessentially Polish landscape from the nineteenth century to the present day, and demonstrating how it has informed one of the most unusual films of the 1990s, Grzegorz Królikiewicz's *Trees* (*Drzewa*, 1995) as well as Agnieszka Holland's more recent *Spoor* (*Pokot*, 2017). Michael Cramer and Jeremi Szaniawski demonstrate that the figuration of nature—whether as transcendent or abject, epic or prosaic—is central to the work of the four greatest Russian auteurs of the post-Soviet period: Alexander Sokurov, Aleksei Balabanov, Aleksei German, and Andrey Zvyagintsev. Finally, Lukas Brasiskis considers the ways the elemental can be harnessed for social and political critique in recent artists' cinema from Slovakia and Croatia.

Though we have tried to ensure the broadest possible coverage in terms of geography and filmmaking practices, this edited volume can only be a start. The chapters included here primarily offer close readings of individual films that have either not received much attention before or have not yet been considered from an ecocritical point of view. We see ample room in the future for an approach that might emphasize institutional practices or take into account the role played by distribution networks and sites of reception. At the same time, we hope that the chapters collected here begin to build up an alternative canon of Eastern European ecocinema—one that reveals new and exciting ways of thinking about the triangulation of the environment, the cinematic apparatus, and human perception.

Masha Shpolberg is Assistant Professor of Film and Electronic Arts at Bard College. Her teaching and research explore global documentary, Russian, Eastern, and Central European cinema, ecocinema, and women's cinema. She is currently at work on a book titled *Labor in Late Socialism: The Cinema of Polish Workers' Unrest*, which explores how filmmakers responded to successive waves of strikes by co-opting, confronting, or otherwise challenging the representational legacy of socialist realism. In addition to this volume, she is also co-editor, with Anastasia Kostina, of *The New Russian Documentary: Reclaiming Reality in the Age of Authoritarianism*, a volume forthcoming from Edinburgh University Press. She holds a PhD in Comparative Literature and Film and Media Studies from Yale University.

Lukas Brasiskis is a film and media researcher and curator, with a PhD in Cinema Studies from New York University. He is an adjunct professor at NYU and CUNY/Brooklyn College and an Associate Curator of Film and Video for e-flux. His interests include eco-media, the politics and aesthetics of world cinema, and the intersections between philosophy, moving-image cultures, and the contemporary art world. His texts were previously published in journals such as *Found Footage Magazine*, *The Cine-Files*, *Screening the Past*, and *Senses of Cinema*. He is a co-editor of *Jonas Mekas: The Camera Was Always Running* (2022).

Notes

1. Lyrics by Vasili Lebedev-Kumach from the popular 1937 song "The Common Soviet Man." Original Russian: "По полюсу гордо шагает / Меняет движение рек / Высокие горы сдвигает / Советский простой человек." Translation by Masha Shpolberg.
2. Heise, "Globality, Difference, and the International Turn."
3. For more, see Adamson, Evans, and Stein, *The Environmental Justice Reader* (2002), Martinez-Alier, *The Environmentalism of the Poor* (2004), and Huggan and Tiffin, *Postcolonial Ecocriticism* (2010) as well as Monani, Arreglo, and Chiu, "Coloring the Environmental Lens."
4. Richard Fleck goes so far as to anoint Prishvin the "Russian Thoreau." See Fleck, "Mikhail Prishvin."
5. Recent years have seen increasing attention to Russian environmental history, reflected in Josephson et al., eds., *An Environmental History of Russia*; Oldfield and Shaw, *The Development of Russian Environmental Thought*; Breyfogle, *Eurasian Environments*; Peterson, *Troubled Lands*; and Moon, Breyfogle, and Bekasova, eds., *Place and Nature*. Another work reexamining Eastern European history from a similar angle is Olšáková, *In the Name of the Great Work*.
6. Kirchhof and McNeill, *Nature and the Iron Curtain*, 3.
7. Zalasiewicz et al., "When Did the Anthropocene Begin?" Other proposed dates for the beginning of the Anthropocene link it to the Industrial Revolution (particularly the invention of the steam engine in 1780s) or the rise of European world empires in the early 1600s. (For more, see Crutzen and Stoermer, "The Anthropocene"; Biello, "Mass Deaths in Americas"; Steffen et al., "Planetary Boundaries"; and Lewis et al., "Defining the Anthropocene."

    Bruno Latour articulates the stakes of these debates well, explaining that the farther away in time we locate the origins of the Anthropocene, the more diffuse the responsibility becomes. If we locate it in 1945, we point to a particular political and economic model that has only grown stronger after the collapse of the Three Worlds system. If we locate it further away in the late 1700s or early 1600s, the culprit begins to look more like human nature than a particular social, political, and economic regime. See Latour, *Facing Gaia*, 138–139.
8. "A Tally of Nuclear Tests." For a detailed history of nuclear testing, see Miller, *Under the Cloud*.
9. McNeill and Engelke, *The Great Acceleration*.
10. Malm, *Fossil Capital*; Moore, *Capitalism in the Web of Life*; and Moore, ed., *Anthropocene or Capitalocene?* Donna Haraway contends that the "Anthropocene" and "Capitalocene" both too easily lead to defeatism and suggests yet another term, the "Chthlucene" (from the Greek *chthonios* for that which lies in the depths the Earth), for the present epoch in which humans will need to learn to "make kin" with other life forms because they act on the world together. See Haraway, *Staying with the Trouble*.
11. Kirchhof and McNeill, *Nature and the Iron Curtain*, 3.

12. For a comprehensive introduction at least to the image of Siberia on screen (if not necessarily Siberian ecocinema), see Sitnikova, "The Image of Siberia."
13. Heise, *Sense of Place and Sense of Planet*, 3–13.
14. Past, *Italian Cinema Beyond the Human*, 3.
15. Kääpä, "Transnational Approaches to Ecocinema," 27.
16. MacDonald, "Toward an Eco-Cinema."
17. Idem., 108.
18. Idem., 111.
19. Brereton, *Hollywood Utopia*, 11.
20. Bozak, *The Cinematic Footprint*, 15.
21. Bozak's *The Cinematic Footprint* (2011) and Hunter Vaughan's *Hollywood's Dirtiest Secret: The Hidden Environmental Costs of the Movies* (New York: Columbia University Press, 2019) embody this latter approach.
22. Kääpä, "Transnational Approaches to Ecocinema," 27.
23. Fay, *Inhospitable World*, 97–127.
24. Past, *Italian Cinema Beyond the Human*, 3.
25. David Ingram, presentation at the conference "Arts and Ecology: Toward an Eco-cinema," Bristol, UK, 28–29 September 2005, as quoted in Willoquet-Maricondi, *Framing the World*, 49.
26. Ibid.
27. Willoquet-Maricondi, *Framing the World*.
28. Dobson, "Building Peace, Fearing the Apocalypse?"
29. Ingram, as quoted in Willoquet-Maricondi, *Framing the World*, 49.
30. For more, see Belmont, "Ecofeminism and the Natural Disaster Heroine"; Sturgeon, *Environmentalism in Popular Culture*; and Gaard, "New Directions for Ecofeminism."
31. Briukhovetska, "'Nuclear Belonging,'" and Lindbladh, "Representations of the Chernobyl Catastrophe."
32. Willoquet-Maricondi, *Framing the World*, 50.

Bibliography

"A Tally of Nuclear Tests." *Reuters Graphics*, 22 September 2017. http://fingfx.thomsonreuters.com/gfx/rngs/NORTHKOREA-MISSILES/010050Y324P/index.html. Accessed April 22, 2023.

Adamson, Joni, Mei Mei Evans, and Rachel Stein. *The Environmental Justice Reader*. Tucson, AZ: The University of Arizona Press, 2002.

Barcz, Anna. *Environmental Cultures in Soviet East Europe: Literature, History, and Memory*. London: Bloomsbury Academic, 2020.

Belmont, Cynthia. "Ecofeminism and the Natural Disaster Heroine." *Women's Studies* 36 (2007): 349–372.

Biello, David. "Mass Deaths in Americas Start New CO2 Epoch." *Scientific American* (11 March 2015).

Bozak, Nadia. *The Cinematic Footprint*. New Brunswick, NJ: Rutgers University Press, 2011.

Brereton, Pat. *Hollywood Utopia: Ecology in Contemporary American Cinema*. Bristol: Intellect Books, 2005.

Breyfogle, Nicholas. *Eurasian Environments: Nature and Ecology in Imperial Russian and Soviet History*. Pittsburgh: University of Pittsburgh Press, 2018.

Briukhovetska, Olga. "'Nuclear Belonging': 'Chernobyl' in Belarussian, Ukrainian (and Russian) Films." In *Contested Interpretations of the Past in Polish, Russian, and Ukrainian Film: Screen as Battlefield*, edited by Sander Brouwer, 95–121. Leiden and Boston: Brill Rodopi, 2010.

Crutzen, Paul, and Eugene Stoermer. "The Anthropocene." *Global Change Newsletter* 41 (May 2000): 12–18.

Dobson, Miriam. "Building Peace, Fearing the Apocalypse? Nuclear Danger in Soviet Cold War Culture." In *Understanding the Imaginary War: Culture, Thought, and Nuclear Conflict, 1945–1990*, edited by Matthew Grant and Benjamin Ziemann, 51–74. Manchester: Manchester University Press, 2016.

Fay, Jennifer. *Inhospitable World: Cinema in the Time of the Anthropocene*. Oxford: Oxford University Press, 2018.

Fleck, Richard. "Mikhail Prishvin: A Russian Thoreau." *The Concord Saunterer* 9, no. 2 (June 1974): 11–13.

Gaard, Greta. "New Directions for Ecofeminism: Toward a More Feminist Ecocriticism." *Interdisciplinary Studies in Literature and Environment* 17, no. 4 (2010): 643–665.

Gustafsson, Tommy, and Pietari Kääpä, eds. *Transnational Ecocinema: Film Culture in an Era of Ecological Transformation*. Bristol and Chicago: Intellect Books, 2013.

Haraway, Donna K. *Staying with the Trouble: Making Kin in the Chthulucene*. Durham, NC: Duke University Press, 2016.

Heise, Ursula. *Sense of Place and Sense of Planet: The Environmental Imagination of the Global*. Oxford: Oxford University Press, 2008.

———. "Globality, Difference, and the International Turn in Ecocriticism." *PMLA* 128, no. 3 (2013): 636–643.

Huggan, Graham and Helen Tiffin. *Postcolonial Ecocriticism: Literature, Animals, Environment*. London: Routledge, 2020.

Josephson, Paul, et al., eds. *An Environmental History of Russia*. Cambridge: Cambridge University Press, 2013.

Kirchhof, Astrid Mignon, and J. R. McNeill. *Nature and the Iron Curtain*. Pittsburgh: Pittsburgh University Press, 2019.

Latour, Bruno. *Facing Gaia: Eight Lectures on the New Climactic Regime*. Trans. Catherine Porter. Medford and Cambridge: Polity Press, 2017.

Lewis, Simon L., et al. "Defining the Anthropocene." *Nature* 519 (March 2015): 171–180.

Lindbladh, Johanna. "Coming to Terms with the Soviet Myth of Heroism Twenty-Five Years After the Chernobyl Nuclear Disaster: An Interpretation of Aleksandr Mindadze's Existential Action Movie *Innocent Saturday*." *Anthropology of East Europe Review* 30, no.1 (2012): 113–126.

Lu, Sheldon H., and Jiayan Mi, eds. *Chinese Ecocinema: In the Age of Environmental Challenge*. Hong Kong: Hong Kong University Press, 2009.

MacDonald, Scott. "Toward an Eco-Cinema." *Interdisciplinary Studies in Literature and Environment* 11, no. 2 (2004): 107–132.

Malm, Andreas. *Fossil Capital: The Rise of Steam Power and the Roots of Global Warming*. New York: Verso, 2016.

Martinez-Alier, Juan. *The Environmentalism of the Poor: A Study of Ecological Conflicts and Valuation*. Cheltenham, UK: Edward Elgar Publishing, 2002.

McNeill, J. R., and Peter Engelke. *The Great Acceleration: An Environmental History of the Anthropocene since 1945*. Cambridge, MA: Belknap Press of Harvard University Press, 2016.

Miller, Richard L. *Under the Cloud: The Decades of Nuclear Testing*. The Woodlands: Two-Sixty Press, 1991.

Monani, Salma, Carlo Arreglo, and Belinda Chiu. "Coloring the Environmental Lens: Cinema, New Media, and Just Sustainability." Special issue of *Environmental Communication: A Journal of Nature and Culture* 5, no. 1 (2011).

Moon, David, Nicholas B. Breyfogle, and Alexandra Bekasova, eds. *Place and Nature: Essays in Russian Environmental History*. Winwick: The White Horse Press, 2021.

Moore, Jason W. *Capitalism in the Web of Life: Ecology and the Accumulation of Capital*. New York: Verso, 2015.

Moore, Jason W., ed. *Anthropocene or Capitalocene? Nature, History, and the Crisis of Capitalism*. Oakland, CA: PM Press, 2016.

Morton, Timothy. "Guest Column: Queer Ecology." *PMLA* 125, no. 2 (2010): 273–282.

Oldfield, Jonathan, and Denis J. B. Shaw. *The Development of Russian Environmental Thought*. New York: Routledge, 2016.

Olšáková, Doubravka. *In the Name of the Great Work: Stalin's Plan for the Transformation of Nature and Its Impact in Eastern Europe*. New York and Oxford: Berghahn Books, 2016.

Past, Elena. *Italian Cinema Beyond the Human*. Bloomington: Indiana University Press, 2019.

Peterson, D. J. *Troubled Lands: The Legacy of Soviet Environmental Destruction*. Boulder, CO: Westview Press, 1993. Republished by New York: Routledge, 2018.

Sitnikova, Alexandra A. "The Image of Siberia in Soviet, Post-Soviet Fiction and Werner Herzog's Documentary Films." *Journal of Siberian Federal University* 4 (2015): 677–706.

Steffen, Will, et al. "Planetary Boundaries: Guiding Human Development on a Changing Planet." *Science* 347 (15 January 2015).

Sturgeon, Noël. *Environmentalism in Popular Culture: Gender, Race, Sexuality, and the Politics of the Natural*. Tucson: University of Arizona Press, 2009.

Willoquet-Maricondi, Paula. *Framing the World: Explorations in Ecocriticism and Film*. Charlottesville and London: University of Virginia Press, 2010.

Zalasiewicz, Jan, et al. "When Did the Anthropocene Begin? A Mid-Twentieth Century Boundary Level Is Stratigraphically Optimal." *Quaternary International* 383 (2015): 196–203.

Filmography

Aleksandrov, Grigori. *The Radiant Path* (*Svetlyi put'*, USSR, 1940).
Andrejew, Piotr. *Tender Spots* (*Czułe miejsca*, Poland, 1981).
Dovzhenko, Oleksandr. *Earth* (*Zemlia*, USSR, 1930).
Dovzhenko, Oleksandr, and Yulia Solntseva. *Poem of the Sea* (*Poema o morye*, USSR, 1958).
Eisenstein, Sergei. *The Old and the New* (*Staroye i novoye*, USSR, 1929).
Gerasimov, Sergei. *By the Lake* (*U ozera*, USSR, 1969).
Guggenheim, Davis. *An Inconvenient Truth* (USA, 2006).
Holland, Agnieszka. *Spoor* (*Pokot*, Poland, 2017).
Kalatozov, Mikhail. *The First Echelon* (*Pervyi eshelon*, USSR, 1955).
——. *The Unsent Letter* (*Nieotpravlennoye pis'mo*, USSR, 1960).
Klushantsev, Pavel. *Planet of the Storms* (*Planeta bur'*, USSR, 1962).
Królikiewicz, Grzegorz. *Trees* (*Drzewa*, Poland, 1995).
Lopushansky, Konstantin. *Dead Man's Letters* (*Pisma mertvogo cheloveka*, USSR, 1986).
Machulski, Juliusz. *Sexmission* (*Seksmisja*, Poland, 1984).
Riazanov, Eldar. *Moscow Does Not Believe in Tears* (*Moskva slezam ne verit*, USSR, 1979).
Schmidt, Jan. *The End of August at the Hotel Ozone* (*Konec srpna v hotelu Ozon*, Czechoslovakia, 1966).
Shepitko, Larisa. *Heat* (*Znoi*, USSR, 1962).
Soderbergh, Steven. *Erin Brockovich* (USA, 2000).
Stoyanov, Svetoslav. *The Last Black Sea Pirates* (*Poslednite Chernomorski pirati*, Bulgaria, 2014).
Tarkovsky, Andrei. *Stalker* (*Stalker*, USSR, 1979).
Vertov, Dziga. *Enthusiasm: Symphony of the Donbass* (*Entuziazm: simfoniya donbassa*, USSR, 1931).
Zdravič, Andrej. *Riverglass: A River Ballet in Four Seasons* (*V steklu reke*, Slovenia, 1997).

Part I
Industrializing the Bloc
Cinema of the Socialist Period

1

Sad and Bitter Landscapes
Ecology and the Built Environment in Czech and East German Photography and Film

Alice Lovejoy and Katie Trumpener

In 1947, the Soviet Union secretly began mining uranium in the German provinces of Saxony and Thuringia—then part of Germany's Soviet Occupation Zone—under the code name "Wismut" (German for the element bismuth). Given the escalating Cold War, the Soviets urgently desired the radioactive ore; by the 1960s, Wismut was one of the world's largest uranium mines, yielding enough ore to build thousands of atomic bombs.[1] As Werner Bräunig noted in *Rummelplatz* (*Fairground*), a novel he composed between 1960 and 1965: "The new recruits . . . without them they wouldn't be able to keep the pit working. . . . Size meant nothing any more, people had lost all sense of scale once the mines appeared, a conglomerate carving itself into the mountainsides across a vast stretch of landscape, from Saxony through to Thuringia, remaking the landscape almost overnight."[2]

In his 1993 documentary *Die Wismut* (*Wismut*), Volker Koepp, in turn, demonstrates how the mine functioned as a state within a state, at times overseen and guarded by the Soviet army. Over its decades of operation, this enormous enterprise employed half a million to a million workers; at the outset, most were forced laborers (some former prisoners) who performed incredibly dangerous work. Koepp quotes horrifying official statistics: during the last six months of 1949 alone, 1,281 workers were killed in on-the-job accidents while another 3,467 required amputations; 16,560 suffered very severe health damage; 11,376 forced laborers escaped; 234 crippled themselves to avoid further labor; and 534 workers, found guilty of "sabotage," were sentenced by Soviet tribunals to long terms of forced labor.

As with the building of the Pyramids or St. Petersburg, Wismut thus consumed many of its workers. For a significant number, moreover, Wismut and the surrounding Ore Mountains (*Erzgebirge* in German; *Krušné hory* in Czech) functioned as a sort of internal Gulag. To citizens across the Soviet Occupation Zone, one 1949 Anglo-American journalistic exposé claimed, the Ore Mountains had become "what the names of Buchenwald and Belsen were to the anti-Nazis of Europe five years ago."[3]

Small wonder, perhaps, that for decades the German Democratic Republic (GDR) suppressed the two most important artistic attempts to depict Wismut, Konrad Wolf's banned 1958 feature film *Sonnensucher* (*Sun Seekers*, released only in 1972) and *Fairground*, Bräunig's unfinished socialist realist novel (harshly criticized in manuscript in 1965, and published to critical acclaim only posthumously, in 2007).[4] The GDR's main feature film about radioactivity, Gottfried Kolditz's 1959 melodrama *Weißes Blut* (*White Blood*) instead indicted the American production of radioactive waste through nuclear bombs and testing. Its protagonist dies of radiation sickness—but not before denouncing American cover-ups and telling the world about the danger of atomic war. *White Blood*, tellingly, made no allusion to the GDR's own large-scale production of uranium, nor its contributions to the Soviet nuclear arsenal.

Koepp's film situates Wismut's postwar history in a long historical and broad geographic context. His soundtrack repeatedly features men singing traditional miner's songs in harmony, especially "Glück auf, der Steiger kommt" ("Come Up Again Safely, The Climber Comes"), sung in the Ore Mountains since the eighteenth century and now the unofficial anthem of miners across Germany. The song's lyrics are movingly stoic, understated. Aware of the acute dangers awaiting "in the night" below, they express fervent hope that the miners will have the luck to reemerge alive; embodying that hope, the "climber" (mine leader) leads the others down into the shaft.

In Koepp's interviews, elderly miners recount their travails: environmental and occupational diseases, sadness over their children's birth defects, friends killed in or by the mine. The miners themselves demonstrate an exceptionally warm, supportive group dynamic. Their sense of profession and calling, of guild identity and solidarity seems both premodern, rooted in centuries of regional mining traditions, and exemplary of the socialist ethos *Wismut* itself embodies in its humane interest in the ways historical circumstances impact working people. Wismut's tragedy lies in the scant heed paid by socialist states—the Soviet Union, and later the GDR—to miners' physical welfare, even their survival.[5] And in retrospect, one interview subject concludes hesitantly—as if it is almost too big to face—the whole frenzied Cold War uranium and arms race was ... completely unnecessary.

Mining, "Glück auf" reminds us, has always been hazardous. Yet Koepp's interview subjects neither hailed from traditional mining villages, nor were they forced conscripts. In the wake of negative international publicity, Wismut's use of forced and convict labor eased after 1949. Thereafter, most who arrived in Wismut did so voluntarily, including newly repatriated POWs or refugee "settlers" (ethnic Germans expelled from other parts of post-1945 Eastern Europe) drawn by Wismut's ready employment offer in the wake of their own displacement.[6] Others doubtless came from the other side of the Ore Mountains, just east of Wismut. These mountains form the natural border between Saxony and Bohemia, and for centuries their rich mineral deposits (coal, silver, gold, lead, copper, tungsten, and uranium) have made them a mining center—on the Czechoslovak side, too, where the famed Jachýmov uranium mines were also a key source of ore for the Soviet nuclear program. Long before the founding of the GDR (or Czechoslovakia), this industry attracted a mixed population of laborers: Germans, Czechs, and bilingual "amphibians" who identified strongly neither with Saxony nor Bohemia.[7] The population of the Ore Mountains had been mixed both on the mountains' eastern and western sides. In 1900, Saxony's foreign population was 90 percent Austrian, and, as Caitlin E. Murdock notes, "overwhelmingly from the northern Bohemian borderlands."[8] And in 1930, conversely, the northwest Bohemian city of Most (Brüx) was over 60 percent German.[9]

World War II transformed the region socially and economically. The 1938 Munich Agreement permitted Hitler to annex the Sudetenland—including the Bohemian side of the Ore Mountains—to the German Reich, precipitating the mass migration and deportation of Czechs from the Ore Mountains to rump Czechoslovakia. Yet geology continued to define life on both the mountains' Saxon and Bohemian sides, as the Nazi government aggressively expanded the region's mining and chemical industries in search of the raw materials no longer available from abroad (between wartime embargoes and domestic autarky policies), as well as their ersatz replacements. Coal was particularly central to Germany's groundbreaking synthetic rubber and oil programs; the lignite fields near Most were nearly as important as the Ruhr Valley's rich seams.[10]

The region's postwar governments adapted this infrastructure for their own mining and chemical industries, the engines of emerging planned economies. At the same time, they initiated fresh population transfers (voluntary and forced) intended to power these industries, and in the Czechoslovak case, to "cleanse" the region of its German past. Thus, after the Sudetenland's ethnic German population was forcibly, in some cases violently, "transferred" to Germany, the borderland region was resettled by Czechoslovaks themselves displaced by territorial revisions to the Slovak/Hungarian border, as well as by Roma and others attracted by the good jobs the industries promised. And as state socialism took hold in the GDR and the Czechoslovak Socialist Republic, the Ore Mountains remained ethnically mixed—albeit with a new population. As Eagle Glassheim astutely observes, the region thus became "not only a laboratory of socialism, [but] also a laboratory of industrial modernity."[11]

This "laboratory" status, as well as the region's uranium deposits and industrial importance, made the Ore Mountains key to both the postwar Czechoslovak and the East German governments, and the focus of documentation (and propaganda) in photography and film. During the 1930s, right-wing Sudeten-German nationalist photobooks like *Sudetendeutschtum in Kampf und Not* (*Sudeten-Germanhood in Struggle and Need*, 1936) by Sudeten German Party (*Sudetendeutsche Partei*, SdP) politician Karl Hermann Frank—later *Gauleiter* of the Sudetenland—had depicted a region in steep economic decline. As coal and mineral yields sank and unemployed ethnic German workers, stuck in slum housing, produced artisanal handicrafts for little recompense or risked their lives in illegal unofficial mines to scrounge heating material, only German nationalist politics, such works argued, could save them.[12] By the late 1940s and 1950s, in contrast, Czechoslovak films and photographs presented the Ore Mountains as a vanguard of the socialist state, advertising the region as a place workers might want to settle. Over time, however, as environmental concerns and ecological movements grew—often unofficially and clandestinely—photography and films began to show something different: the environmental devastation, drastic health consequences, and social fracturing now endemic to the region given the confluence of rapidly escalating resource extraction and population transfers.

This chapter reads socialist-era filmic and photographic depictions of the Ore Mountains against their post-1989 counterparts. In Czechoslovakia and in the GDR, the region's geology sparked not only similar industrial, social, and environmental histories but also comparable visual rhetorics. The works we examine present the Ore Mountains as a region marked by both a heterogeneous, changing population and a deeply sedimented history in which (as Wismut underscores) the ghosts of age-old practices and communities remain visible in the present. At times, in fact, only film and photography can make this sedimentation visible. Joachim Tschirner and Burghard Drachsel's *Die verschwundene Dörfer der Wismut* (*The Vanishing Villages of Wismut*, 2006) thus relies on East German villagers' long-hidden caches of secret photographs documenting the destruction of homes and villages lost to the ever-expanding Wismut mines. As this film and its Czech counterparts underscore, the twentieth century's successive traumas left their corrosive marks not only on the Ore Mountains' natural environment but also on their built environment. Historical landscapes of old farmsteads and baroque churches were leveled or replaced by high-rise apartment blocks, as the inexorably expanding open-pit mines transformed the region's human ecology.

Panorama and *Krajina*

In the 1950s, GDR newsreels about Wismut tended toward the heroic: footage of massive infrastructural machinery and workers descending into or ascending from mine shafts, underscored by equally stirring music (often Beethoven). Official photographic documentation on the Czechoslovak side of the Ore Mountains adopted a similar epic tone. For example, Zdeněk Forman, Vojtěch Jasný, and Karel Kachyňa's photobook *Budujeme pohraničí* (*We Are Building the Borderlands*, 1950) opens with two side-by-side photographs, forming a sweeping panorama of the North Bohemian countryside. The space, the captions announce, is at once ancient and contemporary: the ancestral homeland of early Bohemian clans, its roads recently traveled by Red Army soldiers and by the Czech and Slovak settlers who followed them. The book personifies a series of these settlers, all "builders" of the region's new identity: Slovak children who repurpose abandoned German military material as "children's toys"; the Silesian "re-emigrant" who knits contentedly, seated atop the wing of a downed World War II airplane; the model workers in the "towns, glassworks, mines, ceramics works, and textile factories" left empty by expellees. The book's captions carefully distinguish between the former and current lives of settlers such as "Slovak Ignác Leitavec," "who fought against the occupiers and was imprisoned in a concentration camp," and now works at a glassworks dating from 1427. "In that year," the caption notes, "the Vlachs [Wallachian Sorbs] were invited here. Later, the factory also employed Germans, who needed to be replaced after the May revolution." The region's "new" life, in other words, is also its old life, echoing Czechoslovak Stalinism's common evocation of the links between Bohemian nationalism and Czechoslovak communist identity. Even the postwar population transfers, fraught and brutal as they were, are celebrated as a necessary precondition for building the national-industrial-socialist future the photographs depict.[13]

We Are Building the Borderlands is in this sense a product of its time: an early phase in Czechoslovakia's first Five-Year Plan (1949–1953) that marked the beginnings of agricultural collectivization, the country's devastating show trials, and its version of socialist realism. Accordingly, the book's images are in deep focus, brightly lit, and rarely more magnified than a medium shot. Many, moreover, are situated on facing pages, forming "composed" panoramas whose sweeping, cloudless vistas assert the Ore Mountain landscape's political identity: these hills, farms, mines, factories, and valleys are a slate cleansed of the old order, pregnant with the possibility of the new, which is embodied above all in the resources they contain.[14]

Between 1959 and 1962, Prague photographer Josef Sudek recorded markedly different images of this landscape in a photographic series intended to form a companion to his celebrated photobook *Praha panoramatická* (*Panoramic Prague*, 1959). In 1998, long after his death in 1976, selections from this series (finally publishable after the Velvet Revolution) appeared in a Brno exhibition and accompanying catalog, then in a more extensive, posthumously edited photobook titled *Smutná krajina* (*Sad Landscape*, 1999).[15] The catalog focuses primarily on the presence of new and old industrial infrastructure in regional landscapes crisscrossed by pipelines and exhaust pipes and littered with abandoned heavy machinery; in many of the photobook selections, however, this industrial presence remains only implicit. The photobook opens by contrasting views of the ancient buildings, streets, and squares of Most, a town already slated for destruction to enable mine expansion, with the myriad identical highrise apartment buildings of Most's new town massed like palisades along the river. Housing, these photographs suggest, can itself be conceived as industrial infrastructure.

As Antonín Dufek has argued, Sudek's landscapes were influenced by painter Emil Filla (1882–1953), especially by Filla's early-1950s panoramic paintings of the Bohemian Highlands (immediately southeast of the Ore Mountains and also part of the Sudetenland).[16] Sudek had accompanied Filla on his painting trips, and his subsequent panoramic photographs echo their predecessors' compositions and at times their mood: their slightly off-center compositions, the haze hovering just over their horizon lines, their frequent verticals.

Yet if Filla's images are restrained, portraying the landscape with the measured eye of an artist at the end of his career, landscape takes on different resonances in Sudek's camera. In Filla's "Pnětluky – krajina se suchým stromem, 26.IX.1952" ("Pnětluky – Landscape with dry tree"), for instance, leafless trees overlook an autumnal landscape in late afternoon, a flock of crows alighting from their branches. The same dead trees appear in Sudek's lens—here, however, partly submerged in what appear to be accidental lakes, the by-product of surface mining. As in the image that forms the cover for *Sad Landscape*, there is no overlook, no bucolic village below: the lake continues to a horizon marked by smokestacks, in black-and-white tones that lack the warmth and sense of agricultural productivity evident in many of Filla's paintings—themselves, to be sure, products of the early 1950s, the era of *We Are Building the Borderlands*.

Sudek's photographs, indeed, depart from Filla's paintings and *We Are Building the Borderlands* in depicting the Ore Mountains region as barren and unproductive, its natural and human environment poisoned by industry. This was the reason, Dufek underscores, why the photographs could only be published after 1989; their obvious critical standpoint was incompatible with the official narrative of the Ore Mountains as a powerhouse of the Czechoslovak economy.[17] This criticism was underlined in *Sad Landscape*, where Sudek's images appear with captions (partly composed in the late 1960s, Dufek surmises) by poet Dalibor Kozel, one of the North Bohemian artist-environmentalists who had helped Sudek scout locations for his photographs.

"A ragged path—one must not come nearer with a camera. 1959."

"Former swimming pool at Most. Who would dare swim in the black water of the Běla River! 1959."

"At Humboldtka for the last time, it was pulled down a few days later, 1962."[18]

If Sudek's images are defined by their emptiness, this last Kozel caption underscores this as not just a result of industrial development but also a way of continuing to rewrite the political narrative embedded in the Ore Mountains' landscape: the major 1932 strike at the "Humboldtka" mine drew nationwide solidarity, becoming, in Matěj Spurný's words, "a symbol, a site of memory... [for] the Communist movement and the struggle for social justice."[19] If, as Derek Sayer has underscored, Czechoslovakia's postwar expulsions left "a denuded landscape, shorn of its ethnic and social complexities and ripe for the imposition of a unitary national script," by the early 1960s, even sites of memory central to interwar Czechoslovak communism were being eradicated.[20]

In many senses, then—environmental, historical, social—the North Bohemian landscape captured by Sudek is "sad." This retrospective title, in turn, situates Sudek's book within a centuries-old entwining of landscape, nationalism, and industry in Czech literature and visual culture. Since the late nineteenth-century National Revival, indeed, the Bohemian landscape (*krajina*) has been a central Czech literary trope, invoked as an embodiment of the nation itself in novels including Božena Němcová's *Babička* (*Grandmother*, 1855), with its loving portrayals of the countryside, and Vladislav Vančura's modernist *Marketa Lazarová* (1931), set among the same Bohemian tribes evoked in *We Are Building the Borderlands*.[21] Paired with the adjective "sad," however, the newly coined title of Sudek's posthumous photobook also invokes an older text: Karel Hynek Mácha's 1836 poem "Máj" (May), the cornerstone of Czech Romanticism in which landscape—the same Bohemian Highlands depicted in Filla's paintings—reflects its characters' emotional states, particularly sorrow. The poem's second intermezzo, for instance, pictures the countryside (here "land," or *země*) at dusk as *suffused* with sadness ("rozesmutnivši zem i sebe").[22]

The trope of the "sad" land, or landscape, recurs across Czech literature and cinema: in the chapbook *Smutná krajina* (*Sad Landscape*, 1938), issued after Czechoslovak president Tomáš G. Masaryk's death, as in *Píseň o Podkarpatské rusi* (*Song of Subcarpathian Rus'*), Jiří Weiss's 1937 documentary about Czechoslovakia's semi-colonial relationship to Subcarpathian Rus'—which the film refers to as a "sad land," poor, religious, and unindustrialized. But perhaps the most significant precursor to Sudek's work is Czech graphic artist Ferdiš Duša's 1921 book of woodcuts *Smutná země* (*Sad Land*), which depicts the mines in the Silesian city of Ostrava—built on another coal seam—as sites of poverty, danger, and environmental ruin. In one image, two men sit under a bridge, knives out, waiting for a passing woman; in a pietà, a family mourns a fallen miner; smokestacks choke the air with black smoke, which falls on agricultural fields in the foreground. The human cost of industrialization is clearly visible in Duša's woodcuts. In contrast, Filla's paintings and Sudek's photographs appear empty of people, resorting instead to the long-established allegory of the Bohemian landscape as a bearer of emotion, national and personal.

Krajina, however, can refer to landscape or countryside, or it can refer to scenery, something taken in by a viewer. This idea of the seeing, human eye animates a latter-day invocation of the Ore Mountains: Josef Koudelka's *Černý trojúhelník* (*The Black Triangle*, 1994), a series of panoramic photographs shot after the Velvet Revolution by the recently returned Czechoslovak émigré photographer.[23] Sudek's photopanoramas were first exhibited at the 1994 Prague Castle exhibition of Koudelka's series. The works' sensibilities are strikingly different—yet together they form an important record of ecological deterioration over time, while underlining the belatedness of environmental critique in Eastern Europe.

The Black Triangle explores the layered cultivation, abandonment, and desolation of the Ore Mountains' industrially ravaged landscape. Yet it also shows both industrial and natural forms reverting, in their decay, into sculptural and oddly sublime presences. In its opening image, for instance, a baroque stone statue bisects a smooth series of electrical wires spanning the length of the photograph, as if the harmony of Prague's Charles Bridge (captured indelibly in Sudek's *Panoramic Prague*) is recreated in the hinterland. Here, however, the support on the image's left hand is not another statue but a pair of smokestacks. In later images, the foregrounding of a large, fissured rock, the diagonal slash of a service road across the picture plane, or the torquing of twisted metal toward the middle of the image organizes the landscape for the eye. Sudek's panoramas of building sites and rural industry, in contrast, tend to be decentered, as if refuting the triumphalist symmetry of socialist realist works like *We Are Building the Border*.[24] Underscoring their compositional centering, Koudelka's images are, unlike Sudek's, in full, sharp, continuous focus, with the grain of the photographer's high-speed film—which Koudelka often pushed to be faster—emphasizing their sharpness and at times their subject (as in a photograph depicting a pile of ash).[25] The human eye, the *Black Triangle* photographs seem to promise—the perceiving viewer implicit in *krajina*—can shape even the most degraded industrial or postindustrial landscape, giving sense, beauty, and scale to its surroundings.[26]

In the decades following Sudek's photopanoramic series, the Ore Mountain landscape continued to change. Surface mining not only persisted but expanded, swallowing villages, Most's old medieval center, and, by the early 1980s, much of the city. During the protracted demolition process, thirty thousand Most inhabitants were moved to newly constructed mass housing. As the city was emptied out, its condemned buildings became an often turbulent, semi-lawless refuge for vagabonds and petty criminals. At the same time, the city remained a forum and flashpoint for cultural debate, hosting exhibits by Filla and Sudek, as well as discussions by prominent intellectuals. Both during and after the Prague Spring, preservationists repeatedly published arguments against Most's ongoing demolition—to no avail.[27]

Most's gradual destruction and the transfer of its population also made the city a uniquely appealing setting for films, including Hollywood director John Guillermin's *The Bridge at Remagen* (1969), in which, as Petr Szczepanik details, three city blocks were blown up to approximate the World War II battle of Remagen. *The Bridge at Remagen* was released the same year as Jan Schmidt's post-nuclear-holocaust science fiction drama *Konec srpna v hotelu Ozon* (*The End of August at the Hotel Ozone*, 1966), partly shot southwest of Most, amid the ruins of the depopulated border town of Doupov.[28] Zbyněk Brynych's 1978 crime film *Stíhán a podezřelý* (*Hunted and Suspected*) also set its final cat-and-mouse chase in Most's remaining condemned houses and eerily deserted streetscape.[29] Yet Normalization-era

Czechoslovak documentaries also offered more redemptive images of the city: among them Czechoslovak Television's 1973 *Historie nezanikne* (*History Will Not Die*), uncannily released to coincide with wide-scale architectural razing in Most, and Jindřich Fairaizl's *Jak se stěhuje kostel* (*How to Move a Church*, 1988), showing the complex yet successful transport of Most's most venerable Gothic church to safety, albeit in a no-man's-land outside the new town, formerly the site of an abbatoir.[30]

After 1989, the Ore Mountain mines passed from the Czechoslovak government to the private Czech Coal Group, and documentaries continue to record the region's often surreal landscape, its surface mines abutting baroque castles. These new Ore Mountain documentaries—including Břetislav Rychlík's *Kamenolom boží aneb jeden rok v Severních Čechách* (*God's Stone Quarry: One Year in Northern Bohemia*, 2005) and Martin Dušek and Ondřej Provazník's *Ženy SHR* (*Coal in the Soul*, 2010)—are concerned equally with the region's environmental and industrial history and with its complex social dynamics. Unlike their photographic predecessors, indeed, the films show a *populated* landscape, taking stock of the region's "social laboratory," sixty years after the German expulsions. These sociological dimensions are clearest in *God's Stone Quarry*, which spends a year following residents of Litvínov, a village near Most: an environmental activist, a coal miner, a vintner, a Satanist, a poet whose writing takes inspiration from the region's abandoned German cemeteries, an activist for the preservation of villages threatened by surface mining, and a Roma family. Rychlík interweaves interviews with these figures until the film's final sequence, in which he brings them together in an abandoned chateau above Litvínov to answer the question "What is the biggest problem here?" In contrast with the imposed order and symmetry of Koudelka's photographs, their answer crystallizes around the idea that the landscape is a "permanent struggle"—a fight for community, for history, for ecology in a region fractured by extraction, from the Nazi period to the present.

Coal in the Soul offers a micro-view of this fracturing, following two women from the town of Horní Jiřetín, near Litvínov. Hana Krejčová was born in the nearby village of Albrechtice (now destroyed by mining) and moved to Prague, performing in musicals before returning to Horní Jiřetín to care for Jezeří castle and lobby for the preservation of the region's villages. Her counterpart and fellow townswoman, Liběna Novotná, now works as Czech Coal's spokesperson, advocating the destruction of villages in the interest of energy. While Krejčová has become a local hero—Dušek and Provazník capture her leading an enthusiastic singing of the Czech Christmas carol "Narodil se Kristus pán" (Christ is born) in a church threatened by the mine—Novotná is an outcast, shunned by her community, even by her environmentalist children, because of her work

Figure 1.1. Novotná frames the Ore Mountains' "sad landscape." Ženy SHR *(Coal in the Soul)*. Directed by Martin Dušek and Ondřej Provazník. Prague: Česká televize, 2010. Screen capture by Alice Lovejoy.

for Czech Coal. As Krejčová's rusty refrain of songs from Claude-Michel Schönberg's *Les Misérables* (1980) signals, this is a film in a tragic mode, above all for Novotná, whose destiny, like Horní Jiřetín's other residents', is determined by geology.

Czech Coal, however, would prefer not to see things this way. Midway through the film, a scene depicts its new public relations effort: a "Coal Safari" that brings local residents concerned about the destruction of their homes and environment inside the surface mine. As Novotná says to the filmmakers, stretching her hands to approximate the wide-set frame of a panoramic image, "Look, here's the [mine] shaft and the Ore Mountains above. Isn't that a wonderful sight?" (See figure 1.1.)

Bitter Landscape: East German Environmentalist Film

In early 1960s Czechoslovakia, environmental concerns became widespread, given the translation, publication, and broadcast of parts of Rachel Carson's book *Silent Spring* (1962), and popular science journals' increased treatment of productivism's long-term environmental costs. During the post-1968 period of so-called Normalization, dissident groups continued to be active in environmental issues. Yet as Matěj Spurný has described, Czechoslovak political elites trivialized the country's increasingly palpable environmental deterioration, and by the 1980s, widespread environmental anxieties and anger fueled citizens' growing doubts about the legitimacy and future of state-socialist governments.[31]

East Germany's environmental history holds many parallels. There too, Marx and Engels's influential emphasis on the dynamic transformation of natural landscapes to ensure human prosperity helped justify Stalinist productivism. But the GDR also took shape in the shadow of Nazi techno-nationalism (whose giganticism included a vast military-industrial complex and the Autobahn's reconfigurations of the German landscape). Both as a Third Reich successor state and as a Soviet satellite, East Germany remained as invested in rebuilding heavy industry as in large-scale, visible transformations of the country's human habitat.

Already in the early GDR, to be sure, a few government scientists carefully tracked industrial pollutants. And although the New Economic System promulgated in the mid-1960s emphasized industrial growth, air pollution control systems were built into industrial planning, while the government remained willing to fund research on environmental hazards, even to try fining polluting factories. Those factories, however, successfully countered that such measures would undermine their economic viability. And despite official commitments to balancing growth with conservation, the Party remained fearful of compromising GDR workers' standard of living and access to consumer goods. In practice, then, ecological aspirations were continually sacrificed.[32]

In a 1963 jointly-authored article in *Sozialistische Forstwirtschaft* (*Socialist Forestry*), GDR-based and Prague-based researchers together warned of the danger acid rain posed to forests on both sides of the border. By the 1980s, nonetheless, over half of the trees in the Ore Mountains were dead. The area's increasingly disastrous air pollution levels propelled the GDR and Czechoslovakia into an environmental pact, yet this proved ineffectual even at checking their mutual attributions of blame. And even as the GDR began signing international ecological accords, committing it to lowering pollutant levels, its government resolved, in 1982, to classify its own environmental data.[33]

In 1980, worried by the political success and reformist agendas of West Germany's new Green Party, the GDR government founded its own affirmative ecological group, the Society for Nature and the Environment. Focusing on the enjoyment of nature while ignoring the GDR's obvious ecological crises, the organization was designed primarily to deflect and contain ecological energies among its own citizens. Despite placing many Stasi plants in the group, the government still worried about the potential for infiltration by activists associated with East Germany's Lutheran Church (the country's most influential, if embattled, embodiment of alternative political values). Perhaps unsurprisingly, when a grassroots GDR environmental movement emerged in mid-1980s under church auspices and protection, the government saw it not as a potential environmental ally but as a threat to Party monopoly on power, policymaking, and information.[34]

Wismut, the Ore Mountains, and, just to their west, the heavily industrial area around Bitterfeld—which housed the country's largest concentration of chemical plants—remained central to this independent eco-movement. At the 1983 annual Lutheran conference, when a thousand attendees heard reports from inhabitants from heavily polluted GDR areas, those from the Ore Mountains complained of chemically polluted air, negative health consequences, and forest dieback caused by acid rain.[35] The same year, a newly founded peace/eco group in Berlin-Lichtenberg held, as their inaugural event, a talk on Ore Mountain forest dieback (advertised by a graphic protest poster and postcards of dying and dead trees, over an excerpt from Goethe's famous 1776 poem "Wanderer's Night Song," about the peace of the forest). Many members subsequently drafted and signed a petition to the Ministry of Environmental Protection and Water Management, demanding greater transparency on environmental data and protection measures.[36]

In 1986, the Lichtenberg group established an unofficial "environmental library" (*Umweltsbibliothek*) in a more central location, at East Berlin's Zion Church. The library lasted hardly a year before it was raided and forcibly dismantled by the Stasi in 1987—an act that inadvertently helped publicize and expand the GDR's nascent environmental movement, garnering international coverage and catalyzing scattered protests across the country.[37] In 1987, moreover, a member of the Zion Church environmental group, Michael Belites, managed both to disseminate "Pechblende" (pitchblende, the ore containing uranium), his dissident report on Wismut's ecological damages and dangers, and to shoot surreptitious footage at Wismut, some of which was eventually shown on West German television.[38]

A more finished, widely seen film followed a year later, when members of the GDR's new environmentalist coalition *Arche* (Ark), working with a West Berlin journalist and a West German cameraman, secretly shot and disseminated a documentary about the toxic waste dumps and polluted rivers around Bitterfeld. Such "conspiratorial" cross-border collaboration made these activists potentially liable for lengthy treason or espionage prison sentences. Yet they managed to film unnoticed, smuggle their footage to West Berlin to be edited and synchronized, then sneak the resulting half-hour film back into the GDR, where their *Bitteres aus Bitterfeld. Ein Bestandaufnahme* (*Bitterness from Bitterfeld: A Stocktaking*, 1988), was unofficially screened and discussed in environmental and church circles. Eventually, excerpts were broadcast on two West German television programs aimed at East German viewers, as well as sold to (and broadcast by) foreign news agencies.[39]

Money from these sales helped fund an illegal video camera for the Arche network, which planned to make a video essay to accompany each future issue of its eco-magazine *Arche Nova*. The 1988 issue, on GDR forest dieback, belatedly included an accompanying video about the Ore Mountains, *Über alle Wipfeln ist Ruh: Waldlos auf 2000 zu?* (*Above All the Treetops Is Peace: Towards 2000 Without Forests?*), titled after the first lines of Goethe's "Wanderer's Night Song"). Like *Bitterness*, this film was smuggled out of the GDR and, in spring 1989, shown on West German television—even though Stasi informants within Arche had successfully managed to sabotage, delay, and ruin parts of the film during its shooting and production, prolonging its release and reducing its visual impact.[40]

Bitterness, memorably, had shown noticeably hazy air, ground and water obviously affected by chemical residues. The film centers on an enormous open-air waste dump, a repository for long-discarded World War II armaments and hundreds of open barrels dripping or oozing chemicals. As the barrels' signs warn, their materials are toxic, extremely hazardous, with the potential to cause genetic mutations. Nonetheless they have been left to rot, split, and spill in open air, near or into running water. It is only a matter of time, the voice-over insists, before these chemicals poison the water table itself. They have already, visibly, contaminated the ground—which is cracked, and features oddly textured, pebbled surfaces, as unknown chemicals continue to combine and react. In some places, overflow sludge potentially affects garden allotments, and hence the local food chain. Rusting pipelines, running for kilometers, transport further liquid sludge from chemical factories to waste grounds. Yet in winter, the voice-over explains, these pipes frequently freeze and crack, leaking toxins along their route. In one location, the film demonstrates, a new high-rise apartment block complex is sited right on the edge of the toxic dump.[41]

Throughout the 1950s, 1960s, and 1970s, both documentaries and feature films made at DEFA, the state film studio, had hewn closely to official government rhetoric about the environment. The Stakhanovite norm-breaking and collective self-sacrifice necessary to rebuild heavy industry; the razing of historic if run-down inner cities; the building of new satellite suburbs of densely spaced high-rise apartment buildings: all became established filmic topoi. From the mid-1960s onward, to be sure, a series of New Wave films implicitly questioned all of this: factory and work cultures built around constant worker scrutiny and lurking paranoia about sabotage; razing long-standing, intimately scaled urban neighborhoods, and the untested social experiment of siloing new high-rise districts. Most of these films, however, were banned before or after release.[42] Not until the 1980s was there more sustained filmic attention to the question of environmental damage—and even then, many films were censored or banned.[43]

Among these was a film on forest dieback in the Ore Mountains, proposed in 1983 by freelance director Günther Lippmann (who had grown up in nearby Chemnitz/Karl-Marx-Stadt). DEFA approved the project in 1987, but when Lippmann began filming in 1988 near the Czechoslovak border, he remained under Stasi surveillance. Lippmann argued at DEFA that ecological issues should be less secretive, discussed among wide swathes of the community. Yet although he submitted eight different versions of the film for approval, the studio continued to make objections: too many dead trees; too little optimism; the church presented in too positive a light. At a preliminary screening, the federal Minister of Agriculture exclaimed that the film would "never run in our cinemas"; in the words of another, "the people who live there already know about it, and no one else needs to know." Indeed, the film was never cleared for release in the GDR. Its ninth and definitive version premiered on television only in 1990, nine months after the fall of the Wall. *Wer hat dich du schöner Wald, oder wie ein Film verhindert wurde* (*Who Did This, Beautiful Forest, or How a Film Was Prevented*) both reinserted previously excised footage and recounted the political battles that had prevented the film's approval and release.[44]

Only five years after *Bitterness*, Koepp's *Wismut* experienced no legal challenges in the now-unified Germany, and indeed won numerous awards. Where *Bitterness* and *Above All the Treetops* indicted GDR environmental policies with visual evidence of environmental degradation, *Wismut* focuses on subtler, less visible damage. In the film, former miners reminisce about the mine's boom period (crowds of workers working round-the-clock shifts; living in cramped, makeshift housing; wearing improvised gear underground, then home again), their anecdotes taking on retroactive—radioactive—significance. For years before the mine provided work clothing or on-site showers, miners' clothing and hair inadvertently tracked radioactive dust home. Koepp's challenge is to reconstruct not only a suddenly defunct political and social formation, but also its half-lives, which remain invisible to the camera. Bookending the film are scenes of Geiger counters, meters spinning, making radioactivity *audible*: in some mining villages, these shots show, even the streets contained radioactive materials.

Both before and after 1989, East German ecological documentaries linked industrial damage to natural environments with the state-sanctioned deterioration of historic buildings and cityscapes—a nexus likewise emphasized by the grassroots ecological movement.[45] Kurt Tetzlaff's melancholy longitudinal DEFA documentary *Erinnerung an einer Landschaft—für Manuela* (*Memories of a Landscape—For Manuela,* 1983) thus recorded how GDR coal mining and forced resettlement sealed the destruction of venerable landscapes and villages. After sustained internal studio discussion about whether the film was too depressing, it was released in 1984 in only a few copies (while DEFA, without the director's permission, destroyed large amounts of remaining footage and documentation). Public response to the film was nonetheless powerful.[46]

Tetzlaff focuses on a region, an hour north of the Ore Mountains, whose economy has revolved around open-pit mining since the late 1920s. As with Most, the terrain being mined is continually expanding; to make room, rivers are diverted and—in clear parallel to the destruction of Most—a series of villages, some many centuries old, are demolished. Tetzlaff's film, shot over three years, follows this architectural demolition (as houses, streets, and, most dramatically, village churches are all eradicated) and the process of resettlement (as thousands of displaced inhabitants are moved to new urban high-rise settlements, some named for their lost villages). At moments, the documentary camera captures the poignant social and historical uprooting this represents. The last wedding is celebrated in Magdeborn; the last village child is born there. A village wall sports elegiac graffiti ("It was very beautiful here") anticipating and implicitly critiquing the planned demolition. A church tower is exploded. A two-hundred-fifty-year-old tree, under which Napoleon is reported to have walked, is unceremoniously felled, topples, and is gone. The voice-over explains that the demolition of this tree and town will enable the mining of a coal seam big enough to provide coal for twenty years. A loss of two hundred fifty years, the voice-over continues, to remain coal-powered for another twenty. Our age puts a high premium on coal; the question is one of gains and losses.

Yet this is as outspoken as the finished film gets. It says nothing about coal's environmental costs, nor about possible alternatives to demolishing and resettling village after village (although it does make clear such operations' huge financial and human costs). Nor, unsurprisingly, does it draw the obvious comparison to Nicolae Ceauşescu's 1970s and 1980s "systematization" program, which drew international opprobrium for its attempts to urbanize much of Romania by demolishing ancient (often ethnically Hungarian and German) villages, and resettling villagers in high-rise agro-industrial centers.

Ending five years after it began, Tetzlaff's film concludes that some villagers have healthier accommodation in their tower blocks than in the village, and that over the long run, even some of the elderly have adjusted surprisingly well to transplantation. (There are references to those who have not, but they barely appear on screen.) Unlike its later Czech counterparts—*God's Stone Quarry, Coal in the Soul*—the film suggests that mass transplantation has ensured some continuity in social structure and village solidarity. Moreover, *Memories of a Landscape—For Manuela* uses the device—familiar from Humphrey Jennings's British wartime documentary *A Diary for Timothy* (1945)—of juxtaposing a baby's birth with monumental upheavals in a particular cultural world; the continued thriving and growth of Timothy, then Manuela, symbolically guarantees that the new order, however fraught, will likewise prove tenable.

Nonetheless, much of Tetzlaff's film, shot primarily in grayish light, and scored with elegiac music, registers as mute mourning, even mute opposition to what is unfolding—raising the question, however indirectly, of the government's right to expropriate and, where it deems necessary, to destroy.[47] Much of GDR history, after all, was built atop various large-scale, similarly controversial government actions: the 1945–49 Soviet "land reform" that seized and divided up large estates, itself superseded, bitterly and violently, by forcible 1950s farm collectivization, and the stripping of property rights (following Third Reich precedent) from anyone officially emigrating from or unofficially fleeing the GDR.

By the early 1990s, it was possible to make films more openly skeptical of the GDR's impulse toward architectural clearance. In reunification's immediate aftermath, Tetzlaff himself returned to questions of historical stewardship. His documentary *The Garnison Church: Protocol of a Destruction* (*Die Garnisonskirche—Protokoll einer Zerstörung*, 1993) thus investigated the fate of Potsdam's Garnison Church, a widely influential baroque edifice erected in 1732, partially destroyed in a 1945 air raid, and officially demolished in 1968 to house a new computer facility. Like Tetzlaff's earlier documentary, *Garnison Church* takes as its reigning metaphor the explosion of a venerable church building. Now, however, the changed political situation enables not only retrospective mourning but a full, forensic investigation of the national and local political background to the 1968 demolition.

Burial place of Prussia's kings, this church symbolized the eighteenth-century union of ecclesiastical and military power—and the Nazis used it to stage key ceremonies and propaganda films. Yet one can't blame a building for what occurs in it, a historian now insists to Tetzlaff. (In 1968, he was one of the few city councillors to vote against the already-scheduled demolition.) Tetzlaff intersperses wide-ranging archival footage with interviews with the former mayor and city planners, and the church's parish priest. In 1993, the focus of Tetzlaff's film—like those of other former DEFA documentarians—was ascertaining political responsibility, illuminating GDR chains of command, and ascertaining key historical players' degree of self-examination, self-exoneration, contrition, or regret.

A decade after *The Garnison Church* and *Wismut*, Tschirner and Drachsel's 2006 *The Vanishing Villages of Wismut* uncovers different kinds of demolition, and Wismut stories, with a different mode and lode of historical evidence. Tschirner and Drachsel talk not with the official decision-makers and administrators who dot Tetzlaff's Garnison film, but with organic intellectuals—ordinary villagers who have neither forgotten nor forgiven past injustices, and whose sense of betrayal fueled impressive acts of civil courage. Such acts, Tetzlaff and Drachsel imply, provide the means for a new, more egalitarian, post-GDR mode of documentary filmmaking. Indeed, in lieu of *Garnison*'s heavy emphasis on archival footage, *Vanishing Villages* works primarily with hitherto unseen, decidedly unofficial forms of documentation, as newly available forms of visual evidence.

For both Tschirner and Drachsel, young GDR-trained filmmakers, *Vanishing Villages* represented only one instance of their long-term commitment to ecological filmmaking. Tschirner, a vocal proponent of Glasnost (although in 2011 he was also revealed to have a history of Stasi collaboration stretching back to 1971), made critical long-durée documentaries about East German heavy industry both before and after reunification, and in 1991, he cofounded the new environmental filmmaking initiative "UM WELT FILM."[48] Before *Vanishing Villages*, Tschirner and Drachsel had also produced documentaries about the former Soviet Union's devastated Aral Sea; their later films document the ongoing Wismut cleanup, and worldwide efforts to remediate uranium mining's ecological impact.

Garnison chronicled the demolition of a single, influential, irreplaceable historical structure. *Vanishing Villages* explores a larger, regional wave of demolitions around Wismut from 1951 to the late 1960s. During that period, Wismut expanded and further uranium deposits were discovered. The desire to open more shafts—alongside mining-related landslides and radioactive slag contamination—led to the demolition of seven villages (some with medieval roots) and the partial destruction of seven more. *Vanishing Villages* thus tracks not so much the direct, ecological devastation wrought by uranium mining as its lasting cultural devastation—of lives, communities, and the architectural record. Yet the film also chronicles various attempts by younger villagers to document what was happening to them; ignoring repeated official admonition and threats, they painstakingly photographed the mines' development and encroachment, then their villages' eventual demolition.

In 1951, seventeen-year-old Johannes Weiser began taking photographs of the first excavations in his village of Sorge-Settendorf and of the armed soldiers assigned to guard the site. When Weiser and his brother snuck back to take final pictures of their now-deserted house and their father's gravestone, Soviet soldiers arrested his brother, and opened Weiser's camera to destroy his pictures. Some nonetheless survived; Weiser hid them until after 1989. In neighboring Schmirchau, Soviet authorities arrested a local innkeeper on trumped-up sedition charges, commandeering his inn for their administrative headquarters. A local teenager, Martin Wöllner, took surreptitious photographs of this requisitioning, as well as over two hundred pictures documenting Schmirchau, whose villagers were eventually forced to leave as the mine expanded. Wöllner's photographs thus became key records of the village as it had once been.

Women from neighboring villages also retain clear, angry memories of the human toll their evacuation took. After contamination by radioactive mine waste, the seven-hundred-fifty-year-old town of Culmitzsch was evacuated and razed. Decades later, realizing her children would know nothing about Culmitzsch, Doris Knüppel composed a written chronicle, embellished with surviving photographs, enumerating where specific families had lived in the now-destroyed village, and how they earned their livings. As a young woman in Gessen, Liselotte Lückner secretly took photographs of her village during its demolition. When the authorities noticed and challenged her picture-taking, she insisted that she was (morally) entitled to photograph her own house before it was destroyed. Her actual motivation was not just sentimental: she suspected such photographs would constitute the only irrefutable historical and legal evidence of what was occurring. *Vanishing Villages* honors these photographs as such—and Weiser, Wöllner, Knüppel, and Lückner as unheralded, underground forerunners, critical documentarians.

A Transnational and Transnatural Cinema

What happened to Sorge-Settendorf and Culmitzsch was also, of course, what happened to the many villages mourned in *God's Stone Quarry*: surface mines consumed homes, graves, as well as personal and communal markers of history and tradition, while the industrial projects that accompanied them radically altered the communities' social fabric. The extraction central to the region's chemical industry had similar social, historical, and environmental effects: as *Bitterness* informs viewers, one of the sources of Bitterfeld's environmental devastation was a photographic

Figure 1.2. A woman stands in the door of a historic inn, holding up an old picture of the building even as workers overhead begin dismantling its roof. *Memories of a Landscape—For Manuela* (*Erinnerung an einer Landschaft—für Manuela*). Directed by Kurt Tetzlaff. Berlin: DEFA, 1983. Screen capture by Katie Trumpener.

plant that had been dumping runoff into the local Silver Lake. The plant was part of German photographic giant Agfa's (later Orwo's) complex of factories, built when German chemical companies began to expand beyond the Ruhr to Bitterfeld, drawn by the confluence of inexpensive labor, rivers, and deposits of coal, clay, and potassium. Agfa built its first dye plant in the region in 1895; by 1909, the company had diversified from dyes to photochemicals, and the village of Wolfen became the center of its still and motion-picture stock production. As Orwo, this stock was widely used throughout the GDR and socialist Czechoslovakia.[49]

In this sense, the Ore Mountains' shared geology underpinned not only industrial and social histories on both sides of the Bohemian/Saxon border, but also the material conditions for the region's documentation in photography and film. And—perhaps fittingly, since Agfa produced both photographic and moving-image film—this documentation in both Czechoslovakia and the GDR was characterized by a porousness of media forms. This is visible in sequences from both *Coal in the Soul* and *Memories of a Landscape*. In the former, Liběna Novotná's mimed panoramic photograph of the surface mine threatening Horní Jiřetín attempts to reframe (or perhaps repress) generations of conflict over the North Bohemian landscape. Conversely, in one of *Memories of a Landscape*'s most unsettling sequences, a woman is shown in the doorway of an old inn, mutely holding up a historic photograph of the building (see figure 1.2). As the camera moves back, then pans upward, we notice first that the inn is now quite dilapidated—then that workmen on the roof are already starting to demolish it, tile by tile, even as the woman stands in the doorway below, picture in hand. The sequence and its contrasts register as disturbing, surrealist, allegorical: the photograph she holds seems a guarantor of continuity, and so does her continued presence, even as the house is demolished around her. But when the workmen have finished, there will be nothing left.

These photographs (virtual or real) function differently—the East German woman's as historical evidence, Novotná's, effectively, as fiction. Nevertheless, their interpenetration of the photographic and cinematic is echoed, more broadly, by the dialogue between national media histories this chapter has traced. The chapter, in turn, underscores the importance of an approach to cinema that is not only intermedial but also transnational (and trans*natural*)—with media geography, in this case, a matter not of political borders but of the substances and spaces of life: mountains, trees, rocks, soil, architecture.[50]

Alice Lovejoy is Associate Professor in the Department of Cultural Studies and Comparative Literature and the program in Moving Image, Media, and Sound at the University of Minnesota. Author of the award-winning *Army Film and the Avant Garde: Cinema and Experiment in the Czechoslovak Military* (2015) and coeditor, with Mari Pajala, of *Remapping Cold War Media: Institutions, Infrastructures, Translations* (2022), she is completing a book titled *Militant Chemistry: Film and Its Raw Materials*, which explores the military, colonial, and environmental implications of film stock's entanglement with the chemical industry.

Katie Trumpener is Emily Sanford Professor of Comparative Literature and English at Yale. She is finishing books on film during the Third Reich (and the Nazi occupation of Europe) and on Cold War East and West German film culture. Previous work on Eastern Europe includes essays on Central European modernism; East German film and literature; the photobook under socialism; and the geopolitics of Béla Bartok's ethnomusicology. Other visual culture publications include *On the Viewing Platform: The Panorama between Canvas and Screen* (co-edited with Tim Barringer, 2020), and essays on the modernist picturebook.

Notes

1. Soviet uranium exploration and mining in the Ore Mountains began in 1946; the uranium extracted on the German side was sent to the Soviet Union as war reparations. Wismut was operated solely by the Soviet Union until 1953, when it was transformed into the SDAG Wismut, jointly owned by the Soviet Union and the GDR (German Democratic Republic). On the mine's history, see Naimark, *The Russians in Germany*.
2. Bräunig, *Rummelplatz*, 3–4. Bräunig's novel was written in 1960–65, but first published in 2007.
3. Cited in Murdock, "A Gulag in the Erzgebirge," 794.
4. *Sun Seekers* depicted Wismut as a space in which collaborative work amid danger could forge a new, cohesive German-Soviet industrial community. Despite Expressionist shots showing the cages descending into the mine's depth, and a major accident that takes several characters' lives, leaving another an amputee, Wolf's Wismut also becomes a place where workers find a new home. Yet in spite of its utopian aspirations and pro-Soviet sentiments, Wolf's film was banned before release, given Soviet anxieties about publicizing their atomic-weapons program. (See Pinkert, *Film and Memory*, chapter 7.) *Rummelplatz*'s Wismut becomes a gathering point for still-fascist, anti-social, and progressive miners, allegorizing the nascent GDR. In 1966, Bräunig's massive though still-unfinished novel was attacked by the Central Committee Plenum, then by a government-orchestrated protest campaign, ostensibly organized by rank-and-file miners. Embittered, Bräunig ceased work on the novel, dying of alcoholism in 1976.
5. The neglect of workers' health, Norman Naimark argues, sparked tensions between the Soviet occupying forces and the SED (the Socialist Unity Party, East Germany's Communist Party). Indeed, "even after the founding of the [GDR], the German authorities had no right to interfere in the lives of their citizens in the uranium mining districts of the Erzgebirge. What was worse, they were obligated to hunt down and return workers who escaped." This, in turn, "seriously undermined the formal political and economic goals of [the Soviet] occupation of Germany." Naimark, *The Russians in Germany*, 247.
6. Murdock, "A Gulag in the Erzgebirge," 800.
7. On national identity in the region, see, for example, Bryant, "Either Czech or German."
8. Murdock, "The Politics of Belonging," 59.
9. Glassheim, *Cleansing the Czechoslovak Borderlands*, 128.
10. Idem., 129.
11. Idem., 119.
12. Frank, *Sudetendeutschtum*.
13. Forman, Jasný, and Kachyňa, *Budujeme pohraničí*. On this, see also Spurný, *Making the Most of Tomorrow*, 117.
14. Jasný and Kachyňa became prolific and influential New Wave filmmakers; Jasný's 1969 *Všichni dobří rodáci* (*All My Good Countrymen*), a key film of the

Czechoslovak New Wave, would frame agricultural collectivization very differently.
15. The catalog was published in German as *Josef Sudek—Nordböhmen*.
16. Antonín Dufek, "Sad Landscape," in Sudek, *Smutná krajina*, n.p.
17. Nevertheless, Sudek clearly influenced the contemporaneous, ecologically oriented panoramic photo series made in Moravia by Brno-based botanist, photographer, and filmmaker Miloš Spurný. Spurný's series took a long ecological view, exploring old patterns of land cultivation, plant and geological life, and wetland use. During the Prague Spring, Spurný was offered the chance to publish these photographs as a photobook (with the proviso that it also include images of modern infrastructure and town life). After the 1968 Warsaw Pact invasion, however, publication proved impossible; his photobooks *Sbohem stare řeky* (*Goodbye, Old Rivers*) and *Českomoravská vysočina* (*The Czech-Moravian Highlands*) were published only long after his death in 1979. See Dufek's introductions to both books. Dufek also curated an important 2007 Spurný exhibit at Brno's Moravian Gallery; in 2019, fittingly enough, Prague's Josef Sudek Gallery held a further exhibit, "Miloš Spurný: Disappearing Landscapes."
18. "List of Photographs," Sudek, *Smutná krajina*, n.p.
19. Spurný, *Making the Most of Tomorrow*, 137.
20. Sayer, *The Coasts of Bohemia*, 241.
21. Němcová, *Babička*, 157. Like the woman knitting early in *We Are Building the Borderlands*, *Babička*'s protagonist is a "reemigrant" who left Silesia, returning on foot to Bohemia with her small children. As Jiří Rak writes in *Bývalí Čechové*, these links between land and nationalism originated with a nineteenth-century idealization of the peasant farmer as the bearer of national traditions, in the absence of a Czech aristocracy (which had been destroyed in the Thirty Years' War).
22. "Hasnul požár – bledší – bledší, / až se šírošíré nebe / noční rosou rozplakalo, / rozesmutnivši zem i sebe."
    In Edith Pargeter's translation (http://www.lupomesky.cz/maj/may.html): "Sinks the fire, still waning-waning, / Till the broad and bounteous heaven / Melts in nightly dews of sorrow, / And the earth to grief is given."
23. Koudelka, *Černý trojúhelník*.
24. On Sudek's use of panoramic form as political critique, see Katie Trumpener, "Stalin Boulevard: Panoramic Vistas and Urban Planning in Eastern European Photobooks," in Lovejoy and Pajala, *Remapping Cold War Media*, 17-42.
25. On Koudelka's use, and pushing, of high-speed film in his book *Gypsies*, see Estrin, "Josef Koudelka: A Restless Eye."
26. These are not the only photobooks about the region. Jan Reich's 1983 *Krusnohoří*, published with text in Czech, Russian, German, and English, and thus clearly appealing to would-be tourists, is tentatively environmentalist; Otakar Mohyla's introduction notes that "there are regions of inviolate beauty with which the visitor falls in love at first sight, and there are others in which industry is gradually destroying nature and with which people need more time to become attracted. … Jan Reich's photographs try to show the conflict between

Nature and civilization at least in an abbreviated form and indicate that the path which Man must follow in order to preserve this beautiful countryside for himself will still be long and not always comfortable and easy."
27. Spurný, *Making the Most of Tomorrow*, 50–66, 323–349. Following the social upheavals of the immediate postwar period, in fact, the condemned parts of the city became a de facto Roma ghetto. On the links between anti-Roma racism and Most's shifting historical, social, and national dynamics, see Spurný, *Making the Most of Tomorrow*, 135, and Glassheim, *Cleansing the Czechoslovak Borderlands*, 143–147.
28. Petr Szczepanik, "Hollywood Going East: State-Socialist Studios' Opportunistic Business with American Producers," in Lovejoy and Pahala, *Remapping Cold War Media*, 227–244.
29. Spurný, *Making the Most of Tomorrow*, 64.
30. On the Normalization-era films, see Spurný, *Making the Most of Tomorrow*, 353 and 382–398.
31. See Spurný, *Making the Most of Tomorrow*, 288, 304–322, and Glassheim, *Cleansing the Czechoslovak Borderlands*.
32. Huff, "Die 1950er Jahre—zwei Pioniere," "Die 1960er Jahre—im Windschatten," chapters 1 and 2 in *Natur und Industrie*.
33. Huff, *Natur und Industrie*, 129–250.
34. Huff, *Natur und Industrie*, 129–250.
35. Wernsierski, *Von oben nach unten wächst gar nichts*, 15–19.
36. Huff, *Natur und Industrie*, 355–356.
37. Bastian, ed. *Greenpeace in der DDR*; Jordan and Kloth, eds., *Arche Nova*.
38. On Stasi attempts to scuttle "Pechblende's" publication and investigate the video footage, see Beilites, *Undergrund*, especially pp. 94–95.
39. See also https://www.youtube.com/watch?v=ULaE5o3n3Bc.
40. Huff, *Natur und Industrie*, 373–374.
41. *Das war Bitteres von Bitterfeld* reconstructs the circumstances of filming.
42. *Der Frühling Braucht Zeit* (*Spring Takes Time*, Günther Stahnke), *Berlin um die Ecke* (*Berlin Around the Corner*, Gerhard Klein), and *Jahrgang 45* (*Born in 45*, Jürgen Böttcher) were all banned prerelease in 1966, premiering in 1990. *Spur der Steine* (*Trace of Stones*, Frank Beyer) was banned soon after its 1966 release; rereleased in 1990. See also *Kennen Sie Urban?* (*Do You Know Urban?*) Ingrid Reschke, 1971), *Tauben auf dem Dach* (*Doves on the Roof*, Iris Gusner, banned and ordered destroyed 1973; premiered 1990), and *Die Legende von Paul und Paula* (*The Legend of Paul and Paula*, Heiner Carow, 1973).
43. See Koepp's Wittstock longitudinal documentary series (1975–1997); Tschirner's Maxhütte documentary series (1986–1997); Peter Rocha's Lausitz trilogy (1987-1990); Iris Gusner's *Alle Meine Mädchen* (*All My Girls*, 1980); Warnecke's *Unser kürzes Leben* (*Our Brief Life*, 1982); Zschochke's *Insel der Schwäne* (*Swan Island*, 1983); Kahane's *Die Architekten* (*The Architects*, 1990); Jörg Föth's *Biologie!* (*Biology!*, 1990); and Roland Steiner's *Zeit-Raum – 46 ha Urwald in Böhmen* (*Over Time: 46 Hectares Forest in Bohemia*, 1987).
44. Huff, *Natur und Industrie*, 347–349. The film's title echoed Joseph Eichendorff's 1810 celebratory poem.

45. *Arche Nova* devoted its February 1988 issue to this conjunction; see Jordan and Kloth, *Arche Nova*, 297–363. Arguably, environmentalists' constant evocation of Goethe, Eichendorff, and other icons of high culture suggested that ecological neglect not only ran contrary to German cultural tradition (and nature worship), but threatened the very cultural fabric of German life. Goethe's poem was, of course, also the subject of Theodor Adorno's famous 1951 West German radio lecture "On Lyric Poetry and Society," about the relationship between subjectivity and social pressures.
46. Glass, *Kino ist mehr als Film*, 154; Schenk, *Eine kleine Geschichte der DEFA*, 226.
47. Yuliya Solntseva and Oleksandr Dovzhenko's poetic feature *Poema o morye* (*Poem of the Sea*, USSR, 1958), an important Soviet precedent for Tetzlaff's film, explores the psychic difficulties Ukrainian villagers faced with the inundation of their villages for the sake of progress—the building of the Kakhovka hydroelectric dam, and the irrigation of large areas in Ukraine and Crimea. Such changes are presented as inevitable, but so is the sense of loss that accompanies them and permeates the film form itself.
48. The name involves a pun: *Umwelt* means "environment" in German; "um Welt" for "about the world" or "on behalf of the world."
49. On the history of Agfa's Wolfen plant, including its environmental impacts, see, for example, Karlsch and Wagner, *Die AGFA-ORWO-Story*.
50. Many thanks to Lukas Brasiskis and Masha Shpolberg for their suggestion of the evocative term "transnatural."

Bibliography

Adorno, Theodor. "On Lyric Poetry and Society," *Notes to Literature*. Ed. Ralf Tiedemann, Trans. Shierry Weber Nicolsen. New York: Columbia University Press, 2019, 37-54.

Bastian, Uwe, ed. *Greenpeace in der DDR. Erinnerungsberichte, Interviews und Dokumente*. Berlin: Edition Ost, 1996.

Beilites, Michael. *Undergrund: Ein Konflikt mit der Stasi in der Uran-Provinz*. Berlin: Basis Druck, 1992.

Bräunig, Werner. *Rummelplatz*, trans. Samuel P. Willcocks. London: Seagull Books, 2016.

Bryant, Chad. "Either Czech or German: Fixing Nationality in Bohemia and Moravia, 1939–1946." *Slavic Review* 64, no. 4 (Winter 2002): 683–707.

Estrin, James. "Josef Koudelka: A Restless Eye." *New York Times* Lens Blog, 20 November 2013. https://lens.blogs.nytimes.com/2013/11/20/josef-koudelka-a-restless-eye/. Accessed 15 August 2019.

Forman, Zdeněk, Vojtěch Jasný, and Karel Kachyňa. *Budujeme pohraničí*. Prague: Orbis, 1950.

Frank, Karl Hermann. *Sudetendeutschtum in Kampf und Not. Ein Bildbericht*. Kassel: Bärenreiter-Verlag, 1936.

Glass, Peter. *Kino ist mehr als Film. Die Jahre 1976-1990*. Berlin: A.G. Berlin, 1999.

Glassheim, Eagle. *Cleansing the Czechoslovak Borderlands: Migration, Environment, and Health in the Former Sudetenland*. Pittsburgh: University of Pittsburgh Press, 2015.
Huff, Tobias. *Natur und Industrie im Sozialismus: eine Umweltgeschichte der DDR*. Göttingen: Vandenhoeck & Ruprecht, 2015.
Jordan, Carlo, and Hans Michael Kloth, eds. *Arche Nova. Opposition in der DDR. Das "Grün-ökologische Netzwerk Arche" 1988–1990*. Berlin: Basisdruck, 1995.
Karlsch, Rainer, and Paul Werner Wagner. *Die AGFA-ORWO-Story: Geschichte der Filmfabrik Wolfen und ihrer Nachfolger*. Berlin: Verlag für Berlin-Brandenburg, 2010.
Koudelka, Josef. *Černý trojúhelník, Podkrušnohoří / The Black Triangle, The Foothills of the Ore Mountain / Le triangle noir, La région située au pied des monts métallifères: Fotografie 1990–1994*. Prague: Správa Pražského hradu, 1994.
Lovejoy, Alice. *Army Film and the Avant Garde: Cinema and Experiment in the Czechoslovak Military*. Bloomington: Indiana University Press, 2015.
Lovejoy, Alice, and Mari Pajala, eds. *Remapping Cold War Media: Institutions, Infrastructures, Networks, Exchanges*. Bloomington: Indiana University Press, 2022.
Murdock, Caitlin E. "A Gulag in the Erzgebirge? Forced Labor, Political Legitimacy, and Eastern German Uranium Mining in the Early Cold War, 1946–1949." *Central European History* 47, no. 4 (2014): 791–821.
———. "The Politics of Belonging: Citizenship, Community, and Territory on the Saxon-Bohemian Frontier, 1918–1924." *Austrian History Yearbook* 43 (2012): 59–74.
Naimark, Norman. *The Russians in Germany: A History of the Soviet Zone of Occupation, 1945–1949*. Cambridge, MA: Harvard University Press, 1995.
Němcová, Božena. *Babička*. Prague: Nakladatelství Lidové noviny, 1999.
Pinkert, Anke. *Film and Memory in East Germany*. Bloomington: Indiana University Press, 2008.
Rak, Jiří. *Bývalí Čechové*. Prague: H&H, 1994.
Reich, Jan. *Krusnohoří*. Prague: CTK-Pressfoto, 1983.
Sayer, Derek. *The Coasts of Bohemia: A Czech History*. Princeton, NJ: Princeton University Press, 1998.
Schenk, Ralf. *Eine kleine Geschichte der DEFA*. Berlin: DEFA-Stiftung, 2006.
Spurný, Matěj. *Making the Most of Tomorrow: A Laboratory of Socialist Modernity*. Prague: Karolinum Press, 2019.
Spurný, Miloš. *Českomoravská vysočina*. Brno: Fotep, 2015.
———. *Sbohem stare řeky*. Brno: Fotep, 2007.
Sudek, Josef. *Smutná krajina: Severozápadní Čechy 1957–1962*. Litoměřice: Galerie výtvarného umění v Litoměřicích, 1999.
Vančura, Vladislav. *Marketa Lazarová*. Rev. ed. 1961; reprint, Prague: Dauphin, 1997.
Wernsierski, Peter. *Von oben nach unten wächst gar nichts: Umweltstörung und Protest in der DDR*. Frankfurt: Fischer, 1986.

Filmography

Über alle Wipfeln ist Ruh: Waldlos auf 2000 zu? (*Above All the Treetops Is Peace: Towards 2000 Without Forests?*, Arche Nova video magazine, GDR, 1988).
Historie nezanikne (*History Will Not Die*, Czechoslovakia, 1973).
Beyer, Frank. *Spur der Steine* (*Trace of Stones*, GDR, 1966, rereleased 1990).
Böttcher, Jürgen. *Jahrgang 45* (*Born in 45*, GDR, 1966, premiered 1990).
Brynych, Zbyněk. *Stíhán a podezrelý* (*Hunted and Suspected*, Czechoslovakia, 1978).
Carow, Heiner. *Die Legende von Paul und Paula* (*The Legend of Paul and Paula*, GDR, 1973).
Dušek, Martin, and Ondřej Provazník. *Ženy SHR* (*Coal in the Soul*, Czech Republic, 2010).
Fairaizl, Jindřich. *Jak se stěhuje kostel* (*How to Move a Church*, Czechoslovakia, 1988).
Föth, Jörg. *Biologie!* (*Biology!*, GDR, 1990).
Guillermin, John. *The Bridge at Remagen* (United States, 1969).
Gusner, Iris. *Tauben auf dem Dach* (*Doves on the Roof*, Germany, 1973; banned and ordered destroyed; premiered 1990).
——. *All My Girls* (*Alle Meine Mädchen*, GDR, 1980).
Hällfritzsch, Rainer, Margit Miosga, and Ulrich Neumann. *Bitteres aus Bitterfeld. Ein Bestandaufnahme* (*Bitterness from Bitterfeld: A Stocktaking*, GDR, 1988).
Hällfritzsch, Rainer, Ulrike Hemberger, and Margit Miosga. *Das war Bitteres aus Bitterfeld* (*That Was Bitterness from Bitterfeld*, Germany, 2005).
Jasný, Vojtěch. *Všichni dobři rodácí* (*All My Good Countrymen*, Czechoslovakia, 1969).
Jennings, Humphrey. *A Diary for Timothy* (United Kingdom, 1945).
Kahane, Peter. *Die Architekten* (*The Architects*, GDR, 1990).
Klein, Gerhard. *Berlin um die Ecke* (*Berlin Around the Corner*, GDR, 1966, premiered 1990).
Koepp, Volker. *Der Wittstock Zyklus* (*The Wittstock Cycle*, GDR/Germany; seven films, 1975–1997).
Lippmann, Günther. *Wer hat dich du schöner Wald, oder wie ein Film verhindert wurde* (*Who Did This, Beautiful Forest, or How a Film Was Prevented*, Germany, 1990).
Reschke, Ingrid. *Kennen Sie Urban?* (*Do You Know Urban?*, GDR, 1971).
Rocha, Peter. Lausitz trilogy (GDR; three films, 1987–1990).
Rychlík, Břetislav. *Kamenolom boží aneb jeden rok v Severních Čechách* (*God's Stone Quarry: One Year in Northern Bohemia*, Czech Republic, 2005).
Schmidt, Jan. *Konec srpna v hotelu Ozon* (*The End of August at the Hotel Ozone*, Czechoslovakia, 1969).
Solntseva, Yuliya, and Oleksandr Dovzhenko. *Poema o morye* (*Poem of the Sea*, USSR, 1958).
Stahnke, Günther. *Der Frühling Braucht Zeit* (*Spring Takes Time*, GDR, 1966, rereleased 1990).
Steiner, Roland. *Zeit Raum – 46 ha Urwald in Böhmen* (*Over Time: 46 Hectares Bohemian Forest*, GDR, 1987).
Tetzlaff, Kurt. *Erinnerung an einer Landschaft—für Manuela* (*Memories of a Landscape—For Manuela*, GDR, 1983).

———. *Die Garnisonskirche—Protokoll einer Zerstörung* (*The Garnison Church: Protocol of a Destruction*, Germany, 1993).
Tschirner, Joachum. *Maxhütte Zyklus* (*Maxhütte Cycle*, GDR/Germany; five films, 1986–1997).
Tschirner, Joachim, and Burghard Drachsel. *Die verschwundene Dörfer der Wismut* (*The Vanishing Villages of Wismut*, Germany, 2006).
Warnecke, Lothar. *Unser kurzes Leben* (*Our Brief Life*, GDR, 1982).
Zschochke, Hermann. *Insel der Schwäne* (*Swan Island*, GDR, 1983).

2

From Mastery to Indistinction
Nature in Thaw-Era Cinema

Lida Oukaderova

When the director Mikhail Kalatozov and cinematographer Sergei Urusevsky submitted their second joint feature, *The Unsent Letter* (*Neotpravlennoe pis'mo*, 1960), for review by the Soviet main film production company Mosfilm, in 1959, the reaction of the Communist Party's bureau of the film studio was exceptionally harsh. The film's depiction of an ill-fated expedition to Yakutia to locate diamond deposits, in which three of the four participating geologists die, had little appeal for this particular group of viewers, who perceived the production as anti-humanist to its core. At a meeting to discuss the film, the participants complained that the psychological and emotional depth of the film's protagonists remained unexplored, and the unending struggle between human figures and the Siberian landscape gave an impression of Soviet humanity as feeble: "Although there is ... staunchness in these people, it is one of despairing men who can sacrifice themselves but who cannot resist nature as its master would."[1] If there was any defense of the filmmakers to be offered, it was the natural strain of their work on location, in a climate that was "exceptionally difficult, where it is impossible not only to film but to live."[2] Not only the film's characters, the quote suggests, succumbed to nature, but the filmmakers themselves, who were incapable of besting the wildness of the taiga in their process of shooting. Such overwhelmingly negative criticism was especially striking as it was directed toward arguably the two most celebrated figures in the Soviet cinema of that moment: Kalatozov and Urusevsky's first co-production, *The Cranes Are Flying* (*Letiat zhuravli*), made history at Cannes in 1958 by receiving the Palme d'Or, the festival's highest prize. This accolade seems to have had little influence on Party critiques of *The Unsent Letter;* despite Kalatozov and Urusevsky's national and international reputation, their film's apparent disregard for the established "truth" of Soviet humanity's conquest of nature was understood to be a fundamental flaw.

The critical terms employed in this discussion would be familiar to any student of Soviet history, throughout which the efforts to tame and master the Union's vast land expanse were extensive and ongoing, justified by a conviction that this undertaking was necessary for the success of the socialist project's economic, and thus political, ambitions. If the conquest of nature was intrinsic to the ideology of the Soviet state from start, with major industrial projects beginning to alter the Soviet environments already in the late 1920s, it gained speed in the 1930s and continued after 1945.[3] Although the Thaw reforms of the 1950s and 1960s delivered changes to Soviet politics, economics, and everyday life—easing political oppression and loosening the country's centralized economic organization—they did little to modify the Soviet state's approach to its undeveloped terrain. The images of geologists dying one by one at the forces of the taiga in *The Unsent Letter* (even if these figures successfully located the diamonds that are at the center of the film's plot) could thus not be easily reconciled with the aspirations and beliefs of mastery over nature that had pervaded the Soviet discourse throughout the previous decades.

However, *The Unsent Letter*, with its remarkable portrayal of the geologists' wasting away in the seemingly infinite Siberian landscape, was not the only feature of the Thaw that evaded or questioned Soviet environmental tenets. A growing number of productions during this time took steps, however diminutive, to film nature differently, to escape the static dichotomy of "men/subject/active" versus "nature/object/passive" that Soviet environmental thinking demanded and that had become normative in cultural representations to that point. Such steps were nurtured by cinema's revival during the liberalized climate of the Thaw from the late 1950s and through the mid-1960s, which allowed for much broader experimentations in most spheres of artistic production than had been the case during the Stalinist years. As filmmakers turned their attention to aspects of Soviet life that had been excluded from film screens in the previous decades, and as they sought to record, with precision, people's experiences of everyday life, politics, and history, they searched for new means to deepen the aesthetic and political potential of cinematic expression. Perceiving nature outside of proper Soviet paradigms was part of this process, producing filmic explorations that suspended a familiar masterful gaze controlling the country's natural domain—of which Kalatozov and Urusevsky's work was perhaps the most radical manifestation.

In what follows, I offer a trajectory of shifts in the Soviet screening of nature from the mid-1950s to the early 1960s. I start with Kalatozov's earlier work, particularly *The First Echelon* (*Pervyi eshelon*, 1955) as an example of the normative cinematic treatment of Soviet conquest over its natural environment. Then I move to Oleksandr Dovzhenko and Yulia Solntseva's *Poem of the Sea* (*Poema o morye*, 1958), whose celebration of an industrial project altering nature turns ambivalent because of its extreme diversity of formal and narrative devices. I follow with a discussion of Larisa Shepitko's film *Heat* (*Znoi*, 1962), which not only openly critiques Soviet industrial exploitation of the land but portrays the environment that comes alive only when freed from the state's ends-orientated gaze. Finally, I return to *The Unsent Letter* to discuss the aesthetic and political implications of the film's persistent fusion of human protagonists and Siberian landscape. If the shifts in these filmmakers' approaches to the Soviet landscapes are symptomatic of broader changes in the culture's attitudes toward its land (which I also discuss briefly), film proves a particularly resonant medium through which to explore them. This process was, I argue, a two-way street: just as experimentations with diverse modes of filmic representation led to idiosyncratic images of natural environments, so the desire to grasp and understand nature outside of Soviet ideological constraints resulted in new possibilities for the artistic exploration of the moving images.

Historical Background

To start, a few words on the politics of the natural environment during the Soviet Thaw are necessary. As in the preceding decades, the Soviet demand for an accelerated economic production determined in full the policies and projects of natural exploitation. Nikita Khrushchev's own understanding of the environment was indeed cultivated during the 1930s' militant drive for the subordination of nature to human needs, within which the preservation of natural landscapes and wildlife was considered to be little more than a waste of a significant economic potential. As noted by environmental historians, "the belief that nature was somehow an enemy of socialism—or at the very least should be rapidly transformed into some kind of machine—persisted under Khrushchev."[4] And so the Soviet state during the Thaw years continued to celebrate the scientific and industrial achievements as measured by their success in controlling Soviet ecology and altering the natural order of Soviet territories.

Discussions on the exploitation of natural resources during the 1950s and 1960s were largely dominated by Khrushchev's virgin land campaign—a massive agricultural program focused on developing the untouched "virgin" territories in Siberia and Central Asia, with the goal of increasing the country's grain production. These agricultural endeavors, historians agree, were "unmitigated environmental disasters that resulted in the plowing up and exhaustion of soils followed by a rampant erosion."[5] Furthermore, the widespread use of chemicals in industrial farming, along with the unceasing expansion of heavy industries and military complexes with nuclear capacities, were a central factor in the deterioration of ecological systems across the USSR, with the state giving little thought to how these projects impacted the land. The damage to Lake Baikal's ecosystems, for instance—from overfishing, dumping sewage and industrial waste into its waters, and the construction of nearby hydroelectric stations—significantly accelerated during Khrushchev's industrial push.[6] Similarly, the catastrophic destruction of the Aral Sea in Central Asia, caused by the construction of irrigation systems for the cotton and rice plantation in the steppes that drained the water from the sea, began in the early 1960s.[7]

Yet although the state's unrelenting industrial march to exploit natural resources was left largely unchallenged throughout the Thaw, there were increasing and systematic attempts to tame it. As the historian Laurent Coumel argues, it was during these years that the country experienced a revival in the environmental movements seeking to limit the exploitation of natural resources, preserve undeveloped territories, and protect wildlife.[8] Some of these movements formed from within the state institutions, including the Academy of Sciences and such professional organizations as the Moscow Society of Naturalists and the Geographical Society of the USSR. But there were also independent, nongovernmental organizations that became increasingly more vociferous during the Thaw years, the All-Russia Society for the Protection of Nature (VOOP) most notable among them. As Coumel demonstrates, leading newspapers, such as *Pravda* and *Literaturnaia gazeta*, repeatedly dedicated major articles and editorial discussions to the topic of environmental protection from the mid-1950s on, generating an open discussion that extended beyond the experts, involving known public figures as well as the general population. These efforts gradually crystallized into a call for laws outlining specific measures to curtail human activities within the natural world. While a Russian Federation law passed in 1960, it had little effect on the government's decisions in economic and industrial activities, thus failing to slow down the degradation of ecological systems. Nevertheless, the open public debates preceding the passing of the law raised environmental awareness across a broad swath of the population, sowing the seeds for later state engagement and grassroots environmental organizations. Thaw-era filmic engagements with the natural world, as discussed in this chapter, must be understood within the context of such newly emerging public voices.

The First Echelon

If Kalatozov's *The Unsent Letter* offered one of the most troubling views of the Soviet efforts to master the environment in the post-Stalinist period, *The First Echelon*, made just a few years before, in 1955, had no such critical stance.[9] As the Soviet film journal *Iskusstvo kino* (*The Art of Cinema*) described it, this was "the first fictional film about people conquering the boundlessly vast expanses of the virgin lands in the east. Just this presupposes the epic scope of the film."[10] The epic scope, indeed, portrayed the heroic efforts of young students, who relocate to Kazakhstan to work its pristine but utterly inhospitable lands. Produced after Stalin's death but before Khrushchev's 1956 Party Congress speech denouncing his predecessor's crimes, and before the Soviet film industry began to awaken from its spell of formulaic and predictable productions, the 1955 film is firmly rooted in socialist realist tradition. Its narrative unfolds around the problems of building an agricultural collective, which is complicated by multiple twists and turns, caused by mismatched romantic relationships and, more importantly, by indolent antagonists who lack the skills and commitment necessary for the collective's success in raising the virgin territories.

But all the film's conflicts are resolved by its end: fractures within the group are healed, couples get married, and the group's black sheep publicly recognizes his mistakes before being reintegrated into the collective. Although nature—the wide, unbounded steppes of Kazakhstan—is the driving point of the story, it is so only in the abstract, taking on significance primarily as a medium for the expression of human feats, as a substance to be worked and transformed. And transformed it is: the empty, hostile, snow- and mud-covered areas that grimly greeted the students at the film's outset turn in the course of the film into a pliable, workable space, where tractors tirelessly plow and plants begin to grow. The film does not betray any need to frame Kazakhstan's steppes from any other perspective than that of their economic benefit to humankind; and thus the *cinematic* perspective—the gaze that the film generates while looking at the expansive fields—seamlessly mirrors this relationship, as the camera masterfully and unproblematically oversees the area, celebrating the collective's triumph over nature. Nothing in this landscape remains invisible or unknown; nothing provides a challenge for the socialist gaze. When a sweeping fire toward the end of the film turns the landscape into ashes but does not touch the fruits of the collective labor that has worked it, sparing the lush, tall wheat fields, disaster is considered to be averted. The blackened grounds of the not-yet-"conquered" steppes do not overshadow the film's resolved, happy ending.

Poem of the Sea

Released in 1958, *Poem of the Sea* was directed by Yulia Solntseva, the widow of Oleksandr Dovzhenko, who had developed the script for this production but died before the shooting could begin. The film, as its title suggests, "poeticizes" the construction of the Kachov hydroelectric power station in Ukraine, one of the major Soviet industrialization projects conducted between 1950 and 1956. The construction itself, however, finds only a marginal place in the film, displaced by its focus on a small village that, we gradually come to understand, is about to disappear underwater, intentionally drowned under the "newly built" sea that would bring irrigation to the area. Today, the film comes across as highly awkward and artificial in its poetic composition. Owing much to the conventions of socialist realism, it also attempts to transcend them, displaying a conflicted and motley collection of formal and narrative devices. We experience the film's events through interior monologues and a disembodied voice-over; through animation sequences and overtly symbolic, theatrical shots; through seamless shifts between past and present, or fantasy and reality; and through a frequently stifled, ideologically "proper" speech that occasionally yields to a poignant language of suffering in the most unadorned, non-acted, everyday Ukrainian. Lacking formal stability, as if laying bare a search for its own form, the film unsettles the process of generating a unified, transparent meaning of the historic event at its center.

Nature in particular, as one of the major targets of the film's exploration, fails to be "symbolized" into a singular, overarching image within the unfolding drama of industrialization, which is especially notable as the film's "poetry" works hard to realize a coherent symbolic representation. On a large scale, nature operates in the film as fully under control of Soviet civilization, where even such a wild force as the sea can be, oxymoronically, "built." Manufactured, industrialized, and managed, this nature emerges through human work and will, and is celebrated in the film's final moments with images of the newly abundant waters, whose blue surface and waves, glistening in the sun, look no different from the real, "natural" nature. More than the hydroelectric station, this is the ultimate human achievement—to not only conquer but *produce* the natural environment, and thus establish humanity's absolute mastery over its natural domain.

But there is another nature in the film. Smallish, without any grand wilderness or expansiveness, it takes the form of simple landscapes surrounding the small village, as well as people's gardens with apple, apricot, and pear trees. This nature is intimately bound with human life and with the village inhabitants' individual histories. As the building of the sea advances, the residents have to abandon—or, worse, tear down—their houses and gardens, which some do enthusiastically, in the spirit of industrial sacrifice, but others, especially the aged population, only with pain and agony. In one sequence, for instance, we see an attempt to cut down the last remaining—but strong, age-old, and vibrant—pear tree in the garden of an old woman, the mother of the film's main protagonist. Lacking the courage to destroy the tree, the group decides to simply leave it in place to be drowned by the flood waters. *This* nature is not autonomous from human life but is rather an integrating force within it, and as such becomes a depository of people's personal histories and memories. As the sea begins to fill the area, the camera glances over a few garden trees gradually disappearing underwater—a shot in which the realism of destruction, and not the symbolism of the new construction, becomes most tangible. The film's final images are meant to be a celebration of human mind and power. But it is hard to see the evenly expansive water surface as anything else than a horror machine swallowing all material traces of previous lives, memories, and landscapes. Humanity used to be part of nature, the film suggests. Now, it is nature that is part of humanity, but the transition to this unity is violent, and the result—the blue, reflective, homogenous sea waters—insinuates a sense of pure nothingness, an emptiness that overtakes what should be a joyous socialist landscape.

Heat

A more direct critical shot at the failures of virgin land development appears in Larisa Shepitko's 1962 film *Heat*, which was her first full-length feature, produced as part of her graduation requirements at the Moscow's All-Union Institute of Cinematography (VGIK). Upon release, the film received several national and international prizes, establishing the director as an important new female voice in Soviet cinema. The film is based on

Chingiz Aitmatov's story "The Camel's Eye," an early work by the Kirgiz writer from before his fiction became known for its environmental advocacy. Set in the desserts of Kirgizstan, *Heat* significantly departs from familiarly enthusiastic, conflict-ridden yet happy-ending Soviet films on this topic, such as *The First Echelon*. Instead of *The First Echelon*'s large agricultural collective that successfully transforms empty lands into productive fields, *Heat* focuses on a small, six-person "brigade" that lives in a tiny yurt dwarfed by a homogenous, barren, and seemingly endless desert whose appearance, stubbornly, does not change over the course of the film. The arduous plowing of the area, occurring day after day in an intense summer heat, does not convert the inhospitable ground into a fertile terrain, and the dark, dry soil never shows any signs of growth such as we see toward the end of Kalatozov's production.

Heat, indeed, seems to be disinvested from any sort of narrative progress related to the conquest of nature and more interested in the clash of personalities within the brigade, driven by the authoritarian and misogynistic Abakir, who sarcastically rejects the buoyant attitude of the seventeen-year-old newcomer Kemel. Abakir is thoroughly unsympathetic and pessimistic, and the wickedness of his character is unambiguously established through his treatment of a young female brigade member, whom he abuses physically and exploits emotionally. His attitude toward work is also far from properly "socialist." Although he excels at what he does—and is thus an exemplary worker as far as his skills are concerned—he has no beliefs in the success of the group's agricultural efforts. As he says at one point to Kemel: "Do you still believe in this nonsense [of a better life on earth]? You should believe only your own eyes and hands. Look around, look at this dead soil. Do you know why we need to plow this dust? To prove to our descendants that nothing can grow here." Kemel reacts to these words with evident horror: as a young communist, he is fully convinced in the science of Soviet transformative agriculture. But audiences are offered little to counter Abakir's views, to *not* believe what they see with their own eyes: shot after shot, the camera surveys the dead soil covered with nothing but parched-out thorny bushes, where no sacrificial labor, or socialist magic, succeeds in converting them into life-friendly plants.

Where the landscape does transform, however, is in the sequences of Kemel's enamored encounters with a young horse shepherdess. In an overtly symbolic act, their first meeting takes place at the area's only water spring, which is surrounded by lush vegetation. But also in their later flirtations, as they ride their horses through the landscape, the usually destitute desert acquires liveliness and vitality, exhibiting its appealing curves and shadows and giving rise to a visual harmony between the rac-

Figure 2.1. *Heat* (*Znoy*). Directed by Larisa Shepitko. Bishkek: Kyrgyzfilm, 1962. Screen capture by Lida Oukaderova.

ing couple and their surroundings. In contrast to the predominantly long, wide shots surveying the monotone surroundings for most of the film, the sequences with the shepherdess create a different scenery, one permeated by the unified, mobile energy of the couple and the landscape. The shepherdess in particular is presented in the film as one with nature, moving through the fields with a fluid ease and providing a stark contrast to the brigade's taxing and obsolete labor. No matter how grim the landscape is, it becomes alive and graceful when freed from the human insistence to treat it as a simple means to economic and ideological ends.

With this clear opposition, Shepitko explores how to cast a different gaze onto nature, one that would not subordinate nor deaden the landscape. She does this, primarily, *through* the shepherdess, who emerges in the film as nature's personified figure: shown as an exotic animal of sorts, she does not say a word throughout the film but communicates through gestures, grimaces, masterful horse riding, and occasional laughter. A stranger to the brigade, she appears in the fields often suddenly, conveying the sense of being everywhere and nowhere at once—catching Kemel off-guard and always playing the upper hand in their occasional encounters. Her figure is simultaneously present but distant, material but ephemeral, visible but never knowable to both Kemel and the viewer. An occasional close-up of her face—often slanted, as if imposing the camera's will on her physical appearance—never adds up to an image by which we might grasp, comprehend, or "master" her being. As an integral element of the desert, the young woman becomes a means by which to acknowledge the surrounding space's autonomy, recognizing its inaccessibility and opening up the possibility of a mutual interaction that occurs on the landscape's terms. But if Shepitko succeeds in eliminating the masterful gaze that controls and defines the Kirgiz terrain, she cannot free it entirely from human conceptual dimensions. The revival of the landscape through the shepherdess's figure is tinted with mystified eroticism, even fetishization, of her young, sexualized, and inaccessible body.

The Unsent Letter

If, between the three films discussed here, we can observe a clear tendency in Soviet cinema to suspend the supremacy of the controlling gaze overseeing Soviet territories, *The Unsent Letter* takes this development to another level. The film not only systematically dismantles the validity of such a gaze but imagines the presentation of nature as if seen outside of human vision—or at least outside of a conventional, Cartesian, subject position. Subjectivity itself, the film suggests, has to be rethought, if the human relation to nature is to be changed. This was exactly the issue that a certain Irina Kokoreva took up in denouncing the film at the Mosfilm studio meeting with which this essay opened. While many participants in the Mosfilm exchange blamed Sergei Urusevsky's "formalist" camera work for the film's apparent flaws, suggesting that it run amok by creating "abstract" images of the taiga that were inappropriate for Soviet audiences, Kokareva argued that the problem was not his formalism but the worldviews that his camera expressed—"pantheistic worldviews," specifically—that were simply incompatible with Soviet ideals. "Pantheism," she explains, "inexorably considers people as if dissolved in the world … fused with nature. … This causes a coldness towards man, inattention to his inner nature."[11] Repeatedly stating her core objection, Kokoreva insisted that the film remains completely indifferent to the fate of its protagonists, coldly observing the spaces of the taiga "devouring" them. Such indifference, she suggested, was only possible because the filmmakers considered humanity "as nothing—that is equal with nature itself."[12]

Despite Kokoreva's condemnation of the film, it is hard to disagree with her point of view; images of such a process of "devouring" are indeed plentiful in *The Unsent Letter*, accumulating especially in the film's second half, after a forest fire breaks out. Severing the geologists' connection with "the center," the fire shatters their plans of return, sending the group on an excruciating trudge through the landscape, which turns increasingly

Figure 2.2. *The Unsent Letter (Neotpravlennoye pis'mo)*. Directed by Mikhail Kalatozov. Moscow: Mosfilm, 1960. Screen capture by Lida Oukaderova.

into a blurred, repetitive, and at times flat and abstract surface that fails to offer viewers, or the protagonists, any sense of direction or orientation. If the geologists, in the first part of the film, seem to remake the landscape in their searched for the diamonds, leaving a distinct mark of their work behind them, by the end they become incapable of producing durable traces. We see their footprints rapidly disappearing into the swampy ground or are immediately covered up by the snow; even more, the protagonists' bodies begin to mimic the natural forms of the landscape through which they move, thus negating their distinct identities.

One of the film's most striking sequences in this regard displays the final two protagonists, Konstantin and Tania, settling down for the night on a hill. The sequence begins with them lying together and conversing before falling asleep; the initial nighttime passage, shot in a series of close-ups and from a variety of low angles, alternates between the two protagonists' heads and faces, emphasizing their volumetric forms against the backdrop of the sky. Although the figures are clearly shot to stand out from the flattened, static sky behind them, they simultaneously merge with and in fact take the place of the landscape in which they lie. A slight pine tree blowing above the head of Tania at the sequence's opening, for instance, soon disappears to be replaced by each figure's breezy whisps of hair. Their faces, seen in close-up, are relief-like, characterized by exaggerated volume and extreme physical expansiveness. Viewed at a variety of angles that exclude all surrounding landscape, their profiles appear to be the land itself, a series of craggy cliffs. It is as if they become the very terrain they are trying to traverse.

The film's "pantheistic worldview" is exemplified not only through the images of human figures *becoming* nature, but also in the gaze through which we see this. The camera's dynamic, flexible, handheld mobility (famed for its emotional communication in *The Cranes Are Flying*) suggests an embodied, subjective behavior, but one disconnected from any specific protagonist. Such moments, instead, make tangible the presence of the environment itself, as something that effectively has a body and gaze of its own, a view distinct from that of the human beings who traverse it. The movements of this spatial "body" cannot be motivated psychologically or emotionally—just as its gaze is devoid of the human, psychologically determined interest. It regards the protagonists as a physical matter akin to other natural elements in the surroundings (swamps, cliffs, snow, hills)—as surface rather than depth, thereby excluding their interiority and inviting a pantheistic reading of the film, in which human figures are spatialized and made indistinct from nature itself.

One of the most elaborate sequences in this process takes place with the death of the geologist Tania. She and the expedition's head Konstantin are walking through fields, with Tania becoming increasingly weak, until, as Konstantin suddenly realizes, she is no longer walking behind him. In a series of movements that confuse our spatial orientation, he searches for and finally finds her collapsed on the ground. As he carries her retrieved body, it remains unclear whether Tania is alive or dead. That she has died is suggested through a medium close-up of her static, lifeless face, followed by a gradual fade that at first blends her visage with the surrounding branches and then culminates in a blurred still shot of the frozen surroundings that appears to be a point-of-view shot, a kind of view from the dead. This sequence transitions from her face *as* the environment to her gaze looking out at it, producing a strange inside-out relation. She both gazes at the space that surrounds her and *is*, simultaneously, that very same space. Although Tania is dead within the film's narrative logic, she remains "alive" on a formal level—as nature, still possessing the ability to look.

Such prolonged poetic expositions of the geologists' fusion with space suggests more than just a portrayal of a misfortunate trip. It is better understood as the filmmakers' aesthetic project, the goal of which is to break up a recognizably mapped landscape, to eliminate its conceptual organization, and to propose a different epistemological principle by which to approach and perceive this space: through mimetic approximation of it, by becoming *like* it in the most direct sense, visually and physiologically. It is striking that all three deaths in the film are presented as acts of spatial integration but not one actual dead body is explicitly shown on-screen, perhaps suggesting that the geologists remain somehow alive within the texture of the space that has swallowed them. It is also striking how the film erases politics and ideology from the protagonists' trek through the landscape: what occurs with the fire's breakout in the middle of the film is a process of the group's absolute separation from political and ideological institutions ("the center"), as well as from the structures of vision, perception, and spatial organization they generate.

This is not to say that *The Unsent Letter* is apolitical at its core, but rather that it seeks to reformulate what the Soviet politics of nature might encompass. Instead of human mastery over environments, and the latter's unconditional surrender to the former, this reformulated politics would evaluate the ontological boundary between humans and their surroundings, effecting their greater mutual porosity and boundlessness. This proposition, although raised by less radical means, is also implied by the other films discussed in this chapter: it is suggested by the figure of the shepherdess in *Heat* and by the mutual nurturing of the old villagers and their surrounding gardens and landscapes in *Poem of the Sea*. In all such cases, a relation of reciprocity between humans and nature, in addition to the possibility of their nonhierarchical oneness, is disconnected from the linear progress aspired to by the state—and, more broadly, from a modernity understood to be rooted in the separation of natural and social orders.[13] If these films' interest in the integration of human life into the fold of nature might thus look like an appeal to premodern constructs, it is not an appeal to return to premodern times. Rather, it is a call to consider how such constructs could be accommodated within the modern politics of communities and selfhood that Soviet filmmakers were then beginning to explore.

Lida Oukaderova is Associate Professor of Film Studies in the Department of Art History at Rice University. She is author of *The Cinema of the Soviet Thaw: Space, Materiality, Movement* (2017). Currently she is working on a book titled *In Pursuit of the Common: Soviet and Russian Cinema since the 1960s*. Taking the 1960s as a historical moment when the Soviet socialist ideals of community began to lose their broad acceptance, the book examines the cinematic permutations of "the common" in the cinema of the late socialist and postsocialist period. In addition, she is currently editing a volume on the cinema of the Soviet director Larisa Shepitko for Edinburgh University Press.

Notes

On 6 June 2023, in the midst of the Russia-Ukraine war, an explosion likely set by Russian forces destroyed the Kachov dam and produced devastating flooding to surrounding areas. From a tool of economic development, the dam was turned into a tool of war.

1. "Delo fil'ma 'Neotpravlennoe pis'mo'," 19.
2. "Delo fil'ma," 14.
3. For a detailed survey of Russian and Soviet environmental history, see Josephson et al., *An Environmental History of Russia*.
4. Josephson et al., *An Environmental History of Russia*, 144.
5. Josephson et al., 137.
6. On the industrial projects around lake Baikal, and the environmental movement that emerged in the region, see Breyfogle, "At the Watershed."
7. On the history of the destruction of the Aral Sea, see Kumar, "Aral Sea."
8. Coumel, "A Failed Environmental Turn?"
9. Although Sergei Urusevsky also worked on *The First Echelon* as a cameraman, he joined the crew later in the process, after the original cameraman Yuri Ekel'chik became sick. Urusevsky credits specifically *The First Echelon* as the first fictional film in which he tried out his signature handheld camera movements; on the whole, however, he sought to subordinate his aesthetic vision to that of Ekel'chik. See Merkel, "Effekt Urusevskogo."
10. Ognev, "O Sovremennosti."
11. "Delo fil'ma," 30.
12. "Delo fil'ma," 31.
13. Such a "non-modern" indistinction between humans and their environment has a long discursive trajectory in theoretical writings on modernism, from Walter Benjamin's early twentieth-century essays on mimicry (such as "On the Mimetic Faculty") to Bruno Latour's early twenty-first-century study *The Politics of Nature* (2004), to name a few.

Bibliography

Benajmin, Walter. "On the Mimetic Faculty." In *Walter Bernjamin: Selected Writings*. Vol. 2, pt.2, 1931-1934, edited by Michael W. Jennings, Howard Eiland, and Gary Smith, and translated by Edmund Ephcott and others, 720-22. Cambridge, MA: Belknap, 1999.

Breyfogle, Nicholas B. "At the Watershed: 1958 and the Beginnings of Lake Baikal Environmentalism." *The Slavonic and East European Review* 93, no. 1 (2015): 147–180.

Coumel, Laurent. "A Failed Environmental Turn? Khrushchev's Thaw and Nature Protection in Soviet Russia." *The Soviet and Post-Soviet Review* 40, no. 2 (2013): 167–189.

"Delo fil'ma 'Neotpravlennoe pis'mo'." [File on the Film *The Unsent Letter*], Russian State Archive of Literature and Arts (RGALI), Fond 2453, Opis' 1, delo 664, 19.

Josephson, Paul, Nicolai Dronin, Ruben Mnatsakanian, Aleh Cherp, Dmitry Efremenko, and Vladislav Larin, eds. *An Environmental History of Russia*. Cambridge: Cambridge University Press, 2013.

Kumar, Rama Sampath. "Aral Sea: Environmental Tragedy in Central Asia." *Economic and Political Weekly* 37, no. 37 (2002): 3797–3802.

Latour, Bruno. *The Politics of Nature: How to Bring the Sciences into Democracy*. Cambridge, MA: Harvard University Press, 2004.

Merkel, Maia. "Effekt Urusevskogo." *Sovetskii Ekran* 6 (1977): 18–19.

Ognev, Vladimir. "O Sovremennosti." *Iskusstvo kino* 7 (1956): 10-20.

Filmography

Solntseva, Yulia. *Poem of the Sea* (*Poema o morye*, USSR, 1958).
Kalatozov, Mikhail. *The First Echelon* (*Pervyi eshelon*, USSR, 1955).
———. *The Cranes Are Flying* (*Letiat zhuravli*, USSR, 1958).
———. *The Unsent Letter* (*Nieotpravlennoye pismo*, USSR, 1960).
Shepitko, Larisa. *Heat* (*Znoi*, USSR, 1962).

3

Specters of Ecology in Cold War Soviet Science Fiction Film

Natalija Majsova

The emergence of the Soviet state project coincided with the development of the cinematic medium, giving Soviet science fiction film a very particular genealogy. The medium of film was quickly appreciated for its capacity to serve as a means of surveillance and observation, of propaganda and education, of experiment and reiteration, in short, of monstration and narration of a new world-to-be. As a result, its visualizations of the future constitute something more than mere fantasy, symptom, or flight of fancy. They carried greater weight, offering viewers a new dimension, a perspective, and a voice all at the same time. The genre of science fiction thus came to fulfill a variety of functions in Soviet history, from the normatively prognostic and mnemonic, to the revelatory and introspective.

Considering that both Soviet film and Soviet science fiction as a genre were invested in visualizing, narrating, and arguing for various versions of the future, this chapter focuses on their intersection—Soviet science fiction film—in order to provide a condensed overview of the evolution of this "ecological imaginary of the future." For the purposes of this chapter, evolution should not be understood in terms of linear progression or in terms of a straightforward correlation between visions of the future and the socioeconomic circumstances that might have marked a particular film's production context. Rather, I argue that the broad historical arc that frames this chapter is necessary to bring out the dynamics of this imaginary, and the interplay between its manifest and latent features.

Focusing specifically on Cold War–era cinematography, I use a patchwork of films from various decades in order to highlight the various vectors at the core of the Soviet world-building and terraforming imaginary, accounting for the intertextual dialogue that the cinematic medium offered with regard to these vectors over time. In particular, I interrogate anthropocentrism and the notion of (sociopolitical and technological) progress as the strongest vectors that marked the development of the ecological imaginary of Soviet science fiction. Mapped onto the universe at large and planet Earth in particular, varying constellations of these vectors exposed a range of attitudes toward the environment. In this chapter, the environment is understood in a threefold manner: as *Umwelt*, the term coined by Jakob Johann von Uexküll to describe each individual organism's perspective on its environment, those elements it picks up on because they are crucial to its survival; as nature, understood as a realm that is separate from, but related to, human agency and intervention; and as ecology in the sense of an axiological orientation determining both the abstract understanding of progress and specific attitudes about human intervention in the environment.[1]

I begin by first outlining the contours of the Soviet ideology of world-building as it manifested in the cinema, focusing on its sanctioned interactions between the human and nonhuman world. Then, combining narratological and iconographic analysis, I use the films *Toward a Dream* (*Mechte navstrechu*, 1963) and *Andromeda Nebula* (*Tumannost' Andromedy*, 1967) to demonstrate the limits and the gradual depletion of the anthropocentric and patriarchic ideal of the rational, male, proactive human subject as master of the universe.[2] Alongside this vector, I use *Planet of the Storms* (*Planeta bur'*, 1962) and *The Mysterious Wall* (*Tainstvennaya stena*, 1967) to point to the incompatibility of the aforementioned androcentric and colonial understanding of subjectivity with the basic postulates of scientific inquiry, such as a radical openness to encountering the unknown. Finally, I turn to two later films, *Per Aspera Ad Astra* (*Cherez ternii k zvezdam*, 1981) and *The Moon Rainbow* (*Lunnaya raduga*, 1983) to point to the "dark side" of andro- and anthropocentric ideals of progress and visions of the future that, in their linearity and one-dimensionality, disregard the impact that they have on the environment.

A Man to Fit the World, A World to Fit That Man

Arguably one of the major stakes in Soviet science fiction cinema was a particular perspective on world-building. From the very first Soviet attempt at a science fiction blockbuster, Iakov Protazanov's *Aelita: Queen of Mars* (*Aelita*, 1924) onward, the vast majority of Soviet science fiction films demonstrate, in line with the dominant Communist view on social progress, that a world never develops independently of its subjects and their interactions. Accordingly, up until the 1980s, the subjects of Soviet science fiction were typically human individuals and collectives who strove for a better, socialist future. Moreover, these subjects did not simply wait for the arrival of this future, but worked on their own development, in order to eventually become subjects fit to inhabit this future. In other words, the future entailed as much of a transformation of the material conditions of life, as a transformation of the subjects' hearts. Thus, humanity, individuals, and their surroundings were seen as complementary cogs in the ever improving, progressive machine that was the Soviet socialist future-about-to-come.[3] This was particularly characteristic of those works of Soviet science fiction that tacitly or explicitly adhered to the recommendations of Stalinist socialist realism, the doctrine that had shaped Soviet cultural production from the 1930s until the 1950s; inter alia it involved the recommendation that art represent the Communist future as if it had already happened.[4]

This Stalinist imperative displaced an earlier, vanguard vision of a better, collective future, advanced by local artists and designers, as well as the media, in the first two decades of the twentieth century.[5] A consolidation of visions of the future under Stalinism, and, in the sphere of cultural production, under the postulates of socialist realism, had far-reaching consequences for film production in general and for the genre of science fiction in particular. A set of specific objectives had been set before the film industry: to motivate the masses, to educate them regarding socialism in form and content, to prophesize the future, and to memorialize the early feats of the Revolution and the new Soviet state. Important debates arose around these foci, including about the formal features of Soviet cinema, such as narratives and other possible emphases of screenplays; the organization of the film production and distribution industry in the USSR; and its thematic and genre priorities.[6] Fantasy was not at the top of this last list, considered suspicious on accounts of its reliance on the free flight of the imagination, unbound by ideological imperatives and inclined to other bourgeois indulgences, such as melodramatic twists.

In literature, science fiction under Stalin is chiefly associated with the so-called "near-reach" formula (*fantastika blizhnego pritsela*), that is, the proliferation of narratives that celebrate the graspable, realistic feats of contemporary science.[7] An important undercurrent of such narratives, characteristic of Soviet science fiction films until the late 1960s, remained its clear political statement: Soviet authority was associated with scientific progress and apparently righteous goals, such as improvements in farming and agriculture, whereas scientific progress outside of the Soviet state was linked to war, invasion, heartless imperialism, and colonialism.[8]

Nature and ecology play a remarkably small role in these narratives, the films demonstrating a clearly acceptable and even desirable goal of exploiting it for the benefit of humankind.[9] Moreover, a hierarchy is maintained between the urban space, the countryside, and nature. This distinction between realms permeates Soviet science fiction until the late 1960s; yet, as we shall see in the following paragraphs, it undergoes important transformations. In 1920s-era films, the city is proactive, its structures reaching upward and demanding engagement from the population (something seen as a marker of being both educated and fashionable at the time), while the countryside remains proverbially backward, and magnificent, raw nature waits to be tamed. If Soviet science fiction films from the 1920s–1950s are preoccupied with the growth and development of this world, post-Stalinist science fiction speculates about its completion and its implications; by the 1980s, the latter turns into a major area of concern.

The Dream of Taming Nature

By the late 1950s, the end of the socialist realist dictate signified greater freedom for the genre of science fiction in terms of narratives and screenplays. At the same time, the coterminous early feats of the Soviet space program aligned it with the emergent collective obsession with space exploration—the battlefield of the Cold War, which, in the Soviet imagination, also presented the site of the nearing Communist utopia.[10] While terrestrial Soviet science fiction of the 1960s remained preoccupied with pointing out the lamentable consequences of Western individualism, materialism, and imperialism (*Amphibian Man* [*Chelovek-amfibiya*, 1961] is a good example of this), Thaw-era science fiction offered a screen for projections of magnificent visions of the future.

In particular, late 1950s and early 1960s "space melodramas" should be mentioned for their wholehearted embrace of a "realistic" approach to visualizing Space Age ecology. *Toward a Dream* (1963), a space opera about extraterrestrial contact that combines socialist realist narrative tropes with bold visions of intergalactic communication and collaboration, is a case in point. This production about the far-off future makes use of two devices to emphasize its fictionality. The opening shots are equipped with a voice-over address that dedicates the film "to young dreamers and romantics." Furthermore, we eventually learn that the primary fictional narrative, in other words, the fictional space story, is embedded into the reverie of a future scientist (*Aelita*-style). The society of the future is trying hard to develop a method of contacting alien civilizations. A Soviet and a Western scientist hold opposing ideological positions on the nature of a possible encounter, the Soviet believing in peace, and the Westerner predicting conflict.[11] In this classical socialist realist future, that is, in young scientist Andrei's (Aleksandr Shvorin) present, the weather is great, the water is warm, and everyone does what they are best suited to do. "Fishermen live here, as well as poets, pupils and astronomers, artists and cosmonauts," the narrator explains in the voice-over. This world of the socialist future is rational, compartmentalized, and presents the victory of culture over nature.

Accordingly, in these films, the only argument presented for travel to other planets is the idealistic one: an advanced civilization's "thirst for knowledge." Under the aegis of Soviet reason, the world's scientists, "the collective intellect" of the planet decide to put in enormous effort (delivering impressive amounts of fuel to the intermediate base on the moon, for example) in order to facilitate an expedition to Mars. This feat of cosmopolitan spirit and scientific enthusiasm is represented by an animated sequence of moon-bound rockets, accompanied by one of the two memorable songs: the march-like "Ia Zemlia" (This is I, Earth), performed by an anonymous female lead (presumably Earth herself) and the popular Soviet singer Iosif Kobzon. On Earth, a crew is established and sent off to Mars. Like in most Cold War East European science fiction productions, it is emphasized that the crew is international, gender-diverse, and multi-generational. After a series of mishaps, they locate the alien crew on Mars and transmit evidence of it in the form of a beautiful, blonde humanoid female named Aetania (Tatiana Pochepa), dressed in slightly unusual, modernist attire. In the concluding shots, we see her staring down at the spectators on Earth from a big screen on Gagarin square, the center of our fictional settlement, an idealized hybrid of a metropolis and an upscale rural residential complex. All ends well in this dream, and outside the dream, a spaceship is really sent to Mars.

Toward a Dream belongs to a range of science fiction films justified by the early feats of the Soviet space program (the launch of Sputnik in 1957, Yuri Gagarin's 1961 pioneering flight, Aleksei Leonov's 1965 spacewalk), which were produced with big budgets at some of the most important national film studios (Lenfilm, Mosfilm, Dovzhenko Studios). Moreover, these "A quality" versions "proverbially B productions, such as space op-

Specters of Ecology in Cold War Soviet Science Fiction Film • 69

Figure 3.1. Transmission of alien envoy Aetania's message to Earth and its people. *Toward a Dream* (*Mechte navstrechu*). Directed by Mikhail Karyukov and Otar Koberidze. Odessa: Odessa Film Studio, 1963. Screenshot by Natalija Majsova.

eras," were also released during the Khrushchevian Thaw (1956–1964), which presented a window of relative openness toward the West, and before the USSR's 1973 accession to the Bern convention on copyright.[12] These factors facilitated their exhibition in the United States, where, with producer Roger Corman's blessing, some of them were refashioned to suit the anticipated preferences of the local audience. In an interview for *Kino-eye* in 2003, Corman, who affirmed having bought the rights to the films due to their extraordinary quality, claims to have warned "the Russians" that he would have to adapt the films by cutting out all of the Soviet and anti-American propaganda, and that his assertion was understandingly approved by "the Russians."[13]

Toward a Dream (1963), in particular, was turned into a techno-horror B-movie by Curtis Harrington. The remake, titled *Queen of Blood* (1966), completely disregards the world-building message of the film as unessential to the narrative progress of the story. The version produced in the United States foregrounds the action plot, transforming the Soviet dream within a dream into an American horror story. Harrington's *Queen of Blood*, however, only really begins here. Having excised the melodrama and the ideological framework, the director/editor was left with somber scenes of the space expedition, and intriguing footage of an attractive female alien. The Soviet film never gave an explicit reason to believe that Aetania, the alien, was a kind creature. And, as if poking fun of the Soviets' optimism, *Queen of Blood* transforms her into a vampirical, man-eating monster. Actress Florence Marly was attired in a similar costume to shoot this part of the story. Our lifeworlds are ambiguous and cannot be subordinated to idealist projections, Harrington seems to reply to the Soviets and their innocent reverie.

Notably, the "space voyage as dream" device was only dispensed with in the late 1960s. Yevgeni Sherstobitov's 1967 screen adaptation of Ivan Eefremov's novel *Andromeda Nebula* presents both a case in point and a tipping point with regard to the limits of the Soviet narrative about mastering nature. The far-off future of *Andromeda Nebula* is, in fact, inhabited by new Soviet men and women, who navigate a perfectly balanced, harmonious world, where the most laudable achievements of the past centuries, such as ancient togas, are integrated into a most advanced society, skilled in interplanetary travel and holographic dance parties. In this sense, this 1967 production complies exceptionally well with Evgeny Dobrenko's assessment of the vectors of Stalinist cinema. Dobrenko argues that "in order to master the future, it is necessary, in the first place, to turn it into the past (as it is based on the "known," the past does not scare), and, second, to sacrifice the present (which turns out from this future-directed perspective to be irrelevant, as everything is done "for the bright tomorrow" and "for future generations")."[14] This statement applies to a significant portion of Soviet science fiction films, particularly those that adhered to the socialist realist canon even after the twentieth Party Congress, such as *Toward a Dream* and *Andromeda Nebula*.

Indeed, Sherstobitov's celebration of the Communist project visualizes the fully Communist Earth of the future as a static, monumental, perfectly regulated society. Earth is home to sporty, intellectually capable individuals, who wear outfits that resemble ancient Greek togas, and busy themselves with scientifically (but not socially!) progressive pursuits. These individuals, for instance Dar Veter (Sergei Stoliarov) and his muse, Veda Kong (Viya Artmane), are so advanced that they do not find it problematic to switch between professions with ease, no matter how diverse these professions might be. The only emotions they act upon are dignified, idealized ones that comply with the ideological convictions of Stalinist, Soviet humanism, including its enshrining of masculinity as the rational, dignified, just, and almost infallible gender. And yet the film's dynamic depends on the contrasts between the brightness of idyllic Earth and the enigmatic lure of the depth of space. Just like *Aelita* and *Toward a Dream*, both of which feature mysterious female aliens, *Andromeda Nebula* posits outer space as a female domain. It is in space that mission commander Erg Noor (Nikolai Kriukov) betrays his rational judgment, succumbing to the force of love, embodied by his astro-navigator Niza Krit (Tatiana Voloshina). It is also only in space, in the face of danger, that she allows herself to follow her emotions rather than professional protocols, confessing her love for Noor. Thus, in the realm of science fiction cinema, the appeal of perfectly rational and apparently genderless socialist realist space futures can only be sustained if it is accompanied by its opposite—the mystery of outer space, where femininity is granted agency. In space, the female of Soviet science fiction cinema is not at all the imperfect sidekick of the male scientist or cosmonaut (like in *Toward a Dream*), nor is her role limited to her procreative function. The following paragraphs will highlight several of the many positions, roles, and functions of the female, accessible to her only on the margins of the perfect Communist space future. As we shall see, the outlined dialectic of the exceptionally unrealistic image of the regulated and conflictless Communist future, perfected in *Andromeda Nebula*, and the enticing darkness of the unknown, at the borders of this future, gradually becomes one of the key characteristics of Soviet science fiction cinema after the Moon landing.

To See Is to Capture Is to Master the Nature of the Future

While socialist realism was predicated on progress toward an ideologically overdetermined future, based on the assumption that the new Soviet man will lead humanity into the Space Age, it was also aligned with scientific inquiry as the vehicle of progress toward this future. In the realm of science fiction and cinema concerned with the popularization of science, this translated into a heightened interest in film's capacity to visualize the future. In fact, until the late 1970s, Soviet science fiction films were clearly influenced by special effects master Pavel Klushantsev, specifically his tribute to the history of the Soviet space program, *Road to the Stars* (*Doroga k zvezdam*, 1957). This popular science film, intended to educate the audience about the recent past of space exploration and its future, is an exquisite combination of celebratory, patriotic narration, and footage that both commemorates and expands upon the work of Soviet space scientists.

Produced by the Leningrad popular scientific film studio Lennauchfilm, *Road to the Stars* carefully navigates the border between documentary and fiction, embedding both into a clear ideological context, and using the cinematic medium as the privileged arena for special effects, much like early film pioneers such as Georges Méliès, or Vasili Zhuravlyov in his film *Space Voyage* (*Kosmicheskiy reis*, 1936).[15] However, if Zhuravlyov conceived of spaceflight as a symbol of Stalinism and Soviet power, and mused on spaceflight as a dream, *Road to the Stars*, inspired by the actual developments of the Soviet space program, "dreamt bigger"—not only about a trip to the Moon but also about an entire ecology of manned spaceflight, with satellites, rockets, moon landings, and planetary colonization. Moreover, if Zhuravlyov's film came out in the twilight of early Soviet space enthusiasm, *Road to the Stars* was intended to make the spectator smell the rocket, and to invite Soviet youth to join the ranks of engineers, physicists, and pilots. Not only did this film inspire Stanley Kubrick's 1968 masterpiece *2001: A Space Odyssey*, but it also influenced a series of Soviet productions that followed in its wake.

Klushantsev directed two more successful popular science films, *Moon* (*Luna*, 1965) and *Mars* (*Mars*, 1968), but the fascination with observation of other worlds also permeates his first fiction feature, *Planet of the Storms*, which was released only two days after the first anniversary of Gagarin's flight, on 14 April 1962. This film, which features an international trip to Venus and only slightly pokes fun at the conservative, odd American robot Sir John, also speculates about the possible existence of untamed nature on the surface of Venus, where species might exist side by side and act aggressively toward the Earthlings not out of evil inclinations but rather as a defense mechanism.

Planet of the Storms was reedited by Corman's team into two films: *Voyage to the Prehistoric Planet* (1965) and *Voyage to the Planet of Prehistoric Women* (1968), which also includes inserts from *The Heavens Call* (*Nebo zovyot*), a 1959 Soviet science fiction feature. Interestingly, Corman's first adaptation of this imaginative, visually rich film, *Voyage to the Prehistoric Planet*, was not a great commercial success on the US market. The film's invitation to marvel at natural diversity and at the space crew's first attempts to negotiate a space for themselves on this foreign planet did not go over well. For the second adaptation, Corman hired director Peter Bogdanovich, allegedly for as little as $6,000, to "add some women into the picture," claiming that American-International Pictures was not willing to screen it otherwise.[16] This is how the cult techno-horror space thriller *Voyage to the Planet of Prehistoric Women* was made. Both adaptations made extensive use of Klushantsev's imagery of the Venusian world and those of the space voyage, but all references to the original Soviet mission were omitted.

Moreover, the US adaptations consciously downplayed the question of gender equality, which was highlighted, albeit naively, by the Soviet director, whose mission included a female cosmonaut. In Klushantsev's film, Venus is a strange world, full of unexpected life forms and challenges, which test both the Soviet man and the Soviet woman, not to mention the capitalist robot Sir John. In Corman's adaptation, however, this storyline is completely replaced by the vulgar fantasy of a Venus inhabited by attractive, malicious, and primitive blondes, who finally end up worshipping the robot left behind by the international expedition as their god.[17]

Despite the ideological differences underpinning the two adaptations of Klushantsev's dreamy visuals, the anthropocentrism of the iconography and the plots of all the versions is difficult to ignore. The crews of the Soviet and US spaceship set out to another world to seek similarities, not difference; they evaluate the extraterrestrial world they encounter by terrestrial standards; and their fascination—be it the Soviets' with the Venusian flora and fauna or the presumed Americans' with the "prehistoric women"—is voyeuristic and presupposes the superiority of man over nature, and of humanity over extraterrestrial life. However, the Soviet film concludes in line with the dichotomy between the human and the alien, outlined earlier. As the cosmonauts leave Venus, the camera shifts from their spaceship to a Venusian lake. A mysterious female is reflected on its surface, reiterating the idea of a mysterious, powerful, and alien femininity, familiar to the reader from many of the other Soviet science fiction productions mentioned in this chapter.

In the late 1960s, the special effects that had made earlier Soviet productions interesting for foreign producers such as Corman, began to fall behind. This was due to a number of systemic factors, including the late arrival of personal computers and CGI in the Soviet Union, declining interest in science fiction among directors and scriptwriters, and declining institutional support for the genre, which lacked its own committee within the Soviet Union of Cinematographers until the mid-1980s. Nevertheless, the late 1970s and early 1980s remain a very interesting period for Soviet science fiction cinema, particularly due to the expansion of its temporal and philosophical horizons anticipated by *Andromeda Nebula*.

The World Is as Deep as We Care to Consider: Scrutinizing Otherness

Irina Povolotskaya's debut, *The Mysterious Wall*, produced in 1967, the same year as *Andromeda Nebula*, pioneered an alternative approach to extraterrestrial encounter and the question of interspecies communication. Stylistically influenced by the French New Wave, this production was also one of the first Soviet films to question and lightly mock the authorities. Instead of marveling at the prospects of the Space Age, Povolotskaya interrogates the human capacity to ever really engage with otherness. As if in anticipation of Andrei Tarkovsky's 1972 screen adaptation of Stanisław

Łem's 1961 novel *Solaris* (*Solaris*), the alien Other takes on the form of a mysterious wall that appears at regular intervals in the nowhere of the taiga. When approached by humans, this presence of unknown, possibly alien, origin makes them experience powerful hallucinations that draw on their most intimate memories. In one such episode, we learn, for example, that one of the protagonists, the idealistic, romantic Valia (Andrei Mironov) had once served on a battleship, which had apparently rescued a Canadian writer (Valentin Nikulin) found estranged and alone, at sea. In this episode, the writer, whose appearance and speech indicate a surrealist, and perhaps psychedelic influence, says: "A Martian? No, I am not a Martian. I am no one. I am alone in the ocean. Although, it sounds beautiful. A Martian. Yes, to you, I am a Martian. We are all Martians. We are all naked in the ocean." This episode is key to the film's message regarding otherness. *The Mysterious Wall* provides a strong metaphor for barriers between individuals; this metaphor is further enhanced by the tense relations between the human protagonists that emerge as the main theme of the film, almost overshadowing the strangeness of the recounted events. This emphasis on the epistemic, philosophical aspects of existence was a revolutionary gesture at the time—one that would be picked up by a number of films in the following decade.

The Mysterious Wall delves into the complexities of the human soul in order to question the innermost motives of human conduct. At the same time, it also lays bare the vanity of human struggles for superiority (for example, over humans of different gender or nationality than one's own). Believing that it is one's task to explain away the world and its mysteries, the human subject is perennially incapable of accessing that, which one cannot associate with one's own experience. Once again, radical otherness is represented in this film by the female protagonist. In contrast to the productions discussed earlier in this chapter, she is not an alien. Lena (Tatiana Lavrova) is simply a young woman who visits her fiancé, Egor (Lev Kruglyi), a scientist in the taiga. Her arrival sets up a doubling of disruptive forces. While Lena asks fundamental questions about human relationships that disrupt the male scientists' pursuit of logical, scientific explanations, the wall offers representations that mimic the world as they know and understand it. Yet the purpose of this communication process remains obscure to the men, who are instinctively wary of the Other's motives. Analogously, Lena's thoughts and questions are linguistically intelligible, but remain misunderstood by her male colleagues. Thus, the scientists appear incapable of facing worlds built around logics that differ from their own. As we shall see, the appeal of these very alien worlds increases in the 1970s, as the initial fascination with space-themed science fiction cinema as a visualization of real scientific achievements gradually fades.

From Human to Planetary Agency

The moon landing of 1969 signaled the end of the glorious days of the Soviet space program. The end of Klushantsev's career at Lennauchfilm in 1974, in turn, marked the end of the related era of enthusiasm for the camera's capacity to make the fictional and the hypothetical real by means of visualization. And yet, 1970s-era science fiction cinema remained a privileged genre, though it now became associated with two overarching ambitions: to reflect on the human condition and to convey the ideas of Soviet citizenship to younger generations. Importantly, film directors tended to approach both ideas with an admirable degree of critical reflection, narratively and aesthetically setting 1970s- and 1980s-era productions apart from their predecessors.

Following the Strugatsky brothers' harsh 1967 critique of Soviet science fiction cinema, which, according to the celebrated writers, lacked imagination, direction, narrative skill, and special effects, Tarkovsky's *Solaris* (1972) and *Stalker* (1979) dug deeper than ever before into certain tropes that permeated the very core of Soviet world-building, in practice and in the popular imagination.[18] *Solaris*, inspired by the aforementioned *The Mysterious Wall*, explores the possibilities of conversing with a radically other lifeform, a sentient ocean. In contrast to Povolotskaia's production, which was somewhat axiologically detached, and to the dismay of the novel's author Stanisław Lem, Tarkovsky used the trope of the alien encounter to offer an exploration of the human psyche, seeking redemption in a rather mystical kind of humanism—an aim that was also to characterize *Stalker*, Tarkovsky's adaptation of the Strugatskys' novel *Roadside Picnic* (1972). At the same time, against the backdrop of the older, Soviet canon of optimistic, idealized representations of the future-to-come, *Solaris* and *Stalker* can, in an equally convincing way, be read as criticism of Soviet world-building, including its segmentation of the world into "world" and "zone."[19] The former is epitomized by the utopian society of *Andromeda Nebula*, while the latter belongs to Tarkovsky's outcasts, from Hari (Natalia Bondarchuk) in *Solaris* to Monkey (Natasha Abramova) in *Stalker*. *Solaris* and *Stalker* foreground the recluses and the intermediaries between the zone (of terror, of crime, of exclusion) and the world (apparently peaceful and orderly). In doing so, the two films lead the spectator toward the realization that the zone and the world, separated by rigorously controlled, yet still semipermeable borders, are both products of humanist tenants, such as the idea of radically transforming nature in order to master it. Once such zones become a fact of life, there is no way back to romantic prehistory, to ancient equilibrium.

The teen film *Per Aspera Ad Astra* (1981) went a step further, casting light on the consequences of mindless terraformation for the very first time in Soviet science fiction cinema. The film is set on the planet Dessa, where tyrannical, authoritarian rule has brought about poverty and destruction. The images of the burning planet, evocative of historic, humanmade disasters, such as the drying up Aral Sea, are not just shocking representations of cataclysm. Alongside the female cyborg alien, Niya (Elena Metelkina), the planet itself stars as a protagonist for the first time in Soviet film history. Thematically reminiscent of Nicholas Roeg's *The Man Who Fell to Earth* (1976), *Per Aspera Ad Astra* juxtaposes an unsettlingly idyllic Earth with its dark side, Dessa, which had been turned into one never-ending zone. Ideologically neutral (neither human not outcast) artificial intelligence, anthropomorphic cyborg Niya is presented as an interlocutor between the two realms, advancing the gendered imaginary of Soviet science fiction cinema. This chapter demonstrates that humanoid alien females, such as Aelita and Aetania, and human females, such as Niya and Lena, were typically only granted agency in outer space and remained misunderstood on Earth unless they accepted the function of a sidekick, complementary to the male protagonist. In this respect, Niya, enhanced by technology, plays an unprecedented role, actively intervening in both the world on Earth and the one on Dessa. In doing so, she can be seen as a celebratory symbol of alterity and multiperspectivism.

The remastered 2001 version of *Per Aspera Ad Astra*, completed by the director's son Nikolai Viktorov, stipulates that all footage of Dessa was shot on planet Earth. Goskino censorship had prevented this detail from entering the original film, as the scriptwriter, novelist Kir Bulychev, had initially intended. *Per Aspera Ad Astra* made a very powerful statement for cosmopolitanism and the erasure of borders, and against the uncontrolled, market-oriented exploitation of natural resources. It was also one of the last Soviet science fiction films that believed in the power of humanity to reverse the adverse effects of its activities on the planet.[20]

Bringing Space Back Home: The Zones of the Post-Soviet World

Certain late Soviet productions expanded on the question of planetary futures set out in *Per Aspera Ad Astra*. Georgiy Daneliya's cyberpunk tale *Kin-Dza-Dza!* (*Kin-Dza-Dza!*) from 1986, a sarcastic but not entirely sardonic critique of Soviet utopian thought and its pragmatic politics, the quintessence of what Elana Gomel (2013) has called "utopia in the mud," is an instructive case in point. Its setting, planet Pluke, an analog of Dessa and, by extension, of future Earth, is represented as the site of the conse-

Figure 3.2. The dying planet Dessa. *Per Aspera Ad Astra* (*Cherez ternii k zvyozdam*). Directed by Richard Viktorov. Moscow: Gorky Film Studio, 1981. Screen capture by Natalija Majsova.

quences of human(oid) intervention. The emphasis of the film is not so much on the perils of unbridled technological progress as on the community that inhabits the planet. Pluke's people are portrayed as dirty, slightly bored, petty, and fatalistically invested in observing obnoxious rituals. Like *Per Aspera Ad Astra*, *Kin-Dza-Dza!* is certainly a critique of totalitarian rule, embodied here in the figure of the ruthless dictator "P. Zh." However, if Viktorov's film warns the audience about the consequences of unsustainable and inhumane politics and policies implemented by the political elites, Daneliya points to the social and societal basis—the ordinary people and their habits—that sustain such politics and policies.

One of the leitmotifs of *Kin-Dza-Dza!* is the miserable revelation that there is no one to plead for the "salvation of the protagonists' souls." The same observation had, in fact, already been made by a pre-perestroika production, *The Moon Rainbow* (*Lunnaya raduga*) from 1983. In this eerie account of every traveler's worst nightmare, a number of *kosmodesantniki* (i.e., an international space crew) take a trip to planet Oberon near Uranus and survive a peculiar accident there. On the way back to Earth, they begin exhibiting superhuman qualities: they become capable of affecting magnetic fields but can also temporarily rid themselves of this superpower by placing their hand on a special screen. This screen acts as a receiver, and the release of excessive energy is documented as a black mark on its surface. The film explores the implications of this situation for Earthlings: should the astronauts be considered a threat to humanity? Have they become aliens or are they merely enhanced human beings? Who is to decide? Will humanity ever be able to comprehend the secrets of the universe? The core problem addressed by the film—which does not provide any answers to these questions—is the issue of the individual's place within a system built around notions such as transparency, security, and caution, and guided by the belief that society can function according to the same unemotional, rationalist logic that drives technological progress.

Following prophetic Tallinnfilm productions from the late 1970s such as *The Inquest of Pilot Pirx* (*Doznaniye pilota Pirksa* / *Test pilota pirxa* / *Navigaator Pirx*, 1979) and *Dead Mountaineer's Hotel* (*"Hukkunud Alpinisti" hotel* / *Otel' "U pogibshego al'pinista,"* 1979), this film explored how this kind of social order—could this be a highly reflexive account of how Soviet government might have handled global governance?—might function when faced with unpredictable and uncontrollable situations as well as how it might have dealt with individuals who had the will and the means to overturn established order and rules. *The Moon Rainbow* ends on an ambiguous note. It touches upon existential questions, such as the perilous and uncertain future of all space voyagers, and the pressure it exerts on their loved ones, as well as on the issue of whether *kosmodesantniki*, affected by outer space, should be experimented on or not. Finally, it ponders the significance of the thin line—voiced by astronaut Timur Kizimov (Georgiy Taratorkin) in the film—between "a little bit of caution [that] can do no harm" and "caution for caution's sake," allowing the kosmodesantniki to present their own view of the future of space exploration. Norton (Vladimir Gostiukhin), one of the members of the unlucky crew, concludes: "So who are we? We are people, Dave, and I believe that we can be known. Not at once, it seems. And not in special quarantine zones. We might have retired too early—we could still be of much use. ... I am not at all certain that our generation will understand the essence of how outer space affects us."[21] Although Norton spoke of outer space, his thought can be generalized—and at the same time interpolated—to help us think about the interactions of systems and individuals on Earth.

Tellingly, the trope of quarantine zones exploded in films of the late 1980s, most significantly in Konstantin Lopushansky's *Dead Man's Letters* (*Pis'ma myortvogo cheloveka*, 1986)—a somber film about a post-nuclear-war world, one in which there is nothing left but "zones." An area of underground bunkers, the privileged zone, and the planet's surface, where nuclear smog has long replaced breathable air. The riddle of the environment that had puzzled Soviet visions of progress since the 1920s appears to have been resolved. Humanism, based on the idea of a strong, rational, and versatile human subject, modeled on the basis of an adult male individual, is not the viable answer, all the aforementioned films suggest, adding to the international repertoire of narratives and tropes that can promote environmental awareness and potentially increase people's ecosensibility.[22]

Alternative Perspectives for Alternative Worlds?

This chapter has explored how particular Cold War Soviet science fiction films highlight and scrutinize the formative dissonance between the ideology of Soviet progressive humanism and the rhythms of nature and the environment. I argued that, visualized on cinematic screens, this very dissonance makes the Soviet imagined futures appear unrealistic (think of the optimistic productions from the 1960s), repressive (as in *The Moon Rainbow*), or simply destructive (as in *Per Aspera Ad Astra* and *Kin-Dza-Dza!*). Moreover, the analyses in this chapter lead to the conclusion that these serious shortcomings are, to a notable degree, the byproduct of the underlying ideological tendency to disregard all perspectives on the world but one. In Soviet science fiction film, the world and its future can belong only to one type of subject: the young, potent, intelligent—and, inevitably, male cosmonaut and/or scientist.

At the same time, the socialist realist films acknowledge the uncanny rigidity of perfect Communist futures by juxtaposing them against the alluring darkness of space and its possible inhabitants. Some later films, such as *The Mysterious Wall* (1967) and *Solaris* (1972), actively engage with this otherness, by exploring the origins of its allure, in an attempt to open up the Soviet world of the future to alternative perspectives. Among these, the figure of the female alien emerges as the most intriguing trope. Until the late 1960s, she features as a passive symbol of alterity, and a more or less accessible medium or contact-point, opening the doors to other civilizations. In films like *Solaris* (1972) or *Per Aspera Ad Astra* (1981), however, she becomes more proactive, mediating between different worlds and various positionalities, navigating between humanity, technology, nature, and extraterrestrial intelligence.[23]

Although she is eventually integrated into the rigid framework of typical Soviet endings, which make her almost human (*Solaris*), and even patriotic (*Per Aspera Ad Astra*), the implications of the very presence of this female alien reach far deeper. Films like *Moon Rainbow*, *Kin-Dza-Dza!*, and *Dead Man's Letters* demonstrate the limitations of the normative protagonist of the Soviet future. They emphasize the fallibility, subjectivity, cruelty, and nearsightedness of the rational male subject, painting him as responsible for the conquest, segmentation, and eventual destruction of the natural world. By contrast, the productions that grant agency to their female characters uncover alternative possibilities. In doing so, they do not provide any definite answers or map alternative worlds. However, they do probe the spectator to imagine a worldview that builds on enhancing one's capacity to inhabit multiple worlds and navigate between them, rather than on mastering and possessing a single world as one's fortress.

Natalija Majsova is Associate Professor of Cultural Studies at the University of Ljubljana. Her research interests range from cultural theory and film studies to (post-)Soviet studies and media archaeology. She is the author of *Soviet Science Fiction Cinema and the Space Age: Memorable Futures* (Lexington Books, 2021) and, with Sabine Lenk, the co-editor of *Faith in a Beam of Light: Magic Lantern and Belief in Western Europe, 1860-1940* (Brepols, 2022).

Notes

1. Uexküll, *A Foray*, 119–32.
2. *Toward a Dream* is the literal translation of the Russian title (*Mechte navstrechu*). The film has also been occasionally distributed in the West under the title *Encounter in Space*.
3. Gomel, *Science Fiction*, 70–92.
4. Schwartz, "Die Besiedlung der Zukunft."
5. Siddiqi, *The Red Rocket's Glare*.
6. Belodubrovskaya, "Plotlessness."
7. Schwartz, "Die Besiedlung der Zukunft."
8. See Fedorov, *Ekologicheskaia tema*.
9. In the agitational feature *Napoleon Gas* (*Napoleon-gaz*, Semyon Timoshenko, 1925), the exploitation of nature is presented as something acceptable when it serves a purpose: for example, that of Soviet scientists assuring a greater harvest by exterminating the insect population. It is not acceptable, on the other hand, to use poisonous gases to exterminate an urban population, the way imperialist foreigners do. The Soviet science fiction films of the 1920s are permeated by one key political message: that the Soviet regime is under threat from the imperialists. Nature is primarily associated with territory; it is a canvas to be molded according to the needs of the Soviet people as in *The Death Ray* (*Luch smerti*, Lev Kuleshov, 1925) and *Miss Mend* (*Miss Mend*, Fedor Ozep and Boris Barnet, 1926). Even the notorious "first Soviet science fiction blockbuster," *Aelita*, exemplifies this line of thought. In the 1930s, the narratives change slightly, highlighting the bright future to come, and the transformation that this future will entail, both for the population and the land.
10. See Boym, *Kosmos*. For an in-depth discussion of Soviet cinematic utopias after the collapse of the USSR, see chapter 13 of this volume.
11. In fact, many Cold War–era science fiction productions from the Eastern bloc hint at the imminent demise of capitalism. Productions from the 1960s, par-

ticularly interesting due to the popular preoccupation with space exploration, provide numerous cases in point. For example, both the East German *The Silent Star* (*Der Schweigende Stern*, Kurt Mätzig, 1960) and the Czechoslovak *Voyage to the End of the Universe* (*Ikarie X-B1*, Jindřich Polák, 1964, discussed in chapter 4 of this volume) depict their protagonists encountering the miserable remains of capitalist societies in outer space or on foreign planets. While this trope persists in later productions, films from the late 1970s and 1980s tend to invoke such confrontations between socialism and capitalism in space for a different purpose. In such Soviet films as *The Star Inspector* (*Zvezdnyi inspektor*, Mark Kovalyov and Vladimir Polin, 1980) and *Orion's Loop* (*Petlia Oriona*, Vasili Levin, 1980) or the Polish-Soviet coproduction *Inquest of Pilot Pirx* (*Test pilota Pirksa*, Marek Piestrak, 1970), capitalism does not appear dead or about to collapse. Therefore, encounters between the socialist and capitalist space crews do not serve as a premonition of the eventual triumph of communism the way they did in the 1960s. Rather, they either cautiously warn about the dangers of triumphant capitalism (*Inquest of Pilot Pirx*), use the context of intergalactic capitalism to experiment with fun special effects and innovative plots (*The Star Inspector*), or both (*Orion's Loop*).
12. Yates, "Invasion"; Radynski, "The Corman Effect."
13. Yates, "Invasion."
14. Dobrenko, *Stalinist Cinema*, 6.
15. See Beumers, "Special/Spatial Effects in Soviet cinema."
16. See Yates, "Invasion."
17. The "female shots," shot at Major Studios in Los Angeles, were made during another adaptation of a Soviet science fiction film.
18. Strugatsky and Strugatsky, "Kyda zh nam plyt'?"
19. See Gomel, "Utopia in the Mud."
20. See Fedorov, *Ekologicheskaia tema*.
21. See Majsova, "Articulating Dissonance Between Man and the Cosmos."
22. For more on ecocritical film narratives and aesthetic strategies promoting ecosensibility, see also Ingram, "The Aesthetics and Ethics of Eco-film Criticism."
23. For an overview of females in Soviet and Russian science fiction cinema, see Høgetveit, "Female Aliens."

Bibliography

Belodubrovskaya, Maria. "Plotlessness: Soviet Cinema, Socialist Realism, and Nonclassical Storytelling." *Film History* 29, no. 3 (2017): 169–92.
Beumers, Birgit. "Special/Spatial Effects in Soviet Cinema." In *Russian Aviation, Spaceflight and Visual Culture*, edited by Vlad Strukov and Helena Goscilo, 169–85. London: Routledge, 2016.
Boym, Svetlana. *Kosmos: Remembrances of the Future*. Princeton, NJ: Architectural Press, 2001.
Dobrenko, Evgeny. *Stalinist Cinema and the Production of History: Museum of the Revolution*. Edinburgh: Edinburgh University Press, 2008.

Fedorov, Aleksandr. *Ekologicheskaia tema v rossiyskom kinoiskusstve zvukovogo perioda: problemy i tendentsii*. Taganrog: Izdatel'stvo Kuchma, 2002.

Gomel, Elana. *Science Fiction, Alien Encounters, and the Ethics of Posthumanism*. London: Palgrave Macmillan, 2014.

———. "Utopia in the Mud: Judging Nature in Soviet Science Fiction Film." In *Screening Nature: Cinema Beyond the Human*, edited by Anat Pick and Guinevere Narraway, 162–76. Oxford and New York: Berghahn Books, 2013.

Høgetveit, Åsne Ø. "Female Aliens in (Post-) Soviet Sci-Fi Cinema: Technology, Sacrifice and Morality." *Studies in Russian, Eurasian and Central European New Media* 19 (2018): 41–71. https://www.digitalicons.org/wpcontent/uploads/2019/02/DI19_3_Hogetveit.pdf

Ingram, David. "The Aesthetics and Ethics of Eco-film Criticism." In *Ecocinema Theory and Practice*, edited by Stephen Rust, Salma Monani, and Sean Cubittpp, 43–62. London: Routledge, 2012.

Majsova, Natalija. "Articulating Dissonance Between Man and the Cosmos: Soviet Scientific Fantasy in the 1980s and Its Legacy." In *Ruptures and Continuities in Soviet/Russian Cinema: Styles, Characters and Genres Before and After the Collapse of the USSR*, edited by Birgit Beumers and Eugenie Zvonkine, 183–99. Abingdon and New York: Routledge, 2018.

Radynski, Oleksiy. "The Corman Effect: A Give-and-Take Between Soviet and American Cold-War Science Fiction Film." *Kinokultura* (2009). http://www.kinokultura.com/specials/9/radynski-corman.shtml.

Schwartz, Matthias. "Die Besiedlung der Zukunft. Zur Neubegründung der sowjetischen Science Fiction nach dem ersten Sputnikflug 1957." In *Bluescreen: Visionen, Träume, Albträume und Reflexionen des Phantastischen und Utopischen*, edited by Walter Delabar and Frauke Schlieckau, 105–22. Bielefeld: AISTHESIS Verlag, 2010.

Siddiqi, Asif A. *The Red Rocket's Glare: Spaceflight and the Soviet Imagination, 1857–1957*. Cambridge: Cambridge University Press, 2010.

Strugatsky Arkady, and Boris Strugatsky. "Kuda zh nam plyt'?" *Sovyetskii ekran* 3 (1967). http://www.rusf.ru/abs/books/publ10.htm.

Yates, Steven. "Invasion of the Mutant B-movie Producers: Roger Corman Interviewed about His Work in Europe." *Kinoeye* 3, no. 1 (2003). http://www.kinoeye.org/03/01/yates01.php.

Uexküll, Jakob von. *A Foray into the Worlds of Animals and Humans*. Minneapolis: University of Minnesota Press, 2010.

Filmography

Bogdanovich, Peter. *Voyage to the Planet of Prehistoric Women* (USA, 1968).

Chebotaryov, Vladimir, and Gennadi Kazansky. *Amphibian Man* (*Chelovek-amfibiia*, USSR, 1962).

Coppola, Francis Ford. *Battle Beyond the Sun* (USA, 1962).

Corman, Roger. *Voyage to the Prehistoric Planet* (USA, 1965).

Daneliya, Georgiy. *Kin-Dza-Dza!* (*Kin-Dza-Dza!*, USSR, 1986).
Harrington, Curtis. *Queen of Blood* (USA, 1966).
Kariukov, Mihail, and Aleksandr Kozyr. *The Heavens Call* (*Nebo zovyot*, USSR, 1959).
Karyukov, Mikhail, and Otar Koberidze. *Toward a Dream* (*Mechte navstrechu*, USSR, 1963).
Klushantsev, Pavel. *Planet of the Storms* (*Planeta bur'*, USSR, 1962).
———. *Road to the Stars* (*Doroga k zvezdam*, USSR, 1957).
Kovalyov, Mark, and Vladimir Polin. *The Star Inspector* (*Zvezdnyi inspektor*, USSR, 1980).
Kromanov, Grigori. *Dead Mountaineer's Hotel* (*Hukkunud Alpinisti hotell/Otel' "U pogibshego al'pinista,"* USSR, 1979).
Kubrick, Stanley. *2001: A Space Odyssey* (USA, 1968).
Levin, Vasili. *Orion's Loop* (*Petlia Oriona*, USSR, 1980).
Lopushansky, Konstantin. *Dead Man's Letters* (*Pis'ma myortvogo cheloveka*, USSR, 1986).
Mätzig, Kurt. *The Silent Star* (*Der Schweigende Stern*, GDR, 1960).
Piestrak, Marek. *The Inquest of Pilot Pirx* (*Test pilota Pirksa*, USSR, 1979).
Polák, Jindřich. *Voyage to the End of the Universe* (*Ikarie XB-1*, Czechoslovakia, 1963).
Povolotskaya, Irina and Mikhail Sadkovich. *The Mysterious Wall* (*Tainstvennaya stena*, 1967).
Protazanov, Iakov. *Aelita* (*Aelita*, USSR, 1924).
Roeg, Nicolas. *The Man Who Fell to Earth* (UK, 1976).
Sherstobitov, Yevgeni. *Andromeda Nebula* (*Tumannost' Andromedy*, USSR, 1967).
Tarkovsky, Andrei. *Solaris* (*Solyaris*, USSR, 1972).
———. *Stalker* (*Stalker*, USSR, 1979).
Viktorov, Richard. *Per Aspera Ad Astra* (*Cherez ternii k zvezdam*, USSR, 1981).
Yermash, Andrei. *The Moon Rainbow* (*Lunnaya raduga*, USSR, 1983).
Zhuravlyov, Vasili. *The Cosmic Voyage* (*Kosmicheskiy reis*, USSR, 1936).

Part II
Environmental Crisis and the Nuclear Imaginary

4

Postapocalyptic Landscapes
The End of August at the Hotel Ozone (1966) and the Czechoslovak New Wave

Barbora Bartunkova

In *The End of August at the Hotel Ozone* (*Konec srpna v hotelu Ozon*, 1966), the director Jan Schmidt and the screenwriter Pavel Juráček propose a bleak vision of a postapocalyptic world in the aftermath of atomic war.[1] An older female leader (Beta Poničanová) guides a group of younger women through desolate landscapes and ruined spaces of civilization in search of other people. While the elder remembers life on Earth before the nuclear apocalypse, her followers, who were born after the disaster, lack an understanding of the concepts of history and culture and live outside of any societal norms. Even as they mostly abide by their elder's orders and share her motivation to find others, the women are indifferent to the underlying reason for their quest—the meeting with male counterparts with whom to preserve human life on Earth. When the group finally encounters an old man (Ondrej Jariabek), who inhabits the derelict Hotel Ozone, any hope for humanity's future quickly dissipates. Realizing that he is the sole survivor, the older woman falls ill and passes away, prompting the young women to again embark on their uncertain journey. When they prepare to leave the hotel, one of the women shoots the man in a final gesture of mercilessness, after he refuses to give away his gramophone, the only artifact of a lost civilization that has sparked their interest.

Less concerned with the immediate effects of nuclear destruction, *Hotel Ozone* thus imagines how human subjects might operate in a radically transformed world, while raising the existential question of humanity's survival. Scholars and critics have often interpreted the film as a postapocalyptic sci-fi or a political allegory.[2] Some saw *Hotel Ozone* as the filmmakers' coming to terms with existence under the communist regime and as a testament to intergenerational conflict related to the shifting experience of socialism in Czechoslovakia.[3] The violent behavior of the women and their disregard for social norms have been viewed as a stand-in for the Soviet Union's colonial exploitation of Eastern Europe, which led to a large-scale depletion of natural resources and the erasure of prewar culture.[4] The film's narrative has also been interpreted as a mourning for the loss of the First Czechoslovak Republic's civility and democratic order, disrupted by World War II.[5]

My analysis of the film instead excavates the ground in which these readings are rooted. Accordingly, it brings to light a largely unexamined issue—the cinematic representation of human and nonhuman life and the tensions that emerge from their interactions. When considered in relation to the few films of the Czechoslovak New Wave that touch on nuclear themes, *Hotel Ozone* offers perhaps the most extended meditation on environmental conditions in the post-atomic age.[6] This chapter argues that the film takes the anxieties around the Cold War nuclear struggle as a point of departure for a deeper investigation of human identity in relation to the natural world, while thematizing broader concerns about the crisis of social relations in the face of environmental destruction.

Based on a short story written by Juráček in 1958, *Hotel Ozone* was envisioned by Schmidt and Juráček as their final project at the state film school FAMU in Prague.[7] According to Schmidt, however, the proposal was rejected by the faculty due to the school's limited resources.[8] Nevertheless, the opportunity to shoot the film later arose in the context of the Czechoslovak People's Army, in which Schmidt and Juráček enlisted after their studies. As part of the army's film unit, they worked on newsreels, reportages, and documentaries.[9] In her study on Czechoslovak Army Film, Alice Lovejoy has revealed that the army studio not only produced instructional films and military propaganda but also served as a training ground for a young generation of filmmakers, who would become some of the most well-known figures of the Czechoslovak New Wave.[10] In the 1960s, under the progressive leadership of Bedřich Benda and Roman Hlaváč, the studio allowed for thematic and cinematic forms of experimentation to thrive not only in nonfiction production but also in two fiction features—*Hotel*

Ozone and *Long Live the Republic* (*Ať žije republika*, 1965), a World War II–themed film by Karel Kachyňa, which was co-produced by the state-run Barrandov Film Studios.[11]

Schmidt and Juráček had to face political obstacles in getting *Hotel Ozone* made. Although Czechoslovak Army Film initially agreed to the film's production, the project had to be submitted for approval to the army's political administration department. Schmidt was summoned to the Ministry of National Defense and, in his words, accused of "allowing for the possibility of a third world war and the destruction of the world," which was deemed "not only entirely contradictory to the code of conduct for a citizen of a socialist state but also for a soldier of the People's Socialist Army."[12] The stakes of producing a film addressing the fallout of a nuclear war in the military's film studio were not lost on the Ministry, which claimed that "the army would be sawing off the branch that it was sitting on."[13] It was only after Schmidt leveraged his connections and testimonials from key cultural figures, including Jan Procházka, whose creative team at Barrandov expressed interest in the film for Czechoslovak State Film, that *Hotel Ozone* secured final approval.[14] As Lovejoy has noted, it was therefore partly the rivalry between the state and army film studios that made the film's realization possible, a unique condition in the context of a nationalized Czechoslovak film industry that had promised to efface competition under socialism.[15]

In his account of the resistance he faced at the Ministry, Schmidt pointed out the film's potential "as propaganda material to frighten the Western viewer about the war," speaking to the degree to which Cold War anxieties and tensions between the Eastern and Western bloc informed cinematic production. In this context, the end of the world could only be imagined in the service of unsettling Western audiences.[16] Juráček had fashioned a more utopian vision of a socialist future in an earlier screenplay for the pioneering science fiction film *Ikarie XB 1* (1963) directed by Jindřich Polák.[17] On their mission to explore a planet in the Alpha Centauri solar system in the year 2163, an international spaceship crew encounters the remnants of Western capitalism embodied by a defunct military spaceship from 1987 whose occupants had killed each other. Notably, the spaceship holds nuclear warheads, and an accidental detonation leads to the death of two members of the exploration team. This moment of crisis articulates the haunting threat of the twentieth-century atomic age, while associating capitalism with violence and communism with progress.

Hotel Ozone, by contrast, takes a more complex stance to geopolitical dynamics leading to nuclear crisis. The black-and-white film begins with a long shot of an empty hangar's interior and its geometrically structured steel frame, as a monotonous male voice-over mechanically counts down from ten in English. The image then fades into a white screen. The following shot shows a field of wheat gently swaying in the wind, as another disembodied male voice declares the countdown in Russian. The image once again fades to white. The English and Russian languages, as the first in the otherwise Czech film, instantly evoke the tensions between the two main powers of the Cold War—the United States and the Soviet Union, clearly connecting the film's imagined future in relation to the post–World War II context of the film's making. Yet the ensuing shots complicate this dualistic opposition. Next appears a close-up of a pair of reading glasses placed on top of an open book, with the countdown delivered in Chinese. This time, however, the English voice reemerges, disjointedly interweaving with the texture of the countdown in Chinese, until another fade-out to white at zero. The ensuing take represents a richly adorned interior space of a church, replete with candles, sculptures, paintings, and other religious objects, as two voices, in French and Russian, alternate in spelling out the numbers from ten to one, syncopating the rhythm of the countdown.[18] This series of shots culminates in a multilingual chorus of all the overlapping voices, accompanying a view of a tuft of grass set against a rock formation, until the image ultimately fades into white again. The soundscape of multiple interweaving languages thus not only suggests humanity's shared complicity in the nuclear arms race, but also instills a sense of collective responsibility for environmental destruction.

Certain aspects of this opening sequence resonate with *The Hall of Lost Footsteps (Sál ztracených kroků,* 1960), Jaromil Jireš's graduation project at FAMU. Jireš's experimental short film offers a montage interweaving everyday scenes at a Prague train station and on a train; expressive, dreamlike sequences of a couple affected by a nuclear detonation; and documentary footage of nuclear explosions, aerial warfare, the Holocaust, and the aftermath of the 1945 atomic bombings of Japan.[19] The film's credits are superimposed over a long shot of an empty train station, a "hall of lost footsteps," which later reappears in the film, this time imbued with associations of loss and the disappearance of human life due to an implied nuclear attack.[20] The film's key sequence juxtaposes a romantic encounter between two lovers, rendered in luminous colors, with black-and-white footage of a bomber and a close-up of a ticking clock, which is accompanied by a series of sound snippets of countdowns delivered by off-screen voices in English, French, and German. Following the countdown, a shot of a nuclear explosion introduces a sequence that interlaces red-tinted shots of the couple, disoriented in a haze of radiation, with black-and-white clips of the devastating effects of nuclear war on cities and human bodies.

In a similar manner, the opening and closing sequences of Věra Chytilová's *Daisies (Sedmikrásky,* 1966) include documentary footage of aerial combat, explosions, and bombarded cities to frame the playful yet disruptive adventures of two young female protagonists, who decide to "go bad" because "everything is going bad in the world."[21] In *Daisies*, one of the most provocative films of the Czechoslovak New Wave, the young women reject social conventions and manners, resonating with how *Hotel Ozone*'s female characters engage with their environment in an experimental but more violent way.[22]

In contrast to Jireš and Chytilová, Schmidt's film refuses to deploy charged visual tropes, such as the mushroom cloud or explicit depictions of industrial warfare and mass suffering. Instead, *Hotel Ozone* stages the destruction of the world more abstractly, as a series of erasures. By fading into white, each of the opening shots performs an effacement, first of different aspects of civilization and human culture—modern technology, agriculture, literature, and religion—and, ultimately, of nature. Instead of representing human subjects in their embodied form, the film's opening implies their presence through objects, spaces, and the haunting voices of the countdown foreshadowing imminent annihilation. The final shot of *Hotel Ozone*'s opening sequence further symbolically stages the ultimate disappearance of the human trace on Earth, as a wet footprint on a stone ground gradually fades before our eyes.[23] Its evaporation is dramatically punctuated by a sudden and loud rupture of the earth. As a large fissure widens to reveal a dark abyss, the image fades into a tracking shot closely charting the surface of a geological terrain, onto which the film's opening credits are superimposed. When considered in the context of atomic warfare, the dark evaporating footprint can further evoke both the haunting nuclear shadows of figures and objects in the aftermath of the Hiroshima bombing, as well as the power of the atomic bomb to obliterate humankind and other life forms on Earth.

Here we are reminded again of *The Hall of Lost Footsteps*, which opens with a series of telegraphic paper strips that mark the pivotal events of the atomic age. The first telegraphic message reads: "August 6, 1945 Hiroshima: Human footprints were discovered in the burnt concrete."[24] Jireš's film also concludes with a series of telegraphic strips, which serve as a warning of the dangers of experimentation with atmospheric nuclear testing:

> Dr W. Libby, Member of the United States Atomic Energy Commission, supports test explosions, because atmospheric radioactivity makes weather forecasting more precise. Stop / Atmospheric radioactivity from every explosion of a strategic nuclear bomb anywhere in the world causes the premature death of 100,000 people. Stop / In 1960, 216, 983 children were born in Czechoslovakia. Stop.[25]

While Jireš's film is concerned with the lethal effects of nuclear experimentation, Schmidt brings into relief the significant impact of humankind on the environment by juxtaposing the fading human imprint with geological strata, contrasting the ephemeral trace of human existence with the deep time of Earth's history. As Jennifer Fay has remarked in her analysis of nuclear test films, cinema became a way to record and naturalize the nuclear condition that leaves "clear signals of human-caused planetary change in the geological record," with the first atomic test in 1945 proposed by some scientists as the beginning of the Anthropocene.[26] The visual motif of the human imprint also brings to mind the media theorist Lev Manovich's claim that "cinema is the art of the index; it is an attempt to make art out of a footprint," which highlights the cinematic medium's unique relation to reality due to the photochemical basis of the film image.[27] The opening sequence of *Hotel Ozone* indeed subtly turns toward the medium of film, with the countdown evoking the head leader of a film reel and the fade-out into white laying bare the reflective surface of the projection screen. These self-reflexive gestures can be read as an attempt to highlight the potential of the cinematic medium as a site onto which the relationship between living beings and the environment, presence and absence, past and future, can be "screened."[28]

Following the title sequence, the film cuts to a low-angle shot of the sky and a crown of a tall conifer, the sun shining through its branches. Within moments, the tree appears to collapse toward the viewer. Yet upon a second viewing, it becomes clear that that the tree's felling is an impression constructed purely by cinematic means. The camera dynamically glides upward while zooming into the treetop that comes to fill the screen, as an accompanying loud sound of a falling tree produces the illusion that the conifer is falling. Through this destabilizing and visceral experience, the film directly confronts its audience with the notion of death, while linking the symbolic killing of the tree with the viewer's own vulnerability. It is, however, only a rare instance of rupture and connection between human and nonhuman life in a film that is structured around a series of violent encounters, in which human subjects thoughtlessly kill animals and recklessly damage and exploit the natural world.

In the filmic narrative, the felling of the tree is motivated by the human desire to understand the past and to make sense of the present. After a close-up of a tree cross-section comes into focus, an older woman's hand enters the frame from the right, moving gradually toward the core of the tree trunk, her index finger lightly touching the surface by counting the tree rings. In a reversal of the film's opening countdowns, a female voice-over utters "ten, twenty, thirty, forty, forty-eight, fifty..." to mark the years that have passed since the days "when that other world still existed."[29] The hand then slowly caresses the surface of the tree in an expression of longing and loss, before moving outward. As the woman narrates significant events since the nuclear catastrophe, her index finger highlights the tree rings as markers of temporality. This instance marks the first moment in the film that partly shows an embodied subject. Her still-disembodied voice addresses a yet-to-be-seen "you," aligning the viewer with the subject position of the young women who only now learn about the effects of the nuclear disaster and how their journey began. The cinematic trope of the tree cross-section as a means of exploring identity and memory has famously appeared in Alfred Hitchcock's *Vertigo* (1958) and, perhaps in an even more relevant manner, in Chris Marker's *La Jetée* (1962), a black-and-white short film composed almost entirely of still photographs, which thematizes the experience of time travel in a post–nuclear war experiment.[30] In *Hotel Ozone*, the shot of the tree cross-section is perhaps the most powerful visual metaphor for the film's staging of the relationship between the female protagonists and the natural environment, emphasizing haptic engagement as a model for making sense of the world. This image mediates both collective and personal history, representing the woman's mental landscape, or, as Stanislava Přádná has written, projecting "a 'film' of her life, of her loved ones, of her lived experience."[31] Notably, in the elder's account, the nuclear disaster is not figured as a single traumatic event, but rather as a gradual and prolonged process of death and loss: "It happened somewhere here. Many people survived. There were enough of us—people, animals, and trees. It was only later that everything started to die off—people, animals, and trees. But the cinemas were still playing, the train was still running."[32] What is striking about this description is the insistence on "us"—people, animals, and trees—foregrounding the shared experience of living beings. She also emphasizes that the emblematic technologies of modernity still persist in the aftermath of the nuclear war, which can itself be considered a culmination of modernity's crisis.

Yet *Hotel Ozone* does not offer a redemptive narrative of harmonious interspecies relations in a new world, stripped of the destructive actions of modern civilization. While artifacts of modernity are now scattered in the landscape as relics of the past, the natural environment still remains a site of human exploitation and reckless behavior. For instance, when the young women find a canister of gasoline, they let the flammable liquid spill into the grass, as one of them mischievously lights it on fire and throws live ammunition into it, causing an explosion and a blaze that scares their horses. As the women encounter different beings along their journey, they do not hesitate to commit meaningless and cruel killings: they twist off the head of a snake, slay a stray dog with a firearm, shoot a cow and disembowel her, catch fish with grenades and cut their heads off, and ultimately shoot the old man.

The brutal display of animal killing is the most disturbing aspect of *Hotel Ozone*, deployed by Schmidt to shock his audiences. This cruelty caused an uproar at the Pesaro Film Festival, which the director commented on cynically: "If you kill a dog on screen, they get up and leave in droves, whereas if you think up ten different ways to kill a man, they sit and munch their candy bars."³³ Schmidt refused to acknowledge the highly problematic nature of committing violence against nonhuman animals in his attempt to address the crisis of social relations, claiming that "the ten commandments that you can read in any slaughterhouse is a very humane affair compared to the way people treat one another."³⁴ Such language is echoed in *Hotel Ozone*, when the old man calls the young women "beasts" as they set out to leave Hotel Ozone instead of staying to live with him.

In Schmidt's statements and in writing on the film, the young women have been frequently described as "animal-like" or "behaving like a pack" due to their transgressions of social expectations of normative female behavior.³⁵ If read against the grain of these anthropocentric and misogynist descriptions, the representation of the young women in *Hotel Ozone* can be seen as embracing a more radical position in their indifference to the old order and established norms, as they engage with the world in an experimental manner that tests the limits of their agency in the world. Moreover, their physical prowess and courage to explore the unknown stand in stark contrast with the figure of the old man, who while nurturing and caring is also portrayed as powerless and weak, unwilling to give up his shelter and the comforts of his obsolete manners and artifacts of a long-gone world.³⁶ Yet we cannot extricate these potentially liberating gestures in the film from the oppressive and violent impact on the animals and natural environment as well as from the unequal power relations that the female subjects were subjected to off-screen.

Indeed, the physicality of the women was not only central to their diegetic actions—such as jumping on runaway horses, shooting rifles, and wading through wild waters—but also in their casting and training. The young women chosen for the film from three hundred candidates were mostly non-actors, selected for their physical appearance and ability to master an obstacle course in the Czechoslovak Army Film facilities, where they had to surmount, in Schmidt's words, "various obstacles—water, walls, fire, and trees."³⁷ Milan Jonáš, the assistant director, described the conditions for routine training as follows: "We would wake up before six and bathe in cold water, followed by warm-up exercises and perhaps a conditioning run."³⁸ The women were thus subjected to a near-military-style drill described by Schmidt as "dressage," a term almost exclusively reserved for rigorous horse training.³⁹ This further blurring of boundaries between human and nonhuman terms is troubling here in the sense that it establishes certain notions of animal life as a means to legitimize unequal gender dynamics in the production of the film. Schmidt even regretted that "such a well-trained ensemble" could not be used for further projects in communist Czechoslovakia, lamenting that "a capitalist producer would for sure watch out for this, and would be able to assess very well what a film with such a training regimen would bring him. And many times, the costs of such dressage would be a return on investment."[40]

Apart from *Hotel Ozone*'s intense emphasis on physicality in the representation of female characters, the role of touch and physical engagement with the environment becomes one of the most important tropes in the film. If we recall the image of the wet footprint of the opening sequence, a resonance emerges with Jacques Derrida's meditation on Wilhelm Jensen's novella *Gradiva: A Pompeiian Fancy* (1918), and its analysis by Freud, which traces the archaeologist Norbert Hanold's obsession with finding the traces of Gradiva, an idealized female figure on an antique bas-relief. Derrida foregrounds Hanold's obsessive desire to retrieve Gradiva's footstep in the ashes of Pompeii and his dream of "reliving the other" in "this irreplaceable place, the very ashes, where the singular imprint, like a signature, barely distinguishes itself from the impression."[41] In *Hotel Ozone*, the group's elder is constantly searching for any recognizable trace of past or present human life, even if repeatedly faced with the impossibility of retrieving what she longs for. In one sequence, she discovers a series of abstract images traced in white chalk on the façades of the ruined buildings of an abandoned town, overgrown with wild vegetation. The younger women seem oblivious to the possible meanings behind these images, remaining detached from the experience of loss and an imagined future related to their mission.[42] The elder follows and touches the chalk markings, her fingers becoming dusted with white chalk powder. These traces turn from abstract shapes to a promising human-shaped stick figure, but ultimately the leader discovers that it was one of the members of her group who had chalk hidden in her trousers and was the author of these drawings. As in the sequence with the tree cross-section, the production of knowledge and the limits of knowing are thus foregrounded through the haptic engagement with the environment.

Notably, the film charts territories imbued with unique environmental conditions, while representing historically and politically charged sites. The crumbling buildings and eerily empty urban spaces were shot in the northwestern border region of Czechoslovakia in the town of Doupov, whose German population was expelled in the aftermath of World War II and which was abandoned in 1954 to be incorporated into the largest Czechoslovak military training zone. Only the army's film crews were allowed to shoot in this highly controlled and publicly inaccessible area.[43] Other parts of *Hotel Ozone* were filmed in the depopulated and restricted areas of the Šumava border region in southwestern Bohemia.[44] The filmmakers thus had the rare opportunity to experience and capture the contradictions of these militarized landscapes—both the subject to devastation and contamination by military activity and environments in which biodiversity can thrive due to the absence of human populations and practices such as agricultural production and mining.[45] The film itself portrays the dual status of these contested territories, including the lush vegetation reclaiming the crumbled structures of human settlements as well as the patches of scorched land and a partially flooded underground bunker, from which the women retrieve a barrel of gasoline and ammunition to set them on fire.

In *Hotel Ozone*, landscapes and interiors do not function merely as passive sites serving as backdrops to narrative action, as all intersubjective dynamics are refracted through the environment. While the film is mostly structured around pared-down cinematography to convey a sense of naturalism in the matter-of-fact representation of the group's nomadic journey, it notably provides glimpses into the older woman's subjective experience. In these instances, the environment is activated through point-of-view shots, such as when she contemplates the frescoes on the ornate ceiling of a dilapidated baroque church. In another sequence, she pensively ruminates on the transformed nature of a familiar-looking landscape, which was filmed in the Mohelno Serpentine Steppe, a nature reserve in western Moravia with unique steppe meadows and forests above a meandering river. With a point-of-view shot charting the trees and the glimmer of the river in a valley deep below, the woman's childhood memories are mobilized: "Back then, it rained all summer. Bubbles were appearing on the water. Once my ball floated away. They told me that it will get to the sea, and I stopped crying. I haven't been back since, until now. But it might have been somewhere else."[46] While the old woman experiences spatiotemporal disorientation and a palpable sense of loss, markers of place and time are not associated with any meaning for her young companions. In their view, the river is merely another obstacle to be overcome.

This idyllic valley provides a different kind of site of memory and meaning for the old man, as his refuge, the Hotel Ozone, is nestled at the bottom. In contrast to the wild natural landscape surrounding it, the enclosed spaces of the derelict hotel reflect the man's desire to protect and nurture human life while preserving objects associated with the old world, which have become obsolete and unsustainable. He is preciously attached to relics of modernity and human civilization, such as the last newspaper published before the nuclear apocalypse, an old television, a chess set, and a gramophone with a single record of a polka popularized during World War II.[47] The man's desire to preserve these remnants and isolate himself in the hotel is portrayed as self-centered and unproductive, as the new state of the world demands a radically different mode of engagement.

The old man's overly polite manners appear humorous in the face of the women's experience of nomadic survival, particularly when he proudly opens a parasol on the hotel's patio to serve the women milk, a product of animal domestication that they are unfamiliar with. During this scene, which sets up an opposition of two distinct conceptions of human life in the aftermath of nuclear apocalypse, we glimpse the hotel sign. Its name, Hotel Ozone, can be interpreted as a reference to the temporary presence of humanity on Earth, while gesturing to ozone, a gas whose presence in the stratosphere serves as a key protection from ultraviolet radiation but whose ground-level formation caused by industrial emissions can cause harm to the environment.

The man's efforts to shield himself and the group from the elements is most evident in the bird's-eye-view shot of the parasol that entirely conceals the characters underneath. Here, the filmmakers diverge from their naturalism in the depiction of the narrative in an authorial gesture that points back to the very opening of the film. The concentric stripes of the sunshade evoke the cross-section of the tree, but the umbrella acts as a radically different kind of "screen"—one that creates a division between the viewer and the subjects of cinematic fiction.[48] This effect of defamiliarization echoes the ways in which *Hotel Ozone* refuses to provide access to the younger women's mental and emotional states, with possibly a single exception—when confronted with their leader's death.

The burial of their elder gestures toward the film's opening and the close-up of her hand touching the cross-section of the felled tree. The funeral is introduced by a series of close-ups of the women's hands in different postures, with dirt behind their fingernails. The camera's proximity conveys a rare moment of intimacy and introspection in relation to the young women's experiences. The camera finally rests on the clasped hands of the old man before slowly tracking upward to reveal his face, as he silently utters, "I will plant something here... perhaps a juniper."[49] The man's promise to plant a commemorative tree suggests a continuation of life, the woman's decaying body providing nutrients to another organism within the ecosystem, effacing the boundary between the body and the environment, figure and ground. Unlike the other beings killed in the film, the woman's death is mourned and memorialized on a meadow on top of a hill, which bears two other graves with wooden crosses. Human rituals of mourning and remembrance are thus embedded into the realm of the natural landscape, with the sound of the wailing wind taking over as the group slowly walks away. Yet this elegiac representation of death as part of the cycle of life is followed by a much more cynical ending, as the man is shot after resisting the women's requests to hand over his gramophone.

In one of the preceding sequences, when the elderly woman is ailing in bed, blankly staring at the ceiling, she articulates a critical reflection on humankind's presence on the planet. As a close-up shot closely tracks the surface of the textured white ceiling, she speaks of the world's refusal to continue serving as a resource to people: "Tins are falling apart and cartridges are rusting. Nothing grows, the Earth loathes us."[50] Although the old man in vain attempts to counter her pessimistic vision by arguing that she will be the immortal founder of a new civilization and the mother of humankind, she insists, "We are like vermin. And the Earth loathes us."[51] It is perhaps this deeper realization of humanity's complicity in environmental destruction and the futility of their quest for survival that leads to her death. It is in the film's final part, when the finitude of human life is laid bare, with pathos and absurdity, that *Hotel Ozone* exceeds the contours of its matter-of-fact exploration of conditions of survival, and allows for a decentering of human subjectivity, which is essential for a reenvisioning of the relations between human and nonhuman life.

Schmidt hoped that his exploration of the limits of human life in a postapocalyptic context would elicit a strong affective response in the viewer:

> We are all too used to the usual propaganda proclaiming the danger of those terrible nuclear weapons. It's indifference. And indifference must be feared. ... I attempted to make this film against posters. People are used to reacting to posters and newspapers like masses, in general terms and without feelings, while in my film I tried to affect each viewer individually, so that everyone would feel in their own way.[52]

Contemporary responses to the film varied. The film critic Galina Kopaněvová argued that the psychological dimension of the women's postapocalyptic experience has not been explored in sufficient depth. For her, the thematization of environmental conditions exemplified the film's illustrative narrative: "The warning in the form of a wasteland and towns overgrown with grass is also appalling ... but it cannot be helped, the image of a wasteland of the human soul is always more appalling."[53] For others, the devastating human impact on the environment represented not an imaginary future but "authentic details" of a palpably recognizable reality: "Ruins of buildings, barren plains covered in fragments of military equipment, the youth's wild games with fire and ammunition—that we have all experienced firsthand in 1945."[54]

A broader contemporary reception of the film's vision of a post-nuclear environment cannot be fully assessed, as *Hotel Ozone* had a limited distribution in the Czechoslovak context. Schmidt even claimed that the response to the film was "practically none," as the army "tried to brush it away" by belatedly showing the film a year after its completion and mostly allowing screenings in small cinemas and film clubs.[55]

The film's preview screening was organized by the film club in České Budějovice on 1 December 1966.[56] During an accompanying panel, led by film historian Boris Jachnin, Schmidt insisted that *Hotel Ozone* made a big impact on international journalists at the festival of army films in Versailles. He argued that the press was in awe of Czechoslovak Army Film's ability to produce a feature film, as army studios in the West made only instructional films.[57] The director concluded that the ideological implications of the journalist's comments made "the film a triumph for our army, despite the long debates that preceded its realization."[58] In this manner, Cold War dynamics inflected the way in which Schmidt framed the film to his military and civil audiences. In 1967, the film succeeded at two international film festivals in Italy. At the Pesaro Film Festival, *Hotel Ozone* received the Centro Studi Cinematografici prize, and won the Golden Asteroid at the International Science Fiction Film Festival in Trieste.[59] Having received the award from a representative of the Vatican, Schmidt reminisced over his experience at Pesaro: "I found myself in quite a precarious situation—as a citizen of a socialist republic and representative of the Czech Army, I had received a prize from the Pope."[60] As the film reached Western audiences and began gaining international acclaim, Schmidt seemed to have been only too aware of the uncertain status of his film between the East and the West.

The following year, Slovak director Juraj Jakubisko completed *The Deserters and the Nomads* (*Zbehovia a pútnici*, 1968), a trilogy about the cyclical nature of human violence as exemplified by narratives taking place at the end of both world wars and in the aftermath of an imagined global nuclear disaster.[61] In the final episode, the figure of Death and a young nurse escape an underground shelter to the surface of the earth and seek in vain to find human survivors across plains of cracked earth, lush landscapes, and in an abandoned windmill. Jakubisko's postapocalyptic universe is rendered by means of intense visual stylization. Drawing on Slovak folk culture, an evocative use of bold colors, and at times hallucinatory cinematography, his cinematic approach stands in stark contrast to the pared-down black-and-white aesthetic of *Hotel Ozone*.[62] In his dizzying film, Jakubisko takes the existential dimension of postapocalyptic experience one step further—imagining a world where even Death's life loses meaning, as she ends up having no more people to kill, and ultimately perishes on a green field, amid a dramatic and absurd aerial bombing.

If *Hotel Ozone* opens with the question of humanity's survival in the aftermath of nuclear apocalypse, it concludes with an opening onto more ambiguous possibilities for the future. The final shot reveals an expansive, flattened view of a tree-lined mountainside, its horizon traversed by minuscule female figures that move off-screen. Their presence is overshadowed by the vastness of the mountain and the strong howling of the wind. Such contrast in the scale between the women and the landscape echoes the film's opening sequence, which showed different forms of effacement of the human trace on Earth. The final moments of *Hotel Ozone* imply that as long as the women's journey continues, there may be hope for reimagining the role of humans in the natural world. Ultimately, the film seems to suggest that a decentering of humanity's perspectives is crucial for finding balance within broader ecologies.

Barbora Bartunkova is a PhD Candidate in the History of Art at Yale University, where she specializes in modern and contemporary European art, photography, and film. Her research interests include the intersection of aesthetics and politics, the representations of women and gender, and the relationship between art and ecology. As the 2022–23 Chester Dale Fellow at the National Gallery of Art's Center for Advanced Study in the Visual Arts, she is completing her dissertation, "Sites of Resistance: Antifascism and the Czechoslovak Avant-Garde." Bartunkova holds an MA from University College London (UCL) in the History of Art, where she also completed her BA in French with Film Studies. She was the 2018–19 Mellon Museum Research Consortium Fellow at the Museum of Modern Art in New York, and has held curatorial and museum positions in institutions such as the Royal Academy of Arts in London, the Lobkowicz Collections in Prague, and the Museum of Decorative Arts in Prague.

Notes

1. I am grateful to Masha Shpolberg, Kumar Atre, Meghan Forbes, Laura Phillips, and the CCL writing group (Laura Beltran-Rubio, Hyunjin Cho, Emily Friedman, Nora S. Lambert, Rebecca Levitan, Katherine Werwie) for offering invaluable insights on earlier versions of this chapter.
2. See, for example, Bystrov, "Western z čias po atómovej vojne," Křenková, "Když zítřek umírá"; and Neumann, "*Konec srpna v hotelu Ozon.*"
3. Mohylová, "*The End of August at the Hotel Ozone.*"
4. Mazierska and Näripea, "Gender Discourse in Eastern European SF Cinema."
5. Lovejoy, *Army Film and the Avant Garde*.
6. Several Czechoslovak postwar films address the danger of weapons of mass destruction, including Otakar Vávra's *Krakatit* (1947) and *Dark Sun* (*Temné slunce*, 1980), both based on Karel Čapek's 1924 novel *Krakatit*, the experimental short film *The Hall of Lost Footsteps* (*Sál ztracených kroků*, 1960) by Jaromil

Jireš, and the final part of Juraj Jakubisko's trilogy *The Deserters and the Nomads* (*Zbehovia a pútnici*, 1968). For a comparative study of *The End of August at the Hotel Ozone* in relation to Otakar Vávra's films, see Pospíšil, "The Bomb, the Cold War and the Czech Film."

7. The original story "Konec srpna v hotelu Ozon" was published in the newspaper *Mladá fronta*, no. 38 in 1965 and reprinted in Pavel Juráček as "Filmová povídka," in *Postava k podpírání*, ed. Miloš Fikejz (Prague: Havran, 2001), 103–113.
8. Schmidt, quoted in Liehm, *Closely Watched Films*, 324.
9. Schmidt, "An Interview with Director Jan Schmidt," 5. Schmidt's short documentary films centered around sports, such as football in *Life After Ninety Minutes* (Život po devadesáti minutách, 1965), hockey in *A Game for Guys* (Hra pro chlapy, 1966), and the army's ski jumping team in *Bravery* (Odvaha, 1966). See *Filmový přehled*, no. 17 (May 1, 1967).
10. These figures included Schmidt, Juráček, Jiří Menzel, Jan Němec, Karel Vachek, and others. See Lovejoy, *Army Film and the Avant Garde*, 122–123.
11. Lovejoy, *Army Film and the Avant Garde*, 163.
12. Schmidt, quoted in Holub, *The End of August at the Hotel Ozone*, 6.
13. Schmidt, quoted in Liehm, *Closely Watched Films*, 325.
14. Schmidt, quoted in Holub, *The End of August at the Hotel Ozone*, 6.
15. Lovejoy, *Army Film and the Avant Garde*, 165.
16. Schmidt, quoted in Holub, *The End of August at the Hotel Ozone*, 6.
17. The film was dubbed into English and released in the United States in a significantly edited version as *Voyage to the End of the Universe* (1964). For an analysis of *Ikarie XB 1*, see Uhlířová, "Voyage through Space." On the history of Czechoslovak sci-fi in film, see Adamovič, "Stříbrné komety filmového plátna."
18. By 1966, when *Hotel Ozone* was made, the United States (1945) and the Soviet Union (1949) were joined by the United Kingdom (1952), France (1960), and the People's Republic of China (1964) in manufacturing atomic weapons and expanding their nuclear arsenal.
19. Juraj Jakubisko coauthored the screenplay and even collaborated with Jireš on the film's realization. The expressive use of color and experimentation with dynamic camerawork are also key features of Jakubisko's oeuvre, including his own rendition of the world in the aftermath of a nuclear apocalypse in *The Deserters and the Nomads* (1968).
20. This opening shot is preceded by a series of telegraphic strips that highlight key events of the nuclear age, with the last one establishing a link between the film's title and the ensuing shot of a railway station: "French dictionary: Train station = La salle des pas perdus = the hall of lost footsteps." *The Hall of Lost Footsteps* (Sál ztracených kroků), dir. by Jaromil Jireš (Studio FAMU, 1960).
21. *Daisies* (*Sedmikrásky*), dir. by Věra Chytilová (Czechoslovakia, 1966). Chytilová cowrote the original story for *Daisies* with Juráček, and later transformed it into a screenplay with the screenwriter and set designer Ester Krumbachová.
22. For a reading of *Daisies* as a critique of manners and celebration of laughter, see Parvulescu, "'So We Will Go Bad.'"

23. In the technical screenplay of *Hotel Ozone*, the opening sequence includes a number of other vignettes fading into white, and notably begins with an image that strongly emphasizes the notion of the human trace—a "slice of bread set aside on a workshop drawing, bearing the imprints of human fingers." Juráček, "Konec srpna v hotelu Ozon."
24. *The Hall of Lost Footsteps* (*Sál ztracených kroků*), dir. by Jaromil Jireš (Czechoslovakia, 1960). The next paper strip refers to the first successful French atomic bomb test in the Sahara in 1960, which motivated Jireš to create his cinematic response to the nuclear threat. The subject of French nuclear testing is further thematized in the film by a close-up shot on a newspaper focusing on this news story.
25. *The Hall of Lost Footsteps*.
26. Fay, *Inhospitable World*, 64. This much-debated concept, popularized in the 1980s, advances the idea that the current geological age should be named for the dominant impact of anthropogenic activity on the planet.
27. Manovich, *The Language of New Media*, 295, as cited in Doane, "The Indexical and the Concept of Medium Specificity."
28. For an analysis of the ontology of the screen and the role of screen practices in "screening nature," see Mitchell, "Screening Nature (and the Nature of the Screen)" and Pick and Narraway, eds., *Screening Nature*.
29. *The End of August at the Hotel Ozone*. All translations of the Czech dialogue are mine unless otherwise noted.
30. For an analysis of the iconic sequence in *Vertigo*, see Gunning, "The Desire and Pursuit of the Hole."
31. Přádná, "Poetika postav, typů, (ne)herců," 234.
32. *The End of August at the Hotel Ozone*.
33. Schmidt, quoted in Liehm, *Closely Watched Films*, 325.
34. Liehm, *Closely Watched Films*, 326.
35. Schmidt, quoted in "Vize o konci světa."
36. In her analysis of *Tender Spots* (1981), a late-socialist Polish film by Piotr Andrejew, Eliza Rose has similarly shown how shifting gender dynamics in the face of ecological catastrophe are refracted through the protagonist's crisis of masculinity. See chapter 5 of the present volume.
37. Schmidt, quoted in Holub, *The End of August at the Hotel Ozone*, 7. The only two established actors in *Hotel Ozone* were the Slovak actors Beta Poničanová and Ondrej Jariabek. Poničanová played the role of Stará ("Old Woman")—whose actual name, Dagmar Hubertusová, is first mentioned only as she introduces herself to the old man, named Otakar Herold. The young women were played by Magda Seidlerová (Barbora), Hana Vítková (Tereza), Jana Nováková (Klára), Vanda Kalinová (Judita), Natálie Maslovová (Magdaléna), Irena Lžičařová (Eva), Jitka Hořejší (Marta), and Alena Lippertová (Anna).
38. Jonáš, quoted in "Konec srpna v hotelu Ozón." In this contemporary account, Jonáš claimed that there were in fact four hundred candidates they chose from.
39. Schmidt, quoted in Liehm, "Jiný a přece z nich."
40. Liehm, "Jiný a přece z nich."

41. Derrida, *Archive Fever*, 98–99.
42. Fran Bartkowski similarly perceives the relationship to temporality as the key difference between the characters representing the old and new generation: "where their elders were preserving shards of a past, and searching for a future, they are rather focused on a present." Bartkowski, "Signs of Life," 57.
43. Lovejoy, *Army Film and the Avant Garde*, 166. For an analysis of visual representations of the social, political, and environmental transformations of the broader Ore Mountains region that spans the Czech-German border, see chapter 1 in the present volume.
44. As Schmidt recalled, his assistant director had spent eight years in prison for attempting to cross the border to the West, and paradoxically found himself even closer to the barbed wire while working on *Hotel Ozone*. Schmidt, quoted in Holub, *The End of August at the Hotel Ozone*, 7.
45. For a brief account of the unique characteristics of the ecosystem in the army training area in the Doupov region and on recent efforts to convert former military zones into protected nature areas, such as the Brdy Protected Landscape Area in 2016, see Härtel, "Conservation of Botanical Diversity in the Czech Republic," 435.
46. *The End of August at the Hotel Ozone*.
47. The song "Škoda lásky" (Wasted Love) also known as "Beer Barrel Polka," was composed by Jaromír Vejvoda in the late 1920s and accompanied by Václav Zeman's lyrics in 1934. The song was translated into many languages and became internationally popular.
48. On theoretical investigation and genealogy of the concept of the screen, see Buckley, Campe, and Casetti, eds., *Screen Genealogies*.
49. Buckley, Campe, and Casetti, eds., *Screen Genealogies*.
50. *The End of August at the Hotel Ozone*.
51. *The End of August at the Hotel Ozone*.
52. Schmidt, quoted in "Konec srpna v hotelu Ozón," *Filmový přehled*.
53. Kopaněvová, "Konec srpna v hotelu Ozón," *Lidová demokracie*. Kopaněvová acknowledged the merits of the film's thematic concern with the possibility of atomic war, even if she perceived it as slightly dated, while praising the American director Stanley Kramer's earlier film *On the Beach* (1959), which represented the aftermath of global nuclear annihilation.
54. "Konec srpna v hotelu Ozon," *Rovnost*.
55. Schmidt, quoted in Holub, *The End of August at the Hotel Ozone*, 7.
56. "Zítra: Předpremiéra nového českého filmu."
57. Schmidt, quoted in "Vize o konci světa."
58. Schmidt, quoted in "Vize o konci světa."
59. "Konec srpna v hotelu Ozon (1966)," *Filmový přehled*. https://www.filmovyprehled.cz/cs/film/396700/konec-srpna-v-hotelu-ozon.
60. Schmidt, quoted in Holub, *The End of August at the Hotel Ozone*, 7–8.
61. The realization of *The Deserters and the Nomads* coincided with the Soviet-led Warsaw Pact invasion of Czechoslovakia in August 1968. Jakubisko even incorporated documentary footage of the invasion into the film, and claimed that a Soviet tank accidentally rolled into one of his shots during filming.

Due to the invasion and onset of the "normalization" purges and censorship, Jakubisko's film did not have any substantial reception in the Czechoslovak context until the fall of the communist regime in 1989, as it was locked in a vault and forbidden to be viewed. The film was however shown in 1969 at international festivals in Cannes, Sorrento, and New York.

62. For an analysis of the visual poetics and folk imagery in *The Deserters and the Nomads*, see Owen, *Avant-Garde to New Wave*, 129–156; Přádná, "Poetika postav, typů, (ne)herců," 212–215; and Žalman, *Umlčený film*, 202–208.

Bibliography

Adamovič, Ivan. "Stříbrné komety filmového plátna: Hledání budoucnosti v československém vědecko-fantastickém filmu." In *Planeta Eden: Svět zítřka v socialistickém Československu 1948–1978*, edited by Ivan Adamovič and Tomáš Pospiszyl, 174–193. Řevnice: Arbor Vitae, 2010.

Bartkowski, Fran. "Signs of Life: Questions of Survival." *Synthesis: An Anglophone Journal of Comparative Literary Studies*, no. 1 (2008): 55–58.

Buckley, Craig, Rüdiger Campe, and Francesco Casetti, eds. *Screen Genealogies: From Optical Device to Environmental Medium*. Amsterdam: Amsterdam University Press, 2019.

Bystrov, Vladimír. "Western z čias po atómovej vojne." *Smena* (24 January 1967). Press cuttings folder "Konec srpna v hotelu Ozon, ČSSR: kritiky." Call number IIf-2214, National Film Archive Library, Prague.

Derrida, Jacques. *Archive Fever: A Freudian Impression*, translated by Eric Prenowitz. Chicago and London: University of Chicago Press, 1996.

Doane, Mary Ann. "The Indexical and the Concept of Medium Specificity." *Differences* 18, no. 1 (1 January 2007): 128–152.

Fay, Jennifer. *Inhospitable World: Cinema in the Time of the Anthropocene*. New York and Oxford: Oxford University Press, 2018.

Gunning, Tom. "The Desire and Pursuit of the Hole: Cinema's Obscure Object of Desire." In *Erotikon: Essays on Eros, Ancient and Modern*, edited by Shadi Bartsch and Thomas Bartscherer, 261–277. Chicago and London: University of Chicago Press, 2005.

Härtel, Handrij. "Conservation of Botanical Diversity in the Czech Republic." In *Flora and Vegetation of the Czech Republic*, edited by Milan Chytrý et al., 401–444. Cham: Springer, 2017.

Holub, Radovan. "An Interview with Director Jan Schmidt." In *The End of August at the Hotel Ozone*, edited by Radovan Holub. Facets Cine-Notes DVD booklet. Chicago: Facets, 2006.

Juráček, Pavel. "Konec srpna v hotelu Ozon." Technical screenplay (J. Macák, J. Macháně, J. Schmidt). Czechoslovak Army Film 1730-65, Prague, 1965, 1. Call number S-700-TS. National Film Archive Library, Prague.

"Konec srpna v hotelu Ozón." *Filmový přehled*, no. 17 (1 May 1967).

"Konec srpna v hotelu Ozon." *Rovnost* (7 July 1967). Press cuttings folder "Konec srpna v hotelu Ozon, ČSSR: kritiky." Call number IIf-2214, National Film Archive Library, Prague.

Kopaněvová, Galina. "Konec srpna v hotelu Ozón." *Lidová demokracie* (8 December 1966). Press cuttings folder "Konec srpna v hotelu Ozon, ČSSR: kritiky." Call number IIf-2214, National Film Archive Library, Prague.

Křenková, Jarmila. "Když zítřek umírá: Postapokalypsa na Konci srpna v hotelu Ozon." *Cinepur* no. 107 (October 2016): 68–72.

Liehm, Antonín J. "Jiný a přece z nich." *Film a doba* 13 (1967): 97.

———. *Closely Watched Films: The Czechoslovak Experience*. New York: Routledge, 2016.

Lovejoy, Alice. *Army Film and the Avant Garde: Cinema and Experiment in the Czechoslovak Military*. Bloomington: Indiana University Press, 2014.

Manovich, Lev. *The Language of New Media*. Cambridge, MA: MIT Press, 2001.

Mazierska, Ewa, and Eva Näripea. "Gender Discourse in Eastern European SF Cinema." *Science Fiction Studies* 41, no. 1 (2014): 163–180.

Mitchell, W.J.T. "Screening Nature (and the Nature of the Screen)." *New Review of Film and Television Studies* 13, no. 3 (3 July 2015): 231–246.

Mohylová, Lea. "*The End of August at the Hotel Ozone*: The Social-Political Archetype and Its Allegorical Depiction." *Filmový přehled*, 21 November 2019. https://www.filmovyprehled.cz/en/revue/detail/the-end-of-august-at-the-hotel-ozone-the-social-political-archetype-and-its-allegorical-depiction.

Neumann, Andreas. "*Konec srpna v hotelu Ozon* von Jan Schmidt und Pavel Juráček: Ein dystopischer Science-Fiction-Film der Tschechoslowakischen Neuen Welle." *Zeitschrift des Forschungsverbundes SED-Staat* 40, no. 40 (2016): 130–144.

Owen, Jonathan L. *Avant-Garde to New Wave: Czechoslovak Cinema, Surrealism and the Sixties*. New York and Oxford: Berghahn Books, 2011.

Parvulescu, Anca. "'So We Will Go Bad': Cheekiness, Laughter, Film." *Camera Obscura: Feminism, Culture, and Media Studies* 21, no. 2 (2006): 144–167.

Pick, Anat, and Guinevere Narraway, eds. *Screening Nature: Cinema Beyond the Human*. New York and Oxford: Berghahn Books, 2013.

Pospíšil, Tomáš. "The Bomb, the Cold War and the Czech Film." *Journal of Transatlantic Studies* 6, no. 2 (August 2008): 142–147.

Přádná, Stanislava. "Poetika postav, typů, (ne)herců." In *Démanty všednosti: český a slovenský film, 60. let: kapitoly o nové vlně*, edited by Jiří Cieslar, Stanislava Přádná, and Zdena Škapová. Prague: Pražská scéna, 2002.

Uhlířová, Markéta. "Voyage through Space, Time and Utopian Modernism in *Ikarie XB 1*." In *Czech Cinema Revisited: Politics, Genres, Techniques*, edited by Lucie Česálková, 338–365. Prague: National Film Archive, 2017.

"Vize o konci světa: Beseda s tvůrci filmu 'Konec srpna v hotelu Ozon.'" Interview by Boris Jachnin, in *Jihočeská pravda* (23 December 1966). Press cuttings folder "Konec srpna v hotelu Ozon, ČSSR: kritiky." Call number IIf-2214, National Film Archive Library, Prague.

Žalman, Jan. *Umlčený film: kapitoly z bojů o lidskou tvář československého filmu*. Prague: Národní filmový archiv, 1993.

"Zítra: Předpremiéra nového českého filmu." *Jihočeská pravda* (30 November 1966). Press cuttings folder "Konec srpna v hotelu Ozon, ČSSR: kritiky." Call number IIf-2214, National Film Archive Library, Prague.

Filmography

Jakubisko, Juraj. *The Deserters and the Nomads* (*Zbehovia a pútnici*, Czechoslovakia, 1968).
Jireš, Jaromil. *The Hall of Lost Footsteps* (*Sál ztracených kroků*, Czechoslovakia, 1960).
Polák, Jindřich. *Ikarie XB 1*, Czechoslovakia, 1963.
Schmidt, Jan. *The End of August at the Hotel Ozone* (*Konec srpna v hotelu Ozon*, Czechoslovakia, 1966).

5

Fallow Fields
Crises of Masculinity and Ecology in Piotr Andrejew's *Tender Spots* (1981)

Eliza Rose

Piotr Andrejew's short film *Groping One's Way* (*Po omacku*, 1975) ends with a sequence that invites the viewer to imagine exiting the womb. Bodies traverse a tunnel made of soft, translucent plastic that collapses onto those inside. The eleven-minute film documents outdoor games facilitated by architect and pedagogue Oskar Hansen for his students at the Warsaw Academy of Fine Arts. The exercises hover at a nascent stage of ideation: Hansen's students do not draft or produce objects, and the sole material record of their activities is Andrejew's film, in which no fixed or static shapes appear on-screen. The tunnel's wriggling contours morph with the movements of those inside. In keeping with the Open Form theory underlying Hansen's architectural and pedagogic practice, *Groping One's Way* depicts a suspended state of play, where visual signs have not yet been assigned meaning. Open Form theory critiques models of professional expertise in the applied and fine arts, instead encouraging collective participation and embracing art as process.[1] The semiotic playfulness operative in this brief film would become the seed of Andrejew's authorial idiom, as this chapter will show.

Groping One's Way takes place outdoors but is devoid of nature. High-contrast color bleaches the landscape. In a second exercise, students carry a white parachute that obscures sky and ground. This real yet abstracted monochrome environment anticipates the setting of a feature film Andrejew will direct six years later, *Tender Spots* (*Czułe miejsca*, 1981), which is this chapter's subject. *Tender Spots* opens with a panning aerial shot of lifeless ground resembling a lunar regolith more so than fertile earthen soil. The sole landmarks are abandoned overpasses and cars under dust sheets. Earth is barren, and the activity that once swarmed its surface is at a standstill. A radio voiceover explains the scene: water is scarce. Citizens are advised to stay indoors. The crisis, we learn, is not specific to Poland or the Socialist Bloc. It is planetary, and the prognosis is bleak: Earth will lose its ability to support life within ten years.

Surveying science fiction cinema of the People's Republic of Poland, one is hard-pressed to find films that stay within Earth's orbit. As a genre tradition that came of age during the American-Soviet race to the moon, Socialist Bloc science fiction exhibits a consistent penchant for the cosmic. This remained true decades after the launching of Sputnik 1 in 1957, despite the eventual diminishment of space agency budgets. If a staple figure of 1960s SF was the pioneer cosmonaut charting a galactic terra incognita, then two decades later, this trope was superseded by an under-resourced spacefaring civilization that has expanded beyond its means. This vision comes across vividly in the 1985 film *Ga-ga: Glory to the Heroes* (*Ga, ga. Sława bohaterom*, 1985), set in an overexpanded galactic empire governed from Earth—an obsolescing seat of power. Lacking volunteers willing to take on the risks of space travel, Earth's centralized government sends prisoner conscripts to impoverished space settlements as indentured colonial emissaries.

Of the Polish film industry's major SF releases in the last decade of state socialism,[2] *Tender Spots* is the sole film to remain firmly planted on Earth as we know it.[3] The predicament of living on a transpiring planet whose terminal date has been pronounced may seem a poignant allegory for late socialism in Eastern Europe. *Tender Spots*'s ten-year prognosis for the planet seems prescient of the socialist system's collapse according to that same timeline. The characters' nonplussed attitudes may correspond to that peculiar cognitive dissonance often ascribed to this final chapter in the story of state socialism: awareness of the system's disintegration and, contradictorily, obstinate belief in its permanence. This bivalent mindset, theorized in the Soviet context by Alexei Yurchak,[4] seems no less relevant to Andrejew's portrait of late-socialist Poland. The characters populating *Tender Spots*, indifferent and glassy-eyed in the face of environmental cataclysm, instantiate what Yurchak described as the "hypernormalization" of authoritative discourse—the simultaneous acceptance of and detachment from codified pictures of reality handed down from above.

Tender Spots follows TV technician Jan Zaleski's infatuation with the ravishing but irreverent Ewa. Their dysfunctional rapport, as this chapter will argue, serves up metaphorical fodder for the critique of bureaucratic authority delivered covertly in the film. We first see the protagonists together in the throes of foreplay, with Jan's face pressed to Ewa's breast in an act akin to breastfeeding. A bedsheet balloons overhead, recalling the parachute from *Groping One's Way* and, like its precursor, enveloping those inside in a womblike niche. Indeed, Jan seems to have matured little in his time outside the womb: he lies below Ewa, subordinate to her erotic power. Even when they switch positions, Ewa turns her back to him but remains, decidedly, on top.

This chapter will analyze Andrejew's tale of eco-apocalypse through the masculinity crisis experienced by its protagonist. This private crisis, I argue, reflects broader anxieties of a discredited, male-coded bureaucratic class. Given *Tender Spots*'s production context (Poland in 1980), I believe its satire of male power implicated Party officials in Andrejew's world by casting them as impotent—ill-equipped to gratify their constituents. The film is an epitaph to the "Gierek Decade," coinciding in time with the end of Edward Gierek's term as first secretary of the Polish United Workers' Party. Gierek had opened the decade prior with promises of a rebranded consumer socialism: in lieu of empty shelves and overpriced food staples, there would be affordable Fiats and department stores brimming with luxury imports.[5] Gierek revised the progress narrative embedded in the socialist project: postponement of pleasure to an eventual arrival at full communism was replaced with immediate sensory gratification—a mood satirized in Natalia LL's now-iconic video and photo-cycle *Consumption Art* (*Sztuka konsumpcyjna*, 1972), which depicts a model sumptuously devouring a banana and other suggestive foods.[6]

Gierek opened the next decade with a starkly different message. In a speech delivered on New Year's Day of 1980, he conceded that the Polish economy was in a slump. If *Consumption Art* equated the promise of consumer socialism with sensual gratification, positing the state as phallic pleasure provider, then Gierek's 1980 speech was an admission that the "virile market" had gone limp. Relevantly to this chapter, Gierek blamed the state's diminishing revenue on environmental factors: a severe summer drought and unusually cold winter.

With *Tender Spots*, Andrejew hyperbolizes these climate issues into outright environmental collapse. The film seems to slyly mock Gierek's regime from the perspective of its endpoint for its failure to have pleasured its subjects in the short term or to secure their welfare for the long term. The year of its production, 1980, had been designated at the Twenty-Second Congress of the Communist Party of the Soviet Union in 1961 as the milestone year when standards of living in the Soviet Bloc would finally outstrip those in the United States.[7] *Tender Spots* sounds the alarm on this pleasure prognosis. *Time's up*, it declares, *for the planet and for us*. These grievances are smuggled into a sexual allegory that reduces the political to the interpersonal: the discredited male-coded Party surfaces here as impotent, sterile Jan. Though Jan's character is hardly an avatar for state authority, his labor as a civil servant enables the dissemination of public television broadcasts—a crucial component in the state's infrastructure of control. He inhabits the lowest rung of the male bureaucratic workforce incriminated in the film.

Tender Spots was filmed in 1980, while strikes at the Lenin Shipyard in Gdańsk were laying the groundwork for the formation of the independent trade union Solidarity, later prompting the Polish United Workers' Party to institute martial law in December 1981. Andrejew's film premiered in August of that year, when the state's hostility toward the consolidating opposition was already evident but before it had taken decisive retaliatory action. Rather than reduce *Tender Spots* to a prescient precursor of martial law, I assert a second event as its primary historical substrate. At the Seventh Congress of the Polish United Workers' Party in March 1980, the Party passed the Environmental Protection and Development Act (EPDA)[8] in a belated attempt to mitigate the environmental effects of industrialization. While the pervasive assumption in scholarship that socialist planners disregarded development's environmental costs lacks nuance as a general verdict, it is fair to claim that legislation to protect Poland's natural resources had a slow and staggered lifeline. In 1975, the Party raised environmental protection from its third to first priority but did not complement this show of sentiment with legislative action.[9] This changed in 1980 with the above-mentioned EPDA. There was, in other words, a lag between diagnosis and course of treatment. *Tender Spots* projects this delay into a near-future dystopia where it is too late to reverse the damage done.

Before I proceed to read *Tender Spots* in the context of environmentalist discourse, I want to first acknowledge the myths of failure with which my reading overlaps. The Cold War origins of research on state-socialist environmental management have given rise to the tale of a state system that (1) was too poorly managed to effectively counter localized and system-wide damage, (2) lacked channels for feeding popular critique into its decision chains, and (3) adopted an environmentalist mindset only in belated mimicry of the West.[10] Together, these premises inform a perception of the socialist state as inert, inept, and unresponsive—qualities that all have obvious analogs in the sexual scenario of male impotence. In what follows, I will show how *Tender Spots* formally and narratively riffs on these parallels, dramatizing state failure through the conspicuous emasculation of Jan and other male characters in the film. By offering this reading, I aim not to repeat or validate the total condemnation of socialist environmental protection. I am interested instead in Andrejew's impressively intricate visual code for delivering his critique in response to the anxieties of his time. I will ultimately argue that Western film critics overlooked this code and were therefore blind to the film's nuances. Rather than rehearse the narrative of a sluggish socialist state singularly guilty of ecocide, I will conclude by faulting Western critics for this same "sluggishness" in their unwillingness to perform the interpretive labor called for by Andrejew's aesthetics.

Indictments of environmental management during socialism often veil a dig at Marxism-Leninism for its failure to find partial solutions to local issues due to fixating on a holistic approach to planning. This narrative follows a dual logic that discredits socialist planning on two contradictory counts: socialist planners fail to see the trees for the forest but are equally inept at the systemic perspective requisite for environmentalism (after all, whole-Earth problems call for whole-Earth solutions). The attitude dominating Western historical scholarship locates this ineptitude not in the poor decisions of individuals but in the very logic of socialism.[11] Historian Daniel Cole, for instance, argues that while the Polish United Workers' Party took action to mitigate environmental damage, their efforts were "all hindered by the legal, ideological, economic, and political shortcomings of the (Real) socialism system," with the Party ultimately proving "not powerful enough to overcome the systemic obstacles it had created for its own preservation."[12] Might we instead acknowledge certain inadequacies of environmental management without leveraging them as proof of the innate dysfunctionality of socialist planning? Bearing in mind the obstacles impeding environmental policy under neoliberal conditions of our own historical moment, can we forgo the syntax "it could only have been so," in favor of "what was working, what was not working, and how might the latter have improved"?

A recent interview with Andrejew groups him with Piotr Szulkin, Ryszard Waśko, and others as "calligraphers":[13] filmmakers mutually invested in formal detail. Andrejew cites *Tender Spots* as the peak of his experiments in "calligraphic" style. A parallel can be drawn between calligraphy as cinematic form and the logic of environmental management, for both rest on extrapolation from the molecular to the molar. In what follows, I will first investigate *Tender Spots*'s code of minute yet readable signs and then scale up to a macro-reading of the film within its context of environmental crisis in late socialism.

The agility to connect local malfunction to system failure is precisely what the protagonist of *Tender Spots* requires in his daily work repairing televisions. To perform this work, Jan prods the television interior with his fingers, intuitively reading its mechanisms. He credits his talent at his trade to the fact that he works without the industry-standard tool enigmatically called the "defector." He explains to one client that each television set is linked to central command. The defector's function is to identify linkages between the single set and broader system. Jan must intuit the alignments between system (*ustrój*) and fuse (*bezpiecznik*) to deduce which action will repair the malfunction by relinking node to network. This skill is atavistic, we learn, for the defector has rendered it redundant. Perhaps atrophy of this ability to glide from the particular to the systemic—surely symptomatic of a broader trend—is partially to blame for the decline of human civilization documented in the film. The gadget's pejorative name implicitly ties it to worsening "defects" of human aptitude in Jan's time.

Jan is unique for his retention of this ability to extrapolate from part to whole. This skill, however, is insufficient compensation for his myriad defects, at least in the eyes of his lover Ewa, who ridicules him as a romantic partner. In his signature calligraphic style, Andrejew plants clues underscoring Jan's emasculation in the details of his physical appearance. His compromised masculinity can be traced, for instance, by logging the hats he wears throughout the film. Ewa takes a new lover—Alan—who cruelly hires Jan as technical support for the premiere of a pornographic film starring Ewa. Jan is forced to wear a ridiculous hat to promote the film. The hat resembles a truncated safety cone that is absurdly tall and decorated with infantilizing candy-cane stripes. As a compensatory phallic symbol and crude mutation of the cuckold's horns, the hat emasculates its wearer and, with its bluntly clipped tip, subjects him to symbolic castration as he publicly bears witness to Ewa achieving climax on-screen.

The castration continues in a later scene when Jan dons a beret. The hat's soft shape and tiny woolen stem emasculate Jan further by invoking a host of anatomical connotations: a foreskin, nipple, or miniature penis. Other characters' hats feed into this reading: police officers (aligned with the male-coded state) wear floppy rainhats that undercut their authority, while Ewa, in her final appearance, dons a magnificent white headpiece resembling a peacock's tail. Since ornamental feathers are mating features that only adorn male birds, Ewa's headpiece inverts the typical gendered power balance in a manner consistent with the film as a whole.

If my analysis of the hats of *Tender Spots* seems overzealous, it is because Andrejew trains his viewers to engage in this kind of paranoid reading: one gains entry into the film by ascribing maximal meaning to all on-screen details and trusting in a holistic alignment between fabula,

Fallow Fields • 113

Figure 5.1. *Tender Spots* (*Czułe miejsca*). Directed by Piotr Andrejew. Warsaw: Zespół Filmowy Kadr, 1981). Screen capture by Eliza Rose.

mise-en-scène, and the social critique articulated in tandem by both. Andrejew's calligraphic style can be read as a formal variant of perversion, which was, for Sigmund Freud, the smearing of sexual intensity from its normative locus in the genitals to any number of objects. Perversion entails the drifting of erotic charge to "a woman's breast, a foot or a plait of hair … a piece of clothing, a shoe, a piece of underclothing."[14] Andrejew's clever planting of sexual signifiers in any and all objects—his calligraphic hand—is the logic of fetish rendered as filmic style. This formal technique aptly captures sexuality's new configurations on the terminally ill Earth of *Tender Spots*, due to the newfound obsolescence of the reproductive motive. Birthing a new generation seems unwise given the planet's imminent collapse. Unburdened of pragmatic value as the means of procreation, sexuality oozes into looser shapes.

While the men of *Tender Spots* are in decline, female power flourishes but has no outlet. The damage wreaked on this world by its male leaders is irreversible. Women will not rise to power, for the world they inherit is soon to expire. Men and women both are stymied together in the fallow field of a no-future world sabotaged by those who claimed to govern and protect it. As life moves indoors, women, historically confined to domestic

Figure 5.2. *Tender Spots* (*Czułe miejsca*). Directed by Piotr Andrejew. Warsaw: Zespół Filmowy Kadr, 1981). Screen capture by Eliza Rose.

space, are better prepared for seclusion. In one scene, Ewa rehearses with her all-female ballet class. The dancers are primed to thrive indoors. Inert men in suits watch the ballerinas through a pane of glass. The female ballet instructor, we learn, is in love with Ewa. This incidental detail hints toward a world of female self-sufficiency where men are superfluous, no longer needed to provide pleasure. In another scene, Jan walks through a courtyard and spies on muscular women doing exercises inside their homes. He ogles them from below, where he stands in a puddle of mud. The women regale their Peeping Tom with lewd gestures. They pantomime fellatio and erupt into a fit of shared laughter at Jan's expense. Jan is again ridiculed as a sexual partner, while the women exhibit a self-satiating sexuality. They belong to a closed network of women connected through their windows who perfect their physiques and exchange pleasure among themselves without ever stepping outdoors.

This female ascendance comes filtered through a male director's gaze. Ewa's power lies in her eroticism: her desire and desirability. Yet Ewa's desire and, by extension, subjectivity are opaque: throughout the film, pleasure, grief, and anger flicker incongruently on her face. Her enigmatic subjecthood is accented when she dons a black veil (adding to the film's roster of overdetermined haberdashery). Jan's humiliation has driven him to attempt suicide. Ewa visits his hospital room veiled, mourning a man not yet dead. A child and friend of Jan named Aśka uses a vanity mirror to deflect light onto Ewa's veil. Even under forced exposure, the veil divulges nothing. Her face is a cipher for the mystery of female sexuality described by Jacques Lacan as "the darkness cast upon the vaginal organ." For Lacan, female sexual pleasure is as opaque to the inquisitive male mind as a darkly veiled face. "The nature of vaginal orgasm," he notes, "has kept its obscurity inviolate."[15]

Ewa conjures Jean-Paul Sartre's archetypes of the "frigid woman" and "coquette," who are both profiled as shadow-subjects who will not and cannot access their own desires. The frigid woman denies the pleasure she experiences during sex. This description fits Ewa, who appears to take pleasure in intercourse with Jan but refuses to confirm this verbally. Sartre's coquette, meanwhile, feigns ignorance toward men's sexual designs and divests her lover's words of sexual charge because she herself "does not quite know what she wants."[16] This also accurately describes Ewa, who keeps Jan on a short leash but denies their relationship status, invariably speaking in mixed messages. At Jan's hospital bedside, she delivers two self-canceling verdicts: the promise "I am yours, as I have always been and always will be" comes parceled with the news that this will be her final visit, for her future is with Alan.

At the root of Jan and Ewa's woes is reproductive anxiety. While historically the burden of fertility has fallen on women, here it is Ewa who is blameless: since she spends her life indoors, her uncontaminated body can presumably still bear a child. Jan, on the other hand, walks the streets between clients' homes, exposed to the contaminated air. "Do you think we might have a child?" Jan asks in a moment of postcoital tenderness. To this, Ewa laughs in his face: "A child, with you? With you I could only have a mechanical kitten." Ewa's dismissal of Jan as a reproductive partner implies that his exposure to the elements may have rendered his sperm defunct. His reproductive capacity is voided biologically and socially: his life outdoors has damaged his body, while his gender links him to a bureaucratic class that has sabotaged the planet as our one and only cradle for life.[17] Dejected by this insult, Jan sits on the floor clad in skimpy boys' underwear. His chest and body are hairless. He fiddles with a handmade miniature robot. The image of boyish Jan tinkering with his toys seems to express the emasculation of a technocratic regime that promised progress but delivered catastrophe: a regime of overeager, puerile boys who failed to adequately control their machines.[18]

We can extrapolate from Jan's dilemma to a broader sexual crisis within the world of the film that may comment, in turn, on anxieties in late-socialist society. The masculinity crisis depicted in *Tender Spots* may, in other words, point to a similar dynamic in Poland in 1980—the year the Party finally rallied around environmental protection but offered too little, too late. Environmental crisis is narrated here as a gendered allegory: the devastation of Gaia–Terra–Mother Earth is linked to a blundering, majority-male ruling class that prioritized efficiency over ecology. Procreation is no longer a viable way forward: men are disgraced, and anyway, why bring a child into an expiring world?

With the reproductive function obsolete, sexual interactions in the film revert to the logic of fetish (as argued above) and, more specifically, regress to a childlike state. For Freud, sexual life begins in infancy. If puberty marks a milestone, it is only as the moment when sexual pleasure is decisively linked to the reproductive drive.[19] This drive voided, Jan and Ewa revert to prepubescent sexuality. This may explain why their first interaction consists of Jan mimicking the act of breastfeeding in a womblike tent of bedsheets. The film's title *Tender Spots* (*Czułe miejsca*), also translatable as "tender places," may speak to this diffusely expanded sexuality:[20] relieved of reproductive pressure, sexuality is no longer confined to genital erogenous zones that symbolize and carry out procreation. All parts of the body are reactivated as "tender spots."

The transformation of sexuality in the absence of its reproductive function is documented in the intradiegetic pornographic film starring Ewa and directed by Jan's rival Alan. Close-ups show Ewa's face contorted with pleasure as Alan mounts her on-screen. Jan, as noted above, attends the premier as hired technical support: his task is to monitor the sound levels of Ewa's ecstatic moans. Dwarfed by his ridiculous phallic hat, Jan fingers the nodes on the soundboard to feign control over the pleasure of the partner who betrayed him—the partner whose moans are conspicuously caused by someone else.

Alan reveals his directorial vision to Ewa. He wants to depict a "normal rapport between man and woman—a rapport of our times." What could be the "normal rapport" of man and woman in a world on the brink of planetary extinction? Alan's film disposes with narrative in favor of pure pornography. The pleasure depicted on-screen is without context. The sex scene is set in a public bathroom—a historic cruising site, where what was once transgressive is here asserted as the new norm. Alan's "normal rapport" is sexuality reorganized for a futureless world. Horror, pleasure, and apathy combine on Ewa's face as she reaches orgasm. Lifted free from narrative framing (be it filmic fabula or the narrative logic of reproduction itself, which arcs from conception through the development of an embryo to the transcendent resolution of birth), Ewa's pleasure embodies the Lacanian affinity between jouissance and the death drive. In her and

Table 5.1. Emasculation as the Central Dynamic of Piotr Andrejew's *Tender Spots* (*Czułe miejsca*, 1981)

Visual symbolism (calligraphy)	Phallic imagery
Interpersonal rapport of the characters	Jan's humiliation; Ewa's domination
Gender dynamics in the diegesis of the film	Disgrace of a male bureaucratic class that failed to forestall environmental crisis
Social commentary on gender dynamics in late-socialist Poland	Disgrace of a male bureaucratic class that failed to • adequately mitigate the environmental costs of industrialization; and • deliver the pleasure promised by consumer socialism.

Alan's sex act, futurelessness has finally vanquished the futurist cult of childbirth.

In the interest of clarity, I have reconstructed my argument by separating its layers (see Table 5.1). I propose emasculation as a base dynamic informing the film on several levels. My fixation on emasculation may be legitimated by the film's promotional posters, both of which riff graphically on this theme. The posters were designed by Dana Andreev, who was married to the director at the time. One poster features a loosely coiled tube limply craning upward with a distinctly penile head. A second poster shifts from the phallic to the yonic: two faces mirror one another in Rorschach symmetry.[21] Between them, a vaginal seam sets up a rabbit-duck illusion wherein the faces double as splayed thighs. The image is charged with female power: through the voluptuous lips seeps a black vapor lending the faces a supernatural aura.

The poster stimulates a game of visual decryption that parallels the film itself: just like *Tender Spots*, this Rorschach serves the attentive viewer a bounty of symbolic stimuli open to playful interpretation. The design is an optical enigma from which a host of figures can be reasonably extracted: the vaginal seam between the mirrored faces suggests blackened ovaries discharged from their former function. The seam is a peephole into nothingness rimmed by smoky ink. This may suggest a power vacuum in the wake of the phallus' decline: female power will not fill this vacuum for at least two reasons. The first is inherent to female sexuality, which is portrayed by this male director as indeterminate and disinterested and therefore lacking the necessary substance and thrust to become a surrogate phallus. The second is the film's antinatalist torque: this female power, inheriting a futureless world, spurns its age-old duty to reproduce the social order. The poster's coiling black vapor appears to be emitted from one pair of lips but inserted into that pair's counterpart on the poster's opposing side, where the mouth appears to be either intubated with the dark coil or, alternatively, performing fellatio upon it. Both scenarios seem relevant to the anti-futurist sexuality portrayed in the film.

Queer theorist Lee Edelman has rejected what he calls a universal politics of "reproductive futurism" due to its conservative aim to authenticate and replicate the given social order by transmitting its norms to the future in the vessel of the archetypal Child.[22] He enjoins us to "withdraw our allegiance ... from a reality based on the Ponzi scheme of reproductive futurism."[23] For Edelman, this is a prerogative of queerness, while in *Tender Spots* we witness a society-wide recoil from reproductive futurism. It is not the already queer subject who ushers in this no-future mode but instead the subject queered through its abandonment of posterity.

Indeed, the characters thriving in this futureless world are women of self-satiating sexuality and androgynes. As the pornographic film's auteur, Alan pioneers the new sexual paradigm. His physique is masculinity reconfigured (feminized) for the changing world: he has shapely lips, curled eyelashes, and coiffed hair. Jan has his own "other lover" in the person of Aśka—an androgynous child who follows him around. The child's devotion to Jan may hint toward Jan's regression to a prepubescent stage of sexuality. A second implication of their kinship carries a seed of promise: perhaps Jan's atavistic skill to extrapolate from part to whole links him to a generation born into a condemned world but already acclimating to its altered terms. Aśka outperforms the film's ensemble of adults, who adjust to life indoors with varying degrees of success. The child moves through Warsaw unhindered, traversing its underground passageways on rollerskates, in packs of youthful friends. The viewer first encounters Aśka sitting quietly in their apartment beside a filthy, grease-streaked swan, with whom they share a moment of tranquil reflection. The image links the child to the poisoned planet and its myriad nonhuman casualties. Aśka's love for Jan suggests that his retention of "synecdochal thinking" may offer a possible way out of the planet's predicament.

Tender Spots reached international audiences at the 1981 Gdańsk Film Festival and at Cannes the following year. The formal subtleties I have reconstructed here were lost on Western critics, who expected something else from socialist Poland. One French review reads *Tender Spots* as a message in a bottle from an authoritarian state. Foregrounding martial law as the film's context (even though it was produced prior to December 1981), the critic reproves Andrejew's "total reticence toward confronting current events."[24] Andrzej Wajda's *Man of Iron* (*Człowiek z żelaza*, 1981), awarded the Palme d'Or at the previous year's festival, had been more to his taste, perhaps due to its legibility as a parable about creative captivity under a socialist regime. An American reviewer is similarly dismayed that the film does not deliver a satisfying allegory for life behind the Iron Curtain. *Tender Spots* leaves the critic underwhelmed: "The story limps, and then grinds to a halt midway through the film," leaving the viewer with "unfortunately little else to chew on."[25]

I find it puzzling that neither reviewer mentions the film's intricate visual code. The French critic derides the film's "formal prudence," while the American gives a lackluster salute to its sepia tone but otherwise ignores the visual register altogether. This oversight reveals the critics' unconscious marginalization of the film on two counts: as science fiction (a genre not yet taken seriously as formally complex) and as an Eastern Bloc artifact (expected to deliver Western audiences a readily legible social critique requiring little interpretive labor).[26] By declining to read into visual detail, the critics do not read Andrejew on his terms. In other words, international critics repeated the same error problematized in *Tender Spots*: failure to situate localized details within a macro-narrative.

Let us end where we began, by crawling back into Oskar Hansen's womblike tunnel. I opened this chapter by suggesting that *Groping One's Way* captures ideation in a state of indeterminacy, before forms have been fixed, objects fabricated, meaning assigned, or message conveyed. The swelling and collapsing tunnel sets associative chains into motion without forcing any final marriage of meaning to sign. The calligraphic style of *Tender Spots* may push beyond this pliancy, but in its playful ingenuity it invites the viewer to engage in a game of decryption that is also a game of invention. Like the optical puzzles of Dana Andreev's posters, Andrejew's calligraphy is incomplete without the viewer's input. Perhaps the analysis I outline here can be faulted for its fixation on emasculation. But if, as I argue, the film comments on a deficit of the pleasure promised by consumer socialism, then at least there is pleasure in the game of interpretation. By investing in Andrejew's visual language, the viewer is rewarded with the gratification of coauthorship. She is free to generate her analysis alongside Andrejew's open form, reveling in the pleasure of the text.

Eliza Rose is Assistant Professor and Laszlo Birinyi Sr. Fellow of Central European Studies at University of North Carolina at Chapel Hill. She earned her PhD in Slavic languages at Columbia University. Her current research investigates interactions between art and industry in late socialist Poland. Her articles are published and forthcoming in *Studies in Eastern European Cinema, View. Theories and Practices of Visual Culture, Journal of the Fantastic in the Arts, Science Fiction Studies,* and *Slavic Review.*

Notes

1. See Hansen, *Towards Open Form.*
2. In addition to *Ga-ga*, other notable releases were *The Test of Pilot Pirx* (*Test pilota Pirxa*, 1979) and *Professor Inkblot Goes to Space* (*Pan Kleks w kosmosie*, 1988).
3. The films *Sexmission* (*Seksmisja*, 1983) and *O-bi, O-ba: The End of Civilization* (*O-bi, o-ba. Koniec cywilizacji*, 1985) are exceptions to this statement, but their postnuclear future settings are far removed from real living conditions of the 1980s.
4. Yurchak argues that despite being unable to forecast the Soviet system's collapse, Soviet subjects found that "unbeknownst to themselves, they had always been ready for it." Yurchak, *Everything Was Forever*, 4.
5. For a glimpse into how promises encoded in Gierek's platform infused visual art and film of the 1970s, see Ronduda and Woliński, eds., *Satisfaction.*
6. *Consumption Art*'s iconic status was renewed in 2019, when it was removed from public display at the Museum of National Art in Warsaw along with work by Katarzyna Kozyra on the order of museum director Jerzy Miziołek (a Ministry of Culture appointee). The public contested this decision by demonstrating in front of the museum and brandishing bananas like protest signs. The museum retracted its decision after vehement popular backlash.
7. See Documents of the 22nd Congress o the CPSU, Vol 1: https://archive.org/details/DocumentsOfThe22ndCongressOfTheCpsuVolI (accessed 12 February 2020).
8. "Ustawa o ochronie i kształtowaniu środowiska," *Journal of Laws*, No. 3, item 6.
9. See Cole, "An Outline History of Environmental Law," 322.
10. Historian Sabina Kubeké has worked to qualify these assumptions by recovering a record of Polish environmental experts' work on sustainability from as early as the interwar period. Kubeké documents Polish participation in international environmentalist initiatives in the 1970s (the UNESCO Man and Biosphere program cofounded by Poland; the International Institute of Applied System Analysis) to challenge the misconception that Poland was isolated from an otherwise globally interconnected environmental movement. Kubeké, "Discussing 'Sustainability.'"
11. Anthropologist Michał Murawski has noted how myths of failure informing the discourse on socialist planning are always "ideologically inflected." He argues that "failure-centrism has been elevated into an axiom in the literature on built socialism." Murawski interprets these narratives as remnants of a "Cold War-rooted ideology, which cast socialist modernity as a perverted

version of modernity proper, failure-bound from the beginning." Murawski, "Actually-Existing Success," 909.
12. Cole, "An Outline History," 298.
13. Marecki, "Lekcje kaligrafii."
14. Freud, "Lecture XX," 378.
15. Lacan lays blame for this mystery on "representatives of the fairer sex" who "do not seem to have given their all to remove the seal of secrecy." Lacan, "Guiding Remarks," 612.
16. See Sartre, *Being and Nothingness*, 55.
17. The cult SF film *Sexmission* (1983) also satirizes a dynamic of emasculation through its vision of a near-future world where men have been eliminated. When poet Czesław Miłosz first watched *Sexmission*, he interpreted it as a parody of the "wild masculine anti-feminism of the communist regime." Vladimir Gromov attributes this quote to Miłosz in an article devoted to the film. See "Sexmission—Juliusz Machulski," culture.pl, https://culture.pl/en/work/sexmission-juliusz-machulski (accessed 13 December 2020).
18. A similar sentiment is expressed in Karel Čapek's play *R.U.R.*—the source text of robot science fiction. The character Alquist, builder of robots, laments that today's men, rendered obsolete by machines of their own making, have been disgraced as reproductive partners: "And you expect women to have children by such men? … To men who are superfluous women will not bear children!" Čapek, *R.U.R.*, 35. This same trope appears in an amateur film from 1968–69 titled *Ewa and Her Husband* (*Ewa i mąż*), directed by Krystyna and Józef Czoska at the film club AKF Alka. The female protagonist (coincidentally named Ewa) luxuriates in a state of indulgence (eating in bed, smoking, listening to music) while her robot-husband does the housework. Ewa is portrayed as a woman of infinite desire who can be satiated by no one—man or male-presenting robot.
19. Freud reminds us that it is senseless to suppose children "brought no genitals with them into the world and only grew them at the time of puberty." However, "What *does* awaken in them at this time is the reproductive function, which makes use for its purposes of physical and mental material already present." Freud, "Lecture XX," 385.
20. I am grateful to Masha Shpolberg, coeditor of this volume, for drawing my attention to alternative interpretations of the title.
21. The poster can be viewed online: https://www.mutualart.com/Artwork/Czule-miejsca/764EFBE96C3D3CD0C32B63723F1FA701 (accessed 15 October 2022).
22. See Edelman, *No Future*, 2–3. The antifuturism of *Tender Spots* can be analyzed by complementing Edelman's theory with Yurchak's account of the perception of late socialism as a dysfunctional yet self-replicating system. This mood escalated in the 1980s: societal malfunctions were on full display, but no alternative order was forthcoming. A film of the same period by another "calligrapher," Piotr Szulkin's *O-bi, O-ba: The End of Civilization* (1985), depicts a similar crisis: the destruction of Earth as a viable habitat expresses a crisis in how to visualize the future.
23. Edelman, *No Future*, 4.

24. Codelli, "Czułe miejsca," 86.
25. "Czule Miejsca," *Variety*, 30, 32.
26. The film did receive a warmer response on the genre film festival circuit. It received the Film Critics' Award at the Madrid Film Festival in 1983 and a Special Distinction at the International Fantasy Film Festival "Fantasporto" in Porto the following year.

Bibliography

Čapek, Karel. *R.U.R.: Rossum's Universal Robots*. Trans. by Claudia Novack. London: Penguin, 2004.

Codelli, Lorenzo. "*Czule miejsca* (Des endroits sensibles)/Limuzyna-Daimler Benz (Limousine D.B.)." *Positif—Revue mensuelle de cinema*. July 1982, Arts Premium Collection, 86.

Cole, Daniel H. "An Outline History of Environmental Law and Administration in Poland." *Articles by Maurer Faculty*, Paper 691.

"Czule Miejsca." *Variety* (7 October 1981): 30, 32.

Edelman, Lee. *No Future: Queer Theory and the Death Drive*. Durham, NC: Duke University Press, 2004.

Freud, Sigmund. "Lecture XX: The Sexual Life of Human Beings." In *Introductory Lectures on Psycho-Analysis*, trans. by James Strachey, 375–396. New York and London: W. W. Norton & Company, 1989.

Hansen, Oskar. *Towards Open Form (Ku formie otwartej)*. Warsaw: Foksal Gallery Foundation, 2005.

Kubeké, Sabina. "Discussing 'Sustainability' in Global Epistemic Communities: Polish Scientists at MAB and IIASA in 1970–1990." Conference Paper at ASEEES, 2019.

Lacan, Jacques. "Guiding Remarks for a Convention on Female Sexuality." In *Ecrits*, trans. by Bruce Fink, 610–620. New York and London: W. W. Norton & Company, 2002.

Marecki, Piotr. "Lekcje kaligrafii. Z Piotrem Andrejew rozmawia Piotr Marecki." *Kwartalnik filmowy*, no. 82, 6–16.

Murawski, Michał. "Actually-Existing Success: Economics, Aesthetics, and the Specificity of (Still-)Socialist Urbanism." *Comparative Studies in Society and History* 60, no. 4, 907–937.

Ronduda, Łukasz, and Michał Woliński, eds. *Satisfaction. Sztuka konsumpcyjna w socjalistycznej Polsce lat. 70*. Texts by David Crowley and Jan Verwoert. Warsaw: Centrum Sztuki Współczesnej Zamek Uzajdowski/Archfilm, Piktogram/Bureau of Loose Associations, 2008.

Sartre, Jean-Paul. *Being and Nothingness: An Essay on Phenomenological Ontology*. Translated by Hazel Barnes. New York: Washington Square Press, 1992.

Yurchak, Alexei. *Everything Was Forever, Until It Was No More: The Last Soviet Generation*. Princeton, NJ: Princeton University Press, 2006.

Filmography

Andrejew, Piotr. *Groping One's Way* (*Po omacku*, Poland, 1975).
———. *Tender Spots* (*Czułe miejsca*, Poland, 1981).
Czoska, Krystyna and Józef. *Ewa and Her Husband* (*Ewa i mąż*, Poland, 1968-9).
Gradowski, Krzysztof. *Professor Inkblot Goes to Space* (*Pan Kleks w kosmosie*, Poland, Czechoslovakia, and USSR, 1988).
Machulski, Juliusz. *Sexmission* (*Seksmisja*, Poland, 1984).
Piestrak, Marek. *The Test of Pilot Pirx* (*Test pilota Pirxa*, Poland and USSR, 1979).
Szulkin, Piotr. *Ga-ga: Glory to the Heroes* (*Ga, ga. Sława bohaterom*, Poland, 1985).
———. *O-bi, O-ba: The End of Civilization* (*O-bi, o-ba. Koniec cywilizacji*, Poland, 1985).

6

Catastrophe, Obliquely
Soviet Documentaries about Chernobyl

Masha Shpolberg

For many, the silence surrounding the 26 April 1986 accident at the Chernobyl nuclear power plant was the most egregious part of the disaster. Though Gorbachev had sought to bring greater transparency to the Soviet Union with his policy of glasnost, instituted the previous year, the government famously chose to downplay the event, releasing an official statement only after a tremendous amount of international pressure. The first televised announcement, made a day and a half after the explosion, conceded only that a minor accident had taken place. Gorbachev himself would not acknowledge the accident publicly until 14 May 1986, nearly three weeks later.

Given this information blackout, a Soviet reckoning with Chernobyl on film, in photographs, or in literary works seemed unlikely. One would expect such attempts to have been stymied first by censorship and, later, by the dire economic conditions that prevailed following the collapse of the Soviet Union in the 1990s. Indeed, for many years, the public imagination of the nuclear reactor where the accident had taken place, of the city of Pripyat, which had housed most of the workers, and of the surrounding area was dominated by Western video games and horror films that exploited the setting's genre potential. Recently, those images have been superseded by Craig Mazin's *Chernobyl* miniseries for HBO and Sky UK (2019), which managed to tap into contemporary concerns about human technology—and hubris—transforming the environment in dire, unalterable ways. Together with a succession of critically acclaimed historical accounts from Serhii Plokhy, Kate Brown, and Adam Higginbotham, the series has been credited with reviving wide-scale interest in the disaster.[1]

Yet there were Soviet images, films, and even plays produced immediately in the wake of the event.[2] Despite their initial resistance, Soviet authorities eventually relented and allowed select journalists, photographers, and media personnel into the newly christened "Zone." Among them were two documentary filmmaking teams: one led by Rollan Sergienko and Vladimir Sinelnikov of the Central Studio for Documentary Film (Tsentralnaya Studiya Dokumentalnykh Filmov) in Moscow, and another led by Vladimir Shevchenko of the Ukrainian Newsreel and Documentary Film Studio (UkrKinoKhronika) in Kyiv.[3] The documentaries they produced—*The Bell of Chernobyl* (*Kolokol Chernobylia*, 1987) and *Chronicle of Difficult Weeks* (*Chernobyl: khronika trudnykh nedel'*, 1987)—preceded the first Soviet narrative film by three years.[4] *Chronicle* has also been cited by Craig Mazin as the visual inspiration for his miniseries, lauded as the most "authentic" portrayal of the events to date, and has provided source material for a widely recirculated side-by-side comparison video.[5]

This chapter examines these first two attempts—the earliest in the world—to come to terms with the disaster through filmic means. It focuses specifically on the rhetorical strategies they employ: the metaphors and analogies they draw on, the relationship they set up between sound and image, and their mode of address to the viewer. Specifically, it asks why both sets of filmmakers felt compelled to introduce elements of a mode unused in the Soviet Union for over fifty years—that of the essay film—when faced with an event of such immense proportions. Ultimately, it argues that, even if the approach pioneered by their films failed to set the standard for representations of Chernobyl to follow, it opens up a productive set of questions for the way eco-cinema has developed in our time.

Fatal Films: The Production History

Both sets of filmmakers understood that they were embarking on a suicide mission, and their efforts follow overlapping timelines. Shevchenko was the first to receive permission on 14 May, the day Gorbachev's official broadcast aired on TV. Sergienko and Sinelnikov arrived in Chernobyl just two weeks later, on 28 May. Both operated with a skeleton crew: Shevchenko's team included two additional cameramen, Viktor Kripchenko and

Figure 6.1. Vladimir Shevchenko includes images of himself filming. *Chronicle of Difficult Weeks* (*Khronika trudnykh nedel'*). Directed by Vladimir Shevchenko. Kyiv: UkrKinoKhronika, 1987. Screen capture by Masha Shpolberg.

Vladimir Taranchenko.[6] Sergienko and Sinelnikov had three cameramen (Konstantin Durnov, Vladimir Frolenko, and Ivan Dvoinikov) and two assistants (Vladislav Mikosha and Dmitry Ryzhykh). Shots of the crew in *Chronicle* show them protected only by cloth masks and caps. "Of course, we understood it is a one-way trip," Kripchenko would later say, "but nobody knew when it will end, so nobody thought about the danger."[7] In later interviews, members of each crew would describe others stepping in to protect them, with Kripchenko claiming that Shevchenko had shielded him when they were filming directly above the reactor and Sergienko claiming that Dvoinikov had done the same for him.[8]

The *Bell of Chernobyl* team filmed for one month, from 28 May until 26 June, returning to Moscow, in Sergienko's words, "to look over the material, to understand where we needed to go with it, what else we needed to shoot" as well as to complete work on projects they had abandoned in their rush to Chernobyl.[9] At the end of August, they returned to the Zone for a week of additional filming. The Kyiv-based *Chronicle* team, in turn, shot continuously for one hundred days from May until August. When both had finished, the cameras they had used were buried in the Zone in lead cases. Sergienko also reported studio editors back in Moscow being afraid to handle the negatives and agreeing to work only with the positive print.[10]

The first cut of *Bell* was ready by the end of September; the first cut of *Chronicle*—by November. Unsurprisingly, both were subjected to ruthless censorship. Sergienko and Sinelnikov were reprimanded for shooting a number of "unnecessary scenes," such as a church service, and including "too much Alla Pugacheva" from a concert the pop star had given for the cleanup workers.[11] Shevchenko was similarly ordered to excise a number of politically inopportune moments, such as a strike the crew had captured on camera. In the outtakes of a February 1987 TV interview, Shevchenko would say he received one hundred fifty-two requests for correction, while Igor Malishev, the film's scriptwriter, would reveal that the voice-over had to be rewritten sixteen times.[12] Scholar David Marples, in turn, estimates that of the twenty thousand meters that Shevchenko and his team had shot, only fifteen hundred (or 8 percent) made it into the final version.[13]

Both films found their way to audiences only in March 1987, nearly a year after the accident. Sergienko and Sinelnikov convinced their studio head to allow *Bell of Chernobyl* to be screened at a special international forum in Moscow in February 1987. The German delegation approached the filmmakers after the screening and asked for the film to be screened at the Berlinale.[14] Its resounding success abroad convinced Soviet authorities to distribute the film internally.[15] Sinelnikov also credits renowned director Elem Klimov with intervening on behalf of the film.[16] *Bell* was eventually screened at the 1987 Moscow International Film Festival where it received a special prize "for professional courage."[17] Both directors would become committed to the topic, with Sinelnikov going on to make four more films about Chernobyl, and Sergienko seven.

The release of *Chronicle* took on a far more tragic dimension. Having spent much longer in the Zone, all three crew members had to be hospitalized for radiation sickness after the shoot. Shevchenko suffered the worst fate: already in August, he was diagnosed with lung cancer, but put off surgery to complete the first cut of the film. He eventually went in for the surgery in February and died a month later, on 30 March 1987—before the fate of the film could be known. Though the Soviet government prevaricated regarding the cause of his death, it was eventually acknowledged to have been radiation sickness and widely reported abroad.[18]

Prior to Shevchenko's death, *Chronicle* had received an official screening only in Kyiv. In April, however, *Pravda Ukrainy*, the official Party newspaper of the Ukrainian Republic, ran an article criticizing the film's suppression, and things began to shift.[19] *Chronicle* was shown at the Tbilisi film festival in May 1987 and made its way around the Warsaw Pact countries.[20] Film scholar Jadwiga Hučková cites it as one of the films that shifted the political atmosphere in Poland and made explicit criticism of the USSR feel possible.[21] The film was eventually sold to more than one hundred countries and won nine awards at international film festivals. More surprisingly still, it toured US college campuses as part of the 1989 Glasnost Film Festival, where it was screened alongside two other environmental films from "peripheral" studios—Mikhail Pavlov's *The BAM Zone: Permanent Residents* (*Zona BAM. Postoyannye zhiteli,* 1987), which contrasted propaganda newsreels of the aborted railroad project with evidence of the damage it had caused to the environment, and Igor Gonopolsky's *Scenes at a Fountain* (*Stseny u fontana*, 1986), which documented yearlong attempts to extinguish a fire on a Caspian oil rig.[22] Several years before the actual collapse of the Soviet Union, these films already seemed to invite a retrospective gaze, a reckoning with the environmental dimensions of the catastrophe that had been the Soviet project.

Beyond Propaganda: The Rhetoric of Compromise

Chronicle and *Bell* are, in many ways, similar films. Thematically, both strive to capture as many aspects of the cleanup effort as possible and to reflect on the repercussions of the event—for both the local population and the world at large. True to the communist ethos, they emphasize the labor and self-sacrifice of the cleanup workers, considering not only those directly involved in the heroic work of containing the doomed reactor, but also all those whose labor undergirds theirs, from the nurses and cafeteria workers to the volunteers who came to set up newspapers and radio programs for the crews. These portraits of those who have been thrown in (or who have voluntarily rushed in) to the area are juxtaposed with those who have been thrown out—the inhabitants of Pripyat and the surrounding villages. Sound bites and observational footage featuring these two populations are anchored by interviews with the "experts"—the scientists, medics, and engineers placed in charge of the evacuation and containment efforts. Formally, both films make extensive use of aerial shots to demonstrate the scale of the problem, observational sequences to make the danger and difficulty of the cleanup effort palpable, and languorous pans across lush but now-forbidden landscapes to comment on the uncanny invisibility of radiation and evoke a sense of loss.

The need to satisfy the State Film Board doubtless influenced the films' parallel opening structures. Both seek to legitimize their existence by attaching themselves to Gorbachev's official broadcast—*Chronicle* by opening with a clip from it, *Bell* with a printed quote—as if to suggest that they are, in some way, its continuation. *Bell* even derives its title from Gorbachev's assertion that Chernobyl is but "another sound of the bell, another grim warning" about the "abyss [that] will open if nuclear war befalls mankind."[23] Both films include interviews with scientists speaking about how Chernobyl reflects but a fraction of the damage a nuclear war would cause and conclude with calls for "civilization" to grow wiser and renounce nuclear arms. Finally, both continuously refer to World War II as the primary frame of reference for a national mobilization of this kind. The voice-over in *Chronicle*, for example, reminds us that "this is not the first evacuation this area has experienced" and notes that the long-awaited concrete for the sarcophagus arrives not any random day but on "May 9th, Victory Day."²⁴ It comments on some cleanup workers enjoying "rare moments of rest, as during a pause in the trenches" and informs the viewer that "the word 'heroism' ... in Chernobyl is pronounced rarely, with some embarrassment, in a quiet voice, as back then, at the Front."²⁵ Even the cleanup effort itself is articulated as a battle: "The enemy has been stopped. From defense, very slowly, very carefully, we may pass to an offense."²⁶ The effect, instead of acknowledging the disaster as one of the Soviet Union's greatest failures, is to shift focus to its greatest triumph.

Viewed in this light, Chernobyl is transformed from an embarrassment or a liability into a gift the Soviet Union is holding out to the world. "Medics are aware that a similar catastrophe could have happened in any other country in the world," the voice-over explicitly asserts in *Bell*. In the final scenes of both films, top scientists (Valery Legasov, chief of the commission investigating the disaster in Chronicle, and Andrei Vorobiev of the Soviet Academy of Medical Sciences in *Bell*) claim the rest of the world approves of the Soviet cleanup effort and is learning from the Soviet example. The impact of this scene is amplified in *Bell* by the presence of a simultaneous translator, so that Vorobiev's words are barely decipherable underneath the steady flow of the translator's English. The implication is clear: the Soviet Union is lighting the way for other nations.²⁷ Meanwhile, locally, the films assert, life goes on: both end on notes of uplift, with nearby villagers celebrating Easter in *Chronicle* and evacuees happily resettled in new apartment blocks on the outskirts of Kyiv in *Bell*.

These and even less subtle moments of propaganda are offset by the directors' environmentalist sensibilities. Communist ideology traditionally framed nature in terms of its use value. Moments of cultural efflorescence, when censorship loosened, would offer alternative images, inviting the viewer to regale in nature as an aesthetic experience and, potentially, to see it as something valuable in and of itself. (Hence the sweeping pans of early Soviet poetic documentary and the Thaw-era celebration of the elements.) These later Chernobyl documentaries walk an uneasy line between the two approaches. The cinematography offers lyrical visions while the voice-over often works at cross-purposes, containing them by elaborating on what it all means for human beings only.

This is, in large part, due to the directors' training. Prior to *Bell*, Sinelnikov had worked as a film critic, and his contribution to *Bell* was primarily as a scriptwriter. Sergienko, however, had trained in Oleksandr Dovzhenko's workshop at VGIK, the main Soviet film school in Moscow (graduating in 1963), and clearly carried on both his teacher's love for their native Ukraine and a romantic, somewhat sentimental vision of peasant life. *Bell* consequently devotes extensive screen time to the peasants who have been forced to leave their villages as they mourn the loss and, in many cases, detail their illegal journeys back. Their plight is also conveyed metaphorically, through recurrent shots of a stork leaving and flying back to its nest as the voice-over asks, "How to tear oneself away from one's land?"[28] Time and again, the film suggests an irrevocable, organic tie between the people and their territory. Over visuals that recall Dovzhenko's *Earth*, the voice-over opines:

> This land has grown empty. The people who used to live here will remember their homes as a distant past they can never return to. No one will gather these apples. They will rot, retaining within them their radioactive seeds. The grains of wheat will sprout as a new, radioactive field. Birds will peck at them—they can't be held to boundaries. This land has become the victim of our mistakes...[29]

The primary tragedy here is one of wastefulness; of nature unyoked from its purpose: satisfying human need. The land is also arguably anthropomorphized, the feminine gender of the words "land" (*zemlia*) and "victim" (*zhertva*) in Russian suggesting the image of a female suffering as the result of largely male, human hubris.

Shevchenko, in turn, had come to cinema late, at age forty, having first studied agriculture in Novosibirsk and worked as an agronomist on one of the state farms created during the Virgin Lands campaign. His first film, *Kulunda: Hopes and Anxieties* (*Kulunda: trevogi i nadezhdy*, 1966), was a searing indictment of that campaign's devastating effects on the environment—and was consequently "shelved" for twenty years. Sick in the hospital in 1987, Shevchenko would write in his diary "is my story with Kulunda repeating itself?"[30] *Chronicle* consequently communicates the same concern with the relationship to the land but phrases it as a more positive imperative: "We must leave to our descendants an Earth in flower, filled with the noise of birds, and not cities overgrown with wormwood [*chernobyl'nik* in Russian] and wheat grown wild behind the barbed wire of danger zones."[31] Though the ultimate recipients and beholders of this Earth are human beings ("our descendants"), it is a vision somewhat more aligned with the nature-for-its-own-sake model, one that suggests a particular type of landscape as inherently more desirable than another. Unsurprisingly, however, the positive image is one devoid of any trace of human civilization ("an Earth in flower, filled with the noise of birds"), while the negative one foregrounds the unhealthy intrusion of the natural into the humanmade and vice versa ("cities overgrown with wormwood and wheat grown wild behind ... barbed wire").

Figure 6.2. The iconography of the "zone of exclusion" in *The Bell of Chernobyl (Kolokol Chernobylia)*. Directed by Rollan Sergienko and Vladimir Sinelnikov. Moscow: Tsentralnaya Studiya Dokumentalnykh Filmov, 1986. Screen capture by Masha Shpolberg.

Though many reports at the time focused on the astonishingly long-term consequences of the fallout (Svetlana Alexievich would later say "Chernobyl changed our understanding of time—many radioactive particles will live for a hundred, two hundred, a thousand years"), both films adopt a foreshortened perspective.[32] In both voice-overs, time is measured in generations, bringing reproductive processes of all kinds into focus, from the rotting, radioactive apple seeds and sprouting fields of wheat to the suggested, but unspoken, implications for the human ability to bear children.

Scales of Impact: The Local and The Universal

This is where the similarities end, however. Visually, *Bell* begins to develop some of the iconography that, over time, will become the canonical way of representing Chernobyl, including images of the abandoned city of Pripyat, its Ferris wheel standing still, boarded up villages, forests encircled by barbed wire, signs announcing the "forbidden zone," and Geiger counters ticking madly in otherwise peaceful fields. Its primary way of defining the disaster is thus through the renunciation involved: the land and the (agri)culture that must be given up.

These images stress the local dimension over the universal one and carry hints of a distinctly Ukrainian nationalism defined by strong ties to the soil and religious affect. The latter comes across most strongly in the lengthy sequence of a Sunday service in a nearby church attended almost exclusively by older women. The voice-over justifies the inclusion of this scene, unimaginable before glasnost, by explaining that the parishioners of this church were among the first to donate to the Chernobyl fund, thereby assimilating them to "the Soviet people who, within six months of the disaster, had transferred 520 million rubles to account number 904." The explanation complete, however, the camera lingers in the space, capturing part of the sermon, exploring the faces in the crowd and the icons lining the walls.

Like these parishioners, the film itself seems to turn to religious iconography as a means of processing the disaster. Just before the opening Gorbachev quote fades from the screen, a female voice (possibly Nina Matvienko) begins singing a plaintive, wordless song evocative of a prayer or a funeral dirge. The film eventually cuts to Anna Khodymchuk, the elderly mother of the first person to die at Chernobyl, as she recounts her son's last visit home, and it is to her weary face and the same vocals that it returns at the end. Though the film includes remarkable interviews with some of the workers being treated for radiation sickness and their families, it thus telescopes the human suffering involved primarily through this Madonna-like figure, further consolidating the narrative of self-sacrifice for the greater good.

In attending to the local dimension of the catastrophe and the religious response, *Bell* foretells the way in which the disaster would be progressively "nationalized," becoming a key factor, in the eyes of many historians, in the breakdown of the Soviet Union. As Catherine Wanner explains:

> Chernobyl powerfully and irrevocably destroyed the legitimacy of the Soviet state in the minds of many Soviet citizens who were taken aback by the bureaucracy's blatant subservience to image over real people and real injury. ... During the aftermath of Chernobyl, many Russians and russified Ukrainians agitating for change in Ukraine, who could not relate to the charges of exploitation and cultural oppression that drove independence movements in other areas of the former Soviet Union, saw their republic as a colony for the first time.[33]

Though *Bell* is subtle about the way this Soviet disaster produced a localized Ukrainian suffering, Olga Briukhovetska argues that this point of view would become pronounced in the fiction films that followed.[34] Drawing on the work of Hiro Saito, she demonstrates how, in this, Chernobyl followed the same trajectory as Hiroshima and Nagasaki—articulated first as "an event belonging to the whole of humanity" and, later, as the "founding trauma" of a new nation (postwar Japan in the former case, the newly independent states of Ukraine, Belarus, and Russia in the latter).[35] *Chronicle*, by contrast, continues to operate at the universal level. It devotes only one three-minute sequence to the plight of the peasants who have been forced to resettle, focusing instead on the many different types of activity taking place within the Zone; its "we" oscillates between Soviet citizens and all human beings as such.

Tackling Crisis: The Value of the Essay Form

This difference in scale—*Bell* very much operating at the local level, *Chronicle* seeking to speak to and for all of humanity—extends to their use of the essay film form. Most scholars trace the origins of the essay film to Soviet cinema. In his famous essay on the "camera-pen" or *caméra-stylo*, Alexandre Astruc noted that the first filmic reference to the term "essay" appears to have occurred in Sergei Eisenstein's 1927 notes toward a filmic version of Marx's *Capital*. Closer in time, Timothy Corrigan has cited Eisenstein's elaboration of montage and Laura Rascaroli has cited Dziga Vertov's concept of "the interval" as critical to making the essay film possible.[36] The curtailing of the avant-gardes and the instauration of socialist realism, however, meant that the essay film did not have time to develop properly in the Soviet Union. Both Corrigan and Rascaroli see it coalescing as a distinctive form only in the 1950s, in France.

It is significant that, for both, the rise of the essay film at this time is indelibly linked to the horrors of war. As Timothy Corrigan writes:

> The crisis of World War II, the Holocaust, the trauma that traveled from Hiroshima around the world, and the impending Cold War inform, in short, a social, existential, and representational crisis that would galvanize an essayistic imperative to question and debate not only a new world but also the very terms by which we subjectively inhabit, publicly stage, and experientially think that world. No wonder that Alain Resnais's 1955 *Night and Fog* … becomes an early and widely recognized example of the essay film.[37]

From the outset, the essay film is seen as a response to a crisis, an event so gruesome, and of such proportions, that the narrative clarity offered by more traditional modes comes to seem inappropriate, reductive. What makes the essay film so valuable under these conditions is its ability not to present a definitive version of the event, but to "stage," in Corrigan's words, the process of cognizing, of coming to terms with the event, itself. The central narrative and aesthetic qualities of the essay film flow from there: the self-reflexivity, the privileging of questions over answers, and the narrative or thematic fragmentation. For how can one grasp the unimaginable except obliquely?

It makes sense that, faced with an event of similar magnitude, Soviet directors would turn to this mode.[38] The extent to which they did so, however, varied. *Bell*'s emphasis on local communities meant that its use of the voice-over was limited, with much more time given over to testimony and interviews. The voice-over serves primarily to articulate the film's aims at the beginning, to provide context where needed, and to smooth over the transition between various sections. *Chronicle*, on the other hand, relies heavily on the voice-over, often using it to recalibrate our perception of the images in surprising ways. Though both guiding voices are male, they are not exactly omniscient. Instead, they are clearly identified with the collective voice of the filmmakers and defined by their great, but still partial, knowledge and access. Where traditional "voice-of-God" narration, so common in Soviet documentary, conveyed confidence, these voice-overs betray a deepening crisis of authority. They take viewers behind the scenes, so to speak, revealing the process of their makers' thought rather than presenting them with a finished product, a set take on what has transpired.

In addition to the use of voice-over and the disjunction between sound and image, *Bell* and *Chronicle* borrow several other features from the essay film. Most significant among these is reflexivity: both films draw attention to themselves as manufactured artifacts, foregrounding the conditions of their own production. The voice-over in *Bell*, for example, explains that "this film was shot from May 28th until June 26th, and again at the start of September. Its authors did not set before themselves the task of creating an exhaustive portrait of all that had taken place in Chernobyl. They sought to record the testimony of people immediately affected by the tragedy, whose lessons we have yet to fully grasp."[39] This opening quickly establishes a sense of transparency befitting of glasnost. And, though it starts out in the third person, the narration quickly transitions to a community-building, second-person "we." The reflexivity is not restricted to the voice-over, however. Frames within frames, as when we first see the nuclear reactor through the window of an armored vehicle in *Chronicle*, provide an additional layer of mediation and draw attention to the difficulty with which this film came to be.

Chronicle again takes this aspect further, using the voice-over to explicitly comment on the image. Thus, it tells us as we near the plant that "this very first, short shot was taken when we were allowed to pop out through the hatch of the armored vehicle with the camera for just thirty seconds."[40] And though it acknowledges just how much of this shoot lay outside the filmmakers' control, it finds meaning in happenstance. Thus, the voice-over goes on to say, "Our second camera was loaded with black-and-white film, and therefore the chronicle of the first weeks in the film will be black and white, the colors of our anxiety and our sadness." In its own, minor way, the film thus replicates the process of redeeming an accident by seeking some value in it.

One unexpected outcome of all this reflexivity is that it leads the films toward a new model of representing radiation. Both mention the effects of radiation on the film strip itself. In *Bell*, however, it is mentioned as a sidenote. An important delivery goes awry, leaving the authorities with no choice but to send people out into the zone of highest radiation. In the midst of this dramatic episode, the voice-over draws our attention to the surface of the film, as if to distract us from the unfolding disaster: "physicists explain these flares on the film stock that visited the fourth reactor in different ways."[41] It drops the subject just as quickly, however, returning to the central action. *Chronicle*, on the other hand, makes a point of it. "The mortal enemy who, even from behind our steel armor, pushed the arrows of the Geiger counters beyond their highest mark and, invisible, carried out its evil work in the human body, is radiation," the voice-over intones. "It has no odor and no color. It has only a voice. Here it is. On-screen is one of the shots which the studio had originally labeled as damaged. But this is not damage. It is the visible face of radiation. Look closely."[42] Primed in this way, the viewer begins to hear the static on the soundtrack, to see the white pockmarks on the image. This injunction thus transforms what was previously perceived as noise into a signal, decomposition into composition. For scholar and artist Susan Schuppli, one of the few to write on *Chronicle*, this moment also "collapse[s] the gap between representation and the real, form and content."[43] Where *Bell* had figured the "invisible foe" negatively, in terms of all the renunciation involved, *Chronicle* finds a way of figuring it positively, as a presence actively haunting the image.

The second unexpected outcome of the films' reflexivity is the way in which it allows them to model a more alert and engaged way of being in the world. Like so many essay films, *Bell* and *Chronicle* stage what Corrigan calls "an encounter between the self and the public domain, an encounter that measures the limits and possibilities of each as a conceptual activity."[44] The voice-over in both, but in *Chronicle* in particular, presents a roving consciousness striving to make sense of an event beyond all human measure. The films' direct address to the viewer means that the act of viewing the films becomes an extension of this encounter. "Yes, this is it, the fourth reactor of the Chernobyl nuclear power plant shortly after the explosion," the voice-over in *Chronicle* states, as if anticipating the viewer's question.[45] "When you view this film, the expired reactor will be forever covered by a large structure," the voice-over in *Bell* explains. "Therefore, the shots you see now are already history. It would, fortunately, be impossible to film them again."[46] While these phrases serve to reassure the viewer that the worst is already past, the battle won, they model a way of thinking one's way through events beyond our control and encourage greater implication in the public sphere. "To say 'I' or 'we' is, first, a gesture of responsibility and accountability," writes Laura Rascaroli. "The moment of the essay film is, therefore, politically inflected."[47] The films' direct address to a "you" capable of complex thought and use of the indeterminate, shifting "we" forces viewers to wonder which community is being invoked here and how it is defined. Is it the whole of humanity? The Soviet people? The inhabitants of the surrounding area? Reflecting on this process of interpellation becomes an act of political coming-to-consciousness. It is no wonder that the anti-war and environmental movements Chernobyl launched quickly became movements for national self-determination.[48]

Cracks in the Official Discourse: Bringing in a Polyphony of Voices

While the censorship battle over *Bell* and *Chronicle* was still raging, the Soviet Ministry of Defense ordered its own documentary, *Theater of Operations—Chernobyl* (*Rayon deystviya—Chernobyl*, 1987), devoted entirely to the technological and human exploits of the cleanup effort. Sinelnikov, Sergienko, and Shevchenko's fight would also open up the gates for more documentaries to follow, first among them Georgi Shkliarevsky's *Mi-cro-phone!* (*Mi-kro-fon!*, 1988), which criticized the state for holding back information when thousands had fallen so ill and also traveled widely on the international festival circuit.[49] In the censored outtakes of that 1987 TV interview, Shevchenko says he is beginning to feel that he is "living in this world for naught" since his film "might have been shown four months ago," that it "anticipated certain state and Party decisions," and that it advanced "interesting conclusions" but, by the moment of the interview, had fallen irredeemably behind.[50]

What Shevchenko could not have known at the time and did not live to find out is that, despite no longer being the first, *Chronicle* remained the most original. *Theater of Operations—Chernobyl* and *Mi-cro-phone!* represent opposing poles of how one might have expected the state-subsidized film industry to respond to a disaster of this kind: by focusing either on the bravery of the military and the volunteers or on the plight of the local population (the heroes and the victims). The enduring value of both *Bell* and *Chronicle* lies in the way they eschewed these more obvious (even if, in the case of *Mi-cro-phone!* highly worthy) approaches in favor of something more experimental. *Bell* anticipated the approach that would be perfected by Svetlana Alexievich, prioritizing testimony above all. As Dori Laub wrote in her and Shoshana Felman's seminal book on the topic, preserving and sharing testimony of this kind is important because "the listener to trauma comes to be a participant and a co-owner of the traumatic event."[51] Or, in Lóránt Stőhr's words, "the suffering victims of traumatic events can regain their dignity by giving testimony, and the viewer or listener can share the burden of the memories with the witness by the very act of listening."[52] Still, unlike *Mi-cro-phone!*, *Bell* does not focus exclusively on the victims. It surveys as many of the different actors involved as possible, from the firefighters undergoing treatment for radiation sickness and the local peasants to Party representatives, allowing us to note the different types of discourses generated at each level about the event. It then uses the voice-over—and, with it, elements of the essay film—to stitch these different discourses together into a whole that feels at once lyrical and sober.

Chronicle, likewise, feels polyphonic, but with much of that polyphony internal to the central voice-over. Indeed, the sudden shifts in register give the impression of three competing voices: Shevchenko and Malishevsky's philosophical reflections, the matter-of-fact narration of events, and the moralizing of the Party apparatus. What Shevchenko doubtless saw as the corruption and degradation of his film, however, can be read productively as symptomatic of the times, the lyrical passages streaming forth through the cracks of the tired and spent official discourse.

It is telling that the year *Chronicle* finally reached audiences was the year scholar Mikhail Epstein penned a groundbreaking article in the journal *Voprosy Literatury* titled "The Laws of a Free Genre: The Essay and the Essayistic in Contemporary Culture."[53] There, he asserted that "the essay is one of the liveliest and most rapidly developing genres in contemporary literature."[54] By 1987, the essay form had been in decline in the West already for some time.[55] Its late arrival in the Soviet Union was doubtless made possible by the relaxation of censorship and the new cultural channels opened by glasnost and perestroika. Though the timing may have been an accident, the essay's attractiveness seems anything but. Dialogic in form, it was inherently opposed to the monologism of official Soviet discourse. Moreover, its fragile, tentative, and fragmentary aesthetic must have seemed the perfect antidote to Soviet monumentalism.

Of course, neither *Chronicle* nor *Bell* are essay films in the strictest sense. Both are, to borrow Epstein's term, "essayistic," the former to a greater degree than the latter. Borrowing from the tool kit of the essay film allowed their makers to resist the urge to contain and explain away the unknown, staying with it for some time instead. Though they kowtow to the authorities and draw heavily on preexisting systems of signification (religious iconography, the hallowed Soviet myth of World War II), they also take exploratory steps toward, in *Bell*'s concluding words, "learn[ing] to live and think differently." They model transparency, reflexivity, and a way of actively cognizing the world that encourages greater personal agency and responsibility. Finally, they acknowledge the value of liminal experiences and thinking one's way through events beyond human measure. For it is in wrestling with the colossal that we discover not our insignificance but, rather, our capacity for freedom and our ability to grow and evolve. To quote from Epstein yet again, subjectivity "constantly defining itself ... can never be fully defined."[56]

Masha Shpolberg is Assistant Professor of Film and Electronic Arts at Bard College. Her teaching and research explore global documentary, Russian, Eastern, and Central European cinema, ecocinema, and women's cinema. She is currently at work on a book titled *Labor in Late Socialism: The Cinema of Polish Workers' Unrest*, which explores how filmmakers responded to successive waves of strikes by co-opting, confronting, or otherwise challenging the representational legacy of socialist realism. In addition to this volume, she is also co-editor, with Anastasia Kostina, of *The New Russian Documentary: Reclaiming Reality in the Age of Authoritarianism*, a volume forthcoming from Edinburgh University Press. She holds a PhD in Comparative Literature and Film and Media Studies from Yale University.

Notes

1. Plokhy, *Chernobyl*; Brown, *Manual for Survival*; Higginbotham, *Midnight in Chernobyl*.
2. It is interesting to note that the first approved accounts of the disaster took on a primarily verbal rather than visual form—possibly because these would have been less shocking. Excerpts from Vladimir Gubarev's play *Sarcophagus* were published in *Sovetskaya Kultura* (*Soviet Culture*) as early as September 1986; in January 1989, Sergei Kurginyan was able to stage *Compensation*, a play based on eye-witness testimony at the "On the Boards" (*Na doskakh*) Theatrical Studio in Moscow.

    The most comprehensive account of the disaster, however, came sometime after the collapse of the Soviet Union with the publication of Svetlana Alexievich's *A Chernobyl Prayer* (*Чернобыльская молитва*), first in Russian in 1997 and then in an English translation as *Voices from Chernobyl: The Oral History of a Nuclear Disaster* in 2005. More recently, poets Lina Kostenko, Liubov' Sirota, and Oksana Zabuzhko have become known for their cycles of poems addressing the disaster.
3. During the Soviet period, both filmmakers' names were Russified. Since the collapse of the USSR, they have increasingly been given in their Ukrainian variants, as Rollan Serhienko or Serhiyenko and Volodymyr Shevchenko. Here, I have chosen to use transliterations of their names as they appeared in the films' credits.
4. For more on the narrative films produced both before and after the collapse of the Soviet Union, see Briukhovetska, "'Nuclear Belonging,'" and Lindbladh, "Coming to Terms."
5. On 4 June 2019, after the last episode of the miniseries aired on HBO, Craig Mazin (@clmazin) published a list of books and films that had inspired him

on Twitter, which included Shevchenko's film. The tweets were collected and reprinted in Sharf, "20 Chernobyl Books." The side-by-side comparison video featured scenes from the miniseries next to a variety of footage from 1986, including scenes from Shevchenko's film. See Flight, "HBO's Chernobyl vs. Reality."

6. Alternate spellings: Viktor or Victor Krypchenko and Volodymyr Taranchenko.
7. Peplow, "Chernobyl."
8. Idem.; see also Sergienko, "Eto bylo vpechatlyayushche i strashno: do sikh por" ("It Was Impressive and Terrifying: To This Day"), memoirs collected by the Museum of the Central Studio for Documentary Film in Moscow (30 November 2011), accessed 6 September 2021. https://csdfmuseum.ru/articles/9-роллан-сергиенко-это-было-впечатляюще-и-страшно-до-сих-пор.
9. Ibidem. Original Russian: "Необходимо было отсмотреть материал. Понять, куда двигаться, что доснять." Unless otherwise noted, all translations from Russian are the author's own.
10. Ibidem.
11. Ibidem. See also Brown, *Manual for Survival*, 170. Interestingly, while the scenes with Pugacheva were excised from the film, the church service remained.
12. Vladimir Shevchenko and Igor Malishev in Tereshchenko, *From Kulunda to Chernobyl*.
13. Marples, *Social Impact of Chernobyl*, 136.
14. I am grateful to Dina Iordanova for pointing me to Christian Jungen's biography of Moritz de Hadeln, longtime head of the Berlinale. The biography includes a section detailing Moritz de Hadeln's exchange with Mikhail Shkalikov, then head of the International Department at Goskino, attempting to secure a copy of *Bell* for the festival. Jungen, *Moritz de Hadeln*, 309–326.
15. Sergienko, op. cit.
16. Entry for "The Bell of Chernobyl," Museum of the Central Studio for Documentary Film in Moscow. https://csdfmuseum.ru/films/33-колокол-чернобыля.
17. Ibidem.; Quinn-Judge, "Moscow Festival Reveals New Openness."
18. "A Soviet Film Maker at Chernobyl in '86 is Dead of Radiation." A Reuters news item was widely recirculated here and in many other Western newspapers: "Chernobyl Film-maker Is Dead." Shevchenko's legacy was eventually honored with a memorial plaque on his apartment building in Kyiv. A documentary was also made about him by colleagues at UkrKinoKhronika, titled *From Kulunda to Chernobyl* (1988). Kripchenko and Taranchenko would go on to make an additional documentary short about Chernobyl, titled *An Unpublished Album* (1991), which won prizes at the Krakow, Łódź, and Oberhausen festivals. Bondarchuk, "Ukrainska Studiya."
19. Shanker, "Death, Film Suppression Cloud Soviet Openness."
20. "A Soviet Film Maker at Chernobyl in '86 is Dead of Radiation."
21. Hučková, "Films That Gave Us Boldness," 272.
22. Youngblood, "Review of the Glasnost Film Festival"; Barringer, "Soviet Documentaries That Face Up to Reality."
23. The opening quote in *Bell of Chernobyl* reads: "The accident at Chernobyl showed again what an abyss will open if nuclear war befalls mankind. For

inherent in the nuclear arsenals stockpiled are thousands upon thousands of disasters far more horrible than the Chernobyl one. … We realize that it is another sound of the tocsin, another grim warning." English translation as given in "Excerpts from Gorbachev's Speech."
24. Original Russian: "Эти места уже раз переживали эвакуацию…"
25. Original Russian: "Редкие минуты отдыха, словно передых в окопах"; "Второй раз в разговорах с людьми в нашем фильме звучит слово героизм. В Чернобыле его произносят редко, как бы смущаясь, не громким голосом, как когда-то, на фронте."
26. Original Russian: "Враг остановлен. От обороны пусть медленно, пусть крайне осторожно, можно переходить к наступлению."
27. *Bell* strikes a similar note when Armand Hammer, the American industrialist, is shown saying in a heavily accented Russian, "I would want everyone to see what I have seen so there would be no talk of nuclear war. We need to destroy all nuclear weapons. I hope that when Reagan meets with Gorbachev, they show him your film, and that Reagan goes to Kyiv to see what I have seen."
28. Original Russian: "Как вырвать себя из родной земли?"
29. Original Russian: "Эта земля опустела. Люди жившие здесь будут вспоминать родные дома как далёкое и невозвратимое прошлое. И никто не соберёт эти яблоки. Они сгниют, сохраняя в себе радиоактивные семена. Зерна пшеницы прорастут и снова взойдут радиоактивным полем. Их будут клевать птицы. Для них не установишь границ. Эта земля стала жертвой наших ошибок…"
30. Diary entry dated 22 May 1987, as read aloud by Igor Malishev in *From Kulunda to Chernobyl*, op. cit. Original Russian: "Неужели повторяется моя история с Кулундой?"
31. Original Russian: "Оставить после себя потомкам землю в цвету, в птичьих щебетах, а не города заросшие чернобыльником и пшеницу задичавшую из-за проволоки опасных зон." *From Kulunda to Chernobyl*, the short film made about Shevchenko by his colleagues, traces a concern for the "the over-plowed and unprotected land" from *Kulunda: Hope and Anxieties* all the way to *Chronicle*. Original Russian voice-over in *Kulunda: Hopes and Anxieties*: "распаханной из края в край, ничем не защищённой землёй."
32. Alexievich, "In Search of the Free Individual," 14–15.
33. Wanner, *Burden of Dreams*, 33.
34. Briukhovetska, "'Nuclear Belonging,'" op. cit.
35. Saito, "Reiterated Commemoration," as cited in Briukhovetska, 98.
36. Rascaroli, *How the Essay Film Thinks*, 5.
37. Corrigan, *The Essay Film*, 63.
38. I am indebted to my colleague, Tim Palmer, for first encouraging me to think of these films as essay films.
39. Original Russian: "Этот фильм снимался с 28-го мая по 26-е июня и в начале сентября. Авторы не ставили перед собой задачу показать исчерпывающую картину произошедшего в Чернобыле. Они стремились запечатлеть свидетельства людей, непосредственно причастных к трагедии, уроки которой еще предстоит осознать."

40. Original Russian: "Этот самый первый, короткий кадр был снят тогда, когда из люка бронетранспортёра разрешили подняться с кино-камерой только на 30 секунд."
41. Original Russian: "Эти засветки плёнки побывавшей около четвёртого блока, физики объясняют по разному."
42. Original Russian: "Смертельный враг, который даже за стальной бронёй зашкаливал стрелки дозиметров и, невидимый, вершил в теле человека свою злую работу—радиация. У неё нет ни запаха, ни цвета. У неё есть только голос. Вот он. На экране один из кадров которых студийный отказ сначала задержал как брак. Но это—не брак. Это зримый лик радиации. Вглядитесь."
43. Schuppli, "The Most Dangerous Film in the World," 130.
44. Corrigan, *The Essay Film*, 6.
45. Original Russian: "Да, это он, четвёртый реактор Чернобыльской атомной вскоре после взрыва."
46. Original Russian: "Когда вы будете смотреть этот фильм, погибший реактор навсегда перекроет огромная конструкция… Поэтому кадры которые вы сейчас видите—уже история. Снять их снова, к счастью, невозможно."
47. Rascaroli, *How the Essay Film Thinks*, 5.
48. As Serhii Plokhy puts it: "The mobilization of mass movements first happened around anti-nuclear protests; then the newly formed organizations put independence on their banners" (interview with author, 8).
49. Alternate spelling: Heorhii Shkliarevskyi. According to Kate Brown, the film was released only because Gorbachev saw it as a tool to clear out the Party leadership in Ukraine (Brown, *Manual for Survival*, 170–172). It went on to win the International Federation of Film Critics Award at Oberhausen in 1989 and the Grand Prize at the Freiburg Film Festival in 1990.
50. Vladimir Shevchenko in *From Kulunda to Chernobyl*. Original Russian: "Понимаете что, чувствуешь, что ты начинаешь буквально зря жить на этом свете. Ведь фильм уже четыре месяца можно было показывать. Он шёл впереди решений советских и партийных. Он шёл с выводами какими-то интересными. Сейчас уже состоялся один пленум, второй пленум, одни решения… И мы уже получились в хвосте событий."
51. Laub, "Bearing Witness," 59.
52. Stöhr, "Inside Job," 6.
53. Epstein, "Zakony svobodnogo zhanra."
54. Ibidem. Original Russian: "Эссеистика – один из самых живых и быстро развивающихся жанров современной словесности."
55. Chris Marker's 1983 film *Sunless* (*Sans Soleil*) marks for many the apogee of the essay film. For the rest of the decade, it would be used primarily by avant-garde filmmakers like Su Friedrich eager to explore personal identity, but it would not gather the large audiences commanded by Resnais's films in the late 1950s and early 1960s.
56. Ibidem. Original Russian: "Именно потому, что личность… сама определяет себя, она никогда не может быть до конца определима…"

Bibliography

"A Soviet Film Maker at Chernobyl in '86 is Dead of Radiation." *New York Times*. 30 May 1987: 5.

Alexievich, Svetlana. "In Search of the Free Individual: The History of the Russian-Soviet Soul." Translated by Jamey Gambrell. *2016-2017 Henry E. and Nancy Horton Bartels World Affairs Fellowship Lecture*. Cornell Global Perspectives Distinguished Speaker Series. Ithaca, NY: Cornell University Press, 2018.

Barringer, Felicity. "Soviet Documentaries That Face Up to Reality." *New York Times*. 29 March 1989: C17.

"The Bell of Chernobyl." Museum of the Central Studio for Documentary Film in Moscow. https://csdfmuseum.ru/films/33-колокол-чернобыля.

Bondarchuk, P. M. "Ukrainska Studiya Khronikalno-dokumentalnykh filmiv." [Ukrainian Studo of Chronicle and Documentary Films.] Encyclopedia of Ukrainian History. Institute of Ukrainian History. http://www.history.org.ua/?termin=Ukrainska_studiia.

Briukhovetska, Olga. "'Nuclear Belonging': 'Chernobyl' in Belarussian, Ukrainian (and Russian) Films." In *Contested Interpretations of the Past in Polish, Russian, and Ukrainian Film: Screen as Battlefield*, edited by Sander Brouwer, 95–121. Leiden and Boston: Brill Rodopi, 2010.

Brown, Kate. *Manual for Survival: An Environmental History of the Chernobyl Disaster*. New York and London: W. W. Norton & Company, 2019.

"Chernobyl Film-maker Is Dead." *The Guardian*. 30 May 1987: 6.

Corrigan, Tim. *The Essay Film: From Montaigne, After Marker*. Oxford: Oxford University Press, 2011.

Epstein, Mikhail. "Zakony svobodnogo zhanra." ["Laws of the Free Genre."] *Voprosy Literatury* 7 (1987): 120–152. https://voplit.ru/article/zakony-svobodnogo-zhanra-esseistika-i-esseizm-v-kulture-novogo-vremeni/.

"Excerpts from Gorbachev's Speech on Chernobyl Accident." *New York Times*. 15 May 1986: Section A, 10.

Higginbotham, Adam. *Midnight in Chernobyl: The Untold Story of the World's Greatest Nuclear Disaster*. New York: Simon & Schuster, 2019.

Hučková, Jadwiga. "Films That Gave Us Boldness: East European Documentaries Screened in Poland (1987–1991) as Reflected in the Film Press of the Time." *Images: The International Journal of European Film, Performing Arts, and Audiovisual Communication* 15, no. 24 (2014): 270–276.

Jungen, Christian. *Moritz de Hadeln: Mister Filmfestival*. Berlin: Rüffer & Rub, 2018.

Laub, Dori. "Bearing Witness or the Vicissitudes of Listening." In *Testimony: Crises of Witnessing in Literature, Psychoanalysis and History*, edited by Dori Laub and Shoshana Felman, 221–226. New York and London: Routledge, 1992.

Lindbladh, Johanna. "Coming to Terms with the Soviet Myth of Heroism Twenty-Five Years After the Chernobyl Nuclear Disaster: An Interpretation of Aleksandr Mindadze's Existential Action Movie *Innocent Saturday*." *Anthropology of East Europe Review* 30, no. 1 (Spring 2012): 113–126.

Marples, David. *The Social Impact of the Chernobyl Disaster*. Houndmills and London: MacMillan Press, 1988.
Peplow, Gemma. "Chernobyl: The Real-Life Stories." *SkyNews*, accessed 30 August 2021. https://news.sky.com/story/chernobyl-the-real-life-stories-of-the-worlds-worst-nuclear-disaster-11741751.
Plokhy, Serhii. *Chernobyl: The History of a Nuclear Catastrophe*. New York: Basic Books, 2018.
———. Interview with Andrew Jack of the Pushkin House about *Chernobyl: The History of a Nuclear Disaster*. ASEEES NewsNet (October 2019): 8.
Rascaroli, Laura. *How the Essay Film Thinks*. Oxford: Oxford University Press, 2017.
Saito, Hiro. "Reiterated Commemoration: Hiroshima as National Trauma." *Sociological Theory* 24, no. 4 (December 2006): 353–376.
Schuppli, Susan. "The Most Dangerous Film in the World." In *Tickle Your Catastrophe! Imagining Catastrophe in Art, Architecture, and Philosophy*, edited by Frederik Le Roy, Nele Wynants, Dominiek Hoens, and Robrecht Vanderbeeken, 130–145. Ghent: Ghent University, the KASK (Ghent Royal Academy of Fine Arts), and Vooruit, 2010.
Sergienko, Rollan, ed. Aleksandr Kupny, "It Was Impressive and Terrifying: To This Day," memoirs collected by the Museum of the Central Studio for Documentary Film in Moscow (30 November 2011), accessed 6 September 2021. https://csdfmuseum.ru/articles/9-роллан-сергиенко-это-было-впечатляюще-и-страшно-до-сих-пор.
Shanker, Thom. "Death, Film Suppression Cloud Soviet Openness." *Chicago Tribune*, 18 June 1987.
Sharf, Zack. "20 Chernobyl Books and Movies to Check Out If You're Obsessed with HBO's Miniseries." *IndieWire*. 4 June 2019. Accessed 30 August 2021.
Stőhr, Lóránt. "Inside Job. First-Person Documentary in Trauma Cinema: Balkan Champion (2006)." *Images* 15, no. 24 (2014): 5–18.
Quinn-Judge, Sophie. "Moscow Festival Reveals New Openness in Soviets' View of Film Industry." *Chicago Tribune*, 17 July 1987.
Wanner, Catherine. *Burden of Dreams: History and Identity in Post-Soviet Ukraine*. University Park: Pennsylvania State University Press, 1998.
Youngblood, Denise J. "Review of the Glasnost Film Festival." *The Russian Review* 51 no. 10 (January 1992): 107–109.

Filmography

Flight, Thomas. "HBO's Chernobyl vs. Reality—Footage Comparison," 12 June 2019, accessed 30 August 2021. https://www.youtube.com/watch?v=P9GQtvUKtHA.
Gonopolsky, Igor. *Scenes at a Fountain* (*Stseny u fontana*, USSR, 1986).
Pavlov, Mikhail. *The BAM Zone: Permanent Residents* (*Zona BAM. Postoyannye zhiteli*, USSR, 1987).
Sergienko, Rollan, and Vladimir Sinelnikov. *The Bell of Chernobyl* (*Kolokol Chernobylia*, USSR, 1987).

Shevchenko, Vladimir. *Kulunda: Hopes and Anxieties* (*Kulunda: trevogi i nadezhdy*, USSR, never distributed, 1966).
——. *Chronicle of Difficult Weeks* (*Khronika Trudnykh Nedel'*, USSR, 1987).
Tereschenko, Yuri. *From Kulunda to Chernobyl* (*Ot Kulundy do Chernobylia*, USSR, 1988).

Part III
Animals between the Natural and the Social

7

Is There a Place for the Animal?

Shot Scale, Modernity, and the Urban Landscape in Lithuanian Documentary

Natalija Arlauskaitė

When film scholarship considers the way animals are represented on screen, it is usually in the context of so-called "wild" nature.[1] The analysis focuses on how, using the camera lens, human beings turn the relationship with animals into a colonizing gesture or an exoticizing gaze: how the camera sets up and maintains manifold power structures and hierarchies, how that "wildness" is contained and displayed in specialized institutions—the circus, zoo, or amusement park—and how it is channeled into the taming spectacle while producing a gaze that, according to ethnographic film scholar Catherine Russell, belongs to "an intermediary zone that lies between the pornographic and the ethnographic gazes."[2]

A different strategy can be observed when the kino-eye, above all through montage, acquires narrative structures, "translates" animals into an anthropomorphized visual language, and ascribes to them an anthropomorphic vocabulary of life forms and behavior—family, leisure, care, laziness, crookedness, joy. In such cases, the eye-catching spectacle is not only the life of other species framed by the human way of seeing, but also the conditions of that very visibility, the sheer availability of animal life forms usually hidden from the eye. John Berger, in his seminal essay "Why Look at Animals?," comments on the techniques used to shape these interspecies relationships: "technically the devices used to obtain ever more arresting images—hidden cameras, telescopic lenses, flashlights, remote control and so on—combine to produce pictures which carry with them numerous indications of their normal *invisibility*. The images exist thanks to the existence of a technical clairvoyance."[3] Following this line of thinking, (cinematic) interspecies relationships might be considered a product of visual technologies.

In order to inspect animals in this way, one needs to play around with distance and adjust the scale of the image. However, a close-up or even medium shot of an animal is a tricky endeavor. When in *The Octopus* (*La pieuvre*, 1928) Jean Painlevé films a breathing octopus in close-up, the texture of its body surface, its pulsating membranes, the contractions and expansions of its flesh become a spectacle in and of themselves, freed from the need to illustrate the animal's life circle or any other narrative support. According to Derek Bousé, wildlife documentary, when it uses close-ups, "basically asks us to confront a wild animal in what appears to be our personal, or even intimate space, which we generally reserve for friends, intimates, and loved ones—i.e. those with whom we feel safe (including our pets)."[4] Such an interpretation of the animal close-up is in line with Béla Balázs's reflections. In his *Visible Man* (1924), he mentions that "these shots are the product not so much of a good eye as of a good heart."[5] This "good heart" and the cinematic production of intimacy to the point of tactile closeness is widely used in nature documentary around the world. A recent example in Lithuanian film is *The Ancient Woods* (*Sengirė*, 2017) by Mindaugas Survila, presenting a spectacle of the untouched universe, where the "good heart" is well equipped with extreme patience and all the modern devices of "technical clairvoyance."

However, there is—or rather was—a different "breed" of cinematic animal: one that appears neither in its own environment nor in the places of institutional/domestic taming, but in the modern urban space. Access to this space is nowadays increasingly restricted for animals, but was, until quite recently, still available. These animals enter the cinematic urban space governed by a specific visual regime, defined first of all in terms of the shot scale. They are not pets or strictly domestic animals; they fit somewhere between farm and urban amusement park animals, like horses; they can be companions or loose city inhabitants, like dogs or cats. They mark the cinematic city with their own trajectories and demand a specific mode of looking.

Baltic documentary cinema of the Soviet period, and the Lithuanian documentary school in particular, present a compelling case that allows us to unpack multiple political and social tensions when it comes to animals in urban space, and trace their cinematic figuration. The films examined in this chapter all focus on the layered political temporalities of the city (including Lithuanian statehood, lost in 1940), which become visually intensified and complicated when the animal enters that space. This chapter suggests a relationship between the process of Soviet Lithuanian modernization and urbanization, when animals could still move freely throughout the city, and the scale of the animal shot considered as a part of the cinematic vocabulary of modernity. I intend to show that these particular urban cinematic animals strutting through Lithuanian documentaries tend to favor the medium shot during the great period of urban growth, which began in the mid-1960s and concluded in the early 1990s, when the Soviet political regime collapsed and film production all but ceased for a decade. In a more general sense, the chapter offers a formalist reading of the politics of the urban shot-scale of the animal.

In 1966, Almantas Grikevičius, one of the foremost Lithuanian poetic documentary and feature film directors, produced *Time Passes Through the City* (*Laikas eina per miestą*, 1966), a cinematic poem about Vilnius, the capital of Lithuania, its temporal layers and flows. This film belongs to the long line of "city symphonies," which include Walter Ruttmann's *Berlin: Symphony of a Great City* (*Berlin: Die Sinfonie der Großstadt*, 1927) and Dziga Vertov's *Man with a Movie Camera* (*Chelovek s kinoapparatom*, 1929). As is common for such films examining the rhythms of urban life, Grikevičius's *Time* pictures, catalogs, and variously measures temporal orders as projected onto the city.

To begin with the question of modernity: in the opening sequence of the film, we see the inner mechanism of the bell tower clock atop Vilnius cathedral. Its rhythmically clunking cogwheels not only refer to the mechanically measured abstract time of modernity, but also nod toward the iconic cinematic cogwheels of *Modern Times* by Charlie Chaplin (1936). The film then goes on to present all but an official inventory of different forms and figures of time. The bell tower and

Figure 7.1. *Time Passes through the City* (*Laikas eina per miestą*). Directed by Almantas Grikevičius. Vilnius: Lietuvos kino studija, 1966. Screen capture by Natalija Arlauskaitė.

the cathedral are places where modernity is redirected to the time of grand history: be it a look down to the cathedral's foundations or a look up at the sculptures of the St. Peter and St. Paul Church and inscriptions referring to the 1863 uprising against the Russian Empire.

The temporal order of the life circle is visually distributed between a wedding procession and a shot of a cemetery on All Saints' Day. The political and civic calendars are evoked in the form of the annual commemoration of the October Revolution, while a sequence of students being ritually christened presents a parody of the church sacrament. An icon from the Gate of the Dawn, a place of Catholic pilgrimage, suggests yet another temporality: that of eschatological time.

Reflection on media-specific time and image duration is introduced not only intertextually, as in the reference to *Modern Times*, but also through intermedial montage: from time to time, the documentary footage is intercut with still photographs by Algimantas Kunčius, a prominent Lithuanian photographer. Finally, in this registry of temporalities, the duration of the cinematic image itself is altered: in an episode that has become iconic, a white horse gallops in slow motion in front of a historic building (which became, after Independence, the Presidential Palace), then moves past the columns of the Choiseul Palace on the opposite side of the square.

This horse slowly galloping across an empty Old Town square has become an icon of Lithuanian cinema. It is frequently reproduced on film posters and programs, as well as publications about the history of Lithuanian cinema. In this context, the horse has to be read, first of all, as a ghost of history: it seemed to have just stepped out of the coat of arms emblazoned on Vilnius's baroque buildings. The dreamlike movement of the horse emphasizes the layering and different temporal strata, which is one of the definitions of any urban space. It also has invited a retrospective allegorical reading of the animal's movement through the square as a melancholic expression of the time, nobility, and statehood lost.[6] Despite minor critical remarks during production, the overall structure of the film and the history of its approval by the Soviet institutions of cinematography (*Time Passes* was Grikevičius's diploma film at VGIK) deny this subversive sensibility at the time of creation.[7]

In this *kunstkamera* of orders and forms of time, that of the animal is marked, first, by a sense of astonishment: it presents an unusual movement within the urban landscape.

Second, this particular constellation of temporalities refers to modernity and its apparatus's (cinema's) desire to make time and duration visible. Indeed, this was Eadweard Muybridge's aim in the first photographic experiments dealing with the movement not only of humans or horses, but of all kinds of animal species. In his famous 1887 study *Animals in Motion*, Muybridge categorized animals' movements not according to species but according to the *type* of movement: the walk, the trot, the gallop, the leap, the buck, the kick, and so forth. Muybridge presented these different forms of movement in an abstracted, theoretical space: in some other unmarked place, against either a plain backdrop or a grid. These grids not only remind us of presupposed hierarchies (who subordinates whom) but also add to the scientific ideal of rationality and neutrality created by the illusion of geometric precision.[8]

At the first glance the quality of space in Muybridge's photographs does not depend on the moving being. However, the space acquires different meanings as any statement about nature is always also a statement about culture. Russell summarizes debates about the species, gender, and age of the bodies in Muybridge's photographic catalog of movement in the following way: "[the body] cannot behave like a mute object of study but becomes textual, linguistic, discursive, always alluding to an experience outside the text, prior to its effects of alienation."[9] In other words, the social space created or alluded to by the image immediately corrects both the meaning of the moving animal and its relation to this space.

The horse from *Time Passes Through the City* does not just move through but, as the Russian formalists would say, helps *defamiliarize* the square, bracketing out everyday routine and offering a multidirectional reflection on time—on the historical, biological, or rhythmic structures of urban space. Borrowing the quasi-German word forma-

Figure 7.2. *The Old Man and the Land* (*Senis ir žemė*). Directed by Robertas Verba. Vilnius: Lietuvos kino studija, 1965. Screen capture by Natalija Arlauskaitė.

tion, I call these cinematic animals "animals-out-of-place." They appear in the cinematic urban landscape always as an exception, a slight anomaly, a misunderstanding, a mistake, or a miracle. They create a logical and temporal tension in regard to what the Lithuanian urban scholar Jekaterina Lavrinec calls urban choreography: a "dynamic relationship, first, among spatial structures, second, between the bodily experience of the inhabitants and everyday acts, and, third, between the conventions and rules 'inscribed' into urban spatial organization (the configuration of spatial elements)."[10]

In this case, one of the participants of this urban choreography that helps defamiliarize rules and conventions is the animal-out-of-place. Animals-out-of-place disrupt the usual flow of time, suspend habitual rhythms, bring into doubt mundane temporal coherence. These interventions can take many forms, even fairly straightforward ones such as the didactic symbol of the great break of modernization in *The Old Man and the Land* (*Senis ir žemė*, 1965) by Robertas Verba. In the final scene of the film, the main character travels from his village to the city of Vilnius to order a tombstone for his recently deceased wife. A one-horse cart leaves the Old

City, passes the film posters in the background, and moves through the fields in an extreme long shot as a train rushes past it in the opposite direction. The horse-drawn cart and the train are presented in conflict—the icon of modernization contrasting with that of tradition. The image as a whole becomes iconic, however, not just as an emblem of a singular, historic break, but rather an ongoing shift in the order of movement, speed, and rhythm.

When cinema, the city, and animals come together, the question of scale naturally arises. What does it mean to keep the camera-eye on the fly—the sole character of the film—and to move with it in the town apartment as Darius Žiūra does in his thirteen-minute video *The Fly* (*Musė*, 2007)? Or to film a boxer dog wandering around Užupis, a district just outside the Old Town, which at the time (in 1990) was falling apart and is being rapidly gentrified today? Could we say that the close-up or medium shot of a dog, a fly, or a human still have the same meaning, regardless of the species in question?

What does the scale of the shot used to portray an animal tell us? For example, what does it mean to film an animal in close-up, beyond the greater significance generally attributed to this type of shot? "The laws of cinematic perspective are such that the cockroach filmed in close-up seems on the screen a hundred times more terrifying than a hundred elephants in a long-shot," Eisenstein tells us.[11] There is an important episode in *The Old Man and the Land*, when the horse-drawn cart passes by some film posters in medium shot once again producing an image in which emblems of modernity and tradition cross paths. The question of the politics of the scale comes to the surface once again: the medium shot of the animal-out-of-place contrasts with the close-ups of the posters.[12] At the same time, this tension suggests a kind of "natural" shot scale for each subject.

It might seem that dogs are a species apart. In Soviet times, there were many stray dogs and cats on the street, but in the late 2000s, they ceased being able to move through urban space on their own. Microchipped dogs and cats are now bound to the perimeter of private space. In the mid-1990s, however, the Old Town and other parts of Vilnius were hardly imaginable without them. In the film *Ten Minutes Before the Flight of Icarus* (*Dešimt minučių prieš Ikaro skrydį*, 1990) by Arūnas Matelis, an exhausted boxer dog initiates and concludes the camera's journey through Užupis, which symbolically marks the area where the well-known world, the world of usual order, comes to an end, and transformation is imminent. The boxer dog appears not to "belong" to anyone: she traces her own trajectories, which partially coincide with those of the other, human, inhabitants of Užupis. She moves at her own pace, stopping, turning, and crossing the street. Her solo medium-shot performance at the beginning of the film singles her out from among the other district dwellers. At the end of the film, lost in a more general shot, she blends in with the other human inhabitants of the area. The boxer is an animal-out-of-place until the medium shot accords her an urban and on-screen space of her own. The medium shot allows the animal to occupy the screen in its entirety, the background providing just enough spatial clues but not "leveling" the animal's body with other elements or objects. The moment the boxer finds herself in a longer shot among other moving beings, her status changes. She becomes one of "a hundred elephants in a long-shot," a secondary detail of urban circulation.

This preliminary survey of the role of scale in portraying urban animal life in Lithuanian documentary suggests that the iconography of the animal-out-of-place is established neither through the close-up, which individualizes while eliminating spatial particularities, nor the long shot, which indiscriminately captures a plethora of detail. A medium shot has the advantage of making the entirety of the animal's body visible in a contextualized movement that, through its choreography, plasticity, and other material qualities, creates new dynamics, including a defamiliarized relationship to the urban environment. As Stephen Heath noted long ago, the meaning of any given shot's scale is relative within different films and style systems.[13] However, it seems that historically and stylistically the "animal-out-of-place" has a specific figuration: it manifests itself through the medium shot.

This relationship between the urban landscape in the process of modernization and the visual regime of the "animal-out-of-place" can be traced in Lithuanian cinema to the mid-1960s. From this period on until the 1990s, animals routinely appear in, and then eventually disappear from, urban space. This is a period when the regimes of cinematic visibility for animals in the urban landscape as well as the "moral connotations of the animal in the public domain" are established across a great number of national cinemas, although this process is still ongoing.[14] In Lithuanian documentary this period of the "animal-out-of-place" begins during rapid modernization and ends when public space gets ever more visually controlled and sanitized.

The final step in this sketchy history of the "animal-out-of-place" in Lithuanian documentary film is *Animus Animalis (A Story about People, Animals and Things)* (*Animus Animalis: istorija apie žmones, žvėris ir daiktus*), 2018) by Aistė Žegulytė. The film presents multiple narratives about animals in various states of death and dying, from mortal wounds to flashy decay, stories of taxidermists and hunters, including one about a stuffed animal's competition. The film ends with a reversed trompe l'oeil: a stuffed fox in a zoological museum (yet another space for animals-out-of-life) suddenly moves, leaves its case, and, in a medium shot, goes out on its usual cinematic duty of defamiliarizing an institution of modernity. The reanimated animal adds a new layer to the history of the "animals-out-of-place." Now, this choreography is used to defamiliarize not just the public space and its regimes of visual control, but the institutional staging of the natural habitat. This stage marks the phase when, it seems, meta-games with cinematic animals-out-of-place are still possible and fruitful for the figuration of modern interspecies tensions, but their original history has ended.

Natalija Arlauskaitė is a scholar of Film and Visual Studies and Professor at the Institute of International Relations and Political Science at Vilnius University. Her current academic interests include forms of historical imagination, reflection on war atrocities in film and the arts, and Soviet medical imagery. She is the author of *Key Concepts of Feminist Film Theory* (2010) and *Native and Foreign Canons: Film Adaptations Between Narrative Theory and Cultural Studies* (2014). She also serves as editor-in-chief of the book series "Writings on Film," published by the Lithuanian "Mintis" press and the translator of Sergei Eisenstein into Lithuanian. Her latest book is *Severe Peace: Photographs of Collapsed Regimes in Documentary Film* (2020).

Notes

1. The research is supported by Lithuanian Research Council (MIP-027/2015).
2. Russell, *Experimental Ethnography*, 122.
3. Berger, "Why Look at Animals?," 16.
4. Bousé, "False Intimacy," 130.
5. Balázs, *Visible Man*, 39.
6. In Eastern European cinema, particularly in both Lithuanian and Polish cinema, the white horse is an image inherited from the Romantic period to symbolize the nobility of local aristocratic classes and the lost cause of their doomed rebellions against Imperial Russia. See, for example, the conclusion of Andrzej Wajda's adaptation of Stanisław Wyspiański's *The Wedding* (1975).
7. However, the horse caught the eye of the cinema officials as something inappropriate for the modern urban landscape. Its defense (the last point in the answer to the suggested amendments) cites the necessity for the portraiture of the bombastic nobility, with the "Polonaise" by Michał Ogiński playing in the background. For the overall positive internal reviews, see Kaminskaitė-Jančorienė and Švedas, *Epizodai paskutiniam filmui*, 194–200.
8. Muybridge, *Animals in Motion*, 85.

9. Russell, *Experimental Ethnography*, 73. On Muybridge photographs narrativizing and eroticizing the female body, see Williams, "Film Body," 520.
10. Lavrinec, "Miesto choreografija," 67.
11. Eisenstein, "Krupnym planom," 25.
12. The films are *Stay Alert* (*Jagte Raho*, India, 1956) and *Faithfulness* (*Vernost'*, USSR, 1965). I would like to thank Anna Mikonis-Railienė and Dagnė Beržaitė for their help indentifying films.
13. Heath, "Film and System," 51.
14. Burt, *Animals in Film*, 38.

Bibliography

Balázs, Béla. *Visible Man: The Spirit of Film*. New York: Berghahn Books, 2010.
Berger, John. "Why Look at Animals?" In *About Looking*. London: Writers and Readers, 1980.
Bousé, Derek. "False Intimacy: Close-Ups and Viewer Involvements in Wildlife Films." *Visual Studies* 18, no. 2 (2003): 123–132.
Burt, Jonathan. *Animals in Film*. London: Reaktion Books, 2002.
Eisenstein, Sergei. "Krupnym planom (vmesto predisloviya)." In *Izbrannye proizvedeniya v shesti tomakh*, tome 5. Moskva: Isskustvo, 1968. [Сергей Эйзенштейн, "Крупным планом (вместо предисловия)." In Сергей Эйзенштейн, Избранные произведения в шести томах, V, Москва: Искусство, 1968.]
Heath, Stephen. "Film and System: Terms of Analysis, Part I." *Screen* 16, no. 1 (1975): 7–77.
Kaminskaitė-Jančorienė, Lina, and Aurimas Švedas. *Epizodai paskutiniam filmui: Režisierius Almantas Grikevičius*. Vilnius: Vaga, 2013.
Lavrinec, Jekaterina. "Miesto choreografija: kūnas, emocijos ir ritualas." *Santalka: filosofija, komunikacija* 19, no. 1 (2011): 62–73.
Muybridge, Eadweard. *Animals in Motion: An Electro-Photographic Investigation of Consecutive Phases of Animal Progressive Movements*. London: Chapman & Hall, 1902.
Russell, Catherine. *Experimental Ethnography: The Work of Film in the Age of Video*. Durham, NC: Duke University Press, 1999.
Williams, Linda. "Film Body: An Implantation of Perversion." In *Narrative, Apparatus, Ideology: A Film Theory Reader*, edited by Philip Rosen, 507–535. New York: Columbia University Press, 1986.

Filmography

Chaplin, Charles. *Modern Times* (USA, 1936).
Grikevičius, Almantas. *Time Passes Through the City* (*Laikas eina per miestą*, USSR [Lithuanian Soviet Socialist Republic], 1966).

Matelis, Arūnas. *Ten Minutes Before the Flight of Icarus* (*Dešimt minučių prieš Ikaro skrydį*, Lithuania, 1990).
Painlevé, Jean. *The Octopus* (*La pieuvre*, France, 1928).
Ruttmann, Walter. *Berlin: Symphony of a Great City* (*Berlin: Die Sinfonie der Großstadt*, 1927).
Survila, Mindaugas. *The Ancient Woods* (*Sengirė*, Lithuania, 2017).
Verba, Robertas. *The Old Man and the Land* (*Senis ir žemė*, USSR [Lithuanian Soviet Socialist Republic], 1965).
Vertov, Dziga. *Man with a Movie Camera* (*Chelovek s kino apparatom*, USSR, 1929).
Žegulytė, Aistė. *Animus Animalis (A Story about People, Animals and Things)* (*Animus Animalis: istorija apie žmones, žvėris ir daiktus*, Lithuania, 2018).
Žiūra, Darius. *The Fly* (*Musė*, Lithuania, 2007).

8

Against Interpretation
Animals in Contemporary Hungarian Cinema

Raymond De Luca

Some of the most critically acclaimed works of contemporary Hungarian cinema share an aesthetic and topical interest in animal life. To name but a few: Kornél Mundruczó's *White God* (*Fehér isten*, 2014), which, winning the *Prix un Certain Regard* at the Cannes Film Festival in 2014, follows a mad pack of dogs as they terrorize Budapest; Ildikó Enyedi's *On Body and Soul* (*Testről és lélekről*, 2017), which, having been nominated for Best Foreign Language Film at the Academy Awards in 2017, explores the surreal transformations of human beings into deer; and, of course, Béla Tarr and Ágnes Hranitzky's *The Turin Horse* (*A torinói ló*, 2011), a movie that has already cemented its place in film history by recounting the grim daily routine of a farming family and their obstinate horse as they confront the world's end. These complex, allegorically charged narratives entice us to read their animals figuratively. Given Hungary's vexed sociopolitical history, oscillating between all the major "-isms" of the twentieth and twenty-first centuries—fascism, socialism, capitalism, and, more recently, illiberalism—such readings are readily available. The dogs of *White God* could stand in for the shock troops of fascist or communist mass politics seeking to overthrow the old order. The deer in *On Body and Soul* could signify the dehumanization of the working class in late capitalism, while Tarr's horse seems to embody the failed messianism of every one of these ideological projects, a totalizing symbol of history's end. (*The Turin Horse* was, after all, Tarr's final film.) But what if we resist our impulse to allegorize?

Besides striking us as forced, abstract, and heavy-handed—as allegorism so often does—this sort of figurative thinking has a particularly adverse effect on animals. It threatens to strip animals of their essence in service of human concerns. An animal as a symbol only emerges, as critical theorist Derek Ryan writes, when "anthropocentrism meets anthropomorphism," that is, when a "human-centered analysis depends upon ascribing nonhuman animals with human features or forms," thereby drawing "a sharp line" between humans who are capable of symbolic experience and "animals that are merely objects of symbolic capture."[1] The task of thinking about animal representation, then, is to "stay tuned toward the flesh and blood" of the actual animal lives turned into art.[2] As Donna Haraway teaches us, describing herself as a "philosopher of the mud," animal bodies and the meanings with which human culture freights them co-shape one another; "trope and flesh are always cohabitating" in the "material-semiotic" that is animal representation.[3]

Thus, to understand the animals of Hungarian cinema of the 2010s purely as vehicles for sociopolitical commentaries is to delimit their significance according to our world's preexisting species order. Such an interpretive approach redoubles a mode of human-centric cross-species relations in movies that, ironically, all explore what an unsettling of established interspecies norms might look like. In *Animals in Film* (2002), Jonathan Burt reminds us that "although the animal onscreen can be burdened with multiple metaphorical signifigances ... it is also marked as a site where these symbolic associations collapse" because, as spectators, we are aware of an animal's unawareness of being filmed.[4] That is, we recognize how animals are conscripted against their will into a film and forced to appear in various ways. Watching animals on-screen, our attention is "drawn beyond the image and, in that sense, beyond the aesthetic and semiotic frame of the film."[5]

In this light, the animals of recent Hungarian cinema deserve to be read less abstractly and more literally. What interpretive possibilities are opened up if these animals signify nothing other than themselves? This pivot from "animals-as-content" to "animals-as-form" marks a shift not only in Hungarian but also in Eastern European culture more broadly concerning animal representation. As Eva Plach and Zora Kadyrbekova argue (the latter who focuses on Russian folktales), animal representation in Eastern Europe has been historically loaded with symbolic associations originating in folklore. These animal symbols, for each nation in culturally specific ways, acquired heightened importance under communism for the literary and artistic possibilities they afforded writers, dissidents, and artists in repressive political climates to convey otherwise proscribed ideas and speech.[6] For much of the twentieth century in Eastern Europe, animal representation was precisely to communicate messages beyond animals themselves. Artists behind the Iron Curtain relied on animals as vehicles—Trojan horses—for restricted modes of expression.

By contrast, the animals of contemporary Hungarian cinema frustrate these conventional interpretive strategies. These animals invite us to do what Susan Sontag so many years ago famously called for in her essay "Against Interpretation." Sontag writes: "What we decidedly do not need now is further to assimilate Art into Thought. ... Our task is not to find the maximum amount of content in a work of art. ... Our task is to cut back content so that we can see the thing at all."[7] The politically charged narratives of contemporary Hungarian cinema lure us to understand their animals as pure content—to assimilate them into "Thought"—but these films, as it were, pull the carpet out from under us. They burden their animals so heavily with semiotic possibilities that their animal signs collapse under their own symbolic weight. The films of contemporary Hungarian cinema mount a resistance to animals as objects of symbolic capture. This attack on traditional modes of animal representation betrays a broader interpretive resistance to the totalizing logic that underwrites the destructive ideologies of the twentieth and twenty-first centuries that destroyed much of Hungarian and Eastern European society. The animals of recent Hungarian film are sites of critical rupture. These animals, per Sontag, are "against interpretation."

This chapter approaches the animals of recent Hungarian cinema against the grain in the films *White God*, *On Body and Soul*, and *The Turin Horse*. It shows how these animals' figurative meanings are variously strained by the film narratives in which they inhabit. In turn, these animals disclose several key ideas about animals on-screen concerning agency, vision, and motion that have little to do with "content." Far from being rhetorical devices, animals, these Hungarian movies suggest, are beings unto themselves *who* (not "that") demand consideration as they jointly occupy the world alongside humans. This chapter proceeds from Sontag's exhortation: "The function of criticism should be to show *how it is what it is*, even *that it is what it is*, rather than to show *what it means*."[8] The chapter attempts to bring out the animalness of the animals in contemporary Hungarian film. It concludes by suggesting that, belying figurative thinking via their depiction of animals, *White God*, *On Body and Soul*, and *The Turin*

Horse intimate a trend underway in Eastern European cinema concerning an interest in the material and embodied. A turn to Tarr's *Werckmeister Harmonies* (*Werckmeister harmóniák*, 2000) will finalize such a point.

Canine Agency: *White God*

The film *White God* (2014) opens with a panorama of an empty highway in Budapest. A young girl on a bike with a trumpet in her backpack slowly comes into view with a nervous expression on her face. She's being chased by a pack of dogs. The quietude of what comes to resemble a postapocalyptic city is then interrupted by a din of howls and barks. In a series of alternating shots: close-ups, aerial views, and diagonals, Kornél Mundruczó's cinematographer, Marcell Rév, follows the band of dogs running down the street in pursuit of the girl. She's engulfed from all sides. The erratic camerawork here acknowledges the challenge of capturing the size and vitality of an animal herd on-screen. The camera struggles to keep up with the dogs; it keeps shifting perspective to convey the scale of canine mobilization. This prologue concedes the difficulty of framing animals in all their vitality in the visual field. It even concludes with a rapid-fire sequence of blurred canine bodies sprinting out of the frame; the dogs cannot be contained, cannot be *tamed*, by the film image.

This sequence recalls Gilles Deleuze and Félix Guattari's writings on the animal swarm, such as rats and wolves, who they call "pack animals," in that it concentrates on a multitude of animal bodies rather than on a cohered individual subject. The canine pack presents "a world of intensities, where all forms come undone," where singularity is deterritorialized in favor of a churning mass whose mode of existence is nomadic and restless rather than settled and at peace with itself.[9] The lone girl (played by Zsófia Psotta) is overwhelmed by the ever-changing animal horde, which consumes whatever is around them. For a filmmaker whose work does not often deal with animals, Mundruczó begins *White God* with a striking enactment of a Deleuzian animal-becoming, a process that resists delineated subject-formation.[10] According to Deleuze and Guattari, "To become animal is to participate in movement ... to the benefit of an unformed matter of deterritorialized flux ... animals never refer to a mythology or archetype but correspond solely to new levels, zones of liberated intensities where contents free themselves from their forms."[11] The opening of *White God* is indifferent to what these dogs "mean." Instead, it revels instead in the energy and instability of dog movement.

This sort of insuperable animal liveliness as conveyed by the prologue of *White God*—a film that follows an abandoned mutt, Hagen, take part in

Figure 8.1. The wild dogs "tamed" by the sound of trumpet music, an episode of spectacular dog training and coordination. *White God (Fehér isten)*. Directed by Kornél Mundruczó. Budapest: Proton Cinema, and FilmPartners & Partners Film; Berlin: Pola Pandora Filmproduktions; Mainz: Zweites Deutsches Fernhesen; and Stockholm: The Chimney Pot Sweden, 2014. Screen capture by Raymond De Luca.

a full-blown animal revolt against human society—is the main theme of Mundruczó's film. Forced onto the street by the girl's domineering father, Hagen endures a crucible of cruelty and neglect only to set an army of dogs free from the local pound, whereupon he joins them on a crusade against their former masters, who have been encouraged by the state to orchestrate the mass liquidation of mixed—"mongrel"—breeds across Budapest. The film's plot conjures up the racial hysteria and extermination campaigns of mid-twentieth-century Europe that, motivated by a white supremacist ideology, targeted "non-purebreds" (Jews, Roma, Slavs, and homosexuals, among others). Yet the dogs, appearing at first like resistance fighters, proceed to launch a reign of terror across Budapest so that they themselves come to resemble fascistic streetfighters, Benito Mussolini's Blackshirts or Adolf Hitler's storm troopers. In *White God* there is no clear-cut distinction of who's good and who's bad. Mundruczó muddles the allegorical victim-oppressor binaries that it plainly and continually invites. Only the girl's trumpet can quell the murderous pack of dogs. This arresting image of hundreds of dogs lying down to the sound of music concludes *White God*. Though this ending cries out for a figurative reading—only art can restore peace—it stands out for the way in which it trains and films animals. These dogs are more interesting precisely for what they *do not* represent.

Rather than resorting to computer-generated imagery (CGI) of animals, like so many other contemporary blockbusters, such as Matt Reeves's *Dawn of the Planet of the Apes* (2014), Jon Favreau's *The Lion King* (2019) and *The Jungle Book* (2016), and Darren Aronofsky's *Noah* (2014), Mundruczó's film hired Teresa Ann Miller, a seasoned Hollywood animal trainer, to coach real dogs for *White God*. (Two mixed-breed dogs flown to Hungary from Arizona, Body and Luke, alternated in playing Hagen.)[12] This film, in other words, does not digitally outsource its animals; it relies on living dogs. Indeed, *White God* now holds the record for the most dogs ever used in a single movie. As for the multitude of mutts in the scenes of canine mutiny, they were procured from several of Budapest's animal shelters and trained thereafter. Mundruczó acknowledges these animals by name in the film's credits under the headings: "Our Dog Colleagues" and "Our Dog Friends." Apart from its historical allusions, *White God* raises questions about what it means for animals to act. Its reliance on actual dogs runs against the symbolism baked into the film's storyline.

Acting, for humans and animals, is an assertion of one's autonomy, but it is also performed under someone else's direction and supervision. It is an ambivalent activity relationally negotiated. The dogs in *White God*, mindfully coached by Miller's instruction, were allowed to exert considerable freedom as they were filmed. The ways in which they snarled and stared, lunged, licked, and sniffed imbued *White God* with visceral realistic effects that human direction, on its own, could not have achieved. For instance, an extended sequence early in the film shows Hagen, having been freshly abandoned, wandering around Budapest. He confusedly surveys traffic, gets startled by the sound of a passing ferry, whines over a dog carcass, and greets everything and everyone with a twitchy yet inquisitive slant of head. Rév's mobile camera, vis-à-vis tracking shots and dynamic montage, needed to keep up with Hagen—not the reverse. The dog's spontaneous responses make *him* the star of the show. The camera reacts to Hagen's reactions in real time. Mundruczó lets dogs be dogs in *White God*, notwithstanding the heavy-handed political allegories of his film narrative. Hagen is, in Haraway's terms, more body than sign. Like the superstar dogs Lassie, Toto, and Beethoven, Hagen reveals how dogs generate their own telegenic personalities. Given basic training, *White God*'s canines perform on their own; they train us how to watch them.

If animal agency, as defined by Chris Philo and Chris Wilbert, is not as some innate or static thing which an organism always possesses, but rather in a relational sense which sees agency emerging as an effect generated and performed in configurations of different materials," then anything can "potentially have the power to act, whether human or non-human."[13] Animals exert an effect back onto those in interaction with them just as much humans do on animals. Interpretations of film animals as stand-ins for human-centric concerns minimizes the agency animals have in cross-species encounters. Thus, to approach the dogs of *White God* allegorically is to reduce them to semiotic creatures, what Burt calls "rhetorical animals." Although "there are plenty of *rhetorical* animals on screen—animals as metaphors, metonyms ... much of the film animal derives from the fact that in film human-animal relations are possible through the play of agency."[14] The narrative logic of *White God*, a film about a citywide animal takeover, should curb our anthropocentric impulses before we all-too-hastily anthropomorphize its dogs into figures of political history. *White God* asks us to take seriously its main theme: animal autonomy; content is form here. *White God*'s dogs-turned-freedom-fighters through autonomous recognition of their self-interest are themselves real animal actors, whom humans relied on to make a movie. *White God* is a film about, and a product of, agential animality.

The Animal Gaze: *On Body and Soul*

Like *White God*, Ildikó Enyedi's *On Body and Soul* (2017), which maps the strange metaphysical romance of an abattoir's CFO, Endre, and the plant's new quality inspector, Mária (a role superbly acted by Alexandra Borbély), tempts figurative reading. The film relays a "whodunit" plot after it is discovered that a sample of animal-mating powder, which the abattoir's staff periodically uses to bolster cattle reproduction, is reported missing. Amid the unfolding drama, Endre and Mária, who struggle to socialize in the workplace, begin meeting one another in their dreams, weirdly, as deer. There, as animals, they exhibit a poise and tranquility that is otherwise absent their face-to-face encounters. Indeed, it is only as a stag and a doe that they first consummate their relationship.

Set in present-day Budapest, *On Body and Soul* hints at the dehumanization of the industrial working class. Incapable of social interaction and entangled in the processes of mechanical slaughter, Enyedi's protagonists lose connection not only to themselves but also to the natural world. One worker needs to steal animal hormone supplements to revive his libido. The deer are depicted as ghostly envoys harkening back to a preindustrial world in which nature reigns. While Enyedi, who is best remembered for her late socialist debut, *My Twentieth Century* (*Az én XX. Századom*, 1989), which featured a caged chimpanzee undergo a flashback of the film's heroine at a Budapest zoo, has thematized animals in her work before, also as in her lesser-known film *Magic Hunter* (*Bűvös vadász*, 1994), she has never paid as close attention to them as in *On Body and Soul*.

If understood as symbols for the dehumanization of the industrial working class, the deer in *On Body and Soul* align with the conclusions drawn by John Berger in his seminal essay "Why Look at Animals?" in which he argues that capitalist modernization rendered animals into a kind of phantasmagoric species only encountered as facsimiles of themselves in dreams, zoos, playthings, and cinema. "The cultural marginalization of animals is, of course, a more complex process than their physical marginalization ... instead of being dispersed, [animals] have been co-opted into other categories so that the category *animal* has lost its central importance."[15] Our impulse to look at animals, Berger concludes, is a gambit to restore our severed connection to the natural world. Yet the more we look, the further animals are; animals exist in a perpetual state of vanishing. The relegation of deer to dreamscapes in *On Body and Soul*, a film that takes place in a manifestly modern setting (a factory farm), could be read as a side effect of animals' disappearance from human habitats in the modern era and, correspondingly, as a symptom of human alienation.

Importantly, though, Berger fails to acknowledge that, far from being passive recipients of the human gaze, animals themselves participate in cross-species looking. That is, animals cannot be reduced to receptacles of humanity's sociopolitical angst. Doing so, ironically, only reinforces the process of animals' marginalization in modernity. Berger's critique ends up succumbing to the logic it decries, distancing us from animals evermore.[16] The centrality of the animal eye in *On Body and Soul* complicates the film's symbolic critique capitalism. Enyedi instead invites us to think about what it means to look at animals and, just as crucial, what happens when animals look back.

An overview of *On Body and Soul*'s opening scene reveals how it establishes the motif of looking from its outset. The movie begins with a wintry landscape in which two deer—a stag and a doe—make acquaintances. The doe observes the stag from behind, whereupon the stag turns his head and, registering the doe's appearance, stares motionlessly back at her. This episode transitions to a bullpen of cows, who are peering through the slats of their enclosure at several employees of the abattoir. Close-ups of their furtive eyes and points-of-view shots, captured by Enyedi's deft cameraman Máté Herbai, suggest a nervousness before their execution. A shot of a distant sun as it brightens up the sky (the eye of God?) is then succeeded by two shots of the film's protagonists, Mária and Endre, each looking upward. The image of Mária is an optically intricate one as she is seen staring at the camera through a pane of glass. She turns her gaze back onto Enyedi's viewer across a reflective surface showing her image. The web of gazes, variously cross-cut and interlocking, that begins of *On Body and Soul* brings together humans, deer, and cattle via acts of looking. It will be revealed that the observant stag and doe of the prologue are the animal avatars of Endre and Mária, who spy on each other at work only to start "seeing" each other in their dreams.

The absence of a mutually intelligible form of oral communication between humans and animals makes the look a basis for cross-species rec-

Figure 8.2. One of many close-ups of deer in *On Body and Soul* (*Testről és lélekről*). Directed by Ildikó Enyedi. Budapest: Inforg-M&M Film, 2017. Screen capture by Raymond De Luca.

ognition. "The image of the animal's eye reflects the possibility of animal understanding," Burt writes. "This does not mean that the eye gives any access to what is understood but it does signal the significant participation in the visual field."[17] The animal eye thus marks the boundary where human consciousness recedes. It is no surprise that movies about animals—from David Attenborough's nature documentaries to Bill Viola's *I Do Not Know What It Is I Am Like* (1986)—often explore the nature animal vision as an attempt to connect with the ultimate form of alterity. Humans are equally as enthralled as they are threatened by the radical otherness of animal life. Enyedi's *On Body and Soul* is no exception. The film follows its characters as they shape-shift into deer and are freed from the constraints of the human world. For example, while Endre suffers from an arm injury at work, he effortlessly gallops in his dreams as a stag. *On Body and Soul* decenters the anthropocentric body by way of interspecies looking. The eyes that usher us into Enyedi's film hint at the transformative potential of cross-species looking. Animals and people are constituted by their capacities to see and be seen.

Wide-eyed, Mária herself is deerlike. She shudders at the sound of any sudden disturbance and stands motionless for long periods of time. There are several shots in which her expression rhymes with that of a deer's. Looking into the camera, Mária and the doe train their eyes back onto us. Mária's eyes, and our own eyes as viewers, become the source of interspecies identification. Though Mária works at an abattoir and is implicated in mechanized animal death, she is made *more* human vis-à-vis the animal. The doe instructs her in sociability and sex. Theorizing animals on-screen, Barbara Creed argues that human-animal looks—what she calls the "creaturely gaze"—bear "the potential to break down boundaries, to affirm communicability, between human and non-human animals."[18] The "creaturely gaze" in *On Body and Soul* facilitates interspecies communication; it transforms Mária physically and psychically, hence the title of Enyedi's film. Greater consideration of animal looks, *On Body and Soul* suggests, is a way in which the anthropocentric hierarchies of our modern industrial world can be destabilized. To reimagine human-animal relations, we must let ourselves be seen by animals. That human-animal look can take us out of the operations of language, which has historically been used by human beings as a cudgel to justify animals' lower status and our exploitation of them. It was precisely animals' absence of language that impelled the eighteenth-century philosopher René Descartes to claim that animals have no "soul." In *On Body and Soul*, Enyedi suggests otherwise.

Though *On Body and Soul*'s repressed sexuality is ripe for psychoanalytic critique—Sigmund Freud relied on animal symbols in his studies of dreams (and the film's abattoir hires a psychoanalyst to investigate the stolen mating powder)—Enyedi's human-animal metaphors are all the more enriched by animal eyes. Her shots dwelling on animals' gazes, furs, and bodies should prompt a set of questions beyond "content." What effect does the gaze have on interspecies relations? Why look at animals? The film aptly locates eyes at the heart of cross-species encounters.

Animal Locomotion: *The Turin Horse*

Beginning with the story of Friedrich Nietzsche's mental breakdown in Turin, Italy, when, in 1889, he allegedly lost his mind after witnessing a man flog a horse (an incident that echoes Raskolnikov's nightmare in Fyodor Dostoevsky's *Crime and Punishment*, one of the most famous scenes of all world literature), Béla Tarr and Ágnes Hranitzky's *Turin Horse* (2011), a profoundly grim film shot through with apocalyptic dread, explodes with symbolic possibilities. The film is frequently read not only as a critique of Tarr's contemporaneous historical moment as Hungary, slipping ever further into illiberalism, becomes increasingly hollowed out of cultural promise, but as a renunciation of all the ideological visions that have upended Hungary in the twentieth century.

All of thirty-eight shots, *The Turin Horse* follows two potato farmers, a father and a daughter, subsisting on the edge of a post-apocalyptic society as their world descends into darkness. Unremitting gusts of wind fill the frame for three hours as Tarr's farmers stoically perform daily chores, which are depicted as futile acts of existential survival. The film ends after the girl stops speaking, the father stops eating, and their horse stops moving. The theory of history spun in *The Turin Horse* is one of nihilistic despair. In his statements on the film, Tarr does little to discourage this sort of metaphysical thinking. "The point is that humanity, all of us, including me, are responsible for destruction of the world. But there is also a force above humans at work—the gale blowing throughout the film—that is also destroying the world. So both humanity and a higher force are destroying the world."[19] That *The Turin Horse* was Tarr's self-proclaimed final film only intensifies its seeming profundity in the history of cinema. It itself enacts a kind of "end of history."

An animal stands at the center of Tarr's eschatological vision. No stranger to using animals in film—one shudderingly recalls the tortured cat in *Sátántangó* (1994)—Tarr in *The Turin Horse* forefronts an animal as a character on equal ontological footing with its human companions. All creatures in this apocalyptic world, Tarr suggests, are vulnerable to extinction. They exist in a constant state of survivalism, a form of death in life that amounts to no more than brute endurance.

The opening shot shows a bedraggled horse pulling a carriage down a dirt road, whereas a conclusory shot shows that same horse standing still in a barn, truculently refusing to budge. This horse's journey from mobility to immobility, in fact, performs an inversion of the history of film, which relied on horse locomotion in its earliest stages. The origins of motion pictures, as has been well documented by scholars, is "haunted by the animal figure," especially by horses, whom early filmmakers utilized to experiment with new cinematographic technologies.[20] In his *Sallie Gardner at a Gallop* (1878), for example, which consists of a series of photographs assembled by his zoopraxiscope, Eadweard Muybridge mobilized a static image of a horse, a feat of imaging technology that Tarr inverts in *The Turin Horse*. This film regresses from a motion picture into still-life photography, thereby staging not only an "end of history" but also an "end of cinema."[21] It is telling that Tarr sets his film in 1889, right at the moment of cinema's debut onto the world stage. The animal of *The Turin Horse* takes us back to cinematic prehistory; time moves backward.

Despite the appeal of this reading, Tarr holds our attention on the horse's body. *The Turin Horse*'s first image, rendered by Tarr's cameraman Fred Kelemen, uses a reverse dolly shot to move in tandem with the galloping steed as it lunges into the camera. Kelemen elastically observes its locomotive and strained body as it pulls the carriage forward. The image centralizes a fundamental aspect of animality: movement. As Julian Murphet writes: "The animal moves: it is, in itself, a kind of 'movement-image'. ... Even when it does not move, it moves; its breath and heart-beat, digestion, the twitching of its limbs, the constant circulation of its plasma, all attest to the grounding of this being in movement, and to movement's

Figure 8.3. The truculent horse protagonist who takes viewers back to the earliest days of cinema with Eadweard Muybridge's equine locomotion studies. *The Turin Horse* (*A torinói ló*). Directed by Béla Tarr and Ágnes Hranitzky. Budapest: T.T. Filmmuhely; Paris: MPM FILM; Zürich: Vega Film; Berlin: Zero Fiction Film GmbH, 2011. Screen capture by Raymond De Luca.

exorbitant investment in the animal. ... Movement is animal."[22] The dynamism of the animal is precisely what thrills filmmakers (and filmgoers) with the possibility of capturing it on-screen. Motion-picture technology is a means to discipline animal life, allowing humans to exert control over otherwise unruly animal bodies, to "tame" animals for our spectatorial entertainment. As is well known, celluloid, the very stuff of film, is processed with animal cartilage and bone: gelatin. The history of cinema is contingent upon broken animal bodies.

It is thus significant that Tarr begins *The Turin Horse* not simply with an image of an animal, but with that of a *workhorse*: a beast of burden laden in ropes in service of human economy. This image crystallizes the status of the horse in modernity as an exploitable object for the intersecting ends of cinema and capital. Yet Tarr's horse resists submitting to its place in the established order. It gradually refuses to move, despite the prodding of the farmers. In *The Turin Horse*, Tarr paints a picture of truculent animality. The "movement-image" of the horse is not cudgeled into motionlessness by apocalyptic forces, but it grinds itself to a halt. It elects immobility in protest to its exploitation, rejecting the horse's historical status as a "movement image" to become instead a "time image": a thing, as Deleuze states, of "pure time" that forces viewers to linger on its morose stasis. This horse-as-time, rather than horse-as-motion, replaces its "sensory-motor scheme" with stillness, with "disoriented and discordant" layers of time resistant to history's forward march.[23]

The animal reasserts itself through stasis, by refusing to yield to human demands, thereby upending the superstructures of agrarian labor and imaging technology that exploit animal bodies. Yet what to do with a horse that rejects its own motility? This question is left unanswered by Tarr, whose universe fades to black as the camera lingers on the horse. This is not only an allegorical statement but an epistemological one. How to make sense of a world in which animals no longer move? What comes after the human—humans who, after all, have lost their capacities for language? An end of history, intermixed with an end of cinema, *The Turin Horse* is an end of interpretability.

Conclusion: *Werckmeister Harmonies*

The ways in which animals can frustrate and destabilize symbolic logic is also the center of another of Tarr's films, *Werckmeister Harmonies* (2000), which revolves around a whale carcass that mysteriously arrives at a small Hungarian town as part of a circus. The beast bewilders the townspeople, who, struggling to make sense of it, descend into mayhem. For their part, critics view the whale figuratively, as a retrospective commentary on the unmet promises and fallout of communism and then its ideological replacement, neoliberalism, in the post-Soviet era. The sea monster, whatever its ideological gloss, is said to allegorize Hungary's failed hopes. Yet washing up on the shores of Hungarian cinema right at the turn of the millennium—roughly a decade after the fall of the Berlin Wall in 1989 and a decade before Viktor Orbán's seizure of presidential power in 2010—Tarr's whale is as backward-looking as it is forward-looking. It presages the contemporary illiberal implosion of Hungarian civic society just as much as it recalls Hungary's legacy of unfulfilled political aspirations. It is, in other words, a highly ambiguous signifier straddling historical, ideological, and temporal boundaries that, like many of the other animals discussed in this chapter, collapses under its own semantic weight. It is not by chance that the final shot of *Werckmeister Harmonies* is the leviathan splayed out amid urban debris, as if the wreckage of interpretability. The whale comes to mean everything, so in the end it means nothing.

Tarr's dead whale aptly relays this chapter's larger thesis. In contemporary Hungarian cinema, the animal is often deployed as a floating signifier—equally rooted in the Hungarian past, present, and future; democracy and autocracy; utopia and dystopia. These animals are too multivalent to be read as straightforward "signs." Though appealing to our allegorical impulses, Mundruczó, Enyedi, and Tarr's animals, laden in an excess of semantic possibilities, strain the normatively interpretive process. Similarly, writing about György Pálfi's films, a director who mobilizes animal life and human bodies in fascinating and disturbing ways, György Kalmár argues: "a strategy to avoid, bypass, or radically destabilize logocentric meaning ... Pálfi's films play complex, ambiguous games with meaning and interpretation: they are simultaneously seductive film-texts, calling on interpretation in order to find meaning where meaning is clearly endangered ... they make sure that such attempts can never reach totalizing conclusions."[24] Contemporary Hungarian filmmakers' resistance to allegory is, in fact, a resistance to the totalizing logic of allegorical thinking, a resistance to the dogmatic forms of thought that fueled the destructive ideologies of the twentieth- and twenty-first centuries that are being metaphorized on-screen. Indeed, as Tarr suggests in *Werckmeister Harmonies*, our compulsion to decode, systematize, and reconcile the order of things can lead to violence. That film, like the others described in this chapter, is a postmodern critique, a pastiche, of authoritative discourses that tempt axiomatic readings only to frustrate those very interpretations; they are films against allegory.

The animals of *White God*, *On Body and Soul*, and *The Turin Horse*, more than "content," should call our attention instead to matters of form, which are wrapped up in questions of agency, gazes, and movement. The trained dogs of *White God* reveal how animal agency, especially in the context of acting, is a relational unfolding. These dogs regulate spectatorial perception. The continual recourse to animal looks in *On Body and Soul* not only identifies vision as a fundamental feature of interspecies relations—animals, like humans, are capable of looking back—but also explores the anthropocentrically destabilizing space opened up by cross-species looking, what Creed calls the "creaturely gaze." Finally, Tarr's horse in *The Turin Horse*, beginning as a "movement image," frames mobility as central trait of animality, which, once rejected, ruptures our anthropocentric world; Tarr's horse ends as a "time image." These animals need not signify anything other but themselves; they invite figurative thinking only to, as it were, mongrelize it.

Perhaps because historical allegorism is so readily available for contemporary Eastern European filmmakers (and the route most film commentary pursues) those in Hungary of the so-called Young Hungarian Cinema movement, filmmakers who have achieved international recognition in the postsocialist era, and others have begun turning symbols inside out by way of nonanthropocentric presences: animals, corpses, things, objects, and flesh. This trend is also on display in contemporary Eastern European cinema more broadly, in such films like György Pálfi's *Hukkle* (*Hukkle*, 2002), Szabolcs Hajdu's *Tamara* (*Tamara*, 2004), Aistė Žegulytė's *Animus Animalis (A Story about People, Animals and Things)* (*Animus Animalis: istorija apie žmones, žvėris ir daiktus*, 2018), and Agnieszka Holland's *Spoor* (*Pokot*, 2018). We are witnessing the rise of a wave of Hungarian and

Eastern European directors who have grown sick of history, and sick of its representational pressures, a movement trying to call attention back to the surface of film—to what is in fact *seen* on-screen—rather than plumbing the depths of content. The animals of *White God, On Body and Soul, The Turin Horse,* and *Werckmeister Harmonies* are important solely because they are there.

Raymond De Luca is an Assistant Professor in the Department of Modern and Classical Languages, Literatures, and Cultures at the University of Kentucky. His research and teaching interests include Soviet culture, animal studies, and film theory. He has published widely on cinema in such outlets as *Canadian Journal of Film Studies, KinoKultura, Film Criticism,* and *Slavic and East European Journal*. His current book project, provisionally titled *The New Soviet Animal: Re-imagining The Human-Animal Divide in Revolutionary Russia*, examines how early Soviet artists and ideologues turned to animals as allies of the working class in the building of communism.

Notes

1. Ryan, *Animal Theory*, 31.
2. Cavell, *Philosophy and Animal Life*, 77.
3. Haraway, *When Species Meet*, 4.
4. Burt, *Animals in Film*, 11.
5. Burt, 12.
6. Plach, "Animals in Eastern Europe and Russia"; Kadyrbekova, "Animal Agents in Russian Fairy Tales."
7. Sontag, *Against Interpretation*.
8. Sontag, 10.
9. Deleuze and Guattari, *Kafka*, 13.
10. For more on Mundruczó's oeuvre, see Stőhr, "Conflicting Forces."
11. Deleuze and Guattari, *Kafka*, 13.
12. Tarpinian, "How 200 Dogs Were Trained to Act in 'White God.'"
13. Philo and Wilbert, "Animal Spaces, Beastly Places," 17
14. Burt, *Animals in Film*, 31.
15. Berger, "Why Look at Animals?," 13.
16. For a critique of Berger's essay, see Burt, "John Berger's 'Why Look at Animals?'"
17. Burt, *Animals in Film*, 71.
18. Creed, "Animal Deaths on Screen," 17.
19. Tarr, "Interview with Vladan Petkovic."
20. Lippit, *Electric Animal*, 22.
21. A similar argument is advanced by Laura McMahon in *Animal Worlds*, 95–133.

22. Murphet, "King Kong Capitalism," 153.
23. Deleuze, *Negotiations*, 59.
24. Kalmár, "Local Sensorium, Local Cinema," 211.

Bibliography

Berger, John. "Why Look at Animals?" In *About Looking*, 1–26. New York: Pantheon Books, 1980.
Burt, Jonathan. *Animals in Film*. London: Reaktion Books, 2002.
———. "John Berger's 'Why Look at Animals?': A Close Reading." *Worldviews* 9, no. 2 (2005): 203–218.
Cavell, Stanley, et al. *Philosophy and Animal Life*. New York: Columbia University Press, 2008.
Creed, Barbara. "Animal Deaths on Screen: Film and Ethics." *Relations* 2, no. 1 (June 2014): 15–31.
Deleuze, Gilles. *Negotiations, 1972–1990*. New York: Columbia University Press, 1995.
Deleuze, Gilles, and Félix Guattari. *Kafka: Toward a Minor Literature*, translated by Dana Polan. Minneapolis: University of Minnesota Press, 1986.
Haraway, Donna. *When Species Meet*. Minneapolis: University of Minnesota Press, 2008.
Kadyrbekova, Zora. "Animal Agents in Russian Fairy Tales." *Canadian Slavonic Papers* 60, no. 3–4 (2018): 407–425.
Kalmár, György. "Local Sensorium, Local Cinema: György Pálfi's Sensuous Body Politics." *Acts Univ. Sapientiae, Film and Media Studies* 8 (2014): 203–214.
Lippit, Akira Mizzuta. *Electric Animal: Toward a Rhetoric of Wildlife*. Minneapolis: University of Minnesota Press, 2000.
McMahon, Laura. *Animal Worlds: Film, Philosophy, and Time*. Edinburgh: Edinburgh University Press, 2019.
Murphet, Julian. "King Kong Capitalism." *Animal Life and the Moving Image*, eds. Michael Lawrence and Laura McMahon, 153–170. London: Palgrave, 2015.
O'Key, Dominic. "Bela Tarr's *The Turin Horse*: The (In)Visible Animal." University of Leeds. 2014. http://www.undergraduatelibrary.org/2014/music-film-theater/bela-tarrs-turin-horse-invisible-animal.
Philo, Chris, and Chris Wilbert. "Animal Spaces, Beastly Places: An Introduction." In *Animal Spaces, Beastly Places: New Geographies of Human-Animal Relations*, edited by Philo and Wilbert, 2–36. London: Routledge, 2000.
Plach, Eva. "Animals in Eastern Europe and Russia." *Canadian Slavonic Papers* 60, no. 3–4 (2018): 351–353.
Ryan, Derek. *Animal Theory: A Critical Introduction*. Edinburgh: Edinburgh University Press, 2015.
Sontag, Susan. *Against Interpretation and Other Essays*. New York: Picador, 2001.
Stőhr, Lóránt. "Conflicting Forces: Post-Communist and Mythical Bodies in Kornél Mundruczó's Films." *Studies in Eastern European Cinema* 7, no. 2 (2016): 139–152.

Tarpinian, Katherine. "How 200 Dogs Were Trained to Act in 'White God.'" *Vice*, 25 April 2015. https://www.vice.com/en_us/article/mgp3j8/how-200-dogs-were-trained-to-act-in-white-god.

Tarr, Béla. "Interview with Vladan Petkovic." *Cineuropa*, April 3, 2011. https://cineuropa.org/en/interview/198131/.

Filmography

Enyedi, Ildikó. *My Twentieth Century* (*Az én XX. Századom*, Hungary, 1989).
——. *Magic Hunter* (*Bűvös vadász*, 1994).
——. *On Body and Soul* (*Teströl és lélekröl*, Hungary, 2017).
Hajdu, Szabolcs. *Tamara* (*Tamara*, Hungary, 2004).
Holland, Agnieszka. *Spoor* (*Pokot*, 2018).
Mundruczó, Kornél. *White God* (*Fehér isten*, Hungary, 2014).
Pálfi, György. *Hukkle* (*Hukkle*, Hungary, 2002).
Tarr, Béla. *Werckmeister Harmonies* (*Werckmeister harmóniák*, Hungary, 2000).
Tarr, Béla, and Ágnes Hranitzky. *The Turin Horse* (*A torinói ló*, Hungary, 2011).
Žegulytė, Aistė. *Animus Animalis (A Story about People, Animals and Things)* (*Animus Animalis: istorija apie žmones, žvėris ir daiktus*, Lithuania, 2018).

Part IV
From Communism to Capitalism
Privatization and the Commons

9

Okraina and "Oil Ontology" in Post-Soviet Russian Cinema

José Alaniz

> Oil capital seems to represent a stage that neither capital nor its opponents can think beyond. Oil and capital are linked inextricably, so much so that the looming demise of the petrochemical economy has come to constitute perhaps the biggest disaster that "we" collectively face.[1]
>
> The future of our world is the future of energy. Oil, after water, is the most cinematic and important resource on the planet.[2]

In the early twenty-first century, the rising price of oil and gas on world markets played to the advantage of resource-rich countries like Russia. But as many have noted, Vladimir Putin's absolute reliance on this sector meant less diversification of the economy. Corruption, favoritism, and a neoliberal reliance on a market largely driven by fossil fuels also meant less investment in things like infrastructure, social services for the poor and redress for ever-rising levels of inequality—to say nothing of steep environmental costs.[3] Some, like Alexander Etkind, blamed Russia's devotion to oil and gas, in fact, for holding it back from fully modernizing after the collapse of communism. Etkind writes:

> During the two long post-Soviet decades, Russia had an excellent chance to reshape itself into a European country, a success that would have been hugely beneficial for Russia's people, Europe, and the world. Russia's ar-

> rested development has nothing to do with tradition or inertia. If Russia is still post-Soviet, it is due to a concerted effort of a narrow group that has been actively preventing Russia from becoming a productive, law-abiding, European country. This group has captured Russia's oil and gas, on whose rising prices the development of Putinism has entirely depended. The massive security apparatus and the corrupt, irrational bureaucracy recycle the wealth that is produced, as if by God's will, by holes in the earth rather than by the work of the people.[4]

Cultural representations of this dilemma from the Yeltsin period on often cast it as a center/periphery, have/have-not conflict (which it often is; many of the resources extracted come from places remote to Moscow, such as Siberia); as we shall see, class does play a central role in the works I will discuss.[5]

Given fossil fuel's predominance in the post-Soviet economy, as well as the rise of a Russian environmentalist movement that seeks to bring attention to climate change and the environmental impacts of oil drilling, I will examine how Russian filmmakers of this era have sought to navigate such "tensions," in particular through the motif of oil as the "lifeblood" of the land. But I am also interested in the (so to speak) impossibility of that task.

Following Energy Humanities scholars like Peter Hitchcock and Stephanie LeMenager, I view efforts to "think beyond" petromodernity, defined as "modern life based in the cheap energy systems made possible by oil," as fraught, partial, compromised—in short, as nigh futile.[6] (This makes such efforts no less necessary.) As Hitchcock puts it: "In general, oil dependency is not just an economic attachment but appears as a kind of cognitive compulsion that mightily prohibits alternatives to its utility as a commodity and as an array of cultural signifiers."[7] Focusing on the affective sway of cheap energy for Westerners and others who are born, grow up, and die knowing nothing else, LeMenager in *Living Oil* (2014) poignantly explains her goal as asking more "why the world that oil makes remains *so beloved*, than the more obvious problem of why it is difficult to build an entirely new energy infrastructure."[8]

Our economic and emotional enthrallment to petroleum, what some deem an "oil ontology,"[9] the way our very identities are formed on the blasé incorporation of its many-splendored boons, shapes how we aestheticize it.[10] As LeMenager goes on:

> The representational problem oil presents to the committed artist, be he a socialist such as Sinclair or an environmentalist, has to do with oil's primal associations with earth's body, therefore with the permeability, excess, and multiplicity of all bodies deemed performed *and* given. While the documentary realist can present the immiseration of oil workers or the pollution of environments subjected to oil mining, oil itself retains the indeterminacy and openness to mystification of a living/performing spectacle.[11]

Loving Oil, Russian Style

I see such a "mystification of a living/performing spectacle" operative throughout post-Soviet Russian culture's engagement with oil; contemporary artist Andrei Molodkin, for example, finds in it a labile and endlessly generative raw material that he utilizes as a sort of metaphysical protoplasm. In his *Black Square* (2007), he invokes Orthodox visuality through a three-dimensional plastic container partly filled with oil and hung in a corner like an icon (as was the work it references, Kazimir Malevich's famous 1914 piece of the same name). Molodkin explains, "I use oil as the lingua franca, the political language, which Russia speaks, which the whole world speaks. . . . It's such a virtual image, a kind of God. The God of industry, or its blood. The blood of globalization."[12] Similarly, art historian Maria Engström describes contemporary Russian avant-garde artists who pursue this theme as grappling with "the mystery of the black substance itself, which rules over the post-Soviet and posthuman world."[13] In these and other twenty-first-century Russian cultural expressions, the "black substance itself" functions as material commodity, as metaphor (of connection as well as disconnection from nature), as folklore, as unconscious stratum, as symptom, as polysemous fetish, and much else.

Literary scholar Ilya Kalinin writes about contemporary "petropoetics" in like terms:

> Set in motion under the influence of the public discourse about the role of natural energy sources in the economy and history of Russia, literary petrodiscourse, it would seem, transcends its own cause, symbolically transforming the motif of oil into large-scale chains of metamorphoses, viewing oil alternatively as the "symbolic blood" of postmodernity, or as a peculiar state of matter and consciousness, or as the organic source of existence. However, what emerges as a result is not so much a critical thematization of oil dependency as a gradual ontologizing of it—a dilution of the political economy of the resource-oriented economy in poetic phenomenology and the metaphysics of oil.[14]

Though such formulations to some extent applied to the Soviets as well, it was coal, not oil, that held pride of place in discourses of that era.[15] And despite the state's best propagandistic efforts, the USSR never loved coal the way we (including the Russians) utterly worship oil today. Whether read in terms of LeMenager's affect-driven devotion, or of a postmodern "oil ontology," or of Kalinin's petropoetic mysticism, the theme has proliferated as never before under Putin (the first "petrostate tsar").[16]

The satirist Viktor Pelevin goes so far as to transform the relationship with oil into a kind of ancestor worship in his 2004 novel *The Sacred Book of the Werewolf*, whose heroes pray to coax more yield from a depleted Siberian deposit (on the grounds of a former gulag):

> You are everyone who lived here before us. Parents, grandparents, great-grandparents, and before that, and before that. ... You are the soul of all those who died believing in the happiness that would come in the future. And now you see, it has come. The future in which people do not live for something else, but for themselves. And do you know how we feel swallowing sashimi that smell of oil and pretending not to notice the final ice-floes melting under our feet?[17]

These self-aware characters' supernatural appeal to a "brindled cow" for more barrels per day made up of previous generations, in the face of climate change, is Nikolai Fyodorov by way of Russian folktales and Joseph Heller. But its basic premise—Russia is addicted to fossil fuels and knows it, and moreover will do anything to get them—manifests to greater and lesser degrees in literature and popular culture (including comics, music, and, as we will see, music videos).[18] These representations tend almost exclusively to the oppositional; their makers wish to draw attention to "invisible" oil as a constitutive principle of the nation's social and political system—to deleterious effect. In turning to cinema, I begin with one of the most striking "petro-films" of the Yeltsin era, which couches its depiction of resource extraction within a folkloric mode, the better to address questions of post-Soviet sovereignty and Kalinin's "metaphysics of oil," as expressed through an "oil as lifeblood of the land" motif.[19]

Okraina

The noted screenwriter Pyotr Lutsik released his directorial debut *The Outskirts* (*Okraina*) to mixed reviews in 1998.[20] Its plot could hardly be simpler: a trio of "salt of the Earth" peasants from the Urals, hearing that their land has been sold, journey far from home to find out who they need to appeal to in order to get the land back. They travel from the countryside to increasingly populated centers on their quest, until they reach the summit of national power, an "oil oligarch's" chic office inside a Moscow *vysotka*, or Stalinist high-rise. They get the land back. That description, while accurate, leaves out some crucial components. For one thing, at each stop the men achieve their ends through casual violence and torture, which includes holding a man under freezing water; breaking another's ribs; "gnawing" someone else to death; and a grisly decapitation. They also burn Moscow to the ground as they leave.

Lutsik presents all this through a sophisticated black-and-white conceptualist pastiche made up of remarkably disparate elements: horror,

Stalinist war film, road movie, comedy, snuff, the folktale. As Mihaela Mihailova puts it, *Okraina* "offers a complex intertextual reinterpretation of key genres, texts and archetypes from sources as diverse as the Russian folk tradition, Stalin-era cinema and late Soviet alternative culture."[21] Everything in this film has quotation marks, from the bombastic opening crawl over an endless tracking shot of a ploughed field in close-up (*"Nepravil'niy u istorii khod',"* or, roughly, "history has gone astray") to the men's "folksy" speech patterns to the indeterminate time period: though the plot anchors us in the post-Soviet 1990s, the props and sets hearken to the mid-Soviet era, while our heroes dress in Civil War attire. Furthermore, the talky Safronov (Yury Dubrovin), sadistic war veteran Poluyanov (Nikolai Olyalin), and youngster Pan'ka Morozov (Alexei Pushkin) have almost no interiority; their psychological motivations and outlook on the world exist plainly on the surface.[22] Film critic Zara Abdullaeva aptly called their representation "lubok monumentalism."[23]

Lutsik channels the tradition of 1930s socialist realist cinema in every frame, drawing inspiration from (and at times outright quoting works by) Alexander Dovzhenko, Vsevolod Pudovkin, Mikhail Doller, Ivan Pyr'ev, and Sergei Iutkevich, but most of all from the beloved classic *Chapaev* (1934).[24] The director even had *Chapaev*'s original musical score by Gavril Popov transcribed and rerecorded for his own soundtrack, and he shot on film stock mimicking the look of 1930s film.[25] Finally, *Okraina* takes its title from a 1933 Boris Barnet work of the same name.

Though it earned a 1998 Kinotavr Film Festival prize for its "Bold Search for New Paths in Film Art," *Okraina* divided critics, some of whom called it a "cinematic act of terrorism" and warned it would cause the provinces to rise up against the center in real life (Ivanov, "Okraina").[26] Others seemed to take the film more at face value, like Kirill Razlogov, who wrote that it "merely paid the legacy of the past its due and affirmed its greatness and value in the present and future. True, with elements of *styob*, but more importantly, with a calm dignity and a revival of the epic spirit of the 'great 1930s.'"[27]

In my discussion of *Okraina* as an oil film, I will focus on two chief registers. First, its recurring motif of "the depths" strongly evokes the production processes of oil resource extraction. As argued by Douglas Rogers, discussions of "depth" (especially things emerging out of it), suffused post-Soviet Russian culture in an era of exhumed mass graves and recovered sacred objects and texts, metonymizing the ongoing reassessment of a traumatic twentieth-century Russian history.[28] *Okraina* portrays depth figuratively, as the men steadily climb "up" the social ladder of authority, from settlement to town to megalopolis, encountering ever more lavish furnishings as they go. And of course our heroes—as the film never lets us forget—all hail *iz glubinki* ("from the sticks," or, more literally, "from the depths").

Lutsik also represents the "depth" motif more explicitly, through visual sequences both startling and absurd, as when the men fashion a makeshift tent out of their overcoats and eat, converse, and recite poetry with only a small gas stove (and other ambiguous source) for light; when Poluyanov gnaws his victim to death in a dark, dank basement; and as the trio journeys upward in a cramped elevator on their way to meet the oligarch. The black-and-white photography enhances the dark mise-en-scène, which expands along with the number of nighttime sequences as the film unfolds. It also has the effect of making water look as black as oil when our heroes torture the cooperative chairman Perfil'ev (Aleksei Vanin) by dunking him in an icehole (thus killed, "cleansed," and revived, he joins their cause). All the foregoing reinforces "depth as a shared feature of oil and culture."[29]

The second register of *Okraina* I will discuss involves the portrayal of the unnamed oil oligarch, relatable to Etkind's concept of "petromachismo."[30] He defines it as the product of "synergy between the oil and gas trade and security services," which fosters a "hypermasculine, cynical, and misogynistic culture."[31] Such "oiligarchs," almost all male, and (with the infamous exception of Mikhail Khodorkovsky) all pro-government, dominate the post-Soviet economy like apex predators.[32] The supremely confident oligarch, who brags that his desk alone costs more than our heroes' land, comes off as a swaggering, ludicrous caricature of such men, an impression augmented by the folktale-like staging of the final confrontation. Critic Igor Mantsov even compares the oil tycoon to Khoshchei the Immortal, to the dragon Gorynych and to "evil as such."[33] Note the exchange between the oligarch and Pan'ka, the youngest and by this point the leader of the heroic trio:

> P: We are little people. We recognize your power, your strength. Take what is yours. If you need more, we'll work the land to get it for you. You will always have bread and meat and whatever you wish. What do you need our land for? We plow it. We grow our bread. We've lived on it for a thousand years, and we don't know any other. ...
>
> O: You are good people. Simple people. Only you've sold your land. Nowadays, by the law, everything can be bought and sold. I bought the land lawfully. So the land is mine. For a hundred years, it's mine! Why should I give up what is mine?

The dialogue, which Mantsov writes has the character of "a geopolitical grotesque," continues in this course, as the magnate invites Pan'ka to admire his display of dozens of containers of crude from all over the world; the US variety he dismisses as "so-so" and "watery" (*zhiden'kaya*).[34] In

Figure 9.1. The "oiligarch" (Viktor Stepanov) shows off his wares. *The Outskirts (Okraina)*. Directed by Pyotr Lutsik. Moscow: Goskino, 1998. Screen capture by José Alaniz.

this scene, oil—a formless liquid substance found mostly out of sight and underground—appears in white metallic containers in neat rows: a commodified, corporate product. "It's everywhere," says the mogul. "Always was and always will be. It's like blood—there's veins everywhere. For a whole hundred years, I'll be drilling. All the way down to the heart of the earth will I drill. All the world's blood will be mine!" Cue cackling.

This climactic scene, with its odious vampiric oligarch gleefully boasting that he will literally suck the planet dry, gives clearest expression to the blood/oil motif. The petromachismo framing links the tycoon's lust to a specifically masculine syndrome: the bottomless will to possess and dominate, while the folkloric mode reduces the stakes to a mere contest of good ("simple people") and evil.

Casting also plays an important role here. The film critic Viktor Matizen has noted that during the 1998 Kinotavr screening of *Okraina*, members of the audience were whispering excitedly about the actor who portrayed the oligarch. Specifically, they remarked on his name: Viktor Stepanov, which seemed suspiciously close to Viktor Stepanovich Chernomyrdin, then–prime minister and founder of Gazprom.[35] Though a younger man, Stepanov, with his bald pate, somewhat physically resembled Chernomyrdin too.

The retro-seeming *Okraina* "resurrects the anonymous archetypes upon which Soviet cinema was built: a man with a rifle, vengeance upon the oppressors, peace to all peoples, and land to the peasants," writes

Mantsov. The film also, through its arch conceptualist primitivism, plainly illustrates the functions of what Etkind calls a "hyperextractive state," for whom "the population is superfluous." He quotes a 2012 Facebook post by Alfred Kokh, former head of the State Committee for Property Management: "To the authorities, the general population is an obstacle between them and their oil. Their ideal consists of themselves [ruling over] disenfranchised immigrant laborers, and oil, oil, oil, gas, gas, gas."[36] The statement resonates with Peter Hitchcock's reminder about how "oil proletarianizes—it embodies both extraction from Nature and the value-extraction from labor which is integral to capitalist accumulation."[37] In this sense, oil demodernizes Russia; Lutsik's film, as critic Andrew Horton puts it, mounts "an attack on capitalism which even Soviet cinema in its heyday could not rise to."[38]

In the fantasy realm of *Okraina*, the heartlanders take their vengeance and "demodernize" the demodernizers by strangling them, blowing up their city, and even abducting one of their women (the oligarch's secretary). They literalize "blood for oil." And then they go home. They don't want revolution; they want what is eternally theirs. As Mihailova puts it, "the peasants eventually walk away with their possessions restored in a triumph of wit followed and punctuated—as is this film's wont—by a few grisly murders. ... As the country's corrupt center is ritually cleansed with fire, the outskirts are definitively established as the site of authentic and pure—if imperfect—Russianness."[39]

And yet if we take into account that, as Hitchcock writes, "oil's ubiquity" and "saturation of the infrastructure of modernity" renders it "difficult to represent," we see that *Okraina* cannot avoid the one crushing paradox of oil ontology.[40] Film critic Lev Aninsky, in his negative review, touches upon it when he points out that this supposedly anti-oil film concludes with our heroes triumphantly plowing the land in large combines. "Where did that gasoline come from?" he huffs.[41] Indeed, where did the gas come from which powers the men's motorbike and side seat, which they ride most of the way to Moscow and back? Whence the flammable substances that fuel Moscow's fiery destruction? What lubricates their weapons? How about that hair gel that Pan'ka seems to have used for his meeting with the oligarch? And so on. To recall Menager, loving oil means to love it even when resisting it; there is no outside.

Twenty-First-Century Russian Oil Films

That paradox was carried forth into the Putin era. As Engström notes of oil-focused contemporary Russian artists, so for filmmakers: "They all link oil and other substances from the depths with the discourse of the soil, tradition and war, with archetypal mythological and folkloric plots. They contemplate the fate of this organic chthonic matter in a neoliberal digital modernity."[42]

The theme seemed especially pronounced in music videos, a late-capitalist form oft used for pointed political and nationalist commentary.[43] DJ Smash's "Oil" ("Neft'," 2013), made in collaboration with several performers, embraces "substances from the depths," both literally and figuratively, for what I can only call an EDM oil-as-commodity-fetish orgy.[44] Directed by Marat Adel'shin, the song's video opens (in silence) with a hard-hatted oil worker entering his well-appointed home, where wife and children await. Wide-eyed and delirious, they accept his gift of a small barrel of oil; the next scene shows the wife paying for her shopping purchases by pouring oil from her bag directly into the till. Cue music. Subsequent scenes flaunt the excesses made possible for the rich in a petrostate: a dance party at an expensive club (the sort of place the "oiligarch" from *Okraina* might frequent); women in bikinis by and in a pool; and a parade of products to consume. "As long as Russia has oil, I'm in Milan," coos singer Marina Kravets. "If I'm in Milan, that means Russia has oil."[45]

The three-and-a-half-minute video takes full advantage of oil's splendiferous, polymorphously perverse exchange value, its status as protean thing and symbol: people drink black oil champagne, children eat oil ice cream, women apply oil lipstick.[46] Oil becomes balloons, a swimming pool, sunscreen, a luxury car, and — perhaps belaboring the point — money (including loot with which bank robbers abscond, police in pursuit). The lyrics echo the imagery:

> Oil is a mink coat.
> Oil is a pink Bentley.
> Oil is shopping in Milan. ...
> —Do you love me?
> —I love oil.
> —I am oil.
> —I love you!

Near the end, a group of women in traditional dress dance before a field with oil derricks in the distance. The music video, with its hysterical, breakneck-paced montage, proves the ideal medium for displaying what Etkind calls "the flexible and nimble intermutation that is characteristic of contemporary culture."[47] Explicit where *Okraina* is Aesopian, satirical, and triumphalist in equal measure, the vision in "Oil" of "petro-erotic" hypercapitalist excess advances oil as the paradigmatic substance for "enjoying one's symptom."[48] As the song says, using popular slang for

Figure 9.2. Anastasia Kreslina in "Death No More" ("Smerti bolshe net"). Directed by IC3PEAK/Nick and Nastya. Moscow, 2018. Screen capture by José Alaniz.

sexual intercourse: "Music doesn't pump, oil pumps" (*Muzyka ne kachaet, neft' kachaet*).

What makes oil pump? In closing, I turn to another recurring image in post-Soviet "petro-cinema": the oil-doused human figure. This visual trope appears in documentaries like Murad Ibragimbekov's *Oil* (*Neft'*, 2003) (made up of repurposed period footage) and *Oil* (*Neft'*, 2012), a romanticized portrait of foul-mouthed oil workers in Siberia, edited like a reality show, with a pounding soundtrack of Jan Hammer music. As noted, we may also count *Okraina* if we read the black water in which the heroic trio dunks Perfil'ev as an evocation of oil.

Once more, though, music videos of the Putin era pursue the theme more pointedly and generatively. In the video for Pussy Riot's "Like in a Red Prison" ("Kak v krasnoi tiur'me," 2013), members of the punk collective break into and occupy oil production facilities. At one point, a woman in a balaclava splashes a portrait of Siloviki faction head Igor Sechin (spinning on an oil drill) with a black liquid, dousing him in effigy.[49]

Music videos of the 2010s by the post–witch house/electronic band IC3PEAK, made up of Anastasia Kreslina and Nikolai Kostylev, productively recast both the oil-anointed figure and the oil/blood motif within the genre conventions of horror cinema. In "Death No More" ("Smerti bol'she net," 2018) and "Sad Bitch" ("Grustnaya suka," 2017), both directed by IC3PEAK, one or more of the band members splash themselves with oil or gasoline (in "Death No More," so as to immolate themselves in front of a government building), or else sink in, wallow in, and exude oil-like substances from their mouths.

These black splatter-filled scenes suggest a quasi-Fyodorovian drive behind much oil imagery in contemporary Russian cinema, as Pelevin's apostrophe "you are everyone who lived here before us" asserts. What indeed is oil if not "everyone who lived here before us," including plants, dinosaurs, and other organic matter, all cooked by time? Oil in these representations takes on the qualities of a perverse baptism, of folkloric living water (*zhivaya voda*), in short of animacy, as queer theory and environmental humanities scholars like Mel Chen have conceptualized that term. In brief, animacy refers to how matter *affects* across the life/nonlife divide, blurring such distinctions. Addressing the April 2010 Deepwater Horizon disaster, Chen describes the toxic spill as "a *lifely* thing: lifely, perhaps, beyond its proper bounds. The well itself was alive, and not only because something had flowed out of it with such vivid animation. It was a threat to life in the Gulf, as well as to a *way* of life."[50]

Thus IC3PEAK's videos, which traffic in vampiric and other undead iconography, themselves trouble the life/death border such that substances like water, wine, blood take on a chilling agency. When Kreslina, in "Sad Bitch," sings, "I like mud/It's my high," as she rolls messily about in the muck (in slow motion), the black-gray splashes suggest not only gushing oil but something active, (un)living.[51] The sequence recalls Kalinin's description of oil as "the matter that precedes the thing, the presence given before the emergence of form."[52]

The video for "Death No More" advances the animate agency of oil even more insistently. In it, a viscous black liquid resembling blood (but also oil, given the black-and-white photography) oozes from Kreslina's mouth, and the duo's bodies sink in a swamp (filmed from below, underwater). Most animate of all, oil flares to life as fire. The video opens with the duo and paparazzi standing before the Moscow House of the Government of the Russian Federation (a.k.a. the Russian White House, the former parliament building) in Moscow. Kreslina pours gasoline over herself, while Kostylev lights a match to the lyrics: "I fill my eyes with kerosene/Let it all burn, let it all burn/All Russia is looking at me/Let it all burn, let it all burn." Near the end of the video, we return to the same location, only to find smoldering black ashes where the singers once stood.

Just as it had comically threatened to do when the man almost lights his cigar in DJ Smash's "Oil," just as it does in *Okraina*'s conflagration, which consumes Moscow, and as it does here, oil reveals to Russia its terrifying truth: it is the awakened ancestors whose judgment burns. And worse. In an era of climate change, melting permafrost, mass extinctions, and not-uncommon toxic spills, Russia's oil dependency has far-reaching real-world implications.[53] Yet as argued by Kalinin, the addiction is also cultural:

> Transformed into a systematic motif of contemporary Russian literature (and of culture as a whole), oil acts as one of the central symbolic figures through which the post-Soviet unconscious finds a language—the unconscious that seeks in the bowels of the earth, the depths of memory, and the beginnings of history a resource for the articulation of utopian perspectives, the restoration of historical totality, and the revelation of a metaphysical source.[54]

Or, Icarus-like as it were, the failure to achieve those things.

I want to conclude with another figure doused in oil: a young Russian man who jumped into a pool of black fuel residue (*mazut*) and into minor internet fame in 2015. Various versions of this event and its aftermath, ranging from one to three minutes, circulated on the Runet and were picked up by the Polish blogger To Jest Droga and later the US site Mashable (*Lenta*, "Nyrnuvshiy"). The anonymous man, who in the shaky handheld footage looks to be in his twenties, leaps feetfirst into the ooze, and immediately scrambles back out, completely black, to the laughter of bystanders and those filming. "I can't see a fucking thing!" he yells as he is hosed down by another man, who clenches a cigarette in his lips. The high-pressure hose prompts further complaints, including, "Fuck, that hurts!" (*Blyad' bol'no!*). The dark muck does not come off easily.

In other capitalist cinematic contexts, the figure covered in oil stands for abundance and plenitude, literally striking it rich; hence Jett Rink's (James Dean) euphoria in George Stevens's *Giant* (1956) or Daniel Plainview's (Daniel Day-Lewis) elation in Paul Thomas Anderson's *There Will Be Blood* (2007), when both get completely splattered by black gold in their respective scenes. This is different. In an unnamed town—the *Lenta* report on the incident says only that it happened someplace in "the provinces" (*regiony*)—a working-class everyman walking about with a head-to-toe second skin of oil, spitting out curses, would seem to tragicomically connote the exact opposite of "striking it rich." And indeed it does. But in the process this pathetic scene of absolute abjection succeeds in "making the invisible visible," what W.J.T. Mitchell writes is "precisely the task of photography."[55] (He is alluding here to Walter Benjamin's concept of the "optical unconscious.") So, what invisible thing is it making visible? On the one hand, indelicate as it may sound, I do find the clip rather funny, in a *Jackass* sort of way.[56] Petromachismo laid low. *Ecce homo petroleus*. Even as I laugh, though, I feel a certain sympathy. Moreover, like the explosive revenge of the trio in Lutsik's *Okraina*, the hysterical fetishism of DJ Smash's "Neft'," or the anhedonic violence of IC3PEAK's videos, all fueled by oil, the young man's plunge and regrets hint at a civilization not only beholden to oil but one trying to *become* oil—to meld with the ancestors, with Kalinin's utopian perspectives, historical totality, and metaphysical source. In this sense, the clip once more proves that oil is cinema's Fyodorovian special effect par excellence.

José Alaniz, a professor in the Department of Slavic Languages and Literatures and the Department of Cinema and Media Studies (adjunct) at the University of Washington, Seattle, has published three monographs: *Komiks: Comic Art in Russia* (2010); *Death, Disability and the Superhero: The Silver Age and Beyond* (2014); and *Resurrection: Comics in Post-Soviet Russia* (2022). He has also coedited two essay collections, *Comics of the New Europe: Reflections and Intersections* (with Martha Kuhlman, 2020) and *Uncanny Bodies: Disability and Superhero Comics* (with Scott T. Smith, 2019). In 2020 he published his first comics collection, *The Phantom Zone and Other Stories* (Amatl Comix). His current book project is *Comics of the Anthropocene: Graphic Narrative at the End of Nature*.

Notes

My thanks to the organizers and participants of the inaugural Colby Summer Institute in the Environmental Humanities (2019), which made this chapter better.

1. Szeman, "System Failure," 806–807.
2. Zonn, "Neftianoe," 109. All translations mine unless otherwise indicated.
3. As reported by *The Economist* in 2008: "The competitiveness of the non-oil economy has eroded sharply since the devaluation of 1998. The concept of manufacturing for export scarcely exists, outside the arms industry." "Russia's Uneasy Handover," 13. Incidentally, two *Economist* covers from the 2000s archly capture the country's fossil fuel dilemma. One shows a bear eating oil out of a barrel as if it were honey, with the headline, "The Trouble with Russia's Economy" (1 March 2008); another showcases a gangster-like, fedora-wearing Putin brandishing a gas pump like a tommy gun, pointed westward, with the heading "Don't Mess with Russia" (16 December 2006). For a more detailed picture, see also Gustafson, *Wheel*; Gaddy and Ickes, *Russia's Addiction*; and Rogers, *Depths*.
4. Etkind, "Post-Soviet," 158. Rogers also writes: "It is commonly asserted that Russia's oil boom brought with it a range of cultural transformations—resurgent, swaggering, state-sponsored Russian nationalism; a strong, centralized federal state heavily invested in the performance of its power; and a legal and censorship regime dedicated to suppressing alternatives and challenges in all realms, from the political to the artistic," though he goes on to complicate that portrait. Rogers, *Depths*, 215.

5. See *Depths* for a thorough discussion of the Russian resources extraction industry's effect on the Perm region.
6. LeMenager, *Living Oil*, 67. Also see Boyer and Szeman, "Rise," for a succinct account of the rise of the Energy Humanities.
7. Hitchcock, "Oil," 82
8. LeMenager, *Living Oil*, 69.
9. See, for example, Hitchcock: "If climate change has provoked utopian desires for a world beyond oil, a planet where oil does not and cannot centrally drive its economic activity, then that challenge must include an imaginative grasp of its otherwise abstruse narrative of modernity, not in the mere content of oil's omnipresence, but in the very ways oil has fictively come to define so much of being in modernity, or what is sometimes referred to as an oil ontology." "Oil," 81.
10. As LeMenager cuttingly puts it: "Films, books, cars, foods, museums, even towns are oil media. The world itself writes oil, you and I write it." *Living Oil*, 11.
11. LeManager, *Living Oil*, 92.
12. Molodkin developed these themes further in his 2009 installation "Liquid Modernity."
13. Engström, "Neft'," 257.
14. Kalinin, "Petropoetics," 142. Elsewhere he concludes: "Thus, oil can be defined not only as a natural source of energy. It can also be described as an organic substance from the remote past that, brought into the present, releases an energy that possesses not only a physical but also a historical dimension, as well as a mythical potential" (122).
15. Take, for instance, Vladimir Mayakovsky's 1923 poem "Baku": "If we believe in the future with all our hearts, this is because the thick black blood of Baku flows, to the brim, into the heart of the capitals" (924). In his 1914 poem "My rastem iz zheleza" (We grow out of iron), the poet and political figure Aleksei Gastev writes that "new iron blood" flows into his veins (as quoted in Hellebust, "Aleksei," 505).
16. Engström writes that only in the post-Soviet era does oil become a foundation of petropoetics. "Neft'," 256.
17. Pelevin, *The Sacred Book*, 219; ellipsis in original.
18. A short list of Russian literature touching on oil would include novels like Dmitry Bykov's *ZhD* (Living Souls, 2000); Pelevin's *Ampir V* (Empire V, 2006), in which oil is explicitly likened to blood and capital; Aleksandr Ilichevskiy's *Pers* (The Persian, 2009); and Vasilii Golovanov's *Kaspiyskaia kniga* (Caspian Book, 2014). For comics, see the series *Tyuman* (2016) by Georgy "Gosha" Elaev, a psychedelic, X-rated superhero parody of alienation and oil extraction in Siberia. And for music, see Leningrad's "Neft'" (Oil) from the album *Khleb* (Bread, 2005).
19. Russo-Soviet "energy" films include Nikolai Lebedev and Aleksandr Litvinov's *Oil* (*Neft'*, USSR, 1927); Andron Konchalovsky's *Siberiade* (*Siberiada*, USSR, 1979); and Mikhail Segal's *Short Stories* (*Rasskazy*, 2012), especially the chapter "Energeticheskiy krisis" (Energy crisis).

20. With longtime partner Aleksey Samoriadov, Lutsik wrote the screenplays to *Gongofer* (directed by Bakhit Kilibayev, Russia, 1992), *Children of Iron Gods* (*Deti chugunnykh bogov*, directed by Tamás Tóth, Hungary and Russia, 1993), and *Limita* (directed by Denis Evstigneev, Russia, 1995), among others.
21. Mihailova, "'The Tender Beasts,'" 120.
22. In this sense *Okraina* recalls the work of Andrei Platonov, though Lutsik told an interviewer he had only read two Platonov short stories. Matizen, "Petr Lutsik."
23. "Torzhestvo." Although Lutsik bristled at the suggestion that he created *styob*, saying that he does not like that word. Matizen, "Petr Lutsik."
24. One of the group, Perfil'ev, has the same name and patronymic as Chapaev: Vasily Ivanovich.
25. Mihailova, "'The Tender Beasts,'" 129; Horton, "The Russian Soul." The US director Steven Soderbergh did something similar with *The Good German* (USA, 2006).
26. See the title of Ivanov's review.
27. Razlogov, "Nashe kino."
28. Rogers discusses "the association of deep oil and deep culture" in the Perm region, where the mammoth oil company Lukoil both extracted resources and funded cultural initiatives. See *Depths*, chapter 6.
29. Rogers, *Depths*, 233.
30. The film credits refer to him as "khozyain kabineta" (office boss).
31. Etkind, "Post-Soviet," 162.
32. Rogers, *Depth*, 163. Rogers quotes a former Lukoil-Perm employee: "[When] these oil magnates appeared at the top ... [Ordinary] people's evaluation [of the oil industry] was about as negative as it could be." *Depths*, 215; ellipsis in original. He also notes that of the two hundred richest people in Russia, the vast majority work in oil and gas. *Depths*, 163.
33. Mantsov, "Geopoliticheskaya komediya." In his review, Ivanov compares the heroes to the Three Bogatyrs ("Okraina"). For a thorough discussion of folkloric motifs in *Okraina*, see Mihailova.
34. As Mantsov puts it: "The straightforwardly mythological text works surprisingly well, simultaneously provoking laughter, horror and an awe-struck curiosity: what amount of absurdity is the supporting structure of the film—i.e., the representational system of Soviet cinema—capable of withstanding?" "Geopoliticheskaya komediya."

The scene reminds of an exhibit about the oil industry at the Kungur Regional Studies Museum, which included samples of oil, drilling pipe, maps, and photographs. Rogers, *Depths*, 228. When the tycoon holds up a container of crude from the Urals to show Pan'ka "his oil," the gesture anticipates an August 2020 RBC report in which oligarch and Siloviki leader Igor Sechin presents Putin himself with a glass bottle of "the best oil in the world." See https://www.youtube.com/watch?v=9deXckH6zdU&feature=youtu.be. It also recalls a flourish from the other pole of the ideological spectrum: Rob Hopkins on his YouTube show, holding up a liter of petroleum and saying, "The best place for this is to stay in the ground." LeMenager, *Living Oil*, 67.

35. Matizen, "Petr Lutsik."
36. Etkind, "Post-Soviet," 162.
37. Hichcock, "Oil," 85. On the switch from coal to oil and how it diminished the power of organized labor see Mitchell, *Carbon Democracy*, 21 and Malm, *Fossil Capital*, 356. Engström notes something very similar: "In post-Soviet art on the theme of energy resources and commodities, the laboring man disappears; what is left, as we see, are either the alienated traces of this labor and effort, or only the markers of man's participation in the process of extracting oil from the bowels of the earth." "Neft'," 256.
38. Horton, "The Russian Soul." Also see Etkind, "Post-Soviet," 164.
39. Mihailova, "'The Tender Beasts,'" 125.
40. Hitchcock, "Oil," 81.
41. Aninsky, "Okraina okrainy."
42. Engström, "Neft'," 255.
43. It bears mention that while art films like *Okraina* find their audiences primarily abroad and in the festival circuit, music videos—due to their domestic consumption—can and often do incorporate many more specific "local" references, making for more biting satire. See Vernallis, "Experiencing" on the music video as a consummate "capitalist" form.
44. The credits list Vengerov and Bobina, Zurab Matua, Andrei Averin, Marina Kravets, and others.
45. The video recalls novelist Aleksandr Ilichevskiy's contention in *The Persian* (2009): "Moscow is swimming in oil. In the wearying nocturnal splendor of the dens of iniquity, beauties wash themselves in its streams. The bodies of the dancers on the tower's podiums of the 'Nizhinskiy' club gleam with the lard of the depths. Moscow—all glittering, fluid, tectonically powerful, passionate— only bring a match near, strike it: the slut, the empress will burst into flame" (as quoted in Kalinin, "Petropoetics," 134). In fact, a man in *Oil* does almost light his cigar to the crowd's alarm, until DJ Smash stops him; the moment capitalizes on oil as simultaneously symbol and material flammable object.
46. Such imagery recalls Vladimir Sorokin's conceptualist novel *Norma* (The norm, 1979–1982), with the substitution of oil for shit.
47. Etkind, "Post-Soviet," 120.
48. On the homology between Marx and Freud's approaches to the symptom, see Žižek, "How."
49. To read about Pussy Riot's 2013 "occupy oil objects" tour, see http://pussy-riot.info/blog/2013/7/16/red-prison-tour. The morbid *Cherniy sneg* (*Black Snow*, 2019), a follow-up Pussy Riot music video directed by prominent member Nadezhda Tolokonnikova, addresses fossil fuel extraction's environmental toll on the provinces.
50. Chen, *Animacies*, 227.
51. As LeMenager writes of petro-cinema: "We have learned to expect of oil maximum motility and liveliness, as if it were blood." *Living Oil*, 101.
52. Kalinin, "Petropoetics," 140.
53. The massive May 2020 Norilsk diesel oil spill in Russia's arctic, which drew international attention, prompted numerous videos posted online by Russian

environmentalists. These sought to shed light on the disaster and documented how the authorities stymied such attempts. Images of reddish streams with dead fish predominated.
54. Kalinin, "Petropoetics," 143.
55. Mitchell, *Cloning Terror*, 140.
56. See Nicole Seymour's comments on "irreverent ecocriticism." Seymour, *Bad Environmentalism*.

Bibliography

Abdullaeva, Zara. "Torzhestvo zemledeliia." SEANS. No. 17/18 (1999). https://seance.ru/articles/torzhestvo-zemledeliya/.

Aninsky, Lev. "Okraina okrainy." *SEANS*, no. 17/18 (1999). https://seance.ru/articles/okraina-okrainyi/.

Boyer, Dominic, and Imre Szeman. "The Rise of the Energy Humanities." *University Affairs* (12 February 2014). https://www.universityaffairs.ca/opinion/in-my-opinion/the-rise-of-energy-humanities/.

Chen, Mel Y. *Animacies: Biopolitics, Racial Mattering, and Queer Affect*. Durham, NC: Duke University Press, 2012.

"Don't Mess with Russia." *The Economist*. 16 December 2006. https://www.economist.com/weeklyedition/2006-12-16.

Engström, Maria. "Neft' v sovremennom rossiyskom iskusstve." *Neprikosnovenniy zapas* 126 (April 2019): 255–269.

Etkind, Alexander. "Post-Soviet Russia: The Land of the Oil Curse, Pussy Riot, and Magical Historicism." *boundary* 2, 41 no. 1 (2014): 153–170.

Frith, Simon et al., eds. *Sound and Vision: The Music Video Reader*. London: Routledge, 1993.

Gaddy, Clifford, and Barry Ickes. *Russia's Addiction: How Oil, Gas, and the Soviet Legacy Have Shaped a Nationa's Fate*. Washington, DC: Brookings Institution Press, 2020.

Gustafson, Thane. *Wheel of Fortune: The Battle for Oil and Power in Russia*. Cambridge, MA: Harvard University Press, 2017.

Hellebust, Rolf. "Aleksei Gastev and the Metallization of the Revolutionary Body." *Slavic Review* 56, no. 3 (1997): 500–518.

Hitchcock, Peter. "Oil in an American Imaginary." *New Formations* 69 (2010): 81–97.

Horton, Andrew. "The Russian Soul Fights Back: Peter Lutsik's *Okraina*." *Central Europe Review* 1, no. 1 (28 June 1999). http://www.ce-review.org/99/1/kinoeye1_horton2.html.

Ivanov, Dmitriy. "*Okraina*—kinematograficheskiy terakt Lutsika i Samoriadova." Artifex, no. 36 (March 2018). https://artifex.ru/кино/петр-луцик-алексей-саморядов-окраина/.

Kalinin, Ilya. "Petropoetics: The Oil Text in Post-Soviet Russia" In *Russian Literature Since 1991*, edited by Evgeny Dobrenko and Mark Lipovetsky, 120–144. Cambridge: Cambridge University Press, 2015.

LeMenager, Stephanie. *Living Oil: Petroleum Culture in the American Century*. Oxford: Oxford University Press, 2014.
Lenta. "Nyrnuvshiy v mazut i pozhalevshiy ob etom rossiianin proslavilsia v internete." *Lenta.ru* (March 2017). https://lenta.ru/news/2017/03/03/net_pokoya/.
Malm, Andreas. *Fossil Capital: The Rise of Steam-Power and the Roots of Global Warming*. Verso, 2016.
Mantsov, Igor. "Geopoliticheskaya komediya. Okraina, rezhisser Petr Lutsik." *Iskusstvo Kino*, no. 12 (December 1998). http://old.kinoart.ru/archive/1998/12/n12-article2 .
Matizen, Viktor. "Petr Lutsik: Liudi ukhodiat, a vremia stoit na meste." *Film.ru* (31 October 2000). https://www.film.ru/articles/petr-lucik-lyudi-uhodyat-vremya-stoit-na-meste.
Mayakovsky, Vladimir. "Baku." *Izbrannoe*. Direct Media, 2018: 923–924.
Mihailova, Mihaela. "'The Tender Beasts': Peasant Mythology in Petr Lutsik's *The Outskirts*." *Studies in Russian and Soviet Cinema* 8, no. 2 (2014): 120–137.
Mitchell, Timothy. *Carbon Democracy: Political Power in the Age of Oil*. Verso, 2013.
Mitchell, W.J.T. *Cloning Terror*. University of Chicago Press, 2011.
Molodkin, Andrei. *Liquid Modernity*. Installation at the Tate Museum, 2009.
Pelevin, Viktor. *The Sacred Book of the Werewolf*. Trans. Andrew Bromfeld. New York: Viking, 2008.
Razlogov, Kirill. "Nashe kino. Chernukha stala chernozemom." *Novaia gazeta*, no. 96 (22 December 2003): 18.
Rogers, Douglas. *The Depths of Russia: Oil, Power, and Culture After Socialism*. Ithaca, NY: Cornell University Press, 2015.
"Russia's Uneasy Handover." *The Economist*. 28 February 2008. https://www.economist.com/leaders/2008/02/28/russias-uneasy-handover.
Seymour, Nicole. *Bad Environmentalism: Irony and Irreverence in the Ecological Age*. University of Minnesota Press, 2018.
Szeman, Imre. "System Failure: Oil, Futurity, and the Anticipation of Disaster." *South Atlantic Quarterly* 106, no. 4 (2007): 805–823.
"The Trouble with Russia's Economy." *The Economist*. 1 March 2008. https://www.economist.com/weeklyedition/2008-03-01.
Vernallis, Carol. *Experiencing Music Video: Aesthetics and Cultural Context*. New York: Columbia University Press, 2004.
Žižek, Slavoj. "How Did Marx Invent the Symptom?" *Mapping Ideology*, edited by Slavoj Žižek, 296–331. London: Verso, 1994.
Zonn, Igor'. "Neftianoe myshlenie mirovogo kinematografa." *Problemy postsovetskogo prostranstva* [*Post-Soviet Issues*] 6, no. 2 (2019): 108–128.

Filmography

D.J. Smash et al. Directed by Marat Adel'shin. *Oil* (*Neft'*, Russia, 2013). https://www.youtube.com/watch?v=EucLgHzuZaw&list=RDEucLgHzuZaw&start_radio=1.

Ibragimbekov, Murad. *Oil* (*Neft'*, Russia, 2003). https://www.youtube.com/watch?v=ZCYEGy_xO44.

IC3PEAK. *Sad Bitch* (*Grustnaya suka*, Russia, 2017). https://www.youtube.com/watch?v=zf99kdFw9b8.

———. *Death No More* (*Smerti bol'she net*, Russia, 2018). https://www.youtube.com/watch?v=MBG3Gdt5OGs&pbjreload=10.

Lutsik, Piotr. *The Outskirts* (*Okraina*, Russia, 2004).

Pussy Riot. *As in a Red Prison* (*Kak v krasnoi tiur'me*, Russia, 2013). https://www.youtube.com/watch?v=qOM_3QH3bBw.

10

Upholding the Village, the Beach, the Last Resort

The (Threatened) Idyll in Bulgarian Cinema

Dina Iordanova

In this chapter, I outline the ideology of "return to nature" or the "escape to the village/seaside" that characterizes the specific worldview of many Bulgarians. I link it to long-standing Balkan attitudes, tracing a lineage of cinematic and other art works that evince a fascination with escape from civilization. I want to show that—as far as ordinary people's ideologies of leisure are concerned—there has not been a radical demarcation line between the times of communism and postcommunism. Later in the text, an analysis of the mockumentary *The Last Black Sea Pirates* (*Poslednite Chernomorski pirati*, 2014) illustrates how the seaside idyll comes under threat in the conditions of encroaching neoliberalism.

When I originally wrote this piece, it concluded on an optimistic note— and, as the story of the threatened beachcombers was resolved around 2010, I am keeping the ending unchanged. More recently, however, I could

Upholding the Village, the Beach, the Last Resort • 197

Figure 10.1. A private summer palace built in 2020 on public land with the quiet collaboration of the authorities near Burgas. Exposing the misappropriation of public spaces and the "threatened idyll" often relies on guerrilla-type videos sponsored by anti-corruption bodies. *The Fight with the Untouchable Ahmed Dogan Has Begun*. Directed by Hristo Ivanov, Ivailo Mirchev, and Dimitar Naydenov. Sofia, 2020. Screen capture from YouTube by Dina Iordanova.

not help but notice many fresher instances where the story did not end so well. During COVID-19 I watched the activist video *The Fight with the Untouchable Ahmed Dogan Has Begun* (2020), which shows a private summer palace and a marina built on public land with the quiet collaboration of the authorities on the Black Sea coast near the city of Burgas.[1] It was shot by Bulgarian MPs of the democratic opposition, who resorted to guerrilla filmmaking tactics to expose the existence of the illicit luxury structure. In the video, after having been refused access to the property via the public (yet restricted and heavily guarded) road, the activists are seen descending by boat on the (public but in fact private) beach, where they are treated as intruders and are brutally pushed away by the security personnel. It shows the deplorable state of the rule of law in Bulgarian society today and makes for painful viewing.[2]

Things have grown progressively worse since then. There are reports of deepening corruption on a massive scale, one that penetrates all structures of power and is often linked to supranational gas corporations and political interests, but attempts to fight it are systematically undermined. Many of my fellow Bulgarians have continued seeking an escape in mountain villages or at the seaside, yet everywhere access is becoming more and more difficult. They are either priced out or kept away by the new proprietors of beaches and campsites that were freely accessible in the past. Public spaces have shrunk at the expense of shady, Putin-style capitalism.

Retour à la nature

Attributed widely to the idiosyncratic French philosopher Jean-Jacques Rousseau (1712–1778), ideologies calling for a return to nature share the basic view that society corrupts the individual and that pure moral values can be recovered only there, in solitude. A precursor to many contemporary beliefs about sustainability, Rousseau's writings have gained wide currency in the West, eventually paired up with various Eastern/Buddhist beliefs that call for silent retreat from civilization. In countries like Bulgaria, which have not experienced the strong rationalist tendencies of the Enlightenment and still harbor their share of Orientalist attitudes, embracing Rousseauism in the second part of the twentieth century came somehow naturally. It found an expression in lifestyles—where city individuals would seek to find a place hidden far away in nature to which they could regularly retreat as much as possible. This also led to the creation of respected works of art that are still hugely influential today. I believe that Rousseau's initial call and the drive for retour à la nature, realized through a return to the village (as a gateway to nature) and the restoration of traditional lifestyles in isolated mountain—or other—natural reserves, is key to understanding the place of nature in Bulgarian culture.

This attachment to nature features prominently in the oral tradition, yet it can also be traced to some of the classics of Bulgarian literature and cinema—lying deep in the writings of modern classic Yordan Radichkov (1929–2004) and manifesting powerfully in the writings of Nikolay Haytov (1919–2002) and Georgi Danailov (1936–2017), as well as in the cinema of Rangel Vulchanov (1928–2013). It calls for celebrating and embracing the traditional forms of village life, which are close to nature and thus provide a means of transcending the stress and vanity of urban existence.

A celebrated short story by Haytov from 1967 served as the basis for the eponymous film *A Tree Without Roots* (*Darvo bez koren*, 1974), directed by Hristo Hristov. It tells of the emotional difficulties experienced by an elderly man whose grown children bring him to the city for the winter period. Were he to stay in the city, he would have much better living conditions, and yet he finds it difficult to adapt. He longs for the village and feels like a tree with no roots. In the end, he returns to the village, where he belongs.

Georgi Danailov was a self-confessed Rousseauist and the author of multiple essays connecting Rousseau's philosophy to present-day realities. His views on nature and the escape to the village found their most comprehensive expression in his book-length essay *House Beyond the World* (*Kushta otvud sveta*, 1997). It was his role as screenwriter for director Rangel Vulchanov's cult film *Where Are You Going?* (*Za kade patuvate*, 1986), however, that allowed him to become a major influence on this discourse.[3] The film concerned stressed urbanites escaping from the city and into the magical and dreamlike world of the village.

Notably, both Haytov and Danailov opted for a lifestyle that was in line with the ideology of "the return to the village," respectively basing themselves in the beautiful Rhodope Mountains. Starting in the 1980s, but having its roots in many earlier examples, this became the preferred lifestyle for those employed in the liberal professions, especially those whose jobs permitted them to spend time away from the cities. Kovatchevitsa, where Danailov was based and where the film *Where Are You Going?* was shot, acquired cult standing, and property prices rose higher than the capital. Other remote yet picturesque mountain villages—Leshten, Bozhentsi, Arbanasi—gradually turned into artistic colonies where more houses were owned by writers, painters, and cineasts than by ordinary villagers.[4]

The ideology of "the return to the village" became so entrenched that it is powerfully present also in the cinema of the postcommunist period.[5] A typical plot for many of the Bulgarian films from the last three decades is structured around city dwellers (with the possible variation of protagonists arriving from abroad) who come to the village in search of calm, beauty, mindfulness, and wisdom. The implied message in many of these films is that even if Bulgaria, as a peripheral and underdeveloped country, ranks quite low in the hierarchy of European countries, it is a place where "authentic" values and emotions can still be found, particularly in the remote mountain villages.

This ideological line still runs strong today in the *Getting Lost on Purpose* (*Da se izgubish narochno*, 2018) franchise, which exists as a two-hour film, a twelve-episode miniseries (both available on YouTube), and, more recently, as a book. It is the project of young vlogger Chris Zakhariev, who, along with two other teenage friends, journeys in the course of a summer through various Bulgarian villages in a car that is nearly falling apart. It is a version of the retour à la nature (and to the village) for the millennial generation—the same ideology paired with mobile phone camera aesthetics. The project has been able to bring together a strong fan base, much of it located in the diaspora.

This discourse on the village and nature is one of the key features of the regional psychology and is not limited to Bulgaria, even though I believe it finds a most systematic expression here. Still, echoes and variations of it—featuring the escape from civilization and celebrating the difficult but fulfilling life in close contact with nature—are invariably found in the cinematic traditions of all countries bordering the Mediterranean. Turkish cinema, for example, reveals a similar sensibility in the films of Semih Kaplanoglu (most notably *Egg* [*Yumurta*, 2007], *Milk* [*Süt*, 2008], and *Honey* [*Bal*, 2010]), but directors working in this vein also include Reha Erdem, Nuri Bilge Ceylan, and many others. In Greece, there is Dimos Avdeliodis's *The Four Seasons of the Law* (*I earini synaxis ton agrofilakon*, 1999), an underappreciated masterpiece set in the villages of Chios and focusing on the relationship of people to nature in a wondrous, surrealist tone. Finally, modernity and tradition are diametrically opposed in a number of Italian films set in desolate villages such as Ermanno Olmi's *The Tree of Wooden Clogs* (*L'Albero degli zoccoli*, 1978) and Michelangelo Frammartino *The Four Times* (*Le Quattro volte*, 2010).

Before I go any further, I should underline that the main assumptions of this chapter—as it concerns geography, psychological makeup, and periodization—suggest that Bulgaria may be different from the generally accepted parameters that frame this collection. First of all, Bulgaria's geographical location in the Balkans and close to the Mediterranean positions it in a group that is characterized by a comparable sun-loving, pragmatic, and somewhat insolent Southern European set of attitudes that it shares with its neighboring countries, some of which were never part of the Soviet Bloc. Historically within the Ottoman Empire, the pathways of people living in these parts moved to different trajectories, often stretching into the Aegean Sea, toward Istanbul, the Black Sea, and Asia Minor.[6]

In the period that followed Bulgaria's 1878 emancipation from the Ottomans, a long and influential tradition of writings formed dedicated to analyzing the complex and eclectic national psychology. Many of these specifically reflect on the importance of village life and proximity to nature. The most pertinent are the writings of self-styled ethnologist and anthropologist Ivan Hadzhiyski (1907–1944), whose life was cut short by World War II—but not before he published his influential views on the importance of village roots to the worldview of the Bulgarian. This ideological lineage was continued by Asen Hristoforov (1910–1970), a professor of economics who in 1947 was fired from the university by the Communist authorities and, after spending 1950–1952 in the Belene concentration camp, went to live in the village of Goverdartzi at Rila Mountain. There, he authored a collection of observational essays titled *Matsakurtsi* (1958), which became known as the "Bulgarian *Walden*."[7] Though he honestly reports on the difficulties that a city dweller like him might experience settling into village life, a leitmotif of his writing was the persistent joy of liberation from the confines of urban life. He was followed by many others, such as the aforementioned Nikolay Haytov and, a generation later, the playwright/screenwriter Boyan Papazov (1943–), who was known as a quasi-dissident under communism, then served as a Bulgarian cultural attaché in Washington, DC, in the early 1990s, and finally withdrew into simple village life in the company of his dog.[8]

This longer history suggests that the end of the Cold War and the change in political systems has little bearing on the way Bulgarians relate to nature and the "return to nature" paradigm. The changing political context matters, but not too much as the desire to withdraw from civilization may be triggered as much by the paternalistic communist state as the inequalities of postcommunist capitalism and corruption. Films, likewise, may be set in a specific period, yet there are no substantial ideological differences between features that portray an escape to a dreamy seaside hideout in the 1970s and those made forty years later. They are all about the same thing—finding solace, being left alone.

Oh, the Sea... (Ах, морето...)

While most of the films discussed so far take as their setting remote mountain regions, it is the seaside that features most prominently as the main attraction for such fugitives from civilization. Most Bulgarians make an annual pilgrimage to the seaside to care for their emotional needs. The visit is associated with purifying the body and soul; it is regarded as a meditative, spiritual exchange with sun, sea, and sky, even if often accompanied by abuse of toxic substances.

Historically, those same Bulgarians who shared the ideology of retreating to the villages also took part in a ritualistic annual visit to the Black Sea coast, often displaying special preferences for the season (early September when the beaches are less crowded), the length of the break (a protracted number of weeks), and the mode (as wild as possible).[9] Most importantly, one would develop a preference for a certain isolated outpost and keep returning to it year after year, with some places developing cult standing with the intelligentsia, such as the campground Zlatna Ribka, Varvara, and, later on, Sinemoretz in the south or Kavarna and Krapetz in the very north.[10]

The importance of this annual romantic escape has found expression in various media, but first and foremost in the many popular songs whose lyrics—credited to poets such as Radoy Ralin, Vladimir Bashev, and Nedyalko Yordanov—refer to the special standing of the seaside in Bulgaria's popular imaginary.[11] To this day, songs promote the seaside as a place for romantic or spiritual escape. A typical example is Stefan Vuldobrev's hit "Gentler…" ("Po-poleka," 2018), which talks about slowing down and becoming "pirates," while the videoclip features a group of young people spending the night around a bonfire on a beach.

During the communist period Bulgaria's seaside was also an attractive location for film productions from across the Soviet Bloc. Socialist countries like Hungary, Czechoslovakia, and the GDR did not have access to sunny beaches and warm sands, so many international co-productions, usually with substantial Bulgarian involvement by way of screenwriting (Angel Vagenshtain, Mormarevi brothers), directorial work, or acting (Ivan Andonov, Georgi Kaloyanchev), sought to film on Bulgaria's beautiful shores. Some examples include the romantic comedy *The Ancient Coin* (*Die antike Münze*, Bulgaria/GDR, 1965), the historical fiction *Aesop* (*Ezop*, Bulgaria/Czechoslovakia, 1970), or the sci-fi film *Eolomea* (Bulgaria/GDR/USSR, 1972), all of which contain iconic scenes set against the background of serene sea and abundant sunshine.

However, there was also a parallel tradition of Bulgarian productions in which the seaside setting was of key importance to the film's concept, plot, and aesthetics. Most of the early examples of this lineage are connected with the name of the aforementioned Rangel Vulchanov, like his sophisticated antinuclear chamber piece *The Sun and the Shadow* (*Slantseto i syankata*, 1962), filmed in black and white, co-produced with Poland, and scripted by Valeri Petrov, one of the finest Bulgarian dramaturgs. The film, set on a small island, features a young couple—a handsome but modest Bulgarian man and an anxious foreign woman—spending the day in an erotic but doomed conversation, surrounded by the sea.

The most emblematic early work of Vulchanov, however, is the lighthearted *Escape to Ropotamo* (*Byagstvo v Ropotamo*, 1973), where the proverbial Ropotamo is a slow-flowing, turquoise river lined with water lilies and tall bulrush plants, which runs parallel to the beach on the southern part of the coastline, a site recognized as a "paradisiacal" destination.[12] The film is a romantic comedy that focuses on the resolute escape of a female pop star, whose songs are about longing for the fields, the wind, and the sky. She finds shelter in the derelict hut of an old vagrant at Ropotamo, where she meets another romantic escapee, a handsome Polish seafarer played by Pierre Clementi look-alike Dimitar Tashev, a vegan-breatharian who survives on plankton and who has also sought solace and tranquility in nature. Together, they find freedom and affection on the beach.

Keeping in mind that the large tourist resorts Sunny Beach (near Burgas) and Golden Sands (near Varna) were built in the late 1950s and had already been in place for some years by the time the film was made, *Escape to Ropotamo* is an example of resistance to mass tourism and to the invasion of natural spots by entrepreneurial guides. It pioneered a whole line of films offering visions of a primitive but authentic lifestyle on the beach. The sea and the nature around it become synonymous with an ascent to higher realms, where one's true self can manifest. Not least, *Escape to Ropotamo* also introduced a specific type of secondary but normatively important character found in many later films—an elderly tramp-like figure, often a retired sailor (a "sea wolf") who has settled by the sea, usually in a makeshift cabin amid a coterie of dogs and kittens.[13] Such men have managed to leave aside ego and vanity and have learned to live in the present. *The Last Black Sea Pirates* (2014), which I will consider next, draws precisely on this archetype.

Binka Zhelyazkova's *The Big Night Bath* (*Golyamoto noshtno kupane*, 1980) is also part of this lineage. The film can be considered representative of the "cinema of moral anxiety" trend sweeping across Eastern Europe in the 1970s and early 1980s; it was widely acclaimed at the time and is still considered one of the key moral tales of Bulgarian cinema. Scripted by Zhelyazkova's regular collaborator Hristo Ganev, it follows a disparate group of city dwellers who have been congregating in a remote seaside village for many years; the group dynamic is complex and unsettling. Governed by ennui and restlessness, they engage in a dangerous night game by the sea during which things get rough and a youngster loses his life.[14]

In the early 1990s, Lyudmil Todorov's *The Summer Love of a Shlep* (Любовното лято на един льохман, 1990) reasserted the conceptual and pictorial grammar that was already in place: an idyllic and desolate beach location where simple truths and profound existential realizations can come to light. This time, though, the film is structured around a series of flashbacks belonging to a motley group of friends who reminisce about a romantic and carefree natural existence on the beach in happy togetherness, while mourning the loss of one of their friends. The film is permeated by nostalgia for the last years of state socialism, where the natural stance of young urbanites would be to prefer this kind of life over attempts to achieve socially. The trend continued unabated into the postcommunist period, featuring the same restless escapees. Whatever the changing ills, the sun and sand seemed to provide the antidote. As Greek and Turkish shores became increasingly available, however, films were no longer set in Bulgaria only—Zornitsa Sophia's *Forecast* (*Prognoza*, 2008), for example, features a group of similarly vagrant characters from across the Balkan region who have gathered to windsurf on a small island that happens to be in Turkish territorial waters.[15]

The Last Black Sea Pirates

The Last Black Sea Pirates brings the action to the immaculate Black Sea beach of Karadere. An important recent rendering of the well-established plot, it carries all the basics of the ideology I have described so far. However, it introduces a new element too—the need to resist corporate invasion.[16]

The Last Black Sea Pirates is billed as documentary, and indeed it features a specific spot on the Black Sea coast, its inhabitants, as well as certain—albeit loosely reported—events that jeopardize their way of life. The setting is Karadere, one of the last untouched beaches.[17] Even if not particularly remote—it lies only about thirty minutes to the south of Varna—Karadere is difficult to reach. The beach, some five kilometers long, is sheltered beneath a steep landscape containing a rugged, primeval oak forest, vineyards, and fields, crisscrossed only by dirt roads. During the rainy season, the dirt pathways get eroded. Cars avoid driving there even when the ground is dry, as they may end up stuck or broken. It can be reached only by horse/donkey or on foot. During the summer, there are relatively small numbers of nature lovers who come to spend a quiet vacation there. Only a handful of people, however, have made a permanent home there, and there is not a single residential structure, only a few improvised shacks near the beach. Thus, Karadere has everything necessary for an outlaw idyll. And this is precisely how the filmmakers portray it: as a desolate and spacious wilderness beyond the reach of law—a place where no administrators have ever set foot. Here one can live in immediate proximity to the sea, the sky, and the stars, and where one only takes a few steps on the golden sand to reach a rowboat that can take one out on the serene, blue waters. It is a place where one can sustain oneself by gathering the fruits of the sea and the trees, where one lives surrounded by faithful pets, a silent place where natural, circadian rhythms set the schedule for the day. There are no rules, no taxes, no working hours, and no crime.

The central protagonist of *The Last Black Sea Pirates* is Jack, the king of the beach, a treasure hunter who seems to have lived there forever and is the undisputed leader of a colourful crew of outlaws. None of them are introduced by name; only some are given characterization (the man who abandoned his wife for the sea; the man who "drives" a donkey; the one who likes rowing and fishing; and yet another one who perennially daydreams of hot sex). They all "work" informally and only when they are up to it for Jack, who possesses some secret knowledge regarding a treasure that must have been buried in the area during Ottoman times. The "work" progresses slowly and not in a particularly organized fashion; sometimes

Figure 10.2. A motley crew of outcasts lead an off-grid existence on the Black Sea. *The Last Black Sea Pirates* (*Poslednite Chernomorski pirati*). Directed by Svetoslav Stoyanov. Sofia: Agitprop, 2014. Screen capture by Dina Iordanova.

there is digging and blowing up in the forest, to uncover and inspect some places. Occasionally, metal detectors are used. Nothing has yet been found, though, and one senses gradually that the treasure hunt is more of an excuse to hang out and enjoy the idyllic life outside of civilization. The men savor the warmth of the sea water, the caresses of the sand; they play with their pets and occasionally get the beach barbecue going. The small hardships of no electricity or having to get water from a distant well do not bother them, and life is nice. At moments, when he gets cross, Jack reminds his crew that he is the sole purveyor of cigarettes and booze. But his anger does not last long, and soon they are once again immersed in legends of magnificent sultans, concubines, and treasures…

A subplot that does not appear to intersect with the lives of Jack's gang—a "divertimento" of sorts—is the story of lovebirds Zone and Ilko. She is young and wistful, he is a gentle old alcoholic, and they seem to be utterly dedicated to one another. Living in a makeshift cabin nearby, they are shown in vignettes walking through the nearby fields or at home watching TV soaps, always involved in dreams about their marriage and a wedding dress, preferably pink.[18] The dreams invariably end with the realization that none of it can happen as the couple is so short of money. The replay of these dialogues has an endearingly comic effect. Toward the end of the film, however, Ilko has vanished, and Zone walks through the desolate fields calling his name, in vain.

Dark clouds are gathering. Already in the first part of the film, a strange visitor, who speaks broken Bulgarian with a pronounced foreign accent, is shown flying over Karadere in a balloon. Talking to the camera, he points to different corners of the hilly patch, explaining a plan to build five villages, two of which will be bigger and the other three smaller. There will be a swimming pool, pedestrian pathways, and electric cars, for easy access to the beach below—all for rich people, he specifies. The words of the developer never reach the inhabitants of Karadere, who continue their idyllic existence unaware of his plans. Soon enough, they do hear, and keep on hearing via different channels, about the devilish plan that will jeopardize their fragile paradise.

Jack is shattered: he knows he could never win a standoff with the state, and that his crew will disperse at the first sight of law enforcers. TV footage intercut into the narrative of the film reveals that a celebrity foreign architect, whose exhibition has just opened at the prestigious Gallery for Foreign Art in Sofia, is set to design the project.[19] The opening is attended by none other than the country's prime minister, Sergey Stanishev, who has brought along the Minister of Regional Development. In the film, this part of the plot is developed exclusively through media snippets since Jack does not have a TV. He is shown reading about it in the newspaper and listening to occasional broadcasts on his transistor radio. Things do not look good, especially as Jack is aware that he has no means to resist. Complaining or seeking redress is impossible as he and his "pirates" have no legal claim to the place—they are mere romantics, outlaws by choice.

Jack starts thinking of a way to defend himself and his territory, muttering references to stashed dynamite, if they only dare come any closer. He is determined to resist, but also knows that his resistance will be broken; he is on the weaker, losing side. For the time being, there is nothing to do but wait. The media reports that keep trickling in suggest that the project seems to be on hold, that somewhere far away there are forces fighting against it. It is a faraway battle over corruption, a term that does not mean much to the pirates. For the time being, they are left alone. Fall and winter come and go. Spring is here, and no one has shown up to start construction. The men from Karadere can go fishing, relaxed.

The film is produced by Agitprop—a Bulgarian documentary house fronted by producer Martichka Bozhilova—who have worked out a trademark style over time. Most of their productions feature engaging narratives that loosely tell the stories of real protagonists. These are appealing films: highly scripted, competently edited, and paced in a way that makes them as captivating as feature cinema.[20] The two people behind this specific film—writer Vanya Raynova and director Svetoslav Stoyanov—deploy quite a bit of artistic license. The result is a film that is best described as poetic docudrama. Even if it engages with serious issues of corporate appropriation, it does so tangentially and indirectly; it does not point fingers at any people or institutions.

Like in other films from this region (such as the Bosnian film *An Episode from the Life of an Iron Picker* (*Epizoda u životu berača željeza*, Danis Tanovic, 2013) the protagonists play themselves, often shown in situations that may be somewhat embellished for dramatic effect. The "poetic" feel is particularly important for *Pirates*—the enhanced romantic overtones are achieved by avoiding any scenes that may show the protagonists interacting with the outside world, an approach that enhances the feeling of idyllic self-sufficiency and sustainability. Scenes of the pirates' off-the-grid lifestyle are intercut with panoramic vistas of Karadere, revealing the area's majestic beauty. There are many long takes showing the protagonists at leisurely pursuits such as fishing or cooking on the beach. At moments, the depiction borders on the exotic and the film seems to borrow quite a few of Emir Kusturica's well-tested magic realist devices. For example, there is a scene of a man riding on a donkey that comes along with attached traffic signals and a Mercedes sign on its forehead. One wonders whether this donkey just happened to be "caught" by the camera or whether the trinkets were attached by the film crew specifically for the shot, to heighten the Kusturica-like absurdity of the scene.

The Last Black Sea Pirates presents the ideal seaside lifestyle while simultaneously sketching a confrontation that never takes place. In this way, the film smartly points to the key dilemma that the retour à la nature ideology faces in the times of neoliberalism. Change is, inevitably, coming to all corners of postcommunist Bulgaria—and those who have sought out the remote villages feel its adverse effects. They may have managed to temporarily keep the encroaching bulldozers and tourists at bay, but they are no longer out of reach. A new kind of danger is looming—not one concerning the transition from a state socialist order to a society centered around the idea of private property. The protagonists of the film are neither socialist workers nor capitalist-minded individuals; they are underdogs and would be considered renegades under any kind of social order.

A decade or so since the events depicted in the film, corporate appropriation and corruption in the country has only worsened. Given this context, *The Last Black Sea Pirates* becomes a landmark film. It goes beyond the old paradigm of escape to nature and warns—albeit timidly—of an impending hard landing. The postcommunist change in ownership (of land and other assets) is an issue that is routinely present yet remains insufficiently explored not only in Bulgaria but in the region more broadly, and the film is brave for venturing into this territory, even if, again, it does not go deep enough. All land was state property prior to 1989, but things are far from clear in the aftermath of state socialism. Even if there are constitutional provisions to keep the seaside and other natural resources off limits, many turn a blind eye. Often, business dealings resemble a land grab: whoever has the power to create records is able to simultaneously proclaim and certify ownership.[21] This means that places like Karadere can never be safe. The pirates in the film have also engaged in an undocumented land grab. They can search for treasure as long as no one carrying a piece of paper certifying ownership arrives. The day the person with the certificate appears, however, will be the last day for those who followed in Rousseau's footsteps—knowingly or not. The film ends on a nostalgic note. The men are still there, and nothing has changed—for now.

Protecting the Last Resort: An Existential Crusade

To wrap up this chapter, I want to turn to the present-day reality of Karadere and similar "idyllic" spots. There are three distinct location types on Bulgaria's Black Sea coast. The first consists of the large tourist complexes, the best known of which are Sunny Beach and Golden Sands. These are full of hotels with balconies facing the sea, restaurants, bars, casinos, and other entertainment, and feature crowded beaches. They were first developed by Balkantourist during communist times and were widely used by Soviet and other Eastern Bloc vacationers. In the aftermath, they were all privatized and nowadays cater to low-income mass tourists from the West.[22] The second type consists of holiday homes left over from communist times when enterprises and other organizations were running their own holiday facilities. Most of these were privatized, and a substantial new private base of large houses in various locations was added to it after a protracted construction rush that lasted throughout the 1990s and 2000s; most of these are now privately exploited. They are located near public beaches that provide facilities such as beach bars, umbrellas, and parking; they are used by vacationers mainly from within the country. Neither of these two types of holiday locations are of any relevance or interest to those who share the ideology of return to nature—yet it is these types of locations that occupy more and more of the territory.[23]

The third type of location, which is progressively shrinking, is that of relatively isolated and untouched beaches featuring shantytown accommodations—a dwindling sphere where the escape to the seaside can fully take place and where the sea can be smelled and sensed.[24] Such locations are only accessible to insiders and their friends, and they have remained out of reach for developers. There is only the occasional simple structure, owned by an artist or filmmaker who has made their home there. Only a few such places are left in Bulgaria now.

Even though *The Last Black Sea Pirates* was produced in 2014, the danger to the beach was mainly in the period of 2008–2009, so all references to it in the film relate to a calamity that had already passed by the time the filming took place in 2013. The plan was to build, at Karadere, a 540-acre, one-billion-Euro development, to be named Black Sea Gardens Eco Resort, comprising of five pedestrian hill towns, several artificial ponds, a marina, and leisure areas around the beach. It was backed by a consortium of real estate investors, domestic and international, who had invited the acclaimed British architect Norman Foster to make the sketches for the ecovillage complex. Foster's bureau had followed the brief of their Bulgarian architectural partners, who claimed there were provisions for sustainability (use of local natural resources, a biomass power plant, employment of a local workforce).[25]

Public opinion in Bulgaria mobilized rapidly, and the battle to save Karadere was won by 2009. I speculate that it was successful for several reasons: the people it mobilized shared the ideology of the escape to nature, and many of them now living in diaspora brought in good media and legal connections. Corruption is rife in Bulgaria, but there were several beneficial factors that permitted exposing it in this case. Finally, international channels were used successfully to influence key players to drop out.

The plethora of NGOs that got involved brought to light, through skillful use of the media, several details related to the Karadere project: star architect Norman Foster had never visited the location itself and was clearly misled, not knowing that the project involved the construction of a resort in an area protected under the EU's NATURA law in 2000. It was revealed that the Bulgarian partner-architect was the brother of the then-prime minister Sergey Stanishev, who would have the final say in the land deal.[26] British media covered the struggle in favorable terms; Norman Foster dropped out and the project was shelved.[27]

The outcome is an example of the power of media and of the international reputation of the *Guardian* newspaper specifically, which impacted the situation with the publication of two pieces by freelancer Kate Connolly, one of which appeared in the print edition and the other one a podcast giving voice to various Bulgarians she met camping on the beach in Karadere—members of the "return to the village" set, all fully fluent in English and all articulaten– a "green" lawyer who worked pro bono for the campaign, a violin player and her son, a local "eco"-guide. The *Guardian* publications served as a turning point—not only because they exposed the family ties between the Bulgarian architect and the prime minister, but also in their suggestion that Foster may have made a "mistake" and was probably misled—thus allowing a greatly reputable figure of world architecture like him to elegantly back out.

Karadere's development did not happen in 2008–2009. Unfortunately, it does not mean the battle is over. Reports about new appropriation or construction attempts continue to pop up in the media. A vigilante Facebook group Da spasim Karadere (Let's Save Karadere) is extremely active, with its transnationally based members sharing information and reporting various abuses of public lands nationwide, not only at the beach in question.

Around the time of the battle over Karadere, similar resistance strategies were deployed in Scotland—reputedly, a country with a better-functioning legal system and less corruption. Only here the battle was against the project for a Donald Trump–owned golf course at a protected beach near Aberdeen. As in the case of Karadere, there was evidence of government endorsement bordering on corruption, evidence of destroying a protected natural habitat, violations of the rights of the beach inhabitants whose makeshift dwellings looked very much like those of the "last Black Sea Pirates," as well as extensive public protests—to no avail. The protests were squashed, and construction went ahead, as documented in Anthony Baxter's film *You Have Been Trumped* (2011). Thus, in a wider context, saving Karadere, and, by projection, the Bulgarian intelligentsia's ideology of escape to the seaside, is a true achievement and an existential crusade of sorts. "Not only does Karadere have unique nature, but also a unique culture," says geographer Miroslav Damyanov, referring to the way people who come to the beach behave.[28] Losing Karadere would mean a "loss of human dignity" to them.

I am also one of those Bulgarians who subscribe to the "return to nature" ideology. I always seek to escape the city. Back in time, I would retreat to a village in the middle of the beautiful Stara Planina as often as I could, and every summer we would do our annual pilgrimage to the rocks at Varvara, near the dry tree prop from Binka Zhelyazkova's film. Soon after seeing *The Last Black Sea Pirates* at a festival abroad, I had the chance to go to Karadere, with friends, for a few days of carefree happiness. We arrived on foot, from the village of Byala, four kilometers away. We carried everything we needed on our backs—tents, gear, food. We found a place amid trees to set up camp. Our neighbors were others like us, who we could easily reach out to and join if we wanted to, among the trees or on the beach. Or we could just stay within our own small group. We were sleeping in hammocks under open sky, with the beach a few steps away, so we could swim joyfully in the sea. When we left, again on foot, we carefully packed all our garbage and took it away, aiming to leave no trace. The others did the same. I look forward to finding Karadere untouched, beautiful, and respected when I return, whenever this may be.

Dina Iordanova is a native of Bulgaria where she studied philosophy, aesthetics, and German and worked at the Institute for Cultural Studies. She emigrated after 1989 and subsequently worked in Canada and the United States, before arriving in the United Kingdom in 1998. In 2004, she started the Film Studies Department at the ancient University of St Andrews in Scotland where she spent the bulk of her career while also taking on visiting professorships and serving on international film festival juries around the world. She is now a professor emerita at St Andrews and honorary professor at the University of Hong Kong. Dina Iordanova has written extensively on the cinema of the Balkans and Eastern Europe, including on Bulgarian cinema. She is also a specialist on transnational cinema and film festivals.

Notes

1. Ivanov, Mirchev, and Naydenov, *The Fight with the Untouchable Ahmed Dogan Has Begun*.
2. Streaming such material on YouTube has become the norm for politicians and organizations fighting corruption as they are shut out of mainstream media and the judiciary has a long record of inaction. Bulgarian film scholar Alexander Donev has discussed the commissioning of investigative video by agencies in charge of fighting fraud and exploitation. They often work with filmmakers who sign on anonymously (as for the film *The Eight Dwarves*, 2020, posted by the AntiCorruption Fund on their YouTube channel). See Donev, *Mapping the Untamed Cinematic*.
3. Subsequent films, made by the same team, such as *Where Do We Go from Here?* (*A sega nakade?*, Bulgaria, 1988) and *And Today, Where to?* (*A dnes nakade?*, 2007) also touched on the role of the village in the lives of the next generation of creatives.
4. Even if not directly linked to this Rousseauist ideology and lifestyle, Bulgaria is the home of the Dunovist movement, also known as the White Brotherhood. Followers of philosopher Petar Dunov, they gather in the summer to perform Paneurithmia dance rituals, all dressed in white, in the protected ecological area known as the Seven Lakes in the Rila Mountains. This way of expressing reverence to nature is practiced widely by people of different ages and classes. During the communist regime, Dunovism existed only as an underground movement, but it has grown and flourished in recent decades.
5. See "The Road to the Village" chapter in my *New Bulgarian Cinema*. More recently, Bulgarian film scholar Alexander Donev, writing on indie cinema, noted that while in the 1970s there was a "migration cycle" of films that featured protagonists moving from the villages to the cities, in the post-1989 period there is a trend of filmic narratives where the movement is in the opposite direction, toward the village. See Donev, *Mapping the Untamed Cinematic*.

6. For a more detailed discussion of the key importance of alternative geographies on the region, see my *Cinema of Flames*, 32–45.
7. Sabev, "Matsakurtsi."
8. An inspirational figure of this type of alternative lifestyle is the famous Turkish short story writer Sait Faik Abasiyanik (1906–1954), most often compared to Chekhov—he lived in isolation on the island of Burgazada in the Marmara Sea and preferred to socialize mainly with the locals.
9. It is only after the end of communism that access to beaches in Greece and Turkey became possible for the middle and upper classes. The Halkidiki peninsula in Greece, boasting beautiful beaches and well-developed tourism, is geographically closer for many Bulgarians who have now abandoned the Black Sea coast and vacation there instead.
10. Due to its proximity to the Romanian border, Krapetz is particularly popular with the Bucharest intelligentsia. A feature film romance, Kiril Stankov's *Krapetz* (2012), is set in the village and features, as is usual for the subgenre of "seaside films," themes of disillusionment, loneliness, and escape.
11. Songs were performed by some of the most popular singers such as Margret Nikolova, Lili Ivanova, Emil Dimitrov, Sylvia Katzarova, the Argirovi brothers, Tony Dimitrova, or the Tonika group, which had the special privilege of being based in Burgas and thus closer to the seaside.
12. The "paradisiacal" designation originates from the aforementioned, hugely popular 1962 mambo-marimba song "Ropotamo," which remains an evergreen hit, especially for the intentionally cheesy lyrics by revered satirical poet Radoi Ralin. The film features numerous songs, which, however, never reached the same popularity, lip-synched by the actors but in fact sung by Mimi Nikolova, Boyan Ivanov, and Boris Gudzhunov.
13. In this instance, there are two such protagonists: the film is a vehicle for beloved comedians Konstantin Kotsev and Georgi Kaloyanchev.
14. *The Big Night Bath* was filmed on the cliffs around the village of Varvara—a real-life place of legendary standing with the bohemian crowd, where a special dry tree had been erected for the shoot. After the shoot was over, the tree was left on-site and stood there for many years, serving as a symbolic reminder of the film.
15. Reportedly, the film was shot around Kamen Briag, Tyulenovo, and Krapetz, all small places on the rugged coast north of Varna.
16. The film could be regarded as an updated version of Bill Forsyth's film *Local Hero* (1983), where a large oil corporation sends its representative to a remote village on Scotland's North Sea coast to negotiate with a raggedy beachcomber who turns out to own the oil sands.
17. Karadere, a Turkish word, means "black creek" in translation.
18. They are the only ones who, inexplicably, seem to have electricity in their shack. If the shack is close enough to a property that has electricity, they might have diverted some of the electricity for illegal use. Alternatively, they could have a small generator. In any case, it is not clear from the film itself how is this possible.
19. The footage is from the Norman Foster exhibition opening, which took place in 2007.

20. Other Balkan documentaries follow this same formula—for example the Sundance-winning *Honeyland* (2019), a film that tells the story of a lonely female beekeeper who lives in harmony with nature in the remote mountains near Skopje.
21. Economist Hernando de Soto has persuasively demonstrated this in his book *The Mystery of Capital: Why Capitalism Triumphs in the West and Fails Everywhere Else* (2000).
22. For a perceptive study that tackles postcommunist tourism in Bulgaria, see Ghodsee, *The Red Riviera*.
23. Bulgaria's Black Sea coast in general has been grossly overbuilt in the postcommunist period by developers who sold apartments to a massive number of international owners, mainly Russian middle-ranking members of Putin's nomenklatura. "According to Atanas Krastin, the Bulgarian ambassador to the Russian Federation, a total of more than 300,000 Russians own nearly 450,000 properties in eastern Bulgaria alone, more than 95 percent of which are concentrated on the coast" ("Over Half a Million Russian Properties").
24. Karadere, specifically, had been left out of developers' plans in the past because Soviet submarines were known to dock there and had occasionally used the remote beach for access. Rumour has it that, later, the site was being eyed for purchase by the East German film studio DEFA.
25. For full details on the intricacies of the project, the resistance against it, and general background, see Damyanov, "Save Karadere."
26. Stanishev was a socialist prime minister; he lost power after the 2009 elections, to some extent due to the Karadere situation. Stanishev is now member of the European Parliament and leader of its Socialist faction.
27. Connolly, "Bulgarian Eco-Town"; "Norman Foster Resort."
28. Damyanov, "Save Karadere," 2.

Bibliography

Connolly, Kate. "Bulgarian Eco-Town: 'The Biggest Mistake in Norman Foster's Career,' Say Protesters." *The Guardian*. 14 July 2008.

Damyanov, Miroslav. "Save Karadere: Resisting Relentless Urbanization of a Wild Beach on the Bulgarian Sea Coast." MA thesis. Radboud University, 2015. theses.ubn.ru.nl.

Donev, Alecander. *Mapping the Untamed Cinematic/Kartografirane na filmovata neopitomenost: Post-1989 Bulgarian Independent, Amateur and Alternative Cinema*. Sofia, Art Studies Institute, 2021.

Ghodsee, Kristen. *The Red Riviera: Gender, Tourism, and Postsocialism on the Back Sea*. Durham, NC: Duke University Press, 2005.

Iordanova, Dina. *Cinema of Flames: Balkan Film, Culture and the Media*. London: British Film Institute, 2001.

———. *New Bulgarian Cinema*. St. Andrews: St. Andrews Film Studies with College Gate Press, 2008.

"Norman Foster Resort: Developers Have Been Eyeing It Up since the Collapse of Communism." *Guardian Podcast*. 14 July 2008.
"Over Half a Million Russian Properties in Bulgaria on the Counter, Is There Anyone to Buy Them?" *The European Times*. 13 April 2022. https://www.europe antimes.news/2022/04/over-half-a-million-russian-properties-in-bulgaria-on-the-counter-is-there-anyone-to-buy-them/. Accessed 6 August 2022.
Sabev, Dimitar. "Matsakurtsi—bulgarskiyat Walden." *Bodil.bg*. 21 August 2019. https://bodil.bg/2019/08/21/matsakurtsi/. Accessed 10 June 2020.

Filmography

Avdeliodis, Dimos. *The Four Seasons of the Law* (*I earini synaxis ton agrofilakon*, Greece, 1999).
Baxter, Anthony. *You Have Been Trumped* (United Kingdom, 2011).
Frammartino, Michelangelo. *The Four Times* (*Le Quattro Volte*, Italy, 2010).
Hristov, Hristo. *A Tree Without Roots* (*Darvo bez koren*, 1974).
Ivanov, Hristo, Ivailo Mirchev, and Dimitar Naydenov. *The Fight with the Untouchable Ahmed Dogan Had Begun* (Bulgaria, 2020).
Kaplanoglu, Semih. *Egg* (*Yumurta*, Turkey, 2007).
———. *Milk* (*Süt*, Turkey, 2008).
———. *Honey* (*Bal*, Turkey, 2010).
Kotevska, Tamara, and Ljubomir Stefanov. *Honeyland* (*Medena zemja*, Macedonia, 2019).
Olmi, Ermanno. *The Tree of Wooden Clogs* (*L'Albero degli zoccoli*, Italy, 1978).
Sophia, Zornitsa. *Forecast* (*Prognoza*, Bulgaria, 2008).
Stankov, Kiril. *Krapetz* (Bulgaria, 2012).
Stoyanov, Svetoslav. *The Last Black Sea Pirates* (*Poslednite Chernomorski pirati*, Bulgaria, 2014).
Tanovic, Danis. *An Episode from the Life of an Iron Picker* (*Epizoda u životu berača željeza*, Bosnia, 2013).
Todorov, Lyudmil. *The Summer Love of a Schlep* (*Lyubovnoto lyato na edin lyokhman*, Bulgaria, 1990).
Vulchanov, Rangel. *The Sun and the Shadow* (*Slantseto i syankata*, Bulgaria/Poland, 1962).
———. *Aesop* (*Ezop*, Bulgaria/Czechoslovakia, 1970).
———. *Escape to Ropotamo* (*Byagstvo v Ropotamo*, Bulgaria, 1973).
———. *Where Are You Going?* (*Za kade patuvate*, Bulgaria, 1986).
Yanchev, Vladimir. *The Ancient Coin* (*Die antike Münze*, Bulgaria/GDR, 1965).
Zakhariev, Chris. *Getting Lost on Purpose* (*Da se izgubish narochno*, Bulgaria, 2018).
Zchoche, Hermann. *Eolomea* (GDR/USSR/Bulgaria, 1972).
Zhelyazkova, Binka. *The Big Night Bath* (*Golyamoto noshtno kupane*, Bulgaria, 1980).

Part V
Toward an Eastern European Ecocinema

11

Coming to the Senses

Environmental Ethics and the Limits of Narrative in Contemporary Slovenian Cinema

Meta Mazaj

In the context of East European transitional societies, as well as that of ecocriticism, Slovenia presents an interesting and paradoxical case. In a journalistic discourse, the process of Slovenia's transition in the 1990s is typically described as a small nation success story of postsocialist democratization. After its proclamation of independence in June 1991, the country's threefold transition to national independence, political democracy, and free market economy, has been relatively smooth and peaceful. Slovenia was the first of the EU new members to join the Eurozone and Schengen area in 2004, and the first of new members to hold presidency of the EU Council in 2008. This process of transition and democratizing, coded as "cleaning up" public spaces in Eastern Europe, was closely tied to addressing environmental problems.[1] Slovenia's environmental performance is hailed as similarly successful and fully aligned with the EU environmental legislation and standards. In fact, Slovenia has been fashioned into a flagship in sustainable development in agriculture and tourism. In 2016, the country was named the first Certified Green destination in the world, and its capital city, Ljubljana, as the European Green capital, one of the first ones to be included in the "zero-waste" program. The city boasts numerous green achievements, including the ban on cars in the historical city center, the reduction of noise pollution, the launching of zero-waste retail, the increase in public parks, and the construction of environmentally friendly buildings. Various campaigns and initiatives have been launched in recent years, both on the local and state level, to affirm the country's commitment to environmental agendas in political, economic, and cultural spheres, while sustainable practices and ecotourism have been embraced as the core of the Slovenian image on a global stage. In the cultural sphere, this broader environmental agenda is mirrored in projects such as the Bled Water Film Festival, launched in 2014 in the lakeside town of Bled. The festival fashioned itself as the leading platform for connecting international government organizations, experts, activists, investors, and filmmakers with the general public in order to raise public awareness about water, and provide sustainable solutions toward water resource conservation.

This celebratory discourse surrounding sustainable development, deserving as it may be, often masks and overshadows environmental concerns that Slovenia shares with other postsocialist transition countries. Despite its profile as a tiny country yet a "giant of environmentalism," declining biodiversity, industrial pollution, excessive consumption of natural resources, growth of emissions from transit traffic, a steep rise in extreme weather events, unorganized dumps, and numerous climate change implications, are anything but negligible issues. One would be hard-pressed to find, however, traces of this giant stamp of environmentalism and its flipside—either reflected, refracted, or dismantled—in the imaginary of the country's recent cinematic output. As the editors of this volume point out, cinema is a key part of the public sphere in Eastern Europe that addresses the legacy of industrialization and postwar transformations in the region. It is an important place to register political, economic, and cultural shifts, all of which center around the region's resignified relationship to the material and natural environment. There is no shortage of films from the region, as this volume testifies, that index the effects of rapid industrialization, the decayed spaces of civilization, anxieties surrounding nuclear threat and social transformations, and landscapes as sites of buried historical memory. So how do we account for a relative absence of such works in the Slovenian cinematic landscape—especially in the realm of narrative fiction—even as there is a relatively rich tradition of environmental consciousness, as will be discussed in this chapter, in the area of multimedia, experimental, and performance art?

This apparent gap may tell us something about Slovenia's relatively privileged position in the Eastern European transitional context. Its ethnic homogeneity, developed economy, advantageous geopolitical location, and industrial structure were all factors that enabled a relatively easy and peaceful democratic consolidation and integration into the European Union, without significant traumas that have marked other former Yugoslav republics. The same can be said of its substantial strides toward environmental reforms, which have harmonized rather squarely with a European regulatory framework. A notable absence of narrative fiction films that thematize the environment (together with a similar absence of films about the war) may thus simply be a consequence of the fact that it does not warrant artistic reflection. So much of eco-cinema, after all, seems to be born out of crises, catastrophes, and a sense of urgency stemming from traumatic events, which have not significantly marked the Slovenian landscape.

This absence, however, may also tell us something about the institutional and discursive predicament of "small national cinemas" of transitional societies such as Slovenian cinema (with a population of about two million people and about ten features produced yearly over the past three decades), which have to rely on state mechanisms for its sustainability as well as legibility in a wider European context, where they occupy an invisible or at best peripheral spot. Even though Slovenian cinema has a long and unique history within the broader context of (former) Yugoslavian cinema, it emerged as a distinct national cinema only in the mid-1990s, with the founding of the Slovenian Film Center (originally Slovenian Film Fund) as the new state funding agency for film production. SFC significantly promoted the emerging new talents, backed the debut works of numerous filmmakers, increased the pace of film production (along with TV Slovenia), and contributed to an understanding of Slovenian cinema as a national cinema distinct from the former post-Yugoslav cinema, a broad umbrella under which Slovenian films were traditionally placed. For a country as small as Slovenia, where substantial private investments into film production are still difficult if not impossible to attract, not only because of the country's size but because the potential for domestic commercial return is also small, at least initial support from the national film institution is often a necessary condition before seeking additional funding from the pan-European programs.

The centrality of this institution to a sustainable small national cinema is also its problem, however, when this very institution is marked by structural weaknesses, beginning with a deplorably low production budget. Even though the Ministry of Culture recently approved a gradual increase of its national film production budget (which currently stands at €8.8 milion), and the SFC implemented various mechanisms that would result in a more sustainable and stable film environment, the average annual budget over the last decade has been €4.5 milion. This minuscule budget puts the Slovenian film industry at the very tail end of both the EU and those of former Yugoslav republics and, arguably, accounts for much of its silence. The contemporary art scene, while an active field at first glance (many exhibitions, events, festivals, performances, and multimedia events are produced every year in the visual arts), faces a similar challenge. While Slovenian artists work within the larger international frame and present their projects at biennials, festivals, and international exhibitions, the inadequate allocation of state funding for independent art and its institutions prevent them from becoming serious players in the international art system. In her review of contemporary art in Slovenia, Katja Praznik notes that after the initial period of international financial support after 1989, there was a decrease in funding that, combined with the lack of strategic cultural policies, left the new generation of artists and cultural workers without "financial means, infrastructure, and organization on a systemic level."[2]

Importantly, this institutional predicament is closely tied to a discursive one, whereby the artists' lack of national institutional support and a search for recognition in the wider context often leads to "uncritical adoption of the Western art system," the erasure or marginalization of specifically local problems, geopolitical context, or legacy.[3] The importation of Western neoliberal models into the local models, argues Praznik, not only results in commercialization and depoliticization but also results in the lack of critical reflection and "disappearance of historical memory under neo-liberalism."[4] This politics of recognition also marks the cinematic production. When Peter Stanković, in his review of the national film landscape, notes that Slovenian film "simply cannot draw enough attention if it does not play along with stereotypical Western expectations about the region as exotic and irrational Other to rational West culture," he speaks precisely about the issue of visibility that marks so many small cinemas, a struggle to narrate oneself through film without being reduced to essentializing narrative and aesthetic qualities.[5] Speaking from an ambiguous space that was redrawn as national at the very moment that it became integrated within the transnational European space, the question of self-articulation thus becomes one of enunciative position, narration, and its trappings. How to meaningfully narrate oneself, and rearticulate our specific social experience within the global reality without getting caught in a bind of either mirroring global neoliberal discourses (which will be seen as co-optation) or staging a critique of those discourses (seen as a conservative and nationalist gesture)?

If the question of narration, enunciation, and visibility is key to a small cinema such as Slovenian cinema, this very question also centers many debates on eco-cinema and the Anthropocene. When discussing a phenomenon of the recent proliferation of environmentally oriented film festivals around the world (such as the Bled Water Film Festival) and an increasing currency of eco-cinema, Paula Willoquet-Maricondi argues that, their importance notwithstanding, it is equally imperative to recognize them as part of a trend whose end result may be more about the proliferation and increased visibility of a certain kind of product, and less about a different kind of consciousness and being-in-the-world. Much of what passes as "ecocinema," she notes, frames the issues through narratives that approach the environment as merely another topical issue, and relies on familiar aesthetic and narrative paradigms that "affirm rather than challenge the culture's fundamental anthropocentric ethos."[6]

Claire Colebrook, one of the most cogent critics of the anthropocentric ethos and the posthuman predicament as expressed in popular culture, stresses that *"the* world" in the end of the world narratives is really *"a* world," a threat to man presented as a threat to a highly specific, affluent, over-consuming urban middle-class.[7] Persistently rehearsing the end of the world as the end of *this* (our) world, contemporary cinema "creates 'the human', and a single global perspective, thereby reinforcing the sense of the faux universal 'we' that also subtends climate change discourse: if 'we' are threatened then 'we' must do all we can to survive."[8] While the history of Western civilization has been built on various kinds of extinctions, enslavements, erasures of the Other, "it is suddenly by way of our imagined non-existence that the 'we' has become imperative."[9] Thus, if the global imaginary is a condition for environmental awareness, this imaginary is in fact our own cultural relativism asserted as the ultimate horizon. Implicit in Colebrook's critique of the historical imaginary that forges itself as the world, an imaginary that is crucially shaped by the institution of cinema, is "the world of a narrating and global 'we' who can look upon the loss of other worlds."[10] That is, the imaginary that is expressed in ecocinema is intimately tied with the question of narration, the ability to make meaning, to make sense of the world, and a possible collapse of this sense achieved through the stability and structure of narrativization when faced with a challenge to imagine a different relationality between the human and the world.

It is precisely this question of "a narrating and global 'we'" that I want to highlight, as a pressing question not only for the discourses surrounding the Anthropocene but also for small cinemas that speak on a global stage from the position of the margins or periphery. While one can certainly find more obvious examples of environmental cinema, especially in documentary form (such as *The Undamaged* [*Nepoškodovane*], a 2018 documentary exploring the last remaining wild rivers in the Balkan region), my interest is in ecocritical explorations in the Slovenian cultural sphere that unearth troubling layers otherwise dissolved by the mainstream discourses that address environmental issues within the global neoliberal framework. These writers, artists, and filmmakers have staged politically, ethically, and aesthetically compelling interventions into ecocritical discourses: an independent filmmaker and multimedia artist, Andrej Zdravič, whose prolific body of work explores the audiovisual aspects of natural phenomena; writer, philosopher, and critic Mojca Kumerdej with her novels *Fragma* (2003), *Dark Matter* (2011), and *Chronos' Harvest* (2016); transmedia artist Maja Smrekar with her controversial installations such as *K-9_topology* (2014-2017), and *Survival Kit for the Anthropocene—Trailer* (2014); and filmmakers such as Sonja Prosenc, whose work, rather than directly addressing environmental issues, deploys the cinematic language to disclose a different relationality between the human and the world, between environment and social landscape. That many of these artists are women highlights the importance of understanding environmental critique as part of critical analysis of deeply gendered social, political, and economic inequalities, and of the enmeshed relationship between gender and environment. Their projects all attempt to "think the unthinkable" and undo the epistemological basis that separates nature from human structure to forge a different imaginary. More importantly, because these artists are working across various media—conceptual and multimedia art, experimental video, cinema—putting them in dialogue with each other reveals how the construction of such an imaginary that goes beyond the "narrating and global 'we'" is necessarily bound with the possibilities and limitations of specific representational forms and their relationship with narration.

In one of the foundational pieces of ecocriticism, Scott MacDonald argues that the fundamental job of ecocinema is not a thematization of environmental issues but rather "a retraining of perception" and a construction of alternative media spectatorship.[11] The projects in focus here are compelling not only because they offer alternatives to the anthropocentric ethos but also because they raise important questions about the nature of representation, about how it can "retrain perception," while insisting that the way we engage with artistic representation is inextricably tied to the way we engage with the environment. If the environmental consciousness is about problematizing the common narrative of humanity, as Colebrook insists, it is also about questioning the very prerogatives and limits of narrative as a form that shapes such an imaginary. Given that the process of making sense through narrativization encloses a certain worldview based on the anthropocentric ethos, these projects are generative in that they stage the question of whether, and to what extent, different representational art forms can address the dilemma of representing the nonhuman perspective, whether they can disclose the materiality of the world in different terms—not as a site of narrativity but as an ontology outside of human narrative. Exploring both the possibilities and limitations of technologies of (human) perception to depict the nonhuman, they insist that countering the Anthropocene is a thought experiment that is both restricted within and has to reach beyond the process of narrativization.

Avant-Garde Eyes and Ears of Environmental Consciousness: The OHO Group

An important forerunner to the rise of environmentalist consciousness that posits the retraining of perception as central to such consciousness, was the Slovenian conceptual artist collective called the OHO Group, whose core members were Milenko Matanović, David Nez, Marko Pogačnik, and Andraž Šalamun.[12] The group was active in the late 1960s and early 1970s, and worked across a range of media including film, urban performance, exhibition installation, and land art projects. Their work was represented in the 2015 MoMA exhibition *Transmissions: Art in Eastern Europe and Latin America, 1960–1980*, and its significance extensively discussed by the art historian Ksenya Gurshtein.[13] Their artistic practice, varied as it was and including a range of media, overlapped with environmentalist concerns through its core premise of *reism*, whose philosophical task is to "imagine new relationships between humans and everyday objects," to liberate objects and entities from human appropriation in terms of function and sense, as boundless resources to be exploited.[14] Against the humanistic position, which implies a hierarchical relationship between a subject and a world of objects, OHO wanted to achieve "a world of things," where the distinction between things and people is erased, and where the relationship between people and things is constituted by observation, not action.[15]

Part of the group's "Summer Projects" in 1969, Matanović's *The Snake* featured sticks tied together with strings, which were then lowered into the Ljubljanica river to reveal an otherwise invisible current. In a companion piece, *Paper Path* (1969), he used a large roll of blank newsprint to accentuate the curvature of a hilly landscape outside the city. In Pogačnik's *Water-Water Dynamic* (1969) a clear plastic tube filled with pigment was placed in a riverbed facing upstream, causing the pigment to reveal the rapidity and direction of the current, while in David Nez's *Mirrors* (1969) mirrors were placed in various configurations within the landscape to break up the landscape up into fragments, and make visible what would otherwise be outside of the shot. As Gurshtein notes, OHO artists drew attention to the natural phenomena and sought to render natural forces visible beyond the human way of understanding and structuring them. Showing "a relationship between elements in both static and dynamic modes," projects such as these highlighted "the tension between the sight of the entropic natural phenomenon and the human imposition of order onto it," making both of them equally visible, as well as inextricably bound by perceptual apparatuses that give rise to systems of knowledge.[16] While studies such as Maja Fowkes's *The Green Block* (2015) connect OHO's artistic practice to the rise of environmental consciousness in the 1960s counterculture, it is important to emphasize that their interest was not to thematize environmental concerns within the preexistent perceptive and cognitive paradigms. Instead, their work argues that human order and modes of thought are closely intertwined with technologies of perception, and that this entanglement is at the core of our relationship with the environment, where we are always positioned on the outside looking in or at it—in other words, "having the world" rather than "being-in-the-world." Perhaps the fact that the OHO Group abandoned their artistic practice and the institutional art world, and founded a commune on an abandoned farm in the village of Šempas, desiring to establish a deeper, alternative relationship with the environment, speaks as much to the zeitgeist of the 1960s as it does to the very limits of representational art in expressing the materiality and agency of the world using technologies bound by human perception and sense-making.

The Experimental Ecocinema of Andrej Zdravič

Using video and multimedia installation as his preferred medium to explore a different relationality between the human and the world, Andrej Zdravič is discussed by both Willoquet-Maricondi and MacDonald as an artist whose work is engaged in the retraining of perception. Zdravič boasts a prolific body of work, but his forty-one-minute experimental video *Riverglass: A River Ballet in Four Seasons* (*V steklu reke*, 1997), part of a multiscreen video installation called *Secrets of Soča* (*Skrivnosti Soče*, 1995), has been hailed as one of the most important works illustrating cinema's potential to mediate experiences of natural phenomena. MacDonald and Willoquet-Maricondi showcase it as a noteworthy example of ecocinema in that it does not make the environment into an "issue," nor is it polemical or political. Instead it reframes our experience of representation of nature by challenging our way of seeing and experiencing real and filmic time, thereby opening up a thought space that restructures our relationship with the natural world. Shot over a period of four years with a contraption Zdravič devised himself, the film submerges the camera in the Alpine river Soča (an important national treasure in the Triglav National Park, considered to be one of the most beautiful rivers in Europe) to capture its changing flow through the passing of seasons. On his website, Zdravič asserts that *Riverglass* is not a documentary about the river Soča, but "a poetic river ballet to the music of natural sounds," meant to capture "the magical underwater world of turquoise volumes, flying bubbles, pulsating sun membranes, dancing stones, droplets of snow."[17] Zdravič avoids both the imposition of human narration and the sweeping landscape vistas that define many nature films—an approach that the river Soča, and Soča Valley more broadly, with its distinct emerald color and pristine beauty, would easily lend itself to. The film instead immerses itself in the flow of the river, from within the river, through the span of four seasons, focusing our attention on nothing but its flow, texture, changing levels, and sounds. At the same time, the film, as well as the multiscreen installation it is a part of, also foregrounds the constructed nature of the image by often making visible the technology of recording itself—the glass box that holds the camera, which reveals itself depending on the water level—and the nature of the multiscreen installation that lays bare the framing and linear sequencing of the image. *Riverglass* thus "asks us to see the river in its own terms, not in ours; to experience the river for itself, not for what resources it can provide us," and both exposes and challenges our conditioned relationship to space, time, and narrative.[18]

Undoubtedly, the nature of the medium he is working with, the open aesthetic framework of experimental film and installation art, allows Zdravič to undo the spatial, temporal, and narrative structures that define our perception. From the unique editing rhythm that follows the river's flow and varied water levels; the immersed camera that denies the centered monocular perspective and constructs a more fluid, dispersed, and molecular nature of the image; the unique sonic structure based on the soundtrack of recorded underwater; and the extended duration of the shots that demand sustained attention, the film creates the conditions for a different kind of relationship to the material world. The images here engage with the viewer on the level of affect rather than narration. By undoing the dichotomy between river as object and human as subject, by shifting our own position in relation to the environment, the film not only readjusts our perception but becomes an expression of "being-in-nature." All the while, through the provocative self-reflexivity in moments where the glass barrier between the water and the video camera becomes visible and exposes the process of recording, in addition to the self-reflexivity of the installation that stages a spatial and temporal encounter between the viewer and the images, the film evokes the "collision of natural process and industrial technology."[19] Far from unmediated, the relationship between the human, technological, and natural worlds is revealed as tightly tethered, with the technological perceptual apparatus occupying a central role in both expanding/retraining and limiting/framing our way of seeing and being.

Performing the Limits of Anthropocene: Maja Smrekar's *K-9_topology*

The dilemma of how to deploy both visual and narrative strategies to constitute a different relationality between the human and the world is pushed directly onto the gendered critique of the Anthropocene in the work of Slovenian intermedia artist Maja Smrekar. Her work can be seen in tandem with the tradition of performance art in the region—most famously represented by Marina Abramović—that uses the body as the medium. Merging Western mythology, technological practices, and bioethics to rethink the human being's superior position within the ecosystem and the promises of biotechnological practices, Smrekar performs "the extimacy on the border between nature and culture, between the internal and the external," between human and nonhuman.[20] Her work posits these boundaries as the core of the Anthropocene, and their dissolution as a source of threat, outrage, and "repulsion," but also a possible prospect of a nonanthropocentric world.[21]

Smrekar's most controversial work, the four-part series *K-9_topology* project, was carried out between 2014 and 2017 in cooperation with scientists and technologists. In the first part, called *Ecce Canis*, she thematizes the parallel evolution between humans, wolves, and dogs by showing how through their mutual coexistence, humans and dogs have both developed a neurotransmitter responsible for sociability. Rather than relying on visual or verbal strategies to depict this coexistence, she synthesized her own serotonin and combined it with that of her dog Byron to transform it into an odor that permeated a gallery installation of wolf skins—along with the lab equipment used to conduct the experiment—where the visitors could "smell" the scent of the human-dog alliance. The second project, *I Chase Nature and Culture Chases Me*, took place at JACANA Wildlife Studios in France, where Smrekar was collaborating with animal ethologists and developing a relationship with wolves. Her performance, laying naked on the floor, covered in grease and starch while two wolves sniffed and licked her, was juxtaposed with her childhood memory of living with dogs, and the performance art works of Joseph Beuys and Oleg Kulik (whose whole artistic opus is based on human coexistence with dogs). The

Figure 11.1. Maja Smrekar's *ARTE_mis* installation, part of the *K-9 topology* project. Screen capture by Meta Mazaj from the artist's website.

third part of the project, *Hybrid Family*, was conceived more as a tableau vivant: Smrekar prepared her body using a special diet and a breast pump stimulation to trigger the production of colostrum to be able to breastfeed a dog. Countering the anthropocentric vision of a human, where the human occupies the top of the evolutionary pyramid, the attempt of the *Hybrid Family* attempts to equalize the human and the animal, as well as to demystify the social and ideological instrumentalization of the female body. In the final part of the project, *ARTE_mis* (in reference to the Greek goddess of hunt usually depicted with dog companions), Smrekar fused her own cellular material with that of her dog Ada, using the IVF (in vitro fertilization) technology to produce a kind of "frozen in the process" hybrid that forced the question of "the dangerously troubled multispecies world," and "traditional humanist limitations" in order "to embrace the risks that becoming other-than-human entails."[22]

The installation that shows this hybridization, the petri dish with the magnifying glass, is conceived as an allegorical space that includes all her previous projects and points toward as-yet-nonexistent (or perhaps already extinct) species and intertwining temporalities: future, in that the hybrid species and technology it involves do not yet exist, and past, in that this hybrid species of "wolf-man" (or wolverine) is firmly embedded in the mythology of many cultures, often used to sanction those who are labeled "different." The magnifying glass, a scientific tool through which we observe the world, foregrounds the world itself as an entity molded into a particular perspective. Smrekar's installation—a mother's rocking chair, a window overlaid with fur-covered leather skin, her childhood pictures on the wall, and the lab equipment used in the experiment, among other things—stage the mise-en-scène that ultimately intertwines various kinds of stories: that of her childhood, mythological stories, the master narratives of the humanities and their technological and biopolitical underpinnings. However, this mise-en-scène also points outside itself by both calling attention to the technologically mediated and constructed nature of our human vision of the world, and by redirecting this perception to the hybrid cell as a possible beginning of new (posthuman) life that is organized around a different set of values. This "story" or vision, it suggests, is intertwined with, but cannot be contained or framed within, the limits of existing human narratives.

Coming to the Senses in Narrative Cinema: Sonja Prosenc's *The Tree* (*Drevo*)

While the open aesthetic framework of experimental video and performance art, as in the case of Zdravič and Smrekar, may lend itself more easily to a critique of narrativization, such critique is more difficult to accomplish with a narrative fiction film, a representational form predicated on structures of narrativization. The construction of ontology outside of human narrativity is thus a particularly challenging task for narrative cinema, since its very form, no matter how open and fluid, maintains human agency at the center of cognitive, sense-making processes. It is important, therefore, to highlight filmmakers who take on this challenge within the realm of narrative film. *The Tree* (*Drevo*, 2014), Slovenian director Sonja Prosenc's debut feature film—which premiered at the East of the West section at Karlovy Vary and garnered several international festival awards—is remarkable in that it mounts a critique of the imaginary that is contained by various human structures: nuclear family, nation, as well as narration. The environment becomes a central character in the film that indexes trauma, a disavowal of knowledge, fear, and a painful retreat from material and social reality. At the same time, it also discloses the need for a different, relational understanding between the self and environment.

The Tree is a story about a family of three—widowed mother Milena, her teenage son Alek, and nine-year-old Veli—who are forced to stay in their house under mysterious and evasive circumstances, surrounded by a large concrete wall, seemingly threatened by the outside community. The film is organized in three chapters that constitute three points of view ("Veli," "Milena," and "Alek"), which seem to offer a clear organizational structure and construct at least a semblance of puzzle pieces that, once put together, cohere to complete the puzzle and offer provisional answers to the *who*, *what*, and *why*. However, in the film, this organizational structure and the common narrative prerogatives—the storyline itself, the reasons leading to the exile that would motivate the cause-and-effect logic and the linearity of the drama (it is eventually revealed that Alek is implicated in the tragic accident that led to his friend's death, a conflict that seems compounded by an ethnic dimension since this is an Albanian family living in Slovenia), as well as the role of dialogue—all remain secondary to the film's texture and meaning. Beyond its story of a fractured nuclear family confined to their barren home due to their fear of external, unidentified danger, the film's grounding in the affective, elemental, and psychological, rather than narrative, vectors discloses a vision that stages a potent critique of familial and social bonds, and points to the Anthropocene as a process of recognition, a threshold concept that exposes oneself to the inextricable enmeshment between the self and the environment.

The tension between rigid yet fractured structures (family bonds, relationship with the Other, but also the dictates of storytelling and narrativity) and a desire for a different kind of relationality is set up by the very first scene. The film's opening shot, a medium close-up of the boy Veli, peering out through a hole in a wall, is followed by a slow tracking shot that scans the rich green foliage of the titular tree, as if from within the tree, the wind toying with the leaves and branches that envelop the visual horizon and evoke an open, boundless environment. This shot, which serves both as a point-of-view shot and an expression of desire, is followed by another close-up tracking shot of Veli riding his bicycle. As the camera slowly pans out, the openness and the forward momentum implied by the bicycle ride and the tracking camera movement is revealed as walled-in, enclosed, and circular, mirroring the perceptual limitations of the opening shot's peeping hole. The open environment, movement, and vibrancy invoked by the tracking shot is undermined as such both by the tall concrete wall that circumscribes Veli's movements and the perceptual apparatus of the camera lens depicting it. As Veli gets off the bike to pick up a dead bird on the ground, next to a flower pot with a dead plant, the barren, desertlike ground, the depleted nature of the white wall surrounding the property, mirrored by the grayish sky, imbue the scene with an uncomfortable affect—not so much a concrete emotion but an unexplainable and negative affect of death, dread, depletion, and claustrophobia. Clearly, the fact that the family is confined, that they cannot and are afraid

Figure 11.2. An inhospitable, desertlike environment imbues the film with a discomforting affect. *The Tree* (*Drevo*). Directed by Sonja Prosenc. Ljubljana: Monoo, Nuframe, Staragara Productions, and RTV Slovenia, 2014. Screen capture by Meta Mazaj.

to go out, that what is *outside* is threatening—threatening also because it is unknown—is firmly established, and it is this affect that will haunt the rest of the film, more than the question of what led to it.

Interestingly, however, the concept of what is considered "inside" and "outside" is questioned from the very beginning. The threat is constituted not by the inside/outside paradigm but by the very impossibility of delimiting the space as either this or that. The indoor space of the house, while seemingly offering a safe refuge from the external threat, is as barren and depleted as the outside. As if not lived in, it is sparsely furnished, bland, impersonal, washed out, ambiguous, and ungraspable. Neither space is fully inhabited or depicted, and if the outside is presented as an existential threat, the inside of the house seems to offer no respite or refuge from it. The house, the locus that shelters and nurtures the nuclear family, is here depicted as a space that does not have a location, and is as unfathomable and as uninhabitable as the outside space. The fundamental feature of the film's images is thus an impossibility of secure perspective, unreadability in terms of the question of the scale of space and time, where the material landscape is inseparable from the unboundedness of the psychic space. There is no "it" to confront, to delimit, to fix, or to tackle. The film is thus a constant evocation of space and environment without a stable depiction of the space that—because it is not depictable or intelligible—becomes threatening. It is outside of the system, outside of meaning, and therefore marked by a negative affective value.

The film's emphasis on the negative affective value of the environment—which coexists with a desire for a different relationality between ourselves and the world—exposes what Sarah Ahmed describes as "the stickiness" of affect that informs the connection between values and objects.[23] To be affected by something, to give value to things, "is to shape what is near us," to be open to the incorporation of things into our near sphere.[24] Says Ahmed, "awayness might help establish the edges of our horizon; in rejecting the proximity of certain objects, we define the places that we know we do not wish to go, the things we do not wish to have, touch, taste, hear, feel, see, those things we do not wish to keep within reach."[25] If positive affect is about an orientation toward objects we come into proximity with, that means that atmosphere, environment, is "always already angled" and felt from a specific point of view.[26] To embrace objects thus means an orientation toward those objects as being good. In Prosenc's film, it is precisely this stickiness of affect that is foregrounded, rather than a tangible, concrete external threat. It is not so much that the outside presents the threat, but rather that the affect, the existential angst and fear (hosted by the trauma of the nuclear family/nation), already angles the environment as felt from a specific point of view. The environment is depleted, inhospitable, and unsafe not because it hosts threatening elements—whether these are an ethnic Other or the environment more generally—but because the orientation toward it is shaped by fear and isolation.

Grounded in the affective and elemental, the camera, rather than focusing on "events" or actions that motivate the characters, lingers on objects that constitute the environment, forming a world where human narrative is necessarily intertwined with the narrative of matter itself. The dead bird, the plant, the tree, the concrete wall, the bedroom curtains, are things that construct the characters' environment, but not as a backdrop to their own story or as a vessel to be filled with their actions. Instead, they are endowed with their own agency and materiality—their own "story" that is intensely felt yet unknowable, and therefore discomforting. The materiality of things themselves forms what Serenella Iovino and Servil Oppermann describe as "storied matter," where agency "is not to be necessarily and exclusively associated with human beings and with human intentionality, but is a pervasive and inbuilt property of matter, as part and parcel of its generative dynamism."[27] While the question of "whodunit" certainly informs the film's story, the core challenge of its visual and aural aesthetic is to disclose the legibility of the material world without reducing it to a site of human narrativity. If the world's material phenomena, as Iovino and Oppermann say, are "knots in a vast network of agencies, which can be 'read' and interpreted as forming narratives, stories," then Prosenc posits her cinematic images as an ambiguous medium whose revelation of the world's material phenomena may bring them into our proximity yet renders them unintelligible.[28] They are material narratives that cannot be contained and always reach beyond the filmic narrative.

This ambivalence and tension that result from the collision of intimacy and nearness with alterity and awayness structure both the film's fear and desire. Since for most of the film the origin of the fear and uncertainty is not assigned any scale, and we do not know where it is coming from, the need for shelter and isolation increases, but so does the urgency to face the threat. Veli's older brother's persistent commands—"Leave the curtain closed!" "Get away from the window!" and "Go into the house!"—are in constant tension with Veli's desire to go out, to climb a tree, to climb over the wall, *to be in the world*. The environment is what threatens, what is inhospitable, but it is also what beckons and invites. It is through Veli, who possesses curiosity and an urge to know and exist in the world, that the intense desire for a different relationality is expressed, embodied in the titular image of the lush tree, full of life and vibrancy, and several successive images that show Veli's attempts to infuse his world with color (for example, he spreads blue paint on their white goat, who otherwise blends in, and thus dissolves, with the color of the wall).

One of Veli's favorite preoccupations is incessant counting—counting the cracks on the wall, the number of steps from one side of the wall to the next—and each time he counts a bit further along, as if desperate to measurably enlarge the boundaries of his existence and be inserted into a broader temporality. One night, Veli, unable to fall asleep, begins to tell his mother a story; the story is told in a voice-over, while he remains still in the frame, with his mouth closed, his gaze shifting between the camera and his mother. He tells of a house in the field that stood there for so long that time vanished from it. The boy wanted to find this lost time, so he counted everything he could, but every day was just the same day, the same night, and the boy stayed the same age. So one day he decided to leave in an attempt to find time. In this story, leaving, going out, is posited as a demand for a higher, unpredictable level of self-reflection, which may result in death (after all, the tree in the film is also the site of the original trauma that causes the family's imprisonment and his brother's demise), but it also sustains life, identity, and relationality. It expresses an imaginary that confronts the fear, the constraints of the familial, and our forms of dwelling in the world, and urges for a different relationality with the environment. This alternative relationality is about the ability to neighbor the Other, but in this film neighboring the Other is also posited as neighboring nature, exposing oneself to the inextricable relation between ourselves and our surroundings.

Intertwining the material with the social, perceptual, and psychological, *The Tree* thus insists that the environment is neither a backdrop for human activity nor a safe shelter. It gestures toward both the difficulty and necessity of a relational understanding between the self and the Other, which is posited as an ethical stance toward alterity, toward one's surroundings, toward the material world. In this way, the film not only offers a different understanding of the elemental and agentic forces outside of ourselves, but also points to the possibility of a narrative fiction film to open itself up to the world, to imagine a different ontology, one that operates outside narrative paradigms that rely on possession and mastery of the world through narrativizing it. As Simon Estok argues, coping with the material agency of the world is "the business of maintaining boundaries and, indeed, of maintaining discursive control."[29] To frame a visual aesthetic that captures material agency within the boundaries of a narrative is precisely an attempt to maintain this discursive control over something that is beyond the scope of familiar discourses, to contain the threat of loss of predictability and agency. To impose a stable map onto a film, either visual or narrative, is to deny the fact that landscape and environment are not reducible to manageable property. Prosenc instead emphasizes materiality and affect, which, as Graig Uhlig argues, is always environmental, and resists the stability and structure of narrativization.[30] Her resistance to spatial and narrative mapping posits the cinematic as grounded precisely in the loss of discursive control and limits of representation, which in turn exposes oneself to the inextricable, enmeshed relation between the self and the environment. The great value of the film is that Prosenc uses a fictional narrative—a form more constricted by a "narrative burden" than intermedia art or experimental video—to emancipate the film from the very conditions that delineate its formal possibilities, and exposes those conditions as the core of our troubled narrative of humanity.

That all of the projects discussed here foreground the question of narrative mapping from the perspective of different representational art forms is important not only for our conception of eco-cinema but also for our understanding of the relative (in)visibility of small cinema on a global stage—an issue certainly driving this volume. All these projects come from a small national context, but while the work of Maja Smrekar and Andrej Zdravič echoes strongly in the wider international art sphere (Zdravič's work especially is widely known and discussed in ecocinema scholarship), Sonja Prosenc's work, remarkable as it is and recognized at several international film festivals, has not received a similar kind of critical attention. More than the problem of an individual artist, I believe, this dynamic reveals something about institutional and discursive practices that put pressure on a film narrative to perform the task of "national allegory." In many respects, *The Tree* could be seen as a typical example of art house cinema from New Europe: partially financed by the Slovenian public and private funds, transnationally coproduced, and framed within the art cinema idiom. Nevertheless, it diverges significantly from art house narratives that work more clearly with recognizable, issue-driven stories, and thus gain better visibility on the radar of world cinema (in the context of Slovenian cinema, the films of Damjan Kozole, for example, which address human trafficking, prostitution, and the criminal underworld—issues that translate rather smoothly into a familiar signifier for "genuine" descriptions of transitional societies such as Slovenia). The relative visibility of such narratives points to the extent to which the pressure of a normative narrative of post-1989 collapse of communism and the transition to liberal democracy and capitalism is naturalized and hardened into the very structure of the cinematic environment. It is therefore imperative, as we examine various aspects of the intersection between environmental and Eastern European cinema, to ponder the burden of film narrative—one that *The Tree* carries as well as attempts to unwrap itself from—to capture the essence of national cinema in order to gain visibility.

Meta Mazaj is Senior Lecturer in Cinema Studies at University of Pennsylvania. Her writings on critical theory, new European cinema, Eastern European cinema, and contemporary world cinema have appeared in edited volumes and journals such as *Cineaste, Studies in Eastern European Cinema,* and *Situations*. She is the author of *Once Upon A Time There Was A Country: National and Cynicism in the Post-1990s Balkan Cinema* (2008), coeditor, with Timothy Corrigan and Patricia White, of *Critical Visions in Film Theory: Classic and Contemporary Readings* (2010), and coauthor, with Shekhar Deshpande, of *World Cinema: A Critical Introduction* (2018).

Notes

1. Pavlínek and Pickles, *Environmental Transitions*, 6.
2. Praznik, "A Short Guide."
3. Ibidem.
4. Ibidem.
5. Stanković, "A Small Cinema," 53.
6. Willoquet-Maricondi, "Shifting Paradigms," 47.
7. Colebrook, "Cinemas and Worlds," 39.

8. Idem., 39–40.
9. Idem., 40.
10. Colebrook, "Slavery and the Trumpocene," 44.
11. MacDonald, "Toward an Eco-Cinema," 109.
12. The group's name, OHO, has both local and global connotations. It is a neologism deriving from the Slovenian words for "eye" (*oko*) and "ear" (*uho*), but can also serve as in interjection of surprise or shock.
13. Gurshtein, "The OHO Group."
14. Ibidem.
15. Zabel, "Art in Slovenia."
16. Gurshtein, "The OHO Group."
17. Zdravič, "*Andrej Zdravič.*"
18. Willoquet-Maricondi, "Shifting Paradigms," 52.
19. MacDonald, "Toward an Eco-Cinema," 114.
20. Kumerdej, "Inner Edges."
21. Smrekar's work and its conflicted reception interestingly stages our relationship with the abject as discussed by Julia Kristeva (see *The Powers of Horror*). Mainstream responses to her art that express shock and disapproval, labeling her work as degenerative, disgusting, and morally deplorable, can be understood as the very reaction to the abject and pose interesting questions about the relationship between ethics and artistic practice.
22. Haraway, *Staying with the Trouble*, 6; Herbrechter, "The Posthuman," 2.
23. Ahmed, "Happy Objects," 30.
24. Idem., 31.
25. Idem., 32.
26. Idem., 37.
27. Iovino and Oppermann, "Introduction," 3.
28. Idem., 1.
29. Estok, "Painful Material Realities," 133.
30. Uhlig. "Feeling Depleted: Ecocinema and the Atmospherics of Affect."

Bibliography

Ahmed, Sara. "Happy Objects." In *Affect Theory Reader*, edited by Melissa Gregg and Gregory J. Seigworth, 30–51. Durham, NC: Duke University Press, 2010.

Braidotti, Rosi. *The Post-Human*. Oxford: Polity Press, 2013.

Colebrook, Claire. "Slavery and the Trumpocene: It's Not the End of the World." *The Oxford Literary Review* 41, no. 1 (2019): 40–50.

———. "Cinemas and Worlds." *Diacritics* 45, no. 1 (2017): 25–48.

Estok, Simon. "Painful Material Realities, Tragedy, Ecophobia." In *Material Ecocriticism*, edited by Serenella Iovino and Servil Oppermann, 130–140. Bloomington: Indiana University Press, 2014.

Fowkes, Maja. *The Green Block: Neo-Avant-Garde Art and Ecology under Socialism*. New York: Central European University Press, 2015.

Gurshtein, Ksenya. "The OHO Group, 'Information,' and Global Conceptualism avant la lettre." *Post: Notes on Modern and Contemporary Art Around the Globe* (2016). https://post.at.moma.org/content_items/850-part-1-the-oho-group-in formation-and-global-conceptualism-avant-la-lettre. Accessed 10 November 2019.

Haraway, Donna J. *Staying with the Trouble: Making Kin in the Chthulucene*. Durham, NC: Duke University Press, 2016.

Herbrechter, Stefan. "The Posthuman (2013) by Rosi Raidotti." *Culture Machine* (2012). https://culturemachine.net/wp-content/uploads/2019/05/495-1102-1-PB.pdf.

Iovino, Serenella, and Servil Oppermann. "Introduction: Stories Come to Matter." In *Material Ecocriticism*, edited by Serenella Iovino and Servil Oppermann, 1–17. Bloomington: Indiana University Press, 2014.

Kristeva, Julia, *Powers of Horror: An Essay on Abjection*. New York: Columbia University Press, 1982.

Kumerdej, Mojca. "Inner Edges and Borders of Culture." *Internationale Online* (14 May 2018). https://www.internationaleonline.org/research/politics_of_life_and_death/100_inner_edges_and_borders_of_culture. Accessed 10 November 2019.

MacDonald, Scott. "Toward an Eco-Cinema." *Interdisciplinary Studies in Literature and Environment* 11, no. 2 (2004): 107–132.

Pavlínek, Petr, and John Pickles. *Environmental Transitions: Transformation and Ecological Defense in Central and Eastern Europe*. New York: Routledge, 2000.

Praznik, Katja. "A Short Guide to Contemporary Art in Slovenia." *ArtMargins Online*. 6 January 2010. https://artmargins.com/short-guide-contemporary-art-slo venia-short-guide-seriesq-article/. Accessed 18 June 2020.

Stanković, Peter. "A Small Cinema from the Other Side of the Alps: A Historical Overview of Slovenian Films." *Film History* 24 (2012): 35–55.

Uhlig, Graig. "Feeling Depleted: Ecocinema and the Atmospherics of Affect." In *Affective Ecocriticism: Emotion, Embodiment, Environment*, edited by Kyle Bladow and Jennifer Ladino, 279–297. Lincoln: University of Nebraska Press, 2018.

Willoquet-Maricondi, Paula. "Shifting Paradigms: From Environmentalist Films to Ecocinema." In *Framing the World: Explorations in Ecocritcism and Film*, edited by Paula Wolloquet-Maricondi, 43–61. Charlottesville: University of Virginia Press, 2010.

Zabel, Igor. "Art in Slovenia since 1945." *Artsmidwest: Heartland Project*. 2007. http://web.archive.org/web/20070818053648/http://www.artsmw.org/heartlandproj ect/aspects/essays/zabel.html. Accessed 10 November 2019.

Zdravič, Andrej. *Andrej Zdravič: Riverglass*. 2019. http://andrejzdravic.com/films/independent-films/riverglass. Accessed 10 November 2019.

Filmography

Avguštin, Miha, Matic Oblak, and Rožle Bregar. *The Undamaged* (*Nepoškodovane*, Slovenia, 2018).

Prosenc, Sonja. *The Tree* (*Drevo*, Slovenia, 2014).

Zdravič, Andrej. *Riverglass: A River Ballet in Four Seasons* (*V steklu reke*, Slovenia, 1997).

12

Cinema of the Forest People
From Environmental Consciousness Toward Ecocritical Perspectives in Polish (Post)communist Film

Kris Van Heuckelom

When Poland hosted the United Nations climate summit in December 2018, it was difficult for foreign observers not to comment ironically upon the fact that the Polish "coal capital" Katowice had been chosen as the conference venue. At the same time, as if it were to detract attention from the country's continued dependence on carbon-intensive electricity and energy, the Polish presidency of the summit put considerable effort into foregrounding the crucial role of (re)forestation in reducing the global impact of greenhouse gas emissions (most notably by preparing a "Ministerial Declaration on Forests for the Climate"). At closer investigation, the local organizers' strong preoccupation with forest conservation profoundly resonates with the natural and cultural realities of the host country: not only do forested areas and woodland reserves take up almost one-third of the Polish territory; they have also come to occupy a prominent place in Polish cultural geography and memory, even to the extent that forests have been labeled "a proxy of the Polish nation."[1] Its perhaps most iconic manifestation is the Białowieża Forest located at the border with Belarus, a UNESCO-protected site of natural heritage that has recently become the object of a fierce dispute between the government in Warsaw and the EU Court of Justice in Luxembourg.[2]

Drawing further on the seminal role of forests and woodlands in Polish culture and cultural memory, this chapter seeks to explore the emergence of ecocritical accents in the country's recent cinematic output. At the core of the analysis will be a (con)textual discussion of two post-1989 Polish-language feature films that are set in—more or less remote—forested areas, namely Grzegorz Królikiewicz's *Trees* (*Drzewa*, 1995) and Agnieszka Holland's *Spoor* (*Pokot*, 2017). As I will argue throughout the chapter, the two films under scrutiny mark the gradual transition from anthropocentric (and nation-centered) views of environmental protection toward nonhuman-centered (and transnational) perspectives, especially when it comes to the on-screen representation of typical forest-set activities such as logging and hunting. By way of contextualization, however, this chapter begins with a short historical excursion into the various meanings and functions associated with the "native" woodland, in Polish culture at large and in Polish cinema in particular.

The Polish "Woodland Myth" from Adam Mickiewicz's *Sir Thaddeus* (1834) to Władysław Ślesicki's *Summer of the Forest People* (1985)

Although notable references to the forest in Polish culture can be found as early as in the Renaissance period, the "woodland myth" received its modern shape only after the Polish partitions of the late eighteenth century (when the country disappeared from the European map). One of its primary instigators was the exiled Romantic poet Adam Mickiewicz, whose nostalgia-laden *Sir Thaddeus or the Last Foray in Lithuania: A Story of Life among Polish Gentlefolk in the Years 1811 and 1812 in Twelve Books* (*Pan Tadeusz, czyli ostatni zajazd na Litwie: historia szlachecka z roku 1811 i 1812 we dwunastu księgach wierszem*, 1834) features an elaborate depiction of the mysterious woodlands of the lost home country: within the narrative frame of an engaging hunting scene, Mickiewicz's epic poem portrays the inner parts of the primeval forest as a "sylvan paradise" of sorts.[3] Other partitions-era works of art—such as Artur Grottger's black-and-white drawings devoted to the anti-Russian uprising of 1863–1864—helped disseminate images of the "native" forest in its various guises, not only as a place of refuge and shelter against foreign oppression, but also as a battlefield and a place of mourning. The semantic ambivalence surrounding forested areas in Polish culture extended well into the twentieth century, when new forms of clandestine resistance against foreign—Russian and German—rule and aggression reactivated the myth of the forest, as a *locus amoenus* and a *locus terribilis* alike.

As a quintessential twentieth-century medium, cinema has had a considerable part in the perpetuation and reconfiguration of these tropes. In one of the very few scholarly articles devoted to the subject, Alicja Kisielewska argues that "the motif of the forest has been used in Polish filmmaking from its early beginnings, mainly as a landscape that offers the backdrop against which heroes are shown or events take place."[4] In all its vagueness, Kisielewska's statement captures well the anthropocentric character of forest portrayals in Polish cinema, many of which may be said to navigate between collective and personal levels of human experience. Its varying parameters may be aptly described by looking into the rich afterlife of one of the most popular "forest books" ever written in Polish, namely Maria Rodziewiczówna's novel *Summer of the Forest People* (*Lato leśnych ludzi*, 1920). Revolving around the initiation of a city boy—under the guidance of three experienced "forest people"—into the (dis)comfort of living and working in the wilderness, the book had numerous reissues throughout the twentieth century and eventually received a screen adaptation in the mid-1980s (directed by Władysław Ślesicki).

Divided into five episodes that loosely follow the structure of the literary source text, the TV version of the book transplants the action from interwar Poland to the People's Republic of the 1980s and ostentatiously reflects the global rise of environmental awareness from the 1970s onward (not the least behind the Iron Curtain). Time and again, the young protagonist's summertime stay at a remote forester's lodge—far away from modern technology and machinery—is set in contrast with the harmful and reckless behavior of car- and motorcycle-driving city dwellers (some of whom, apart from causing environmental and noise pollution, also engage in poaching activities).[5] At the same time, the serial's prominent focus on various forms of small-scale pollution in a state-protected woodland reserve may be said to draw attention away from the large-scale environmental degradation and atmospheric pollution that had been inflicted by the communist project of industrial modernization.[6] What is more, Ślesicki's adaptation offers a very interesting example of how Polish cultural practices have tended to conflate the issue of forest protection and cultivation with various forms of memory management—or "forest mythopraxis," as this cultural paradigm has been aptly called by Agata Agnieszka Konczal.[7] In the concluding fifth episode, the young boy's initiation culminates in a long-awaited encounter with the legendary Polish partisan Odrowąż (who turns out to be his grandfather). The close link between ecological awareness and the remembrance of wartime resistance is reinforced on the level of montage, as the TV series combines the aestheticizing impulse characteristic of wildlife documentaries with repeated flashbacks to the underground partisan struggle during World War II. As a result, in spite of the environmental consciousness that obviously permeates *Summer of the Forest People*, Ślesicki's work "affirms, rather than challenges, the culture's fundamental anthropocentric ethos."[8]

At the opposite side of the spectrum of anthropocentric perspectives, one could situate another literary adaptation that came out in the twilight years of state socialism, namely Witold Leszczyński's 1985 reworking of Edward Stachura's cult novel *Axiliad, or the Winter of the Forest People (Siekierezada, albo zima leśnych ludzi)*. The story centers around Stachura's literary alter ego Janek Pradera, a lonesome wanderer who takes up seasonal work as a logger in a remote Polish village. Both the soundtrack and the camerawork of the film serve to showcase the snow-covered woodland as a sacred space of sorts where the horizontal (earth) and the vertical (heaven) meet. Along these lines, the forest's firmly established role as a witness to national history and a bearer of collective memory gives way here to a very personal story of existential despair and metaphysical longing, in which the surrounding hibernal nature appears to mirror the inner landscape of the human soul. Importantly, although the tender Pradera puts much effort into bonding with the local "forest people," he continues to long for his lost beloved one (whom he usually calls "Gałązka Jabłoni," or "Twig of the Apple Tree") and ultimately ends his life by jumping under a train that passes through the forest. In keeping with the countercultural and existentialist spirit of Stachura's poetic prose, Leszczyński's film decidedly moves away from nation-centered forms of "forest mythopraxis" and memory management, although the overall narrative perspective is unmistakably anthropocentric. Quite symbolically, the closing sequence of *Axiliad* does not show Pradera's suicide itself, but ends with a shot of a falling pine tree, which adds to the strong (poetical) identification between the predicament of man and that of inanimate nature.

Bringing Down the Forest: Grzegorz Królikiewicz's *Trees* (1995)

If ecocriticism—as Pietari Kääpä reminds us—"approaches humanity as part of the diversity of the ecosystem, on par with all the other organisms and processes that comprise its complex structures," then its untimely appearance in Polish cinema should be related to a film production from the early postcommunist period that has largely remained unnoticed until today, namely Grzegorz Królikiewicz's experimental feature project *Trees* (1995).[9] Partly financed by the Provincial Fund for Environmental Protection in Łódź, the film offers a very loosely organized story set in the immediate surroundings of a seaside forest. The female protagonist is a heavily pregnant scientist (Ewa) who uses a well-equipped laboratory in the garden next to her house to conduct extreme neuropsychological experiments on plants and juvenile trees. With the aid of a sophisticated oscilloscope, the woman manages to register and analyze the plants' varying responses to experiences of torture, pain, and affection, which makes her increasingly aware of their humanlike dispositions. For the purpose of these experiments, Ewa closely collaborates with an authoritative professor of the Academy of Sciences (played by Leon Niemczyk), with whom she has coauthored a book under the telling title *Stepmother Earth* (*Macocha Ziemia*). As the woman's elderly supervisor and superior, Niemczyk's character fashions himself as a Faust-like figure who shamelessly manipulates the outcome of her scientific research, for his own benefit and glory. Tellingly, the professor makes his first on-screen appearance in a TV broadcast during which he warns the viewers of the "dangerous and expansive psyche of plants" and their "destructive force." In a narrative setup replete with references to the book of Genesis and the story of the Fall, he comes to embody a proto-Darwinian view of nature that propagates destructive competition with other life forms and species—rather than mutual empathy and coadaptation—in order to secure the privileged (God-like) position of humanity. The professor's "venomous" character is exemplified by a huge snake wrapped around his neck and by the conspicuous appearance—on the wall of the TV studio set—of three chemical formulas that refer to poisonous substances (arsenic trioxide, hydrogen cyanide, and potassium cyanide).

Another narrative thread in *Trees* centers around Ewa's husband Paweł, a dedicated biology teacher actively engaged in protecting the local woodland. The storyline takes an increasingly dramatic turn, however, when two people get crushed under a falling tree, as a result of which a herd of enraged locals, armed with axes and chainsaws, turns itself against the defenseless plants. Significantly, whereas Paweł eventually switches sides and takes part in the violent "revenge" on the "dangerous" trees, his wife firmly dissociates herself from the anti-ecological stance of her academic supervisor and his hubristic manipulations. Right after her final encounter with the professor, she leaves behind the artificial setup of her lab and makes her first diegetic appearance in the nearby forest, in a sequence of shot reverse shots that seem to establish a mystical bond between the heavily pregnant woman and the surrounding trees. This connection comes full circle when we see her going into labor on the floor of the now empty lab, while shifting oscilloscopic lines give visual form to her suffering. Inasmuch as she refuses to acknowledge the primacy of human beings over other (sentient) species and refuses to perceive the interactions between them as a zero-sum competition, the woman comes to embody what may be called a post-Darwinian Franciscan stance: an empathic awareness of the interdependence of all beings that is grounded in the shared experience of suffering, pain, and regeneration (rather than in the belief of jointly taking part in the divine plan of creation). What is more, by using a plural noun in the title of the film—rather than a collective noun, such as "forest"—the makers may be said to foreground the inherent worth of each singular being, albeit within the larger fabric of a shared community.

Characteristically, throughout the film, Królikiewicz deploys atypical and unusual camera perspectives that make it difficult for the viewers to identify with the "human" actors, urging them to readjust and retrain their perceptual habits. This applies, for instance, to the first environmentalist action in which Paweł engages in the forest (some five minutes into the film): a disorienting vertical low-angle shot that goes on for forty-five seconds shows the teacher being fiercely attacked with an ax by a clandestine logger (while giant treetops tower above their two bodies leaping to and fro). The opposite perspective is repeatedly used in the "revenge on the trees" sequence toward the end of the film: in a series of vertical high-angle shots—taken as if from a treetop—we see one tree after another collapsing and creating havoc on the ground below. On the aural level, in turn, much of Królikiewicz's film is fraught with ominous string music (partly taken from Andrzej Panufnik's violin concerto *Arbor Cosmica*), as if it were to convey onto the viewer a thriller-like sense of suspense and tension. What is more, as early as in the opening credits—which are interspersed with images of trees that resemble human bodies and their intimate parts—the very idea of human exceptionalism is subverted by various instances of anthropomorphizing inanimate nature. Generally speaking, this strategy may be linked to the makers' obvious intention to put "arboricide" on a par with "homicide" (or "ecocide" with "genocide," for that matter). Significantly, in various versions of the screenplay—the first version as well as the final shooting script—the massive destruction of the trees is explicitly described in terms of a war scenery: "The forest has been cut down almost entirely. It completely looks like a battlefield covered with corpses of wood."[10]

As ensues from a long interview published a couple of years before Królikiewicz's death, the enigmatic man/tree equation in *Trees* bears particular relevance for the timeframe in which the film came into being, namely the turbulent period of socioeconomic and political transformation ("shock therapy capitalism") right after the demise of state socialism.[11] A special role in this political reading of the film is attributed to the professor whose imbrication in the communist-era secret services is repeatedly alluded at and whose "experimental" collaboration with Ewa resembles the seemingly inevitable introduction of a "survival of the fittest" ethos in early postcommunist Poland. In her perceptive analysis of the film, Sylwia Borowska-Kazimiruk convincingly draws further on this line of argument by interpreting Ewa's scientific "torture chamber" as a sui generis "laboratory of history" that exposes the weakest and most defenseless beings to immoral experiments.[12] Taking the professor's complicity in both communism and neoliberal capitalism back to the ecological level, the film's (eco)critical stance may be related to both systems' reliance on the modern idea of human domination over (objectified) nature (or "Stepmother Earth," as the book coauthored by Ewa and her supervisor is symbolically called). In the closing sequence of the film, the apparent failure of the modernity project of mastering nature is exemplified by the appearance of a miniature globe within the diegesis. First, we see the globe standing prominently on Ewa's desk in her study room, but in the final shot, it ends up being carried away by the waves of the nearby sea (continuing to be a plaything, but no longer, so it seems, under human control).

As some of the aforementioned authors have rightly observed, the complete critical failure of Królikiewicz's film should be closely linked, among other things, to the makers' failed attempt to find a nonanthropocentric artistic formula that would be nevertheless intelligible and digestible for Polish spectators and critics in a time of turbulent socioeconomic and political transformation.[13] In the aforementioned interview, the director himself comments upon the untimely appearance of *Trees* in the following way: "*Trees* was made too early. In this tormented country of ours, where horrible things have been happening, this entire narrative about hypersensitivity is something unacceptable and non-tactical. Who is going to think about tree leaves in the face of the Smoleńsk tragedy?"[14] With the explicit reference to the presidential plane crash in 2010—which, seventy years after the Katyń massacre, has turned another Russian forest into a Polish place of trauma—Królikiewicz's remark unequivocally underscores the difficulty of moving beyond nation-centered narratives of environmental awareness and activism—a critical diagnosis of which the Polish tradition of "forest mythopraxis" bears obvious evidence.

Transnationalizing the Forest: Agnieszka Holland's *Spoor* (2017)

Although Królikiewicz's *Trees* goes against received binaries such as man/woman, culture/nature, mind/body, and reason/feeling, the film undeniably comes with certain ecofeminist undertones, especially in its portrayal of Ewa's emancipation from her male supervisor and her subsequent (life-affirming) return to the "womb of nature." The intricate connection between patriarchal hegemony and the lethal exploitation of nature is much more explicitly dealt with in Agnieszka Holland's award-winning thriller *Spoor* (2017), one of the first Polish feature films ever to be explicitly labeled with the prefix "eco."[15] Based on the acclaimed novel *Drive Your Plow Over the Bones of the Dead* (*Prowadź swój pług przez kości umarłych*, 2009) by Nobel Prize winner Olga Tokarczuk (who also collaborated on the screenplay), *Spoor* centers around Janina Duszejko, a retired civil engineer who lives in an isolated cottage adjoining a big forest in the Kłodzko Valley (close to the Polish-Czech border). When the nearby town is affected by a series of brutal murders (all of them inflicted on local hunters), the eccentric Duszejko puts herself in the role of private detective and tries to convince the local police that vengeful animals are behind the cruel homicides. It should not come as a surprise, then, that *Spoor* has been seen as a particular blend of a thriller, a mystery film, and a revenge-of-nature story. From an ecocritical (and an ecofeminist) perspective, however, it may be more productive, first of all, to approach the film as a highly interesting and irony-laden subversion of the classic model of wildlife filmmaking. As Luis Vivanco has observed, the conventional characteristics of nature documentaries include, among other things, "a didactic stance involving the use of paternalistic and disembodied male voiceover narration," "the close association of the film's knowledge claims with scientific authority," and "a narrative style that emphasizes natural cycles, often focusing on an individual member of a species."[16] What is more, as Vivanco adds, these productions typically display the wildlife habitat as a "self-contained and self-regulating domain standing apart from human history," seemingly devoid of any kind of human presence and intervention.

In many ways, *Spoor* may be said to undermine (and ironically reverse) the classic wildlife film's disembodied androcentric and scientifically objective gaze directed at the self-contained "natural" world. Throughout, Holland's feature film is narratively framed by Duszejko's (female) voice-over and by a series of intertitles that mark the subsequent phases in the (male) Polish hunting cycle. In her footsteps (and partly through her eyes), we follow the events that take place in the "habitat" of the Kłodzko Valley over the course of approximately one year, with particular attention to the unlawful activities undertaken by local hunters and poachers. By doing so, Holland's story foregrounds a "degenerate" form of hunting geared at exploitation and slaughter rather than being based on a noble bond with nature and the natural order.[17] At the same time, as a highly unreliable embodied narrator, Duszejko imposes her idiosyncratic worldview onto the spectator, offering a particular blend of ecological and astrological insights combined with occasional references to William Blake (the poet of Romantic imagination par excellence). Along these lines, the ecocritical preoccupation with patriarchal exploitation—vis-à-vis women and nature alike—runs like a thread through her interactions with the local hunters. The most prominent target of ecofeminist critique is undoubtedly the local fox farm owner Wnętrzak who, already on his very first encounter with Duszejko, clumsily pushes his (phallus-shaped) gun bag in her face. Other women—most notably Wnętrzak's girlfriend Dobra Nowina and the "playboy bunnies" at his fox farm—turn out to be exposed to much less allegorical forms of sexual harassment and exploitation.

As such, *Spoor* targets not only the very principle of hunting but also the "toxic" form of homosocial Polish masculinity that goes along with it (the biased depiction of which—as has been observed by many critics—borders on the caricatural and the grotesque). By way of contrast, the less "toxic" men who sympathize and side with Duszejko are given more psychological depth (partly through flashbacks). What is more, not unlike Duszejko who, as a former expat, represents a cosmopolitan sensitivity, her male "helpers"—an elderly neighbor of Polish-German parentage, a Czech entomologist doing fieldwork in Poland, and a young expert in information and communications technology who used to work in Berlin—do not easily fit into narrow and fixed categories of national belonging.[18] As such, the film's ecofeminist stance vis-à-vis exploitative Polish masculinity comes with undeniable undertones of transnationalism. As Simon Lewis rightly observes, this sense of "border-crossing worldliness" also pertains to Holland's particular portrayal of the Kłodzko Valley, where "nature is colorful, expansive, and borderless, in contrast to the short-sighted parochialism of national culture" and where "wild animals are pictured frequently, wandering in the forest and meadows, crossing roads and other artificial demarcation lines, such as inter-state borders."[19]

Importantly, already from the opening sequence of the film, it is suggested that Duszejko's subjective (gynocentric) narration goes along with instances of zoocentric focalization: some two minutes into the opening credits, the camera frames four stags in a meadow looking in the direction of the lens, after which the angle switches again to the surrounding valley. The entire film features a dozen of similarly arranged shots and montages of animals looking back on their "environment" (and taking over, as if it were, the camera perspective). Duszejko's strong identification with the animal viewpoint takes on a very literal (zoomorphic) shape in the final part of the film, when she attends a fancy dress party in a wolf costume. The animals' implied presence in the story (and the "human" world at large) does not only rely, therefore, on mere observation, but also on active intervention. Throughout the film, Holland puts much effort into portraying the Kłodzko Valley—its mountainous forests, meadows, cottages, and the nearby town—as a space where the human and the nonhuman constantly intersect and interact (animals and human beings encroaching on each other's privileged territories). Its most obvious example is the hunting activities of the local men in the forest. Remarkably, however, the film does not portray the act of hunting in a direct and straightforward way—since there is not a single shot in which we *see* a hunter shoot—but rather focuses on its immediate impact on the animals (who are repeatedly framed while being startled by the *sound* of shotguns).

Along similar lines, the traditional hunting ritual to which the title word *pokot* alludes—defined by Polish dictionaries as "the game killed during a hunt and displayed in a specific order according to the hunting hierarchy"—is given considerably little diegetic attention (taking up less than fifty seconds of the entire running time of the film). As perhaps another example of the film's blending of the anthropomorphic and zoomorphic, it could be argued that the storyline of *Spoor* actually revolves around another kind of hierarchically ordered "game display," namely that of the five Polish men that die over the course of the story. Starting with a local poacher and ending on the town's priest, the narrative focus gradually shifts from the margins to the center of masculine power. Not coincidentally, the mystery story reaches its climax during a church-set celebration of Saint Hubert, at the occasion of which the priest vehemently exposes the ideological foundation (and religious justification) for man's primacy and power over the animal world (and over nature at large). By acting out revenge on behalf of the animals, Duszejko, in turn, radically contests the moral codex of Christianity ("Thou shall not kill"), as it refuses to include weaker beings in its moral community ("Thou shall not kill animals"). Ultimately, the very fact that the woman turns out to be behind the serial murders (and not the animals with whom she sympathizes) confirms her zoophilic worldview (which goes along with some misanthropic undertones).[20]

The woman's radical antihunting stance undoubtedly explains why *Spoor* has met with very critical reactions, up to point of being called "the apotheosis of ecoterrorism."[21] What some critics seem to ignore, however, is the subtle sense of irony that casts an ambiguous shadow over Duszejko's unusual trajectory of radicalization. While the subjective form of narration and camerawork fosters strong identification with the main character's position and that of her allies, the viewer is simultaneously made aware that Duszejko should not be trusted and that her zoophilic worldview comes with obvious flaws, gaps, and distortions (as indicated, for instance, by her repeated reliance on horoscopes and astrological wisdom). As it appears, the dreamlike closing sequence of *Spoor* adds one more reflexive twist to Holland's tongue-in-cheek portrayal of Duszejko. After one more obligatory reference to astrology, Duszejko's voice-over solemnly announces the advent of a new cycle: she and her friends have

Figure 12.1. Duszejko strolls through a sunlit meadow, right before fading from view. *Spoor* (*Pokot*). Directed by Agnieszka Holland and Kasia Adamik. Warsaw: Studio Filmowe TOR; Köln: Heimatfilm; Prague: nutprodukce; Bratislava: nutprodukcia; Stockholm: The Chimney Pot Sweden, 2017. Screen capture by Kris Van Heuckelom.

managed to escape from Kłodzko Valley and now live in what seems to be an Edenic resort (where human and nonhuman animals peacefully appear to coexist). Significantly, in the very final shot of the film, the camera frames three white-tailed deer fawns in a summer-lit meadow, while Duszejko passes by behind them (and eventually fades from view, as a ghostlike figure). With this obvious nod to *Bambi*, Holland not only urges the viewer to read *Spoor* in relationship to the profound controversy that has surrounded Walt Disney's antihunting animation film for decades; Holland also helps lay bare one of the prominent blind spots in Duszejko's sentimental zoophilic worldview, namely her anti-Darwinian belief that nature in itself—without human intervention—constitutes a benign community free from predation and interspecies violence (which is usually called the "Bambi syndrome").[22]

In Lieu of a Conclusion: Globalizing the Forest in Jerzy Skolimowski's *Essential Killing* (2010)

As we have seen, both Królikiewicz's *Trees* and Holland's *Spoor* convey explicit messages of ecocritical awareness that subvert the long-standing (hu)man-centered outlook on nature and add a particular twist to col-

Figure 12.2. The blood-stained white horse in the closing sequence of *Essential Killing*. Directed by Jerzy Skolimowski. Warsaw: Skopia Film and Syrena Films; Bekkestua: Cylinder Productions; Dublin: Element Pictures; and Budapest: Mythberg Films, 2010. Screen capture by Kris Van Heuckelom.

lectivist (nation-centered) forms of "forest mythopraxis." In view of the rapidly growing social and political salience of climate change on a European and a global scale, it seems inevitable that twenty-first-century Polish cinema will increasingly draw attention to environmentalist and ecological issues. Meanwhile, in keeping with the steadily expanding scope of ecocinema studies, it may be equally productive to widen the focus to include film productions and projects that one may initially not think of in ecological terms. A notable case in point is Jerzy Skolimowski's award-winning *Essential Killing* (2010). Even more than Holland's *Spoor*, Skolimowski's engaging manhunt thriller suggests that the "native" forest is increasingly losing its national features and turning into a site where local, national, transnational, and global interests (and discourses) intersect. Whereas some of these multiple layers—Polish Romanticism, East-West antagonism, the "war on terror," biopolitics—have been extensively discussed, the film's highly elusive thematization of intra- and interspecies violence, which ultimately ends with the apparent demise of man, against the sublime backdrop of a snow-covered landscape (with horse!), invites particular comparison with the growing body of films that envision a posthuman future for our planet.[23]

Therefore, in spite—or perhaps because—of not being an obviously eco-themed film, *Essential Killing* is very well suited to be treated in tandem with an explicitly ecofeminist production like *Spoor*. While Skolimowski's highly unromantic take on humankind and nature radically differs from *Spoor*'s ironically sentimental portrayal of benign nature, both productions offer a compelling cinematic account of human-animal continuity that ultimately leads up to the diegetic disappearance of the (fe)male protagonist. Or to put it, by way of ultimate conclusion, differently and more generally: some thirty years after the demise of the Polish People's Republic and the advent of a new world order, there are hopeful—and much less hopeful—signs in the air that global warming will not leave the summers (and winters) of the Polish "forest people" unaffected.

Kris Van Heuckelom is Professor of Polish Studies and Cultural Studies at KU Leuven, Belgium. He specializes in late modern Polish culture, with a particular focus on comparative and transnational perspectives, and has published several books, edited volumes, and anthologies in these domains. His most recent books are *Polish Migrants in European Film 1918–2017* (2019) and *Nostalgia, solidarność, (im)potencja. Obrazy polskiej migracji w kinie europejskim (od niepodległości do współczesności)* (2022). Over the past few years, he contributed book chapters to volumes such as *Being Poland: A New History of Polish Literature and Culture Since 1918* (2018), *The Routledge World Companion to Polish Literature* (2021), *European Film Remakes* (2021), and *Rethinking Modern Polish Identities* (2023).

Notes

1. Blavascunas and Konczal, "Bark Beetles," 113.
2. Barcz, *Environmental Cultures*, 189–207.
3. Schama, *Landscape and Memory*, 53–60; Mytych, *Poetyka i łowy*, 145–148; Barcz, *Environmental Cultures*, 200–204.
4. Kisielewska, "Las jako przestrzeń symboliczna," 249.
5. Both in terms of narrative and of setting, the serial has some similarities with a short documentary Ślesicki made in the early 1960s, *Płyną tratwy* (*The Rafts Sail On*). Set in the Augustów Primeval Forest in northeastern Poland, the documentary revolves around the coming of age of a country boy whose fascination with the local wildlife gradually gives way to the awareness (and acceptance) of the exchange value of nature.
6. Manser, *Failed Transitions*.
7. Konczal, "Trees."
8. Willoquet-Maricondi, "Shifting Paradigms," 47.
9. Kääpä, *Ecology*, 5.
10. Jankowski and Królikiewicz, "Drzewa. Scenariusz Filmowy," 37; Jankowski and Królikiewicz, "Drzewa. Scenopis Filmu Fabularnego (Roboczy)," 107.
11. Kletowski and Marecki, *Krolikiewicz*.
12. Borowska-Kazimiruk, "Awangarda wrażliwości."

13. Kletowski and Marecki, *Krolikiewicz*; Borowska-Kazimiruk, "Awangarda wrażliwości."
14. Kletowski and Marecki, *Krolikiewicz*, 317.
15. In the opening credits of *Spoor*, the film is presented as "an Agnieszka Holland film." However, Holland made the film together with her daughter, Katarzyna ("Kasia") Adamik, who is acknowledged in the closing credits. For simplicity's sake, I will refer to *Spoor* as "Holland's film" or "Holland's story" in this chapter, but I wanted to note Adamik's contribution to the film as a co-director here.
16. Vivanco, "Penguins," 111.
17. Mytych, *Poetyka i łowy*, 208–211.
18. Lewis, "Border Trouble," 539.
19. Idem., 359.
20. Symbolically, by becoming a "hunter" herself and by turning the hunters into "game," Duszejko becomes the on-screen embodiment of the legendary character that makes its appearance in the second half of the story: at the aforementioned fancy dress party, Duszejko hears the local legend of the Night Hunter, an avenger who—aided by animals—hunts down and kills evil people.
21. Lewis, "Border Trouble," 539.
22. Bruckner, "Bambi and Finding Nemo."
23. Ladegaard, "On the Frontier of Politics"; Whitehall, "The Biopolitical Aesthetic"; Mazierska, "Framing a Terrorist."

Bibliography

Barcz, Anna. *Environmental Cultures in Soviet East Europe: Literature, History and Memory*. London: Bloomsbury Academic, 2020.

Blavascunas, Eunice, and Agata Agnieszka Konczal. "Bark Beetles and Ultra-Right Nationalist Outbreaks: Myth, Propaganda, Reality." In *Environmentalism under Authoritarian Regimes: Myth, Propaganda, Reality*, edited by Stephen Brain and Viktor Pál, 96–122. New York: Routledge, 2018.

Borowska-Kazimiruk, Sylwia. "Awangarda wrażliwości. O 'Drzewach' Grzegorza Królikiewicza." *Widok. Teorie i praktyki kultury wizualnej* 22 (2018): 211–235.

Bruckner, Lynne Dickson. "Bambi and Finding Nemo: A Sense of Wonder in the Wonderful World of Disney?" In *Framing the World: Explorations in Ecocriticism and Film*, edited by Paula Willoquet-Maricondi, 187–208. Charlottesville: University of Virginia Press, 2010.

Jankowski, Jerzy, and Grzegorz Królikiewicz. "Drzewa. Scenariusz Filmowy." Warsaw: Polish Film Archives, 1995. S-26688.

———. "Drzewa. Scenopis Filmu Fabularnego (Roboczy)." Warsaw: Polish Film Archives, 1995. S-26688.

Kääpä, Pietari. *Ecology and Contemporary Nordic Cinemas: From Nation-Building to Ecocosmopolitanism*. London: Bloomsbury Publishing, 2014.

Kisielewska, Alicja. "Las jako przestrzeń symboliczna—na przykładzie 'Brzeziny' Andrzeja Wajdy i 'Siekierezady' Witolda Leszczyńskiego." In *II Ogólnopolska Konferencja pt. "Las w kulturze polskiej." Materiały z konferencji*, edited by Wojciech Łysiak, 249–254. Poznań: Wydawnictwo "Eco," 2002.

Kletowski, Marek, and Piotr Marecki. *Krolikiewicz: Pracuję dla przyszłości*. Kraków: Korporacja Ha!Art, 2011.

Konczal, Agata Agnieszka. "Trees That Must Remember: Polish Foresters as Guardians of the Nation." 13 February 2018. https://www.eurozine.com/trees-must-remember/. Accessed 19 December 2019.

Ladegaard, Jakob. "On the Frontier of Politics: Ideology and the Western in Jerzy Skolimowski's *Essential Killing* and Jim Jarmusch's *Dead Man*." *Studies in Eastern European Cinema* 4, no. 2 (2013): 181–197.

Lewis, Simon. "Border Trouble: Ethnopolitics and Cosmopolitan Memory in Recent Polish Cinema." *East European Politics and Societies and Cultures* 33, no. 2 (2019): 522–549.

Manser, Roger. *Failed Transitions: The Eastern European Economy and Environment since the Fall of Communism*. New York: The New Press, 1994.

Mazierska, Ewa. "Framing a Terrorist: The Politics of Representation in *Ici et Ailleurs* (1970–1974), *Four Lions* (2010), and *Essential Killing* (2010)." *Framework* 55, no. 1 (2014): 102–120.

Mytych, Beata. *Poetyka i łowy: o idei dawnego polowania w literaturze polskiej XIX wieku*. Katowice: Wydawnictwo Uniwersytetu Śląskiego, 2004.

Schama, Simon. *Landscape and Memory*. New York: Vintage, 1996.

Vivanco, Luis. "Penguins Are Good to Think with: Wildlife Films, the Imaginary Shaping of Nature, and Environmental Politics." In *Ecocinema:Theory and Practice*, edited by Stephen Rust, Salma Monani, and Sean Cubitt, 109–127. New York: Routledge, 2012.

Whitehall, Geoffrey. "The Biopolitical Aesthetic: Toward a Post-Biopolitical Subject." *Critical Studies on Security* 1, no. 2 (2013): 189–203.

Willoquet-Maricondi. "Shifting Paradigms: From Environmentalist Films to Ecocinema." In *Framing the World: Explorations in Ecocriticism and Film*, edited by Paula Willoquet-Maricondi, 43–61. Charlottesville: University of Virginia Press, 2010.

Filmography

Holland, Agnieszka, and Kasia Adamik. *Spoor* (*Pokot*, Poland, 2017).
Królikiewicz, Grzegorz. *Trees* (*Drzewa*, Poland, 1995).
Skolimowski, Jerzy. *Essential Killing* (*Essential Killing*, Poland, Norway, Ireland, and Hungary, 2010).
Ślesicki, Władysław. *Summer of the Forest People* (*Lato leśnych ludzi*, Poland, 1985).

13

Beyond the Utopian Landscape in Post-Soviet Russian Cinema

Michael Cramer and Jeremi Szaniawski

Кому на руси жить хорошо? (Who lives well in Russia?) asks Nekrasov's tale. Russia has, ever since its inception, marked its imaginary with the idea of man having to conquer and deal with a hostile environment, and, further, a hubristic desire to defy said environment, in addition to a pride or delight in enduring brutal winters and intemperate elements. Taken together, these attitudes suggest a kind of unstable dialectic between human action as overcoming or taming the land, and, conversely, the land as something that simply must be endured; when the latter is emphasized, human heroism takes on a kind of negative dimension, as though its greatest glory could simply come through a kind of dissolution or identification with something that cannot be conquered or mastered, a landscape that subsumes or incorporates the human into itself, at once negating it and allowing for its transcendence. We need only look at a few historical examples to see this dialectic at work. We find another dialectic internal to the motif of overcoming the environment, in which human attempts to master the landscape result in untold suffering and destruction, regardless of their success or failure: think of Peter I's project of turning the swamps of the Baltic Gulf into his imperial capital. The trauma of Petersburg's foundation and creation resonates in Pushkin's *Bronze Horseman* (1837) and its combination of flood, devastation, and madness—tropes later rehearsed in Gogol and Dostoevsky, exhibiting the quandaries of life in the phantasmagoric city as well as outside of it.

All these early modern reflections on the most modern of cities can be said to foreshadow the horrors of the twentieth century, finding their echoes in the irrigation plans, dams, and the Belomor canal under Stalin. These quixotic and monstrous undertakings are consubstantial with the country's gigantic size, and the imaginary that attaches to it. They thus contain within themselves the idea of a landscape that cannot ever ultimately be conquered, one that will inevitably reduce the human to a small, even pathetic figure, but which also contains possibilities for its absorption into something greater. The vastness of its landscape has preoccupied Russia for centuries, as attested in its thought and aesthetic production—philosophy, painting, literature, music, and, of course, cinema. Already old church Slavonic chronicles accounted for the difficulties of dealing with the elements (crossing a river, for instance, an eminent trope), and one of Ilya Repin's most famous paintings—*Barge Haulers on the Volga* (c. 1873)—exhibits the plight of the underclass toiling at inhuman labor and working against the elements. It has also been suggested that while the Tatars were undeterred by Russia's expanses at first, their stronghold on the country dissolved also because of the impossibility of extending their rule over such a large territory. Later, Napoleon's army and Nazi Germany's alike would tumble and get bogged down in the endless, muddy or snowy expanses of Russia. Here, though, we begin to see the positive valence of this vastness, which serves as a kind of protection or enclosure for those who inhabit it, one that could not be matched by any human effort. The rub, of course, is that Russians themselves are at the same time largely subject to it in the same way their invaders were.

The dialectic between the conquering of the landscape and submission to it (both in positive and negative terms) has persisted, and of course takes on new dimensions in the twentieth century, as the failed Soviet utopia, the apex of humanity's effort to produce its own history, crumbled into something stubborn, intransigent, or frozen. This failure, however, leads in many different directions as far as the landscape and its relationship with humanity is concerned: on one hand, we find the retreat into mysticism, in which this relationship becomes one of a transcendent or spiritual utopianism, in the case of Andrei Tarkovsky, with the poet/artist responsible for achieving a kind of union with the landscape that overcomes and ultimately reveals as illusory both history and time. On the other hand, and for most of the filmmakers considered here, it becomes a reminder of that history and of an ongoing submission and humiliation to both human and natural forces. The representation of landscape, in short, becomes the ground upon which man's relationship (both objective and subjective) with history itself is articulated, in a wide range of different tones and affects; there is no "nature" here after all, as landscape becomes an allegorical stand-in for something far more human, yet continues to point toward the possibility of whatever would transcend it. Here we are concerned with landscape in the work of the most prominent post-Soviet auteurs, whose works range from mystificatory ideological propositions (Andrey Zvyagintsev), and attempts at the enclosure of the forces of history within finely wrought aesthetic forms (Alexander Sokurov), to a more conscious grappling with the concrete ruins of the Soviet utopia and their sign as a kind of halted or failed history (Aleksei Balabanov) and of history's brutal materiality—one that is still with us and in which we are implicated (Aleksei German). In the first two cases, we see a kind of panicked effort to contain or understand history through a largely unconscious allegorical function of landscape, while in the latter two, we are aggressively confronted with questions that cannot be contained or answered, in which the materiality of the landscape allegorizes the material processes of history itself and the way that they refuse any reassuring mastery or transcendence. Yet in all these cases we still find something like a utopian impulse at work, albeit one that is blocked or prematurely closed off in the cases of Sokurov and Zvyagintsev, treated with doubt and cynicism in Balabanov, and, finally, manifested in terms of ugliness and disgust in German.

From the very beginnings of Russian cinema we find articulated a clear and significant relationship between the human subject (as an individual or as a collective) and its environment. Early Russian cinema and its bourgeois or decadent inclinations (one thinks of Bauer, of course) is dominated by the urban setting (a function of its production modes), associated with a kind of comfort or safety, which will be promptly swept aside by early Soviet cinema wherein the environment becomes once more a frontier to conquer and rationalize—something that remains "unfinished" or incapable of responding to human needs, yet ultimately a source of profound value. This exaltation of the Russian landscape and its potentialities is enabled by modern technology and sheds the mysticism or obscurantism of yore to present at last, with lyricism and ecstasy (from Vertov to Eisenstein), a landscape in the service of the Russian/Soviet man. However, this joint act of suppression and harnessing of the mystical and the environment, followed by outright repression under Stalin, will lead in later years to a resurgence of the melancholy or contemplative inclination, drudging through swampy or slushy expanses. Man no longer evolves in the impeccably dried swamps (now turned into fields of flowers or wheat, or lush gardens) of socialist realist aesthetics, but is confronted with the reality of nature's cycles.

The cinema of the Thaw thus reminded viewers of the harsh realities and insubordinate qualities of nature. This did not, however, forbid a different kind of utopian element, which we find in the films of Andrei Tarkovsky: here, transcendence comes through the negation of man by landscape, standing in for ultimately invisible spiritual forces. Instead of something that must be mastered or overcome, landscape becomes a sign of the failure of that overcoming, yet offers another kind of transcendence by way of a retreat into counterrevolutionary mysticism. Whereas the draining and rerouting of water was paramount in early Soviet cinema, we find in the 1960s and beyond a fixation on wet or saturated landscapes, beginning with Tarkovsky. Gilles Deleuze is keen to point out this quality of "wetness" in the director's work, which leads him to ask, "what is Russia . . . ? The seed seems to be frozen in these sodden, washed, and heavily translucent images, with their sometimes bluish, sometimes brown surfaces, while the green environment seems, in the rain, to be unable to go beyond the condition of a liquid crystal which keeps its secret."[1] The ground is always in the process of being washed away, melting beneath one's feet and revealing only the barest, most abject character, yet at the same time seems to hold some redemptive "secret," and thus calls us to draw it out. "Tarkovsky's wash," Deleuze writes, "the rains that provide rhythm for each film . . . constantly bring us back to the question: what burning bush, what fire, what soul, what sponge will staunch this earth?" Fire, which is of course another key motif in Tarkovsky's films, seems to cleanse the land, turning its status as a sign of the failure of the Soviet project into something that transcends the human, like a burned offering to God. This fire is also that of history, of humans still animated and evolving, resiliently, in the inhospitable landscape.

But Tarkovsky's mystical orientation obscures the historicity of the films themselves, which bear witness to the impossibility of ever making landscape anything other than historical. His attempts at escape or transcendence remain the inventions of an artist, expressing an unfulfilled utopian drive—albeit one that is blocked or whose ultimate end is mystifyingly represented by God. Tarkovsky's treatment of landscape finds clear echoes (often parodic ones) in post-Soviet cinema: the motifs of wetness, muddiness (both suggesting a kind of middle state, between liquid and solid), the fascination with the Russian landscape, and the question of how it might antagonize or transcend any human projects, remain at the forefront of the subsequent works of major auteurs, all of whom align these issues with the question raised by Deleuze, namely "what is Russia?"

Tarkovsky finds his most immediate successor (both chronologically and in the sense of fulfilling a similar "official" cultural function) in Alexander Sokurov. Born in 1951, Sokurov began his filmmaking career in the late Stagnation period under Brezhnev—a period during which most of his films were shelved—and was hailed an important Soviet filmmaker during Perestroika. Jeremi Szaniawski has posited that Sokurov's elevation to the status of prime "Sovexport" figure had to do with the passing of Tarkovsky in 1985, as the two men knew each other and Sokurov was the closest "next of kin," in his idiosyncratic and often contemplative cinema, to Tarkovsky.[2] But as Fredric Jameson argues, the two filmmakers are entirely different, once one looks beyond the motifs present in both oeuvres.[3] For Jameson the difference is not to be found merely in formal intricacies or motifs but in the directors' rapport with history. We can detect these differing orientations toward history through their respective uses of landscape. To put it briefly, Tarkovsky deploys a more egotistical approach, in which, despite his mystical pretensions, the landscape is always ultimately there for man (and indeed ends up completely submitting to the projections of the solipsistic director, even as he disingenuously imagines the transcendence of the human). Sokurov's landscape, by contrast, is more collective or even geological, as the human becomes something far smaller, and the land something far less fertile or subject to redemption or cleansing.

The differences between the two directors' respective adaptations of the Strugatsky brothers' *Stalker* (*Stalker*, 1979) and *Days of Eclipse* (*Dni zatmeniya*, 1988) provide an exemplary illustration of this point. The category of the "geological" is particularly apt for characterizing the treatment of landscape in the latter, which ends with a vast arid expanse of land after all human presence or trace has vanished from it. To the fixation on wetness (marshes, brooks, rivers, pools, etc.) in Tarkovsky, Sokurov opposes a sepia-hued landscape where even water does not quite seem liquid, but rather thick, oily, or clay-like; flow and movement (also present in Tarkovsky's elaborate camera movements) are arrested; things are not so much sullied or waiting to be dried out as they are already completely extinguished, as though the utopian dimension (reactionary though it was in Tarkovsky) had withered away during the final years of the Soviet Union.

This historical reading is further supported by the fact that Sokurov's first two features, *Lonely Voice of Man* (*Odinokiy golos cheloveka*, based on Platonov's *The Potudan River*) and *Mournful Unconcern* (*Skorbnoye bezchustviye*, loosely based on G. B. Shaw's *Heartbreak House*), made in 1978 and 1982 respectively, feature many scenes involving bodies of water, often of an abject kind (the useless mopping of a shopkeeper's wet storefront in the debut, the swamp in the sophomore feature). There seems, therefore, to be a connection here between wet, abject landscapes in Sokurov,

Tarkovsky's mystical ones, and the political climate of Stagnation, with which Sokurov associates wet and dank atmospheres. Conversely, after his friend's death and the coming into being of a very different late Soviet cultural landscape, Sokurov's landscapes alter dramatically with his shift to the emptied-out, unconquerable desert dryness of *Days of the Eclipse* (where human bodies and even water become afflicted by a stifling heat and are turned into "drier" entities—a fate only narrowly escaped by a child whose brow sweats clearer water, and is filmed in color instead of being filtered through the sepia tone used in much of the film). Sokurov depicts the equally dry Caucasus in his *Madame Bovary* adaptation, *Save and Protect* (*Spasi i sokhrani*, 1989) and even dry snow in the northern-located *Second Circle* (*Krug vtoroi*, 1990). Interestingly enough, wetness (often associated with washing or purification, but of a useless kind) will reemerge in his post-Soviet practice: think of Chekhov's ghost's bath in *The Stone* (*Kamen'*, 1992), of Lenin's ablutions in *Taurus* (*Telets*, 2001) or of the laundry/bathhouse scene in *Faust* (2011). In each and every case, the bath or washing are associated with something useless, incapable of stopping or even delaying disappearance, death, or eternal damnation.

We might begin to find a different historical dimension, however, if we look to how Sokurov seems to respond to or "contain" this situation, a move that is of course a deeply ideological one. Diane Arnaud has analyzed Sokurov's cinema in terms of enclosing structures.[4] These are particularly characteristic of Sokurov's post-Soviet work, where even open landscapes are somehow framed, transformed, anamorphosed, foregrounding their artificiality: suffice it to think of the film that established the Russian director as a leading art film figure in the West (and takes place mostly outside), *Mother and Son* (*Mat' i syn*, 1997), as well as the one that brought him a measure of notoriety beyond the niche of cinephiles (and takes place primarily indoors), namely, *Russian Ark* (*Russkiy kovcheg*, 2002). In the former, the perambulations in oneiric countryside landscapes give the viewer the sense of watching stills or paintings, inspired by those of Caspar David Friedrich, as though stilling or mastering what can no longer bear any fruit in the real world within the compensatory realm of the aesthetic, diverting the utopian drive away from history and toward the mastery of the artist himself.[5]

This sense of containing the expansiveness and intransigence of the landscape is reinforced by the fact that most shots are long and motionless, but also by a very elaborate sound design—which combines the sound of wind; a variety of birds whose singing is rendered in a shrill, quasi-metallic pitch; and treated romantic musical tracks sounding distant, as though heard through a wall or down a tunnel—all giving the very clear sense of enclosure identified by Arnaud. This mode in Sokurov is repeated in outdoor sequences in the 1999 film *Moloch* (Hitler's picnic) and the 2001 film *Taurus* (Lenin's and Krupskaya's ruminations in the meadow). In *Russian Ark*, meanwhile, the sense of enclosure is obviously thematic: the characters enter the Hermitage museum, a repository for Western culture that in order to be preserved must also be enclosed, all the more so given that it is sailing through the rocky or murky waters of history. To the progressive and deeply stimulating engagement with history that Jameson had identified in *Days of the Eclipse*, Sokurov's Yeltsin- and Putin-era films suggest a withdrawal from and pessimism vis-à-vis history. We can detect this in a variety of aspects of the filmmaking, including in the treatment of the landscape itself, which becomes in *Russian Ark* something that must be resisted at all costs through the enclosure and preservation of a history that is no longer moving at all, a boat that goes nowhere.

In contrast to Sokurov's aesthetic containment of landscape and history, we find a more transparently ideological form of containment in the films of Andrey Zvyagintsev, which rail against the injustices of contemporary Russia by casting them in spatial terms. Wilderness and human developments alike are equated with a form of Wild West (or Wild East?) lawlessness, but the different players at work can nonetheless still be contrasted through their respective spaces and their relationship to them. Examples abound in his oeuvre, from the socioeconomic divide, articulated through the space of bus rides and the contrast between wealthy and poor peoples' apartments in *Elena* (2011), to the plot of *Leviathan* (*Leviafan*, 2014) as a whole, which hinges on contested space. What connects the urban locales and outdoor spaces of *Elena* and *Leviathan*'s rough northern outpost—besides Zvyagintsev's keenness on overusing music by Philip Glass—is a rapport between water and death, both of which seem to be omnipresent in his Russia.

In *Elena*, water is mostly evoked in the swimming pool scene—one which seems fairly anecdotal, yet which lingers with the viewer. The "civilized" water of the pool (in *Loveless* [*Nelyubov*, 2017] we find echoes of this, when the police go looking for the missing child in an old abandoned Communist sports and culture complex with an empty, derelict swimming pool) contrasts with the furious and crashing dark waters of the northern sea with which *Leviathan* opens. To this one can add the murky underwater images in the opening credits of *The Return* (*Vozvrashcheniye*, 2003) and the emphasis placed on the element throughout the film, telling the story of a wayward father's trip to the northern wilderness with his two estranged sons (the boat rides and fishing scenes while on the Baltic island). When the film earned the Golden Lion in Venice and gained its director worldwide recognition, the media were keen on reporting on the tragic fate of one of the actors, who had died by jumping into a lake.

Expanses of water, in Zvyagintsev, are always connected with a sense of doom—drowning, crashing, hypothermia, and so forth seem to inhabit them. Both stagnation and cleansing here give way to a portrayal of bodies of water as an analog to the criminal underbelly of Putin's Russia, in which even the most bucolic or comforting landscape will undoubtedly yield something sinister and fatal (*The Banishment* [*Izgnanie*, 2007]).

Yet the director's surface critique of the ills of Putin's Russia (corruption, nepotism, social inequality), on which he made his bread and butter (yet another filmmaker who capitalizes off of a Western desire to consume critiques of the non-Western other), hides something far more nefarious as well. In Zvyagintsev, the land is crucial to understanding the psychology of characters (it is overdetermined in every one of his films), but we have to go further than this obvious statement. The anxiety or deadliness associated with water seems to bespeak a concern with limits (it delineates the limits of the land, of Russia, or, perhaps, of Western civilization, all the while suggesting a limitless beyond), and hence bears traces of an imperial and indeed nationalist consciousness that is not so far removed from the very thing it seems to critique. To put it differently, the primary political term here is land itself, and whether it is taken literally or in a more metonymic or metaphorical sense, this results in a narrow and limiting political perspective in which the physical ownership and domination of space or territory inevitably constitutes the "ground" that underpins any conflict. This angst concerning limitation is replicated in the landscape itself, whose expansiveness suggests the possibility of an infinite realm, yet the desire for such is made all the more absurd by the sterility of the territory. Examined more closely, the entire premise of *Leviathan* appears deeply arbitrary. As we remember, the entire conflict at the center of the film has to do with businessmen and corrupt politicians vying for the protagonist's plot of land (where his ramshackle home stands), upon which they want to build an Orthodox church. The protagonist will not budge, and, in the end, will be destroyed by the system (convicted for his lover's murder).

The film ends with the sobering images of caterpillars razing down the old home, the church being erected on that plot of land, and a service being held there, enshrining a new or renewed social order from which the rogue or maverick element has been removed. There are certainly echoes here of the far-right American ideology of the "sovereign citizen" and his inalienable right to land as property. Just as in everywhere through Zvyagintsev, the concern is with territory, both literal and metaphorical: the rat race for money and finer living quarters (*Elena*), the expansion of a business or institution (*Leviathan*), the will to impose a quasi-mythological or archaic imprint on the body as contained in the land (*The Banishment*), the desire to roam the land in search of a hidden treasure (*The Return*), or the desire to disappear into the landscape (*Loveless*).

Zvyagintsev's cinema, in short, is one of an unresolved libidinal drive for territory, a morbid and beastly élan vital that replicates the rapaciousness of the movie industry itself. Even if the director seems to critique this drive, his critique conceives of political conflict in the same territorial way. If there is any utopian drive here, it is surely both imperial and, in its emphasis on ruthless competition, neoliberal. It is surprising, thus, to see that the least artistically compelling or intellectually appealing of the four directors discussed here may also be the one who most closely produces a landscape that allegorizes the medium of film itself (in the sense that it engages with the power struggles and commercial concerns endemic to film production, and not only in Putin's Russia). But this allegorical dimension does not seem to be an intentional one, and more likely can be explained as the unconsciously articulated truth content behind an impotent critique that cannot transcend the terms of its own object.

In a more cogent and focused fashion, not to mention a far more historically conscious one, Aleksei Balabanov dedicated his oeuvre to depicting the fate of the subject relegated to a decaying or irretrievably corrupt environment; here, while history may not move forward, it also does not disappear but instead remains as a kind of static ruin in which all action takes on a gratuitous, and ultimately fatal, character. Both in his depictions of Soviet and post-Soviet cities as they were during the time the films were made, and in his more allegorical efforts, Balabanov sees the human subject as produced by his surroundings in a dark twist on Marx's dictum, "it is not the consciousness of men that determines their being, but, on the contrary, their social being that determines their consciousness." This is epitomized by *Cargo 200* (*Gruz 200*, 2007), one of the most sobering portraits of social and philosophical decay in the late Soviet Union. Every environment portrayed in the film bears the traces of a historical stalemate or stasis: from the supine military man's balcony where the tiling is peeling off the wall, to the apartment of Zhurov, the psychopathic policeman who tortures a girl from the *nomenklatura*, showering her with corpses (those of her boyfriend killed in Afghanistan, brought back to town on the titular cargo 200 airplane, and of a local drunkard initially brought there to rape her). The point where all these elements converge is the parodic utopia created by a former associate of Zhurov's. This man lives on an abject farm where he peddles *samogon* (homemade vodka), a brutal parody of Tarkovsky's rural utopias (the Stalker's "Zone" most notably, but also the farmhouse in *Mirror* [*Zerkalo*, 1975]). Yet this reference is not an instance of postmodern pastiche, or a simple overturning for the sake of thumbing one's nose at the father; instead, Balabanov's intention is to convey a deeper meaning through the bleakness of his representations, one that has a clear and revealing historical dimension.

Beyond the failure and collapse of a system represented through human corruption and decay of the built environment, we find in Balabanov's landscapes a sense of history's inescapability: hence the heavy skies and the drab, hopeless expanses of land. In such a context, it is unsurprising that a sense of absurd Beckettian waiting or repetition (Balabanov's first feature, *Happy Days* [*Schastlivye dni*, 1991] was directly inspired by Beckett) connects with the surface realism (which is in fact very allegorical) of his later films. This is nowhere clearer than in *Stoker* (*Kochegar*, 2010), where finely choreographed repetitions and perambulations emphasize the futility of human undertaking, as movements that go nowhere or are bound to be lost in the inhospitable landscape of post-Soviet Russia: characters keep on moving through the same wintry landscape, which doesn't move or change. Indeed, we might say the same of the characters themselves, who, despite their seeming motion, exhibit little more than a kind of death drive. For the inhabitants of this post-Soviet landscape, mobility provides an illusory sense of agency and order, or the reassuring quality of a forward-moving traditional narrative, but in fact leads nowhere.

The titular character of *Stoker*, Ivan Scryabin—a shell-shocked war hero rendered abject—spends his days in the repetitive and seemingly endless stoking of a furnace. Meanwhile, his less traumatized fellow veterans have turned hired guns in a social environment determined by lawlessness and violence, with their repeated, seemingly pointless murders aligning with Ivan's stoking of the furnace. Balabanov makes the connection quite clear, as these soldiers-turned-mobsters take advantage of the stoker's Myshkin-like "holiness" to burn the corpses of their victims (including Ivan's daughter) in the ovens of the old decaying factory. The film's repetitive score and mise-en-scène (tracking shots of people trudging through a wintry urban landscape) productively take precedence over its minimalist plot of senseless violence, highlighting the philosophical quality of the liminal urban landscape as opposed to the events of the lurid plot. Drifting away from the diegetic and toward the discursive, this emphasis brings cinema and reflexivity back to the fore, not least in the short story the stoker is trying to write (a tale of cruelty imparted by an ethnic Russian onto a Yakut household), powerfully echoing the motif of senseless exploitation and a corrupt, decaying society, as well as doubling the present-day plot of the film. Through this juxtaposition of two stories, we begin to see how this landscape is not only or uniquely a post-Soviet one (although this does not mean that Balabanov is not sensitive to the specificities of the situation he depicts, even if he approaches it with a kind of transhistorical fatalism). The stoker's story, connecting nineteenth-century colonial violence and

Figure 13.1. A foreclosed, negative utopia: a typical "Balabanovyan" terminal wintry landscape and the famous "Tarkovskyan" motif of a church bell tower in ruins. *Me Too* (*Ya tozhe hochu*). Directed by Aleksei Balabanov. Saint Petersburg: CTB, 2012. Screen capture by Michael Cramer and Jeremi Szaniawski.

greed with that of late twentieth-century mobsters and oligarchs, gives us a sense of the repetitiousness of history. And what connects past and present, here, is of course the landscape—very often represented, in Balabanov (indeed, in half of his output!), as wintry and snowy.

Winter, in Balabanov, is associated with something terminal, nuclear, and dominant (his take on a Tarkovskyan Zone, in *Me Too* [*Ya tozhe hochu*, 2012], is set in an eternal wintry landscape). This wintry quality suggests that the present remains frozen or stuck within both material and metaphorical remnants of the past—that actions do not function "historically" in a Hegelian or Marxist manner, but simply repeat past trauma. The character of the locales that Balabanov represents so frequently, and the heaps of dirtied snow to be found in them, only reinforces the sense of hopelessness, of something that does not move, and is unlikely to be dislodged by a thaw of any kind. Unlike in Tarkovsky, the key dyad is not fire and water but fire and snow. Fire, in *Stoker*, is bereft of the mystical association Deleuze attributed to it in Tarkovsky: it is basely material despite being evanescent. It does not warm people's souls; it warms only their fragile or dying bodies. And the stoker's fire, while used to cremate corpses, can never melt the winter of a derailed history. Even when a thaw does occur, it simply seems to continue the repetition of violence, enabling the propagation of a form of "evil": think of the pornographer Yogan drifting away on a piece of broken ice on the Neva at the close of *Of Freaks and Men* (*Pro urodov i lyudey*, 1998).

Like Sokurov, then, Balabanov adopts a disillusioned approach to history, but to the withdrawal or enclosure of space in the former, he proposes a pessimistic approach that consists of opening it up: in Sokurov, space is disorienting in its cinematic decoupage—and deliberately so. Balabanov, on the contrary, adopts the rules of Hollywood continuity editing and subverts them: the clarity in his treatment of interior space makes it all the more disturbing in enhancing our intimacy with the heinous acts taking place therein (the abduction and rape in *Cargo 200*), and the spectator is not given the luxury of imagining that s/he exists in a separate space or time from the characters. Some of the settings that Balabanov favors, however, still retain a measure of inscrutability: take, for instance, the endless snowy expanses of *Morphine* (*Morfiy*, 2008) or *Me Too*, or the perilous mountains of Chechnya in *War* (*Voina*, 2002), which seem to still stand in some way outside of history, albeit in a way that is self-consciously ironic. Most important, however, is the specific quality and allegorical function of his most typical setting, namely the suburban—a space between interior urban areas and the country, with its disaffected postindustrial zoning, courtyards, and roads. In the liminal and "impure" quality of these landscapes, there still remains a sense that time exists and holds meaning: space, as Eisenstein well knew, is also temporal, and bears upon it the signs of uneven development, and hence inevitably reminds us that history is a process rather than a constant, even if it grinds to a halt. The possibility of utopia is thus still conceivable outside of the aesthetic realm, but only as something negative, foreclosed, or reduced to parodic form (the bell tower in *Me Too*). While Sokurov has, later in his career, put his conservative, preservationist concerns (sometimes considered reactionary) into action in order to protest and critique the expansion of postmodern spaces such as gaudy malls and hotels—to the detriment of architectural landscapes—in St. Petersburg, Balabanov extols the putrid beauty of the decaying urban landscape, which he connects with forms of oppression in the flux of history. Whereas Sokurov clearly separates the urban/modern and the countryside/traditional, Balabanov shows them as deeply interconnected. History thus is still with us, and refuses any containment, not to mention any delineation of truly "separate" spaces.

History is surely still with us, albeit in a very different way, in the films of Alexei German, whose use of landscape (and snow and mud in particular) is at once the most allegorically loaded and at the same time most concrete of all the filmmakers described here. German's technique, particularly in *My Friend Ivan Lapshin* (*Moy drug Ivan Lapshin*, 1984) and *Khrustalyov, My Car!* (*Khrustalyov, mashinu!*, 1998), hinges on a simultaneous closeness and distance from the landscapes of the past. On one hand, both films distance us from the past through the use of voice-over, or, rather, force us to be in two places at once. On the other, their use of the camera (particularly in the latter, as in *Hard to Be a God* [*Trudno byt' bogom*, 2013]) is resolutely anthropomorphic: the camera moves and gazes like a human being, and those in the images confront it as it weaves around them, always at risk, it seems, of bumping into something (here we might note how telling it is to compare this camera movement to the always ghostly, disembodied one of Sokurov). This same movement that seems to put us into the past, in a bodily sense, at the same time makes it ungraspable. As Fredric Jameson notes, "what this kind of movement does is to obliterate scenic distance along with perspective itself ... the difference between these places and settings, these spaces and architectures, is virtually wiped out, as in a landscape seen from a moving train."[6] There is thus a constant tension between a sense that we can fully inhabit the past (or, indeed, space altogether) and one that it eludes our grasp or understanding. It is also worth noting that, like Balabanov, German does not hesitate to implicate the viewer in what he depicts: we are not only there, but we have adopted a gaze of surveillance (however imperfect) akin to that of the Stalinists in *Khrustalyov*. The relationship between ourselves and the past is thus, among other things, one of complicity.

With German more than in any of the other directors considered here, landscape and the elements exhibit an unstable quality, not only in their incessant movement (as though they were animated not through natural forces but through the movement and action of what Jameson calls the "figure in motion"),[7] but also through their transitional or evanescent character. On the one hand we are confronted with the resolute materiality of snow and mud (to whose crucial importance we will shortly return), yet on the other the landscape and the humanmade objects that populate it often fade into the mist, as the whiteness of the wintry landscapes blots out everything that inhabits them. Yet if there is a kind of absorption of the human here, a union between man and nature, it is a profoundly ironic and abject one, unlike the transcendent one that Tarkovsky seeks. Nothing actually dissolves or disappears; it only fades from our view, as attested to by German's emphasis, in tension with disappearance or evaporation, on the resolute persistence and materiality of mud and snow. Just as the train on which the General is riding at the end of *Khrustalyov* seems about to vanish into the white landscape (a motif we have already seen several times in the film), the frame freezes, as though insisting on cinema's ability to prevent this disappearance or dissolution just as much as its capacity to depict it. It is this materiality, and cinema's ability to convey it with such palpability and force, that provides another form of connection between the spectator and history.

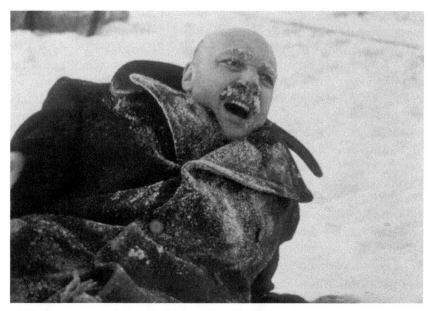

Figure 13.2. A striking and palpable image: The Doctor (Yuriy Tsurilo) gets a taste of snow, mud, and blood as he is confronted with the materiality of a History that hurts and stains. *Khrustalyov, My Car!* (*Khrustalyov, mashinu!*). Directed by Aleksei German. Saint Petersburg: Lenfilm, Studiya pervogo i eksperimentalnogo filma, and Petroagroprombank; Moscow: RTR; and Paris: La Sept and Canal+, 1998. Screen capture by Michael Cramer and Jeremi Szaniawski.

In German, mud and snow, which comprise the majority of his landscapes, are not only images or landscapes but simply matter as such, and are hence continuous with the same "substance" or materiality of human beings. We find the relationship between the human body and these elements articulated in German's frequent use of images in which snow or mud is thrust into a character's face, often with the aim of forcing them to eat it. These are some of the most striking and palpable images in his films, and perhaps the greatest source of the disgust with which they are often met. Landscape becomes a kind of projectile, something to literally shove in the viewer's face (a function that is perhaps that of the films as a whole, as suggested by the early scene in *Khrustalyov* when Aleksei spits at his own image in the mirror). The elements bear a kinship with bodily fluids, and the human body itself, in their capacity to spatter, shatter, and change shapes, and indeed to be incorporated into one another, as suggested by the ubiquitous motif of ingestion.

On a literal level, we might argue that this characterization of the land as a kind of manipulable, even weaponizable, materiality simply suggests that it is the irreducibility of matter itself that ultimately connects us with the past—and, most importantly, with its atrocities. While this is surely true, it would be a mistake to see German's snow and mud as simply depictions of brute matter. Instead, we might turn to Jameson's observations about the repulsive nature of German's work, which he characterizes as an attack on the aestheticization of daily life (something like a *very* late modernist gesture).[8] With this in mind, we can begin to see how what appears to be "brute matter" here is not that at all, but rather stands in (as it does in Balabanov) for something like the repulsiveness and pain of history itself (the "imaginary" setting of *Hard to Be a God* only underscores this effect, insofar as it is conceptualized precisely in terms of a Hegelian-Marxist and materialist conception of historical development). We cannot flee from this history that hurts through the pleasure of the beautiful image; landscape represents an element that persists because we have not yet moved beyond that history, and indeed not yet fulfilled its promise. But we might ask here whether German's conception of history, as expressed through landscape and the elements, is ultimately a fatalistic or cynical one, as in Balabanov: are we simply living in an abject landscape from which we can never emerge, that can never change? The aesthetic, despite Jameson's characterization of German's films as "not aesthetically accessible at all,"[9] still plays some role here: indeed, German is not, for all the talk of his films' repulsive character, entirely averse to the beautiful image (as attested to in the fades into the mist of *Khrustalyov*, the painterly and almost Sokurovian first image of *Hard to Be a God*, and a panoply of images in *Ivan Lapshin*).

There is thus always a sense that there is something of value (whether real or imagined) in the past; to be seduced by this would be entirely reactionary, yet to couple these moments of beauty with grime and brutality, shoving them in our faces, constitutes an unresolved dialectic between an in fact properly utopian refusal to let the past dissolve into glossy images or a fetish object (as in Sokurov), and an insistence on its status as a source of utopian drive (if we think of the beautiful image, much like the ugly one, in abstract or allegorical terms, rather than a literal reference to pastness), calling our attention to the way that that drive has continually been thwarted. There is something in history that haunts us, but also something that we long for, in a way that cannot be fully contained by the concept of nostalgia, namely the utopian. Of course, when that utopian drive fails not only on earth but also on the distant planet of Arkanar, it is hard not to see a concession to fatalism. At the same time, the ability of the spectator to continue to feel or sense both beauty and ugliness, transcendence and abjection, in the very fabric of matter itself, suggests that somehow what we see on the screen represents unfinished business.

Perhaps what is most important, then, in thinking about the utopian dimension of landscape within the post-Soviet context, is that utopia is no longer a project to be undertaken, nor is it a matter of somehow harnessing the power of the land, whether in spiritual or materialist terms. Only in Zvyagintsev does land represent something literal to be obtained or kept (in other words, the site of a political squabble that has little interest in anything other than power itself in its most primitive forms), while with all three of our other filmmakers, it represents a more abstract historical challenge, calling upon the viewer to consider what Russia was and what it is now. If Sokurov's aestheticizing approach represents a kind of backward-looking fetishism, in which any utopian elements are now lost and can only be compensated for through art (quite literally, in *Russian Ark*) and through beauty, Balabanov and German force us to see the ugliness of the land and the history whose allegorical image it is. It is, then, ugliness, simply in its acknowledgment and direct presentation to the viewer, that still bears the utopian impulse: first, because, as Jameson reminds us, utopian thought has always been more concerned with "the alleviation and elimination of the sources of exploitation and suffering, rather than at the composition of blueprints for bourgeois comfort"[10] — and it is indeed only in ugliness that we can find the acknowledgment of this exploitation or suffering, which far exceeds (and indeed is perversely minimized) by the (seemingly) liberal objections of a Zvyagintsev. And second, because these two filmmakers, and German in particular, carve out a space where, in the realm of cinema, all "bourgeois comforts" are refused and revealed to be the palliative narcotics that they really are, a means of forgetting history. To truly confront history demands that the filmmaker quite literally throw it in our face, like a clod of mud.

Michael Cramer is Associate Professor of Film History at Sarah Lawrence College. He is the author of *Utopian Television: Rossellini, Godard, and Watkins Beyond Cinema* (2017), and the co-editor of *Fredric Jameson and Film Theory: Marxism, Allegory, and Geopolitics in World Cinema*, with Jeremi Szaniawski and Keith B. Wagner (2022). His work has been published in venues including *October*, *New Left Review*, *Senses of Cinema*, and *1895*.

Jeremi Szaniawski is Associate Professor of Comparative Literature and Film Studies, and the Amesbury Professor of Polish Language and Culture at the University of Massachusetts at Amherst. He has published extensively on the topic of Russian cinema, including in his monograph *The Cinema of Alexander Sokurov: Figures of Paradox* (2014), and the coedited volume *The Global Auteur: The Politics of Authorship in 21st Century Cinema* (2016). He has also translated the book by Alexander Sokurov *В центре океана* into French, under the title *Au cœur de l'océan* (2015).

Notes

1. Deleuze, *Cinema 2*, 75.
2. Szaniawski, "*Days of the Eclipse.*"
3. Jameson, "Soviet Magic Realism."
4. Arnaud, *Le cinéma de Sokourov.*
5. See Jacques Rancière, "Le cinéma comme la peinture?"
6. Jameson, "Suffocating Kinesis," 152.
7. Idem., 153.
8. Idem., 150.
9. Ibidem.
10. Jameson, *Archeologies of the Future*, 12.

Bibliography

Arnaud, Diane. *Le cinéma de Sokourov. Figures d'enfermement.* Paris: L'Harmattan, 2005.

Deleuze, Gilles. *Cinema 2: The Time Image*, translated by Hugh Tomlinson and Robert Galeta. Minneapolis: University of Minnesota Press, 1989.

Jameson, Fredric. "On Soviet Magic Realism." In Fredric Jameson, *The Geopolitical Aesthetic: Cinema and Sace in the World System*, 87–114. Bloomington: Indiana University Press, 1995.

——. *Archeologies of the Future: The Desire Called Utopia and Other Science Fictions.* London: Verso, 2005.

——. "Suffocating Kinesis: The Late Films of Aleksei German." In *The Global Auteur*, edited by Seung-hoon Jeong and Jeremi Szaniawski, 149–159. London: Bloomsbury Academic, 2016.

Rancière, Jacques. "Le cinéma comme la peinture?" in *Cahiers du cinéma* 531, 30-32, January 1999

Szaniawski, Jeremi. "*Days of the Eclipse*—A New Hope?" In *100 Years of Soviet Cinema*, edited by Daniel Fairfax. LedaTape Organization, 2019.

Filmography

Balabanov, Aleksei. *Happy Days* (*Schastlivye dni*, USSR, 1991).
——. *Of Freaks and Men* (*Pro urodov i lyudey*, Russia, 1998).
——. *War* (*Voina*, 2002).
——. *Cargo 200* (*Gruz 200*, Russia, 2007).
——. *Morphine* (*Morfiy*, Russia, 2008).
——. *Stoker* (*Kochegar*, Russia, 2010).
——. *Me Too* (*Ya tozhe hochu*, Russia, 2012).
German, Aleksei. *My Friend Ivan Lapshin* (*Moy drug Ivan Lapshin*, USSR, 1985).

———. *Khrustalyov, My Car!* (*Khrustalyov, mashinu!*, Russia, 1998).
———. *Hard to Be a God* (*Trudno byt' bogom*, Russia, 2013).
Sokurov, Alexander. *Lonely Voice of Man* (*Odinokiy golos cheloveka*, USSR, produced in 1978, released 1987).
———. *Mournful Unconcern* (*Skorbnoye bezchustviye*, USSR, produced in 1983, released in 1987).
———. *Days of the Eclipse* (*Dni zatmeniya*, USSR, 1988).
———. *Save and Protect* (*Spasi i sokhrani*, USSR, 1989).
———. *The Second Circle* (*Krug vtoroi*, USSR, 1990).
———. *The Stone* (*Kamen'*, Russia, 1992).
———. *Mother and Son* (*Mat' i syn*, Russia, 1997).
———. *Moloch* (*Moloch*, Russia, 1999).
———. *Taurus* (*Telets*, Russia, 2001).
———. *Russian Ark* (*Russkiy kovcheg*, 2002).
———. *Faust* (2011)
Tarkovsky, Andrei. *Mirror* (*Zerkalo*, USSR, 1975).
———. *Stalker* (*Stalker*, USSR, 1979).
Zvyagintsev, Andrey. *The Return* (*Vozvrashcheniye*, Russia, 2003).
———. *The Banishment* (*Izgnanie*, Russia, 2007).
———. *Elena* (*Elena*, Russia, 2011).
———. *Leviathan* (*Leviafan*, Russia, 2014).
———. *Loveless* (*Nelyubov*, Russia, 2017).

14

Recycling, Citroën Cars, and Roma Refugees in Boris Mitić's *Pretty Dyana* (2003)

Alice Bardan

In his essay "The New Citroën," Roland Barthes suggested that the Citroën DS model introduced in 1955 at the Paris Motor Show was the modern equivalent of a sacred item. Enchanted by the beauty of the French-made car, the critic famously remarked that one could compare it to Gothic cathedrals and that consumers would appropriate it as a magical object. The DS belonged to the stuff of fairytales, an object able to captivate modern audiences in the same way in which *Nautilus*, the legendary submarine that allowed captain Nemo to glide through the sea in Jules Verne's novels, was able to enthrall nineteenth-century audiences. The linguistic connotations of the DS, pronounced *Déesse* in French, encouraged consumers to associate it with a goddess, the divine coming from heaven.

Describing the intensity of the sensation when touching the DS, Barthes remarked:

> One keenly fingers the edges of the windows; one feels along the wide rubber grooves which link the back window to its metal surround. There are in the DS the beginnings of a new phenomenology of assembling as if one progressed from a world where elements are welded to a world where they are juxtaposed and held together by sole virtue of their wondrous shape.[1]

The exaggerated femininity, supported in French by the grammatical gender of *la voiture*, provided the car with grandeur and gentleness. The DS was more feminine, softer, lighter, and without virile bumper bars and radiator grills. In order to suggest that it was gliding, the car was often showcased at trade fairs without its wheels. The associations of space travel, femininity, and religious glory alienated the object from its worldliness and transformed it into a container for the imagination.

The documentary film that I examine here, Boris Mitić's *Pretty Dyana: A Gypsy Recycling Saga* (*Lijepa Dyana*, 2003), foregrounds a group of Roma refugees living in a cardboard settlement on the outskirts of Belgrade who express their love for old, rusty-looking Citroën 2CV and Citroën Dyane cars with the same exuberance that Barthes showed in his mythicization of the DS.[2] For them, all the recycled Citroën models are simply "Dyanas," feminized vehicles invested with potential and hope. Tracking the Roma's ingenious ways of modifying and repurposing old Citroën cars as recycling vehicles that enable them to work faster than those who recycle with push carts, the film uses their stories of resourcefulness as a way of providing a broader perspective on their realities. Most importantly, it reveals how essential these cars are for the Roma's resilience and survival. I argue that the documentary powerfully challenges viewers to reconsider received ideas and assumptions about the Roma, promoting them as unsung recycling heroes by revealing the wit and grit they employ to collect the city's waste. Drawing on Levi-Strauss's figure of the *bricoleur* and on the Chicano scholar Tomás Ybarra-Frausto's theorization of *rasquache* as a means of empowerment for the downtrodden, I first explore the documentary's emphasis on the Roma's assertive display of their modified cars and link it with other films and documentaries that foreground the agency of vulnerable subjects. I then consider the film's invitation to reflect on the history and environmental legacy of the Citroën cars in Europe.

Eschewing the solemnity that often characterizes aesthetic encounters with poverty, *Pretty Dyana* develops a humorous gaze that constantly shows its complicity with the Roma's own ironic stance toward their challenging situation. As displaced refugees, they are forced to be on the move after having been caught in the dramatic interethnic conflict between the Albanian and the Serbian segment of the Kosovo population. In 1999, when NATO attacked Yugoslavia's aerial defenses in support of the Albanian population, the Kosovar Liberation Army, an ethnic Albanian separatist militia, expelled from Kosovo a large number of Romani people whom they considered allied with Serbs. In order to escape death, the latter took refuge in central Serbia, settling around Belgrade's city dumps or on the edge of construction or industrial areas, where there was little risk of eviction. Given the absence of official papers to legitimize their status and the almost complete lack of income-generating options due to their uncertain position, the Roma protagonists in the film resort to sorting out the city's garbage. They have few, if any, material possessions, and their home is an improvised shelter made of tarps and scraps.

The documentary reveals how despite the Roma's hard efforts to work rather than engage in begging to survive, their labor is low-paid and thankless. An absence of formal contracts, coupled with discrimination that often locks Roma out of other job opportunities, leaves the scrap collectors open to exploitation by companies who purchase what they collect for next to nothing. *Pretty Dyana*, however, foregrounds how by modifying Citroën cars to transport recyclables, the Roma families in the film become examples of true survivalists in a world where people ignore them and where "nobody gives them anything." A moving scene in the film reveals Adem's frustration with being excluded from a community that doesn't recognize people like him: "Yugoslavia won the gold medal . . . but they didn't give anything to the poor. Why don't they give something to us, refugees? A bag of flour, at least! We also cheer for Yugoslavia! We, too, have the will to win! Even greater than the Serbs!" While the film's subject matter is serious, it doesn't take itself overly seriously, thus avoiding pedantry and self-righteousness.

Since the Roma/Gypsies occupy a central place in the imagination of the West as objects of both revulsion and fascination, their representation in a documentary about the recycling of strange-looking cars raises important issues regarding the production and consumption and images of the subordinate Other.[3] Dina Iordanova has pointed out, in this respect, that the persistent interest in "Gypsies" has prompted critics to probe questions of stylization and exoticization raised by many filmmakers' exploitation of the "visual sumptuousness of colorful Roma."[4] In her critique of *Dallas Among Us* (*Dallas Pashamende*, 2005), a fiction film about a group of poor but spirited Gypsies living on a heap of waste in Romania, Iordanova describes the "rough realism as exotica" genre, a genre driven by filmmakers' apparent social concern for vulnerable people which, in turn, masks their exploitation of the stereotypical framework of Gypsy passions and surreal imagery.[5] Probing representations of Romani people in cinema, Anikó Imre notes that many documentary films from the Balkans featuring Romani themes tend to either "correct the record" by emphasizing images of exploited Romanies or "celebrate the nonconventional" by exoticizing Romani lifestyles.[6]

From this perspective that recognizes the difficult task of documentary filmmakers' attempts to avoid the exoticization of Romani lifestyles, I read Mitić's *Pretty Dyana* as a documentary able to skillfully negotiate the burden of representing marginal identities. I suggest that the film's foregrounding of how the Roma families proudly boast about their "pretty" modified cars marks them as subjects who are able to resignify their deprivation in order to showcase skills and practices associated with the Levi-Straussian figure of the *bricoleur*. Underscoring their constant preoccupation with sorting and recycling garbage and their ability to reuse and recombine things in ingenious ways, Mitić's documentary celebrates the Roma's environmental agency and their extraordinary resourcefulness. As the director points out, the Roma are like alchemists who transform old cars into "symbols of power, freedom, and style."[7] Ingenious and creative in myriad ways, they customize their Dyanas by painting them and fitting them with radios, alarms, and even cigarette lighters. Moreover, they skillfully demonstrate how one can use the cars' batteries as power supplies that allow one to charge their phones, listen to music, and even watch television for hours.

At the beginning of *Pretty Dyana*, a few English subtitles provide viewers with a context for the story they are about to watch: "Between 1948 and 1990, Citroën has produced 6,806319 2CV, Dyane, and Ami cars that reached a cult status worldwide. Twelve hundred of them are still cruising in Belgrade... But that's only according to official statistics..." The rest of the film depicts the strong affective bonds that the Roma build over time for each of their repurposed cars, tracing the process of how the Dyanas are acquired, torn up, and transformed. Mitić foregrounds the Roma as hardworking laborers and road "heroes" who, at times, enjoy the thrills of speed afforded by driving their cherished possessions. The opening scenes showcase teenager Touche proudly demonstrating how fast his Dyana can go, even though the speedometer is broken. He then explains, standing and looking at the camera, that he is going against the regular traffic on a side road to avoid the policemen who could fine him for driving a vehicle without a valid permit and required paperwork. Since one does not usually need a license plate to operate a farm vehicle, the Roma completely remove the hoods of their Dyanas in the hope that the policemen will turn a blind eye. However, the police often wait for them as they return to their camp at the end of the day, fining them and even beating them up. "We tell them we can't get proper papers because we are illiterate, but they say they don't care," Goran laments.

At the end of the film, when Touche proudly asserts that he will continue working and driving his beloved Dyana while others are still afraid of being caught by police, Imer's wife casually remarks, "He's young, he's never been busted. He doesn't know how it feels to be beaten!" She thus exposes how normalized punitive measures against the vulnerable Roma have become and the real impact that they have on poor families. When

Figure 14.1. *Pretty Dyana: A Gypsy Recycling Saga* (*Lijepa Dyana*). Directed by Boris Mitić. Belgrade: Dribbling Pictures, 2003. Screen capture by Alice Bardan.

Imer returns from prison, his young daughter walks away from him, pretending not to recognize him with short hair. Although this is a small incident, the tension it generates reveals the real-life consequences of criminalizing the Roma's waste management efforts rather than supporting them. A visibly hurt Imer looks embarrassed and nervously laughs, ashamed of the fact that his own daughter has rejected him.

Some of the most poignant aspects of the vicissitudes endured by the Roma protagonists emerge from things that are left unsaid while they are in the process of describing their love for their Dyanas. In one scene, Adem explains that he had to sell his first Dyana to pay for his wife's Cesarean operation, and his second one for a trip in search of his mother, who drowned off the coast of Montenegro, on a boat to Italy. He is then quick to admit that he would never make the mistake of selling his most beloved possession again, since his identity and freedom are tied to having a means of transportation and a sense of owning something.

Even though Mitić touchingly exposes the frustrations experienced by the Roma for having been abandoned by authorities and by society in general, he ultimately refuses to dwell on their suffering. Balancing moments of sadness with scenes in which the Roma are shown engrossed in the process of tearing up and refitting the cars with whatever means they have available at hand, the film incorporates a series of Dyana songs by Hüsker Dü ("Diane"), Ferid Avdic ("Dijana ljubavi"), Paul Anka ("Diana") and

Michael Jackson ("Dirty Diana"), which add a humorous tone and encourage viewers to empathize with the protagonists.

Emphasizing the Roma's sense of agency derived from owning a recycled car, the documentary traces the process through which these people acquire a sense of dignity and the role that their Dyanas play in their perceptions of themselves as winners rather than losers in life. In one scene, Imer addresses the camera explaining that he sends his son to school "so that . . . he doesn't have to wander, like me. So that he learns something and gets a job," and then proudly exclaims that his son can already drive better than him. His eyes light up with a sense of pride that, as a father, he had something to teach his son: "For those of you who only watched on camera, he drove all the way around the block, and he came back to the square. There you go! My eight-year-old son, Sultan!"

Pretty Dyana's playful look at its Roma families neither exoticizes nor derides them for their infatuation with their customized cars. Instead, it exposes the discrepancy between the high value that the Roma place on their metamorphosed cars and the small amount of money earned from recycling with the help of their improvised means of transportation. At the beginning of the film, Imer, one of the Roma protagonists, remarks that he only makes "two to three euros per shift: one for the fuel and one for me, just enough to say that I am not working for free." Later on, Touche reveals that after the hard work of collecting and uploading a truck full of cardboard, the money he receives from the waste collection barely covers his gas and a few beers.

The very first images of the film introduce us to a group of Roma children surrounded by strewn garbage materials. They are playing a hand-clapping game while singing a children's rhyme. The choice to begin the film with children playing around a rusty recycled Dyana works to normalize the car as a friendly possession. Images of children punctuate the film, but the director doesn't ask us to pity them. We see them either observing or helping their parents fix their cars, doing homework, happily jumping into a pile of shredded paper, or chasing chickens around. In one scene, a child even drives around the block in a Dyana filled with laughing children enjoying the ride.

This filmic approach stands in stark contrast to the way in which a range of recent ecological documentaries such as *The 11th Hour* (2007), *Crude* (2009), *Trashed* (2012), *Waste Land* (2010), *The Baby Needs Some Fresh Air* (*La bambina deve prendere aria*, 2009), *Beautiful Country* (*Biùtiful cauntri*, 2008), and *A Mountain of Bales* (*Una montagna di balle*, 2009), which seek to raise environmental awareness by projecting an impending environmental catastrophe of trash. Karl Schoonover underscores that such films tend to rely on shock value to highlight the proximity of dangerous waste.

Often, they use aerial photography that minimizes the human subject, tracing the disappearance of human subjectivity as it is consumed by the menacing reality of the garbage. Moreover, Schoonover points out:

> Think of the highly rhetorical function of images of children in these documentaries: a child plays in dumping grounds in *Crude*; hunts for Easter eggs on a lawn dotted with lesions left behind by fracking in *GasLand*; drinks from polluted streams in *Trashed*; or tries to breathe through pollution in *La bambina deve prendere aria*.... In the repetition of the endangered child, the toxic's virulence—its destabilization of the psychical integrity of spaces and bodies—leans on the traditional emblem of human reproduction and hope for the future.[8]

While many eco-documentaries prefer to use the image of a figure disappearing into an inanimate mass of junk, Mitić's film privileges low-angle shots that make his subject look more important and dignified. Often, his protagonists appear in close-up or medium shots, speaking directly into the camera. Eschewing a rhetoric of othering that constructs the Roma as unclean or unhuman, the documentary foregrounds the trash surrounding the Roma families as simply a part of their environment, not as squalor. Adem recognizes at one point that the Romas burn a lot of things that may bother people, yet he admits that once the construction of the church nearby is finished, their families will move to another place.

Recent scholarship that theorizes waste has brought attention to "wasted people" treated poorly because of their association with it, critiquing the idea of waste as being disgusting and examining how trash builds up around certain groups of people. Maite Zubiaurre's *Talking Trash* (2019), for instance, decouples waste from vilification and disgust to reveal a much wider wealth of meanings and interactions. Susan Signe Morrison's *The Literature of Waste* (2015) argues for giving dignity to things in order to bring more dignity to people. In *Wasted Lives* (2003), Zygmunt Bauman suggests that the border politics of globalization categorized many people as human waste, dumped into the refuse heaps of asylum seekers, refugee camps, or urban ghettoes. His book, however, offers no redemption, highlighting a sense of the impossibility of agency and resistance on the part of those who are designated as human waste. Gillian Wylie comments in this respect that to suggest that such people "have 'learned the futility of resistance and surrendered to the verdict of their own inferiority' suppresses alternative stories" in which people demonstrate their ability to strategize and use their agency to surmount various obstacles.[9]

Each Dyana, the film intimates, is as precious for the Roma families as the stolen bicycle in Vittorio De Sica's *Bicycle Thieves* (*Ladri di biciclette*, 1948), the famous postwar neorealist film that Bruce Bennett reads as "a fable of mobility, masculinity, and economic precarity."[10] Indeed, one can read *Pretty Dyana* in line with a series of films that seem to *recycle* and indirectly cite *Bicycle Thieves*, or who use De Sica's film as a sort of "narrative and thematic chassis."[11] A film that follows such a template is Theodoros Bafaloukos's *Rockers* (1978), which offers an account of the impoverished lives of Rastafarian Jamaicans. The plot centers on a drummer whose motorcycle that helps him sell records of reggae music is stolen after he stops to visit an open-air dance. To give another example, in Ousmane Sembène's *The Cart Driver* (*Barom Sarret*, 1963), a poor but kind cart driver working in Senegal's capital ends up being pulled over by the police after a malicious customer obliges him to enter an area where carts are banned. Since he cannot afford the fine, his cart is impounded, leaving the driver a humiliated man who dreads seeing his wife and child without money.

It is important to stress that *Pretty Dyana* does not simply ask spectators to "take mercy on the pitiful," as Karl Schoonover points out in his analysis of *Bicycle Thieves*.[12] Much like Sebastian Antico's *The Nexus* (*El nexo*, 2005), a science fiction film made on the cheap by dwellers in a slum in Buenos Aires, Argentina, and Federico Leon and Marcos Martinez's *Stars* (*Estrellas*, 2007), which began as a documentary about the process of filming *El nexo*, Mitić's film deploys a perspective that works against the "melodrama of poverty" (a phrase coined by Mexican critic Carlos Monsiváis with reference to Latin America), throwing into relief how the reappropriation of destitution can be linked to alternative forms of social and artistic agency.[13] Both *Stars* and *The Nexus* highlight deprivation and restage social inequality by advancing inventive modes of action. In *The Nexus*, slum dwellers imagine a science fiction film in which aliens who invade earth land on a slum rather than on a perfectly manicured lawn, as they do in American films. Dressed in white plastic bags, aliens descend from a spaceship that "looks a lot like a classic Citroën CV," only to be defeated thanks to the special water of the slums.[14] As Víctor Goldgel-Carballo suggests, in this film the slum dwellers become "heroes of the abject" who use rotten water and their degraded material conditions as their main weapons.

Stars documents a collective acting project and a casting agency for the inhabitants of a shantytown in Buenos Aires. The goal of the project "Arte Villa" is to provide the film industry with actors who "act" their own poverty, an act that "makes explicit the idea of the collapse of all distinctions between 'being' and 'performance.'"[15] Insisting on creating *villero* heroes and on bringing a *villero* point of view to a public sphere saturated by narratives and images of criminalized poor, the shantytown dwellers in the film disrupt some of the rules by which the poor are spectacularized. This process involves their assertive display of poverty as they capitalize on their appearance as a way of reappropriating their status for monetary gain. In his insightful analysis of the documentary, Gabriel Giorgi comments that it "literalizes and, at the same time, turns paradoxical the relationship between precarity and subjectivity: it illuminates a mechanism by which social exclusion can be viewed as a proprietary, appropriable resource capable of being inserted in the marketplace of images."[16] Indeed, this sense of subjectivity acquired through a process of aesthetic re-appropriation of poverty can also be helpful in thinking about the power of Boris Mitić's documentary. Moreover, I suggest that we can also think about the Roma's agency and subjectivity developed through the process of modifying old cars not by associating the Roma's works with the "dark art" of Edward Burtynsky, who has become famous for his photographs of toxic waste, industrial areas, and recycling plants, but by drawing on Chicano scholar Tomas Ybarra-Frausto's theorization of the *rasquache*.

Ybarra-Frausto uses *rasquache*, a Mexican Spanish slang term that refers to something tacky, of bad taste, of "no value," a leftover, to describe rasquachismo, a conceptual aesthetic category that expresses an underdog perspective in working-class Chicano communities. For Ybarra-Frausto, *rasquachismo* is a view of the downtrodden that uses elements of hybridization and juxtaposition as a means of empowerment and resistance and as an attitude of survival and inventiveness. "Neither an idea nor a style, but more of an attitude or a taste,"[17] *rasquachismo* is a sensibility describing "the politics of making do, of cobbling together makeshift solutions, using whatever's at hand, more often than not the cast-off junk of the conspicuously consuming upper classes."[18] To perform *rasquache* is to use recycling in an environment that is always on the edge of coming apart, employing one's resilience and resourcefulness to deal with a social reality where one finds oneself poor, disenfranchised, and mired in elemental daily struggles for survival. *Rasquachismo* entails being unfettered and unrestrained, favoring the flamboyant, bright colors over muted tones, and using whatever coping strategies one uses "to gain time, to make options, to retain hope."[19] As a textbook example of *rasquachismo*, the lowrider car, customized by Mexican Americans in the US Southwest who were outsiders to the commodity spectacle and popularized by Hollywood movies such as *Selena* (1997), *Napoleon Dynamite* (2004), and *Straight Outta Compton* (2015), can be a useful comparison to the Citroën cars transformed by the Roma in Mitić's film.[20]

A similar point of view that foregrounds the inventive ways in which outsiders manage to "make do" with cars chronically on the verge of mechanical collapse is highlighted in David Batty and Francis Jupurrurla Kelly's *Bush Mechanics* (2001), which consists of five half-hour television episodes first made in 1998. These episodes explore the relationship to cars of a group of young Aboriginal men from the Yuendumu community in remote Australia, emphasizing the bush mechanics' clever hacks to showcase their ingenious approach to mechanics. While the Roma in *Pretty Dyana* hook up a Sprite bottle as fuel reservoir or connect a brake pedal to the handbrake lever with a piece of antenna cable, the bush mechanics similarly use unusual methods to fix their cars, repairing a puncture by lifting the car onto a jerry can or stuffing the tire casing with spinifex grass. Their story is told by men who speak directly to the camera and who use humor and self-deprecation to explain their enthusiasm for cars.

Reflecting on this Australian film's provocation to viewers, Gay Hawkins asks us to consider the human agency driving the practice of *bricolage* by drawing on what Bruno Latour refers to as "the networked quality of things." The representations of practicality of the bush mechanics' repair techniques, Hawkins suggests, "continually foreground the heterogeneity of things in the world and the fluidity of their classifications; things are continually open to new uses and frames of understanding."[21] Keeping the car on the road therefore "involves a radical openness to the technical possibilities of anything and everything."[22] In other words, trash for the bush people is not just rubbish but something available for transformation. In this respect, drawing attention to the fact that we are increasingly presented with cars as "sealed objects" that we are discouraged to tinker with, Georgine Clarsen insightfully points out that nowadays cars have become objects given by experts, designed with no room to move except for the kind of authorized movement already built in them. This flattening of possibility, she insists, no matter how much it is justified in the name of progress, "also embodies political choices about how lives should be lived, how we may act, and who can take responsibility for what. From this perspective, *Bush Mechanics* offers a timely reminder of the contingent nature of the technological worlds we inhabit."[23]

Indeed, it is important to remember that many companies nowadays use planned obsolescence (the deliberate design of products to artificially limit their lifespan) to encourage or require consumers to replace products prematurely. We live in an environment that rewards planned obsolescence rather than product longevity. While within the American legal system there are currently no federal laws that prohibit planned obsolescence, in Europe France is the first and so far only country that has addressed this problem "by defining, prohibiting it, and penalizing it."[24] Even though many countries have shown concern about the issue though policy, warranty, and regulatory initiatives focused on consumer rights or repairs, they have not legally defined obsolescence and only in recent years the "right to repair movement"[25] has increased attention to the issue.[26]

Ther reason why the Roma in *Pretty Dyana* choose to recycle the 2CV and the Dyane Citroën models (produced from 1967 to 1983) is because they are the only ones from which one can remove the shell without damaging the chassis. The Citroën 2CV (*deux-chevaux* [*vapeur*] translated as "two-steam horsepower") was specifically designed by architect-engineer Pierre-Jules Boulanger to democratize car ownership. Manufactured between 1948 and 1990, this "people's car" helped motorize the large number of farmers still using horses and carts in 1930s France and became an example of innovative engineering and straightforward utilitarian bodywork. Legend has it that Boulanger came up with the idea of producing a "TPV" (*Toute Petite Voiture*, a "Very Small Car") after having been stuck on a narrow French lane behind a farmer's slow-moving horse and cart. Boulanger asked the question: why not offer French farmers a better mode of transportation, a cheap, reliable, low-maintenance car that was easy to drive and would meet their needs? At the time, he had just been made president of the French car company following the sudden death of its founder, André Citroën, in 1934. After creating the company in 1919, Citroën launched the first mass production of cars outside the United States. By the early 1930s, his company became the fourth-largest automaker in the world.

Citroën himself must be credited here for his drive to change society. His ideal was a civilization and a factory built on harmony between the classes, united in mass production and the consumption of goods. A man who understood the consumer's needs, he always championed efficiency and highly specialized mass production. Citroën was the first to institute a five-day workweek and to introduce paid holidays before they became mandatory. Not only did he envision a workers' city with shops, medical facilities, laundry, a pharmacy, a nursery, and a canteen, but he also drew attention to the gender wage gap and advocated for equal pay for men and women, in addition to maternity leave.[27]

After Citroën's death, Boulanger brought Citroën's vision for a people's car to fruition. Influenced by the German concept of *Existenzminimum* (minimum dwelling or subsistence dwelling)—a radical social project developed during a housing crisis in Germany after World War I that set the conditions for a dignified and healthy existence—he conceived the 2CV as a deceptively primitive-looking car featuring a sophisticated design.[28]

During the 1950s, the 2CV had enormous success in France, but it failed in the United States and Australia, where high comfort levels were expected. At the same time, however, it was enthusiastically adopted by many Argentineans, Chileans, Iranians, Vietnamese, and Czechoslovakians, who set up plans to build the car under license. In Yugoslavia, the 2CV model, nicknamed "Spaček" (little freak), was considered to be, along with Citroën's Dyana, the car of the liberated generation of the 1960s and 1970s. As a symbol of 1968, the Citroën 2CV is prominently featured

Figure 14.2. *The Gendarme and the Gendarmettes* (*Le Gendarme et les gendarmettes*). Directed by Jean Giraud. Neuilly-sur-Seine: SNC, 1982. Screen capture by Alice Bardan.

in Želimir Žilnik's *Early Works* (*Rani radovi*, 1960), a film concerned with exposing the ideological limitations of the 1960s political radicalism. Citroën 2CV appeared in many films, but two instances deserve mention. In 1981, the model reached filmic fame with James Bond in *For Your Eyes Only*, which contains a dramatic chase scene through the countryside. In Jean Giraud's *The Gendarme and the Gendarmettes* (*Le Gendarme et les gendarmettes*, 1982), featuring comic actor Luis de Funès, a stunt-driving nun, Soeur Clotilde, manages to drive her Citroën 2CV even after the car breaks in two. What these films foreground is the car's extraordinary versatility as well as its ability to fly in the air, land on its wheels, and function despite having some of its parts missing. With a keen eye for publicity, Citroën himself sought to promote these attributes, as he skillfully advertised his creation by performing elaborate crash and safety tests (a novelty at the time) in which the car tumbles down a hill but quickly regains stability.[29]

By showcasing the afterlives of old Citroën cars in the postsocialist world, which can now be seen in various stages of dilapidation, abandoned in parking lots, accumulating dust, and taking up space, Mitić's documentary functions as a reminder of the legacy of the French manufacturer in Eastern Europe, especially in countries such as Romania and former Yugoslavia. Moreover, the images of cars left to rust away in neighborhoods challenge viewers to reflect on the over-accumulation of secondhand cars from the West after 1989, activating, at the same time, powerful memories related to East Europeans' affective bonds with the cars produced in their own countries. Once ubiquitous under socialism, these cars, inflected with nationalist pride, began to look more and more obsolete until buyback schemes promised to get rid of them and their polluting effects. In Romania, the "Olcit" model emerged after a partnership between the Romanian communist authorities and the French automaker Citroën that began in 1977.[30] The car's name was a portmanteau word that referenced Oltenia, Ceausescu's native province, and the French Citroën.[31]

I began this chapter with the image of a Citroën DS that created a sensation when it was first introduced at the 1955 Paris Auto Show. In 1993, Mexican artist and sculptor Gabriel Orozco created one of his best known and most spectacular works, "La DS," a modified Citroën DS sculpture for which he transformed the iconic French car from the 1950s by slicing it vertically in three, removing a portion from the center of the car, and then putting the remaining parts together again to generate a new shape and a new experience. Even though part of the body of the car is missing, the artist contends that "it is still present in our bodily-cultural memory of the object."[32] Natasha Amadou suggests that Orozco literally opens up sculpture and places the body so as to inhabit it from within, like architecture, inverting the traditional perspective of the visitor who looks at an object situated vis-à-vis himself or herself in the exhibition space."[33]

In 2013, Orozco created another work titled "La DS, the Cormaline," a scarlet red replica of the same model, inspired by his stay in Havana, where vintage cars are ingrained in the Cubans' culture. I conclude with a Swiss artist's provocative invitation to see one of Dyanas used by the displaced Roma community in Belgrade as an objet trouvé reminiscent of the readymades of Marcel Duchamp. In 2008, Johannes Gees, an installation and performance artist, contacted Mitić to arrange for the shipment of a modified Citroën Dyane from 1978 to Switzerland, where it was first used in the exhibition "Moral Fantasies" (2008) at the Thurgau Art Museum. After that, "Final Fantasy," was put on display in busy city centers all over Switzerland as a reminder not only of "the first automobiles and the beginnings of gasoline-driven mobility, but also of the apocalyptic visions of the Mad Max movies."[34] The website created for the "Final Fantasy" exhibition, which includes movie clips, texts, and images that give insight into the history of this work, suggests that it could be read "as a vision of the last vehicle in this world that is being propelled by gasoline," urging spectators to reflect on our relationship to mobility and gasoline-operated cars. Most importantly, the artwork's history reminds us not only of the ethos behind the car's original creation but more specifically of the ingenious design that allowed the exiled Kosovar Romanies in Belgrade to transform the vehicle to meet their needs.

Alice Bardan holds a PhD from the University of Southern California and now works as an Assistant Professor at Mount Saint Mary's University, Los Angeles, where she teaches film and literature courses. Her work has appeared in several edited collections, including *The Berlin School and Its Global Contexts: A Transnational Art Cinema* (2018); *Prostitution and Sex Work in Global Visual Media* (2017); *Work and Cinema: Labor and The Human Condition* (2012); *The Cinemas of Italian Migration: European and Transatlantic Narratives* (2013); *Not Necessarily the News? News Parody and Political Satire across the Globe* (2013); *Entertaining the New Europe: Popular Television in Socialist and Post-Socialist Europe* (2013); *The Blackwell Companion to East European Cinema*; *Transnational Feminism in Film and Media* (2012); and in the refereed journals *Feminist German Studies*; *Northern Lights: Film and Media Studies Yearbook*; *The European Journal of Cultural Studies*; *The Journal of Popular Television*; *Popular Communication*; *Flow*; and *New Cinemas*.

Notes

1. Barthes, "The New Citroën," 88.
2. "Gypsy" is a racialized, derogatory, and disparaging term used by outsiders to define the Roma people, the most discriminated and disadvantaged group in Europe. The introduction of the term "Roma" reflects an attempt to break away from social stigma and to produce a more positive image.
3. Gay y Blasco, "Picturing 'Gypsies,'" 297.
4. Iordanova, "Mimicry and Plagiarism," 307.
5. Iordanova, 308.
6. Imre, "Screen Gypsies," 18.
7. Mitić, "The Last of the Dyanacheros."
8. Schoonover, "Documentaries Without Documents," 497.
9. Wylie, "Human Waste?" 64.
10. Bennet, *Cycling and Cinema*, 68.
11. Bennet, 68.
12. Schoonover, *Brutal Vision*, 171.
13. Goldgel-Carballo, "The Reappropriation of Poverty," 117.
14. Goldgel-Carballo, 115.
15. Giorgi, "Improper Selves," 76.
16. Giorgi, 77.
17. Ybarra-Frausto, "Rasquachismo," 80.
18. Dery, "Rasquache Futurismos," 3.
19. Ybarra-Frausto, "Rasquachismo," 86.
20. Chappell, *Lowrider Space*, 2.
21. Hawkins, *The Ethics of Waste*, 88.
22. Hawkins, 88.

23. Clarsen, "Still Moving."
24. Bisschop et al., "Designed to Break," 278-279.
25. For more on the "Right to Repair" Movement see https://repair.eu/.
26. Bisschop et al., 286.
27. Schweitzer, "Rationalization of the Factory," 28.
28. Jonathan Glancey emphasizes that the car's brilliant simplicity was a hallmark of French design at the time, reflected, for instance, in the work of architect-engineer Jean Prouvé, who pioneered new structural techniques that would permit the efficient and inexpensive construction of buildings with prefabricated components, or that of locomotive engineer André Chapelon, who brought a rigorous scientific method to the design of steam locomotives. Glancey, "Objects of Our Time: Citroën 2CV," 23.
29. See, in this respect, Fabien Béziat's documentary *Renault versus Citroën: La Course du siècle* (*Renault versus Citroën: The Race of the Century*, 2011).
30. For a history of the Citroën in Romania during the 1980s, see Gatejel, "A Socialist–Capitalist Joint Venture."
31. Otoiu, "Automobile Metempsychoses," 203.
32. Orozco quoted in Amadou "Shade Between Rings of Air," 404.
33. Amadou, 404.
34. A website dedicated to the project can be found at https://finalfan.wordpress.com/about/.

Bibliography

Adamou, Natasha. "Shade Between Rings of Air: Architecture as Sculpture: Carlo Scarpa/Gabriel Orozco." *Sculpture Journal* 25. 3 (2016): 401-419.

Anderson, Maria. "A Lesson in 'Rasquachismo' Art: Chicano Aesthetics & the 'Sensibilities of the Barrio.'" *Smithsonian Insider* (2017). https://insider.si.edu/2017/01/lesson-rasquachismo-chicano-asthetics-taste-underdog/.

Barthes, Roland. "The New Citroën." In *Mythologies*, translated by Annette Lavers. New York: The Noonday Press, 1972 [originally published 1957]: 88–99.

Bennet, Bruce. *Cycling and Cinema*. Cambridge, MA: MIT Press, 2019.

Bisschop, Lieselot, Hendlin, Yogi, and Jaspers Jelle. "Designed to Break: Planned Obsolescence as Corporate Environmental Crime." *Crime, Law, and Social Change* 78 (2022): 271-293.

Chappell, Ben. *Lowrider Space: Aesthetics and Politics of Mexican American Custom Cars*. Austin: University of Texas Press, 2012.

Clarsen, Georgine. "Still Moving: *Bush Mechanics* in the Central Desert." *Australian Humanities Review* 25 (March 2002). http://australianhumanitiesreview.org/2002/03/01/still-moving-bush-mechanics-in-the-central-desert/.

Dery, Mark. "Rasquache Futurismos." *Review: Literature and Arts of the Americas* 48, no. 1 (2015): 3–5.

Gatejel, Luminita. "A Socialist–Capitalist Joint Venture: Citroën in Romania During the 1980s." *Journal of Transport History* 38, no. 1 (2017): 70–87.

Gay y Blasco, Paloma. "Picturing 'Gypsies' Interdisciplinary Approaches to Roma Representation." *Third Text* 22, no. 3 (2008): 297–303.
Giorgi, Gabriel. "Improper Selves: Cultures of Precarity." *Social Text* 31, no. 2 (2013): 69–81.
Glancey, Jonathan. "Objects of Our Time: Citroën 2CV." *Architects' Journal (London)* 184, no. 33 (1986): 20–32.
Goldgel-Carballo, Víctor. "The Reappropriation of Poverty and the Art of 'Making Do' in Contemporary Argentine Cultural Productions." *The Global South* 8, no. 1 (2014): 112–127.
Hawkins, Gay. *The Ethics of Waste: How We Relate to Rubbish.* Lanham: Rowman & Littlefield Publishers, 2006.
Imre, Anikó. "Screen Gypsies." *Framework* 44, no. 2 (Fall 2003): 15–33.
Iordanova, Dina. "Mimicry and Plagiarism: Reconciling Actual and Metaphoric Gypsies." *Third Text* 22, no. 3 (2008): 305–310.
Mitić, Boris. "The Last of the Dyanacheros." In *"Pretty Dyana*: Info Kit." Dribbling Pictures. http://dribblingpictures.com/wp-content/uploads/2012/03/PRETTY-DYANA-info-kit.pdf.
Morrison, Susan Signe. *The Literature of Waste: Material Ecopoetics and Ethical Matter.* New York: Palgrave Macmillan, 2015.
Otoiu, Adrian. "Automobile Metempsychoses in the Land of Dracula." In *Autopia: Cars and Culture,* edited by Peter Wollen and Joe Kerr, 199–209. London: Reaktion, 2002.
Schoonover, Karl. *Brutal Vision: The Neorealist Body in Postwar Italian Cinema.* Minneapolis: University of Minnesota Press, 2012.
———. "Documentaries Without Documents: Ecocinema and the Toxic." *NECSUS* 2, no. 2 (2013): 483–507.
Schweitzer, Sylvie. "Rationalization of the Factory, Center of Industrial Society: The Ideas of André Citroën." *International Journal of Political Economy* 24, no. 4 (1994): 11–34.
Wylie, Gillian. "Human Waste? Reading Bauman's *Wasted Lives* in the Context of Ireland's Globalization." In *Enacting Globalization,* edited by Louis Brennan, 57–66. New York: Palgrave, 2014.
Ybarra-Frausto, Tomas. "Rasquachismo: A Chicano Sensibility." In *Chicano and Chicana Art: A Critical Anthology,* edited by Jennifer A. González et al., 85–90. Durham, NC: Duke University Press, 2019 [originally published in 1989].
Zubiaurre, Maite. *Talking Trash: Cultural Uses of Waste.* Nashville: Vanderbilt University Press, 2019.

Filmography

Agrisano, Nicola. *A Mountain of Bales* (*Una montagna di balle,* Italy, 2009).
Antico, Sebastian. *The Nexus* (*El nexo,* Argentina, 2005).
Bafaloukos, Theodoros. *Rockers* (Jamaica, 1978).
Batty, David, and Francis Jupurrurla Kelly. *Bush Mechanics* (Australia, 2001).

Berlinger, Joe. *Crude* (United States, 2009).
Brady, Candida. *Trashed* (United Kingdom, 2012).
Calabria, Esmeralda, and Andrea D'Ambrosio. *Beautiful Country (Biùtiful cauntri,* Italy, 2008).
Conners, Leila, and Nadia Conners. *The 11th Hour* (United States, 2007).
De Sica, Vittorio. *Bicycle Thieves (Ladri di biciclette,* Italy, 1948).
Giraud, Jean. *The Gendarme and the Gendarmettes (Le Gendarme et les gendarmettes,* France, 1982).
Glen, John. *For Your Eyes Only* (United Kingdom and United States, 1981).
Gray, Gary F. *Straight Outta Compton* (United States, 2015).
Hess, Jared. *Napoleon Dynamite* (United States, 2004).
Leon, Federico, and Marcos Martinez. *Stars (Estrellas,* Argentina, 2007).
Mitić, Boris. *Pretty Dyana: A Gypsy Recycling Saga (Lijepa Dyana,* Serbia, 2003).
Nava, Gregory. *Selena* (United States, 1997).
Pejo, Robert Adrian. *Dallas among Us (Dallas Pashamende,* Hungary, 2005).
Prudente, Barbara Rossi. *The Baby Needs Some Fresh Air (La bambina deve presendere aria,* Italy, 2009).
Sembène, Ousmane. *The Cart Driver (Barom Sarret,* Senegal, 1963).
Walker, Lucy. *Waste Land* (United Kingdom and Brazil, 2010).
Žilnik, Želimir. *Early Works* (Rani radovi, Yugoslavia, 1960).

15

Foggy Past, Windy Present
Elemental Critique in Recent East Central European Artists' Films

Lukas Brasiskis

Elements surround us in various shapes and forms. From the atmospheric forces such as wind, fire, and water, to material remnants of natural phenomena, we make choices about how to coexist with elements—how to use them and how to face misuses of them.[1] Despite a recent turn toward the studies of connections between elements and mediation (or, simply, elemental media) exemplified by the works of Nicole Starosielski, Jeffrey Jerome Cohen, John Durham Peters, Yuriko Furuhata, Jussi Parikka, Melody Jue, and other scholars, the representation of elements in moving-image art has only recently started to be discussed in the field of film studies.[2] As Kristi McKim writes in her book *Cinema as Weather (2013)*, although throughout the history of the moving image medium weather has continually informed films' narratives and spectatorial experiences, images and sounds of elemental forces have not had much agency in film stories.[3] This is not because atmospheric or material elements on-screen are hard to notice, but because they have too often been taken for granted as a meaningless feature or, in a best-case scenario, a backdrop for suspenseful or melodramatic stories centered on human characters.

However, the consideration of the state of elements is changing in both film theory and film practice. With the rise of ecological awareness, the visualization of natural environments and atmospheric elements has become a closely scrutinized and widely discussed academic topic. For instance, in his article "Visualizing the Anthropocene," Nicholas Mirzoeff demonstrates how the interconnection of visibility and power determines the imaging of natural environments. In his words, the theory and practice of the conquest of nature has become integrated into the special place Western aesthetics has for the depiction of the natural realm. He suggests that the desire to depict natural environments through the beautification or instrumentalization of elemental forces—as if they existed just for entertainment and consumption, above history as well as cultural and sociopolitical contexts—is a remnant of imperialistic and colonizing views. Elemental visuality of this type is a representation of the position of power that controls the visibility of elements while ignoring the specificity of contexts that elements are situated in and disregarding the subjectivity of the filmic perspective itself.[4]

Mirzoeff's critique of elemental visuality can be applied to the analysis of postcommunist East Central European moving image art. As a number of contributors to this collection demonstrate, in the socialist period, many filmmakers from Eastern Europe conceived the depiction of the elemental world as a device to help activate, embellish, or spiritualize human-centered stories. Notable directors of art house cinema, such as Andrei Tarkovsky, Alexander Sokurov, and Sergei Parajanov, regularly relied on images of elements to employ the second and the third of the above-mentioned narrative functions. Their films celebrated the sensations of elements as an escape from political and social reality—associated with state control—into something transcendent that belonged to characters' inner lives and was meant to outlast the Soviet Union. The perception and assessment of the pristine and metaphysical nature of the elemental world in East Central European films, however, have shifted in tandem with changing political systems. Since the collapse of the Soviet Union and its satellite states, the everyday, often loaded with tangible traces of the past, has been considered to be the most productive setting for critical films and videos—whereas in the new, capitalist-era, abstract portraying of the elemental world as an escapist realm lost its critical potential.

As Mirzoeff points out, the aestheticization of the elemental for our admiration distracts us from sociopolitical concerns, "allow[ing] us to move on, to see nothing and keep circulating commodities."[5] Whereas "elemental countervisuality," to use Mirzoeff's term, first and foremost relies on the critical assessment of specific contexts that define elemental relations. This critical gesture—or, as I refer to it in this chapter, elemental critique—is performed without adhering to an immaterial and context-independent imaging of elements that embraces the position of the privileged and ignores the hierarchies that continue to produce one-sided and partial global visions of the world.

The relations between ideology and material infrastructures have to be brought to focus in order to understand the special role that elements played in East Central European countries during the transition from communism to capitalism. In the late 1980s and the early 1990s, the transformation of ideological functions of socialist-built infrastructures—industrial sites, political monuments, and urban architecture—marked the failure of dreams of communist progress. In the early 2000s, after coming to terms with the drastic changes caused by the collapse of the communist system, a number of East Central European moving image artists started to focus on (pointed their cameras at) the material remnants from the communist past. Ieva Epnere (Latvia), fantastic little splash (Ukraine), Ana Hušman (Croatia), Flo Kasearu (Estonia), Deimantas Narkevičius (Lithuania), Ilona Németh (Slovakia), Ilona Kristina Norman (Estonia), Oleksyi Radynski (Ukraine), Emilija Škarnulytė (Lithuania), Sophia Tabatadze (Georgia), and Krassimir Terziev (Bulgaria) are just a few of the many artists from postcommunist East Central Europe who, in their works, have focused on the material remnants freed from ideological tasks imposed on them during the communist times.

In contrast to traditional filmic representations of elements as background for anthropocentric stories, films by the aforementioned artists evoke the perspective in which material remnants, humans, and elements are inextricably woven together—a perspective in which they all are equally impacted by the new postcommunist sociopolitical context. Through the lenses of these moving image artists, endangered and obsolete, outmoded or simply wrecked environments acquire eco-materialist autonomy from their previous ideological roles. In their films and videos, spectral memories are embedded in the elemental surroundings that have continued to linger after the communist epoch passed. Importantly, these works concentrate on ex-socialist landscapes and infrastructures not just to document their alteration or disappearance but also to assess their critical implications on today's sociopolitical and environmental realities.

In this chapter, I focus on Ilona Németh's *The Fog* (*Hmla*, 2013) and Ana Hušman's *Almost Nothing* (2016), two artists' films that neither employ elements simply as backdrop for anthropocentric stories nor offer answers as to what elements are or what they do for us. Rather, they deliver critique *with* elements.[6] In what follows, I suggest that the films by these two acclaimed artists reflect Jeffrey Jerome Cohen's and Lowell Duckert's proposition that "human form is simply one composition among many, not the measure of the world" and portray what they call "elemental relations"—human and nonhuman entanglements that expose ubiquitous associations between elemental forces, material infrastructures, and humans.[7] According to Cohen, elemental relationships result in narrative involvement, creativity, and co-composition.[8] In Németh and Hušman's work, this narrative involvement contributes to a reevaluation of the transition from communism to capitalism.

Critique of Memory Politics in Ilona Németh's *The Fog*

During the communist era, successive leaders erected thousands of monuments in city squares to support their new myths and history. Statues honoring communist heroes went up all over the East Central European countries, erasing the collective memory of the pre-communist past. As Svetlana Boym writes, intentional erection of monuments made a claim not to the real past but to the immortality and eternal youth of communist history, to victory over time itself.[9] However, as Birgit Beumers and many others note, with the fall of the communist regimes, the material supports of collective memory irretrievably lost their ideological bearing.[10] Consequently, in the beginning of the 1990s, the majority of the monuments were dismantled, marking the mortality of these mnemonic supports of communist history across the region. The implications of this process of de-monumentalization have become a captivating subject for East Central European moving image artists who have started to contemplate, investigate, or criticize the monumentalization of the past and the transition from one political and economic system to the other. Ilona Németh, a Slovak artist of Hungarian origin, is one example.

Born in 1963, Németh is one of the most active figures in the first postcommunist generation of Slovak artists. Her works have been featured in numerous galleries and museums including Showroom in London, the United Kingdom; the Museum of Modern and Contemporary Art in Rijeka, Croatia; and Kunsthalle in Bratislava, Slovakia, among others. Known for her video installations, land art, and public activism, in *The Fog* Németh combines video, urban performance, and installation art. Installed in a number of contemporary art venues in Slovakia and around the world, *The Fog* is a single-screen video projection accompanied by textual information. The projected video begins with the image of a sculptural fountain positioned in the middle of a wide public square. Over the film's five-minute runtime, fog renders the entire square opaque before the fountain completely vanishes from sight. The slowly intensifying haze

Figure 15.1. *The Fog*. Created and directed by Ilona Németh. Bratislava: Slovak Ministry of Culture, 2013. Screen capture by Lukas Brasiskis from the artist's website.

around the monumental environment triggers an affect not unlike what one senses during early morning strolls through foggy urban sites. However, to recreate a sublime or melancholy experience of disappearing architecture is by no means the artist's ultimate goal.

The artist's statement accompanying *The Fog* highlights that what the viewer sees on-screen is a creative documentation of a public action that Németh organized and carried out in 2013. The intervention took place and was recorded in Bratislava, the capital of Slovakia, at the centrally located Freedom Square over the course of two early mornings in September. Layers of fog in the square were gradually unleashed by Németh herself, who used the artificial smoke grenades often applied by the law enforcement to combat public protests. The video of Freedom Square shrouded in a coating of what seems to be natural but is, in fact, manufactured fog alludes to the elimination of the architectural limitations of movement and expression that political powers impose on public spaces. According to Németh's artist statement, her intervention and its documentation were informed by the complicated history of the location where she filmed her video. Therefore, the historical context is crucial for comprehending the critique produced with elements in *The Fog*.

As Marián Potočár writes, in the early twentieth century, the centrally located square was an important site for events organized by a short-lived right-wing Slovak nationalist movement. From 1939 through 1945, the square hosted nationalists' rallies and mass rituals, as well as pro-Nazi military parades.[11] Whereas, in 1948, when the Czechoslovak Communist Party took power after the end of the Second World War, the square was renovated and renamed for Klement Gottwald, an early Czechoslovakian Communist Party leader. In the years that followed, communist authorities used the square as a place for their official events. The monumentalization of the square reached its peak in 1979, when a statue in memory of Gottwald and the huge steel Fountain of Unity were erected. During the last two decades of communist rule in Czechoslovakia, the square hosted a number of significant state-organized events, parades, and celebrations. Following the fall of socialist Czechoslovakia in 1992, Gottwald's statue was removed and the square regained its previous name. However, the colossal fountain that formerly symbolized the achievements of Czechoslovak socialism remained.

According to Potočár, various projects for new monuments in Freedom Square have been proposed over the past thirty years, but due to the so-called memory wars—the unsolvable disagreements about how the material heritage from the communist era should be approached—none of the proposals for a substitution to the fountain and the former Gottwald memorial have been realized. Due to lack of maintenance, the fountain stopped working in 2007 and has been out of order since then. Self-organized flash mobs in support of keeping the square for community use and against its re-monumentalization were confronted by counterprotests in support of erecting a new monument to victims of the communist regime. As a consequence, the deteriorating square has remained vacant and has become a site of encounter for contradictory discourses on the treatment of the past. The ideological discourse that formerly dominated the square has yet to be replaced by a new one.

This dramatic history of the square informed Németh's work. Through temporary effacement of the monumental architecture, *The Fog* questions the top-down narrative-based memory politics that strive to establish and maintain a monolithic understanding of the past. By performing the encounter between the atmospheric element and the dysfunctional ideological infrastructure, Németh's film not only reminds us of the ephemeral status of the material supports of dominant memory, but also acknowledges that the function of the public monument is always ideological and that there is no such thing as a site of memory that produces an objective version of the past. Indirectly referring to the antagonistic debates about the spectral importance of the communist past for the capitalist present and taking to task current political inclinations to memorialize the recent past by reterritorializing existing public spaces, the work criticizes the hierarchical attempts of new governments to instrumentalize history. Thus, due to its performative action—the activated collision between the fog and the humanmade structure, Németh's film can be seen as an elemental critique of memory politics in the postcommunist region.

Ana Hušman's *Almost Nothing*: Wind of Today

Ana Hušman's *Almost Nothing* (2016) is a similar case study.[12] Films by Hušman, a leading moving image artist in postcommunist Croatia, have been presented in various film festivals, as well as solo and group exhibitions, including the 9th Gwangju Biennale in Korea, the Ludwig Museum of Contemporary Arts in Hungary, the Doc Leipzig Festival in Germany, and the International Film Festival Rotterdam in Netherlands. The artist is known for her formal investigations of the possibilities for film to articulate the realities of the postcommunist everyday.

In *Almost Nothing* Hušman combines digital and analog footage to produce a critique of the capitalization of natural environments on the Croatian island of Korčula. After the demise of the communist Yugoslavia, the real estate on Korčula was privatized and new tourist infrastructures were built. By the early 2000s, the island, known for its picturesque landscapes, became a widely advertised tourist destination. The shift in administration of natural environments that accompanied the change of economic and political systems is one of the film's central concerns, expressed with an emphasis on the element of wind.

The film presents various manifestations of wind—from its consumer-oriented imagery produced for tourist consumption, to the audio recordings of wind and visual documentation of its effects on the ecosystem of the island. Structurally, Hušman's film is split into two parts. The first part examines the interiors of the tourist apartments situated on the island's coast. The second part introduces outdoor images of the island's flora. The indoor scenes are presented in long, static takes, recorded with a digital camera using the 16:9 screen aspect ratio, in empty hotel rooms whose stylized interiors (paintings, furniture, various souvenirs) refer to the natural and elemental imagery of the island's flora and fauna. While observing the standardized, kitschy images made from cheap materials and produced for the tourism industry indoors, one hears recordings of sounds of the wind blowing through the island and notices the swaying branches of trees outside of the hotel. A monotonous voice-over provides technical weather reports (based on the Beaufort Scale) emphasizing the wind's effects on the flora and fauna of the island.

The second part of *Almost Nothing* is shot outdoors on 16mm film using the 4:3 aspect ratio. In contrast to the static indoor shots, the camera here is shaky and unstable, opening more room for contingent images to oc-

Figure 15.2. *Almost Nothing*. Directed by Ana Hušman. Zagreb: Studio Pangolin, 2016. Screen capture by Lukas Brasiskis from the artist's website.

cupy the frame. Although the images in the second part of the film speak to both the wildness and tranquility of nature, the superimposed textual information disclosing shooting locations, typologies of wind heard, and classifications of plants, breaks the viewer's aesthetic appreciation of nature by meta-critically referring to human attempts to tame and quantify the contingency characteristic of natural environments. In this way, the film juxtaposes these contingent landscapes with new capitalist infrastructures that control and exploit elements, as emphasized in the first part of the film. As Hušman writes in her artist's statement, the pleasure of experiencing elements and nature "has been a political question since the birth of Europe. … The idea of a landscape has nothing in common with the idea of unspoiled nature. Landscapes are formed in planned processes of afforestation, controlled and planned planting influenced by economic, health and other policies documented in the systematic and taxonomic languages of the land registry."[13]

Thus, through the bipartite structure of her film, Hušman invites us to think about the interconnection between the natural elements that subsume human activities and human ambitions to capitalize and master nature. Although the hotel apartments' interiors are devoid of human characters, the human desire to administrate and manage nature is distinctly evident through the camera's emphasis on representations of domesticated natural elements, as well as the descriptive captions laid over the images of elemental forces . Hušman emphasizes this in her text about the film: "mapping the flora of the island, recording the resistance of the vegetation to the wind, and recording the sounds of friction, I document the sound signals that reflect the changes, fashions or economic conditions of a particular location. These cultivation policies remind houses and apartments like the wind, producing a complex feedback loop between interior and exterior space."[14]

Almost Nothing thus exposes elemental relations by repositioning the atmospheric element from "almost nothing" into a meaningful agent of critique that implicates the policies underlying the management of space and opposes the over-aestheticized views of the island that circulate in the travel market. Through contrasting visual and aural layers, the film critically exposes the contradictions of the postcommunist economic and political administration of nature. It reveals the anthropocentric view of nature and the aesthetics that implies. The film points out that the beautification and stylization of the elemental world goes hand in hand with the promotion of national identity and the economic exploitation of landscape. *Almost Nothing* thus focuses on the element of the wind to expose the mechanisms by which natural landscapes have been monetized.

In Lieu of Conclusion

In *The Marvelous Clouds* (2015), John Durham Peters suggests that elements themselves should be conceived of as media.[15] In his view, despite the fact that they surpass linguistic codes of communication, elements convey meanings. One of the uses of moving image art can thus be to expose viewers to elemental meanings. Affirming the importance of elemental relations—the interconnections between humans, materials, and elemental forces—the artists' films analyzed in this chapter exemplify the potential of the elemental critique. The stylization and staging of elemental forces in order to either reflect on dominant memory politics (as in the case of *The Fog*) or to expose capitalist exploitation of nature (as in the case of *Almost Nothing*) defies the traditional on-screen depiction of the elemental world. In these works, fog and wind do not only manifest themselves in their affective capacity, but also exert their power to critique the present as shaped by a particular historical context.

Through the application of elemental critique, both artists suggest that assumptions about natural sites and elemental forces are conditioned by the sociopolitical context informed by the official ideology of land management. It is as if their works state that elements, understood as something untouched by humans, can only exist where humans have chosen to set them up as spectacle. These films do not produce overtly environmentalist messages, but rather focus on the context-specific relations between human and environment, emphasizing the acceptance of impurity of the nature as a necessary strategy for elemental critique.

To conclude, I want to return to the question of elemental countervisuality. According to Mirzoeff, it cannot be produced while thinking in linear logic. According to him, it is achieved "in moments of rupture, resonance with similar moments in the past it suddenly becomes perceptible. We learn in such moments what it is to learn and what history might mean for those who are not the traditional victors."[16] Following this line of thought, I propose that through visualization of elements shaping the material remnants as critique rooted in specific historical conditions, Ilona Németh's and Ana Hušman's films offer a new perspective on a complex period of transition from communism to capitalism in Slovakia and Croatia, respectively. Relying on context-informed recording of elemental forces, they critique the standardization, management, and regulation of the material and natural environment. Both moving image works exemplify a view that refuses to adhere to clearly defined boundaries between human and nature, past and present, and instead recasts the discussion in terms of elemental relations within a particular historical context. They manage to produce affects and concepts that induce new political subjectivities, allowing us to revisit the failed project of Eastern European communism in times of exploitative capitalism.

Lukas Brasiskis is a film and media researcher and curator, with a PhD degree in Cinema Studies from New York University. He is an adjunct professor at NYU and CUNY/Brooklyn College and Associate Curator of Film and Video for e-flux. His interests include eco-media, the politics and aesthetics of world cinema, and the intersections between philosophy, moving-image cultures, and the contemporary art world. His texts were previously published in journals such as *Found Footage Magazine*, *The Cine-Files*, *Screening the Past*, and *Senses of Cinema*. He is a coeditor of *Jonas Mekas: The Camera Was Always Running* (2022).

Notes

1. As Melody Jue and Rafico Ruiz put it, the elemental evokes both ancient and contemporary sensibilities to include not only the four Greek elements, earth, air, wind, and fire, but also elements in the material structures, synthetic substances, or even the precarious melting of glaciers. Jue, *Wild Blue Media*, 5.
2. The recent spike in scholarly journal projects dedicated to this topic—including *Media+Environment*, a transnational and interdisciplinary ecomedia

research platform published by the University of California Press, and *The Journal of Environmental Media*, a scholarly platform to bridge work in environmental studies and screen media, published by Intellect—exemplifies the growing field of environmental media studies.
3. McKim, *Cinema as Weather*, 4.
4. Mirzoeff, "Visualizing the Anthropocene," 219.
5. Idem., 217.
6. I use the term "artists' films" to define films made by contemporary artists to avoid the terminology-related confusion related to the common misuse of the term "video art" perfectly described by Erika Balsom in the introduction to her book *After Uniqueness*, 7–8.
7. Cohen and Duckert, *Elemental Ecocriticism*, 12.
8. Cohen, "Elemental Relations," 58–59.
9. Boym, *The Future of Nostalgia*, 78.
10. Beumers, *World Film Locations: Moscow*, 7.
11. Potočár, "A Monument," 22–24.
12. Although *Almost Nothing* has been presented as both a single-screen film and an installation, here I focus on the single-screen version. Per the artist's website, the film, initiated in 2013, came about in the framework of a project entitled *Almost Nothing—Ferrari Dalmatia* that was dedicated to French composer Luc Ferrari, who, during his visit to the Korčula island in 1968, produced his best-known composition titled, "Almost Nothing No. 1. Dawn on a Seashore," in which he portrays the wind of the island by means of field recording. Ana Hušman's personal website, accessed January 30, 2021.
13. Ana Hušman's personal website, accessed January 30, 2021.
14. Ibidem.
15. Peters, *The Marvelous Clouds*, 6–10.
16. Mirzoeff, "Visualizing the Anthropocene," 229.

Bibliography

Balsom, Erika. *After Uniqueness: A History of Film and Video Art in Circulation*. Columbia University Press, 2018.
Beumers, Birgit. *World Film Locations: Moscow*. London: Intellect Publishing. 2014.
Boym, Svetlana. *The Future of Nostalgia*. New York: Basic Books, 2001.
Cohen, Jeffrey Jerome. "Elemental Relations." *O-Zone: A Journal of Object-Oriented Studies* 1 (2014): 53–61.
Cohen, Jeffrey Jerome, and Lowell Duckert. *Elemental Ecocriticism: Thinking with Earth, Air, Water, and Fire*. Minneapolis: University of Minnesota Press, 2015.
Demos, T. J. *Against the Anthropocene: Visual Culture and Environment Today*. New York and Berlin: Sternberg Press. 2017.
Jue, Melody. *Wild Blue Media: Thinking through Seawater*. Durham, NC: Duke University Press, 2020.

McKim, Kristi. *Cinema as Weather: Stylistic Screens and Atmospheric Change*. New York: Routledge, 2013.
Mirzoeff, Nicholas. "Visualizing the Anthropocene." *Public Culture* 26, no. 2 (2014): 213–232.
Peters, John Durham. *The Marvelous Clouds: Toward a Philosophy of Elemental Media*. Chicago: University of Chicago Press, 2015.
Potočár, Marián. "A Monument and a Blindspot – On the Precarious State of Modernist Architecture in Bratislava." *Field Journal* 6, no. 1 (2014): 19–36.

Filmography

Hušman, Ana. *Almost Nothing* (Croatia, 2016).
Németh, Ilona. *The Fog* (Slovakia, 2013).

Index

Abasiyanik, Sait Faik, 212n8
Abdullaeva, Zara, 181
Adel'shin, Marat, 185
Agrisano, Nicola: *A Mountain of Bales* (*Una montagna di balle*), 276
Ahmed, Sarah, 231
Aitmatov, Chingiz, 55–56
Alaniz, José, 4, 12
alterity, 76, 79, 166, 232, 233
Amadou, Natasha, 283
Andrejew, Piotr
　Groping One's Way (*Po omacku*), 107–8, 109, 119
　Tender Spots (*Czułe miejsca*), 10–11, 108–19
animals
　animals-out-of-place, 11, 151–52, 155
　Animus Animalis (Žegulytė), 154–55, 171
　On Body and Soul (Enyedi), 158–60, 164–67, 171, 172
　in Hungarian cinema, 158–72
　in Lithuanian documentary, 147–55
　The Old Man and the Land (Verba), 152–53
　Ten Minutes Before the Flight of Icarus (Matelis), 153
　Time Passes Through the City (Grikevičius), 149–52
　The Turin Horse (Tarr and Hranitzky), 158, 159, 160, 167–70, 171, 172
　Werckmeister Harmonies (Tarr), 161, 170–72
　White God (Mundruczó), 158–59, 160, 161–64, 170–71
Aninsky, Lev, 184
Anthropocene
　beginning of, 3, 14n7, 92
　definition of, 3
　ecocinema and, 220–21
　film noir and, 8
　K-9_topology (Smrekar) and, 226–28
　narrativization and, 221–23
　Survival Kit for the Anthropocene Trailer (Smrekar), 222
　The Tree (Prosenc) and, 229
　usefulness as critical framework, 4, 14n10
　"Visualizing the Anthropocene" (Mirzoeff), 289
Antico, Sebastian: *The Nexus* (*El nexo*), 278
antifuturism, 121n22
Arlauskaitė, Natalija, 11–12
Arnaud, Diane, 258
Astruc, Alexandre, 133
Avdeliodis, Dimos: *The Four Seasons of the Law* (*I earini synaxis ton agrofi lakon*), 200

Bafaloukos, Theodoros: *Rockers*, 278
Balabanov, Aleksei, 262–65, 267–68
　Cargo 200 (*Gruz 200*), 261, 264

Happy Days (*Schastlivye dni*), 262
Me Too (*Ya tozhe hochu*), 263–64
Morphine (*Morfiy*), 264
Of Freaks and Men (*Pro urodov i lyudey*), 263
Stoker (*Kochegar*), 262–63
War (*Voina*), 264
Balázs, Béla, 148
Barthes, Roland, 271–72
Bartunkova, Barbora, 10, 11
Batty, David: *Bush Mechanics*, 279–80
Bauman, Zygmunt, 277
Baxter, Anthony: *You Have Been Trumped*, 210
Benda, Bedřich, 88
Benjamin, Walter, 62n13, 188
Berger, John, 148
Berlinger, Joe: *Crude*, 276, 277
Berlin Wall, 5, 170
Beumers, Birgit, 291
Borowska-Kazimiruk, Sylwia, 244
Bousé, Derek, 148
Bozak, Nadia, 7–8
Brady, Candida: *Trashed*, 276, 277
Brasiskis, Lukas, 13
Bräunig, Werner: *Fairground* (*Rummelplatz*), 21, 22, 42n4
Brereton, Pat, 7
Briukhovetska, Olga, 11, 132
Brown, Kate, 125, 141n49
Brynych, Zbyněk: *Hunted and Suspected* (*Stíhán a podezrelý*), 29
Bulgaria, 196–211
  Black Sea coast, 12, 196–97, 201, 204–8, 213n23
  Dunovist movement (White Brotherhood), 211n4
  geopolitics, 200
  Karadere, 204–10, 213n24, 213n26
  periodization and, 200–201
  See also Vulchanov, Rangel
Burt, Jonathan, 159, 163, 166
Burtynsky, Edward, 279

Calabria, Esmeralda: *Beautiful Country* (*Biùtiful cauntri*), 276

calligraphy, cinema as, 111–13, 119
Čapek, Karel: *R. U. R.*, 121n18
Capitalocene, 4, 14n10
cars, 271–83
Citroën cars, 271–83
Carson, Rachel, 31
Chaplin, Charlie: *Modern Times*, 149
Chen, Mel, 187
Chernobyl Island nuclear accident, 3–4, 11, 124–25
  The Bell of Chernobyl (Sergienko), 125–30, 136
  Chernobyl (Mazin), 124–25, 138–39n5
  Chronicle of Difficult Weeks (Shevchenko), 125–30, 132–37
  iconography of, 131–32, 137
  Mi-crophone! (Shkliarevsky), 136, 141n49
  nationalization of, 132
  Theater of Operations—Chernobyl (Ministry of Defense), 136
Chthlucene, 14n10
Chytilov, Věra: *Daisies* (*Sedmikrásky*), 90–91, 101n21
Citroën, André, 281
Citroën cars, 271–83
Clarsen, Georgine, 280
climate change, 3, 9, 178, 180, 187–88, 190n9, 218, 221, 249–50
Cohen, Jeffrey Jerome, 288, 290–91
Colebrook, Claire, 221
colonialism and imperialism
  beautification of elemental forces and, 289
  The End of August at the Hotel Ozone (Schmidt) and, 88
  postcolonial turn, 2
  science fiction and, 67, 80n9, 88, 108
  scientific progress and, 67
  Stoker (Balabanov) and, 262–63
  subjectivity and, 65
commons, the, 12, 196–97, 201, 204–8, 213n23
Conners, Leila: *The 11th Hour*, 276
Conners, Nadia: *The 11th Hour*, 276
Connolly, Kate, 209

Corrigan, Timothy, 133, 135
Coumel, Laurent, 52
COVID-19 pandemic, 197
Cramer, Michael, 2, 13
Creed, Barbara, 166–67, 171
Croatia, 13, 291, 294–96, 297
Czechoslovakia and Czech Republic
    Barrandov Film Studios, 89
    FAMU, 88–89, 90
    New Wave, 88–89, 91
    Normalization era, 29–30, 31, 103–4n61
    See also Dušek, Martin; Ore Mountains; Rychlík, Břetislav; Schmidt, Jan

D'Ambrosio, Andrea: *Beautiful Country (Biùtiful cauntri)*, 276
Damyanov, Miroslav, 210
Danailov, Georgi, 198–99
Daneliya, Georgiy: *Kin-Dza-Dza!*, 76–77, 79
Deepwater Horizon oil spill, 187
Deleuze, Gilles, 161, 169, 256, 263
De Luca, Raymond, 12
Derrida, Jacques, 95
De Sica, Vittorio: *Bicycle Thieves (Ladri di biciclette)*, 277–78
disaster film, 10–11
    documentaries about Chernobyl Island nuclear accident, 125–37
    The End of August at the Hotel Ozone (Schmidt), 10, 11, 29, 87–100
    Tender Spots (Andrejew), 10–11, 108–19
DJ Smash, 185
Dobson, Miriam, 10
Donev, Alexander, 211n2, 211n5
Dostoevsky, Fyodor, 167, 254
Dovzhenko, Oleksandr, 181
    Earth (Zemlia), 3, 130
    Poem of the Sea (Poema o morye), 10, 45n47, 51, 54–55, 61
Drachsel, Burghard: *The Vanishing Villages of Wismut (Die verschwundene Dörfer der Wismut)*, 25, 38–39

Duckert, Lowell, 290–91
Dufek, Antonín, 26, 27, 43n17
Duša, Ferdiš, 28
Dušek, Martin: *Coal in the Soul (Ženy SHR)*, 30, 37, 40
dystopianism, 10, 110, 170. *See also* utopianism

Eastern Europe, use of the term, 6
ecocinema
    Anthropocene and, 220–21
    crises and, 219
    defining, 7–9
    experimental ecocinema, 224–26
    global ecocinema, 8
    goal of, 7, 222
    imaginary in, 221
    inclusive, process-oriented vision of, 8
    national traditions of, 12–13
    regional approach to, 6–7
    scholarship, 2, 7–9, 10, 233, 249
    Siberian cinema and, 6
    use of the term, 7
ecocriticism, 11, 13, 217
    Polish cinema and, 238–50
    regional approach to, 6–7
    Slovenian cinema and, 222
Eisenstein, Sergei, 255, 264
    on close-up shots of animals, 153
    contributions to essay film, 133
    The Old and the New (Staroye i novoye), 3
elemental critique, 288–97
    capitalization of natural elements, 294–95
    elemental countervisuality, 289, 297
    elemental relationships, 290–91, 296–97, 299
    elemental visuality, 289
    infrastructure and, 290–91, 293, 294–95
    monuments and, 291–94
Engelke, Peter, 4
Engström, Maria, 179, 184, 192n37
Enlightenment, 198

environmental films, 7, 127–28
Enyedi, Ildikó
   On Body and Soul (*Testről és lélekről*), 158–60, 164–67, 171, 172
   Magic Hunter (*Bűvös vadász*), 164
   My Twentieth Century (*Az én XX. Századom*), 164
Epstein, Mikhail, 137–38
essay film, 133–37
Estok, Simon, 233
Etkind, Alexander, 177–78, 182, 184, 185
European Union, 5, 12, 209, 217, 219–20, 239

Fay, Jennifer, 8, 92
Felman, Shoshana, 136
Filla, Emil, 26–27, 28, 29
film noir, 8
Forman, Zdeněk: *We Are Building the Borderlands* (*Budujeme pohraničí*), 25, 26–29, 43n21
Fowkes, Maja, 224
Frammartino, Michelangelo: *The Four Times* (*Le Quattro Volte*), 200
Frank, Karl Hermann, 24
Freud, Sigmund, 95, 113, 116, 121n19, 167
Furuhata, Yuriko, 288
futurity, 8
Fyodorov, Nikolai, 180, 187, 189

Gees, Johannes, 283
gender
   Anthropocene and, 222, 226
   in disaster film, 10, 115–16, 130
   matriarchy, 11
   in petro-cinema, 272
   in science fiction film, 70–76, 94–95
   wage gap, 281
Gerasimov, Sergei: *By the Lake* (*U ozera*), 3
German, Aleksei, 2, 255, 264–68
   Hard to Be a God (*Trudno byt' bogom*), 265, 267
   Khrustalyov, My Car! (*Khrustalyov, mashinu!*), 264–67
   My Friend Ivan Lapshin (*Moy drug Ivan Lapshin*), 264, 267
German Democratic Republic (GDR), 4, 6
environmentalist film, 31–39
   Ore Mountains and, 22–25, 32–40, 42nn4–5
   Wismut (Soviet uranium mine), 21–25, 33–35, 38–39, 42n1, 42n4
Gierek, Edward, 109
Giraud, Jean: *The Gendarme and the Gendarmettes* (*Le Gendarme et les gendarmettes*), 282
Glancey, Jonathan, 285n28
Glass, Philip, 259
Glassheim, Eagle, 24
Glen, John: *For Your Eyes Only*, 282
Global South, 2
Goldgel-Carballo, Víctor, 278
Gonopolsky, Igor: *Scenes at a Fountain* (*Stseny u fontana*), 128
Gorbachev, Mikhail, 4, 124, 125, 128, 132, 139–40n23, 140n27, 141n49
Gottwald, Klement, 293
Gray, Gary F.: *Straight Outta Compton*, 279
Great Acceleration, 4
Grikevičius, Almantas: *Time Passes Through the City* (*Laikas eina per miestą*), 149–52
Guattari, Félix, 161
Guggenheim, Davis: *An Inconvenient Truth*, 7
Guillermin, John: *The Bridge at Remagen*, 29
Gurshtein, Ksenya, 223, 224
Gustafsson, Tommy, 8

Hajdu, Szabolcs: *Tamara*, 171
Hansen, Oskar, 107, 119
Haraway, Donna, 14n10, 159, 163
Hawkins, Gay, 280
Haytov, Nikolay, 198–99, 201
Heath, Stephen, 154
Heise, Ursula, 2, 6
Herzog, Werner, 6

Hess, Jared: *Napoleon Dynamite*, 279
Higginbotham, Adam, 125
Hiroshima atomic bombing, 91, 132, 133
Hitchcock, Alfred: *Vertigo*, 93
Hitchcock, Peter, 178, 184, 190n9
Hlaváč, Roman, 88
Holland, Agnieszka: *Spoor* (*Pokot*), 13, 171, 239, 244–48, 249, 251n15
Horton, Andrew, 184
Hranitzky, Ágnes: *The Turin Horse* (*A torinói ló*), 158, 159, 160, 167–70, 171, 172
Hristoforov, Asen, 200–201
Hristov, Hristo: *A Tree Without Roots* (*Darvo bez koren*), 198
Hučková, Jadwiga, 127
Hungary, 158–72. *See also* Enyedi, Ildikó; Hranitzky, Ágnes; Mundruczó, Kornél; Tarr, Béla
Hušman, Ana: *Almost Nothing*, 294–96, 298n12
hybridization, 227, 279

Ibragimbekov, Murad: *Oil* (*Neft'*), 186
IC3PEAK, 186–89
Ilichevskiy, Aleksandr, 192n45
imperialism. *See* colonialism and imperialism
industrialization, 1–3, 8–9, 28, 54–55, 110, 117, 218
Industrial Revolution, 14n7
Ingram, David, 9, 11
Iordanova, Dina, 12, 273
Iovino, Serenella, 231–32
Ivanov, Hristo: *The Fight with the Untouchable Ahmed Dogan Had Begun*, 197

Jachnin, Boris, 99
Jakubisko, Juraj: *The Deserters and the Nomads* (*Zbehovia a pútnici*), 99, 103–4n61
Jameson, Fredric, 257, 259, 265, 267–68
Jasný, Vojtěch
  All My Good Countrymen (*Všichni dobří rodáci*), 42–43n14
  We Are Building the Borderlands (*Budujeme pohraničí*), 25, 26–29, 43n21
Jireš, Jaromil: *The Hall of Lost Footsteps* (*Sál ztracených kroků*), 90, 91, 102n24
Jonáš, Milan, 94
Jue, Melody, 288, 297n1
Jupurrurla, Francis: *Bush Mechanics*, 279–80
Juráček, Pavel, 87, 88–89

Kääpä, Pietari, 6, 8, 241
Kachyňa, Karel, 42–43n14
  Long Live the Republic (*At' zije republika*), 89
  We Are Building the Borderlands (*Budujeme pohraničí*), 25, 26-29
Kadyrbekova, Zora, 159–60
Kalatozov, Mikhail
  The Cranes Are Flying (*Letiat zhuravli*), 50, 60
  The First Echelon (*Pervyi eshelon*), 10, 51, 53–54, 56, 62n9
  The Unsent Letter (*Nieotpravlennoye pis'mo*), 10, 49–51, 58–61
Kalinin, Ilya, 179–80, 187–88, 189, 190n14
Kalmár, György, 170–71
Kaplanoglu, Semih, 200
Karyukov, Mikhail: *Toward a Dream* (*Mechte navstrechu*), 65, 67–71, 80n2
Khrushchev, Nikita, 51–52, 53, 69
Kirchhof, Astrid Mignon, 3, 5
Kisielewska, Alicja, 240
Klimov, Elem, 127
Klushantsev, Pavel
  Planet of the Storms (*Planeta bur'*), 65, 72–73
  Road to the Stars (*Doroga k zvezdam*), 71–72
Koberidze, Otar: *Toward a Dream* (*Mechte navstrechu*), 65, 67–71, 80n2
Koepp, Volker: *Wismut* (*Die Wismut*), 21–23, 35
Kolditz, Gottfried: *White Blood* (*Weißes Blut*), 22

Konchalovsky, Andrei, 6
Konczal, Agata Agnieszka, 240
Kotevska, Tamara: *Honeyland* (*Medena zemja*), 213n20
Koudelka, Josef: *The Black Triangle* (*Černý trojúhelník*), 28–29, 30
Kozel, Dalibor, 27
Kozole, Damjan, 234
Kripchenko, Viktor, 125–26
Królikiewicz, Grzegorz: *Trees* (*Drzewa*), 13, 239, 241–44, 248–49
Kubeké, Sabina, 120n10
Kubrick, Stanley: *2001: A Space Odyssey*, 72
Kumerdej, Mojca, 222

labor strikes, 27, 110, 127
Latour, Bruno, 14n7, 62n13, 280
Laub, Dori, 136
Lavrinec, Jekaterina, 152
LeMenager, Stephanie, 178–79, 190n10
Leon, Federico: *Stars* (*Estrellas*), 278
Levi-Strauss, Claude, 272, 274
Lewis, Simon, 246
Lindbladh, Johanna, 11
Lippmann, Günther, 35
Lithuania, 5, 11–12, 147–55. *See also* Grikevičius, Almantas; Matelis, Arūnas; Verba, Robertas; Žegulytė, Aistė
Lopushansky, Konstantin: *Dead Man's Letters* (*Pisma mertvogo cheloveka*), 3, 11, 78, 79
Lovejoy, Alice, 6–7, 9–10, 88, 89
Lu, Sheldon H., 8
Lutsik, Piotr: *The Outskirts* (*Okraina*), 180–84, 188–89

MacDonald, Scott, 7, 222, 224
Mácha, Karel Hynek, 28
Machulski, Juliusz: *Sexmission* (*Seksmisja*), 11, 120n3, 121n17
Majsova, Natalija, 10
Malishev, Igor, 127, 137
Malm, Andreas, 4
Manovich, Lev, 92

Mantsov, Igor, 182, 183–84, 191n34
Marker, Chris
  La Jetée, 93
  Sunless (*Sans Soleil*), 141n55
Martinez, Marcos: *Stars* (*Estrellas*), 278
Marx, Karl, 32, 133, 261
Marxism, 32, 111, 263, 267
Masaryk, Tomáš G.: *Sad Landscape* (*Smutná krajina*), 28
masculinity, 70, 109, 112, 116, 118, 121n17, 246–47, 277
  petromachismo, 182–83, 188
Matanović, Milenko: *The Snake*, 223
Matelis, Arūnas: *Ten Minutes Before the Flight of Icarus* (*Desimt minuciu pries Ikaro skrydi*), 153
Matizen, Viktor, 183
Mazaj, Meta, 12
Mazin, Craig: *Chernobyl*, 124–25, 138–39n5
McKim, Kristi, 288
McNeill, J. R., 3, 4, 5
memory politics, 291–94, 296
Mi, Jiayan, 8
Mihailova, Mihaela, 181, 184
mining. *See* Ore Mountains
Mirchev, Ivailo: *The Fight with the Untouchable Ahmed Dogan Had Begun*, 197
Mirzoeff, Nicholas, 289, 297
mise-en-scène, 112–13, 182, 228, 262
Mitchell, W. J. T., 188
Mitić, Boris: *Pretty Dyana: A Gypsy Recycling Saga* (*Lij epa Dyana*), 272–83
Molodkin, Andrei, 179
Monsiváis, Carlos, 278
Moore, Jason W., 4
Morrison, Susan Signe, 277
Mosfilm, 51, 58
Mundruczó, Kornél: *White God* (*Fehér isten*), 158–59, 160, 161–64, 170–71
Murawski, Michał, 120–21n11
Murdock, Caitlin E., 23
Murphet, Julian, 168
music videos, 12, 185–86, 192n43, 192n49

Muybridge, Eadweard, 151, 168

Nagasaki atomic bombing, 132
Naimark, Norman, 42n5
narrativization, 221–23, 228–29, 232–33
Natalia LL: *Consumption Art* (*Sztuka konsumpcyjna*), 109, 120n6
nationalism, 8, 24–28, 32, 43n21
    cars and, 283
    Eastern European cinema and, 8
    land and, 260
    music videos and, 185
    Slovakian, 292
    state-sponsored, Russian, 189n4
    transnationalism, 244–48
    Ukrainian, 131
Nava, Gregory: *Selena*, 279
Naydenov, Dimitar: *The Fight with the Untouchable Ahmed Dogan Had Begun*, 197
Nazi Germany, 23, 30, 32, 37, 254, 292–93
Nekrasov, Nikolai, 253
Němcová, Božena: *Grandmother* (*Babička*), 28, 43n21
Németh, Ilona: *The Fog* (*Hmla*), 290–94, 297
neoliberalism, 111, 170, 177, 185, 196, 207, 220, 222, 244, 261
Nez, David: *Mirrors*, 223–24
nongovernmental organizations (NGOs), 52, 209
Norilsk diesel oil spill, 192–93n53
nuclear power plants, 1, 4. *See also* Chernobyl Island nuclear accident
nuclear war, 10, 22, 78, 89, 90, 93, 103n53, 128, 139–40n23, 140n27
    The End of August at the Hotel Ozone (Schmidt), 10, 11, 29, 87–100

oil industry. *See* petro-cinema
Olmi, Ermanno: *The Tree of Wooden Clogs* (*L'Albero degli zoccoli*), 200
Oppermann, Servil, 231–32
Ore Mountains, 6–7, 9–10, 22–25, 40–41, 42n1

geopolitics, 25, 27
mine strikes, 27
nationalist photobooks and newsreels, 24, 25
population demographics, 23–24
post-1989 documentaries, 21–22, 30, 33–35, 37–39
post-1989 photographs and paintings, 25–30
socialist-era documentaries, 33–37
Wismut (Soviet uranium mine), 21–25, 33–35, 38–39, 42n1, 42n4
Orozco, Gabriel, 283
Others and Otherness, 8, 73–74, 220–21, 229, 231–33, 273
Oukaderova, Lida, 6, 10

Painlevé, Jean: *The Octopus* (*La pieuvre*), 148
Pálfi, György: *Hukkle*, 171
Papazov, Boyan, 201
Parikka, Jussi, 288
Past, Elena, 6, 8
Pavlov, Mikhail: *The BAM Zone: Permanent Residents* (*Zona BAM. Postoyannye zhiteli*), 127–28
Pelevin, Viktor, 179–80, 187
Peters, John Durham, 288, 296
petro-cinema, 4, 177–89, 192n51
    depths motif in, 181–82, 184–85, 188
    oil-doused figures in, 186–88
    The Outskirts (Lutsik), 180–84
    Putin-era Russian oil films, 184–89
petromachismo, 182–83, 188
petromodernity, 178
petropoetics, 179
Philo, Chris, 163
Plach, Eva, 159–60
Plokhy, Serhii, 125, 141n48
Pogačnik, Marko: *Water-Water Dynamic*, 223
Polák, Jindřich: *XB 1*, 89
Poland, 238–50
    Environmental Protection and Development Act, 110
    forest motif and, 238–50

Lenin Shipyard strike, 110
masculinity and, 109, 112, 116, 118, 121n17
See also Andrejew, Piotr; Holland, Agnieszka; Królikiewicz, Grzegorz
postcolonial studies, 2
postcolonial turn, 2
Potočár, Marián, 292–93
Povolotskaya, Irina: *The Mysterious Wall* (*Tainstvennaya stena*), 65, 73–74, 75, 79
Prague Spring, 29, 43n17
Praznik, Katja, 220
Prosenc, Sonja, 12, 222
The Tree (*Drevo*), 228–34
Protazanov, Iakov: *Aelita: Queen of Mars* (*Aelita*), 66, 68, 70, 76, 80n9
Prudente, Barbara Rossi: *The Baby Needs Some Fresh Air* (*La bambina deve presendere aria*), 276
Pushkin, Alexander: *The Bronze Horseman*, 253
Pussy Riot, 186
Putin, Vladimir, 177–78, 179, 184, 186, 189n3, 191n34, 198, 213n23, 259, 260, 261

quarantine zones, 78

Radichkov, Yordan, 198
Rak, Jiří, 43n21
Rascaroli, Laura, 133, 135–36
Razlogov, Kirill, 181
Reagan, Ronald, 4, 140n27
reflexivity, 133, 134–35, 137, 225–26, 262
Reich, Jan, 43–44n26
Repin, Ilya: *Barge Haulers on the Volga*, 254
"return to nature" ideology, 196–210
Rousseau and, 198–99, 208, 211n4
See also Vulchanov, Rangel
"return to the village" ideology, 198–99, 209

Roeg, Nicholas: *The Man Who Fell to Earth*, 76
Rogers, Douglas, 181, 189n4
Roma people, 44n27, 272–83
Rose, Eliza, 10–11, 102n36
Rousseau, Jean-Jacques, 198–99, 208, 211n4
Ruiz, Rafico, 297n1
Russell, Catherine, 147, 151
Russia. See Soviet Union and Russia
Ruttmann, Walter: *Berlin: Symphony of a Great City* (*Berlin: Die Sinfonie der Großstadt*), 149
Ryan, Derek, 159
Rychlík, Břetislav: *God's Stone Quarry: One Year in Northern Bohemia* (*Kamenolom boží aneb jeden rok v Severních Čechách*), 30, 37, 39

Sadkovich, Mikhail: *The Mysterious Wall* (*Tainstvennaya stena*), 65, 73–74, 75, 79
Šalamun, Andraž, 223
Sayer, Derek, 27
Schmidt, Jan: *The End of August at the Hotel Ozone* (*Konec srpna v hotelu Ozon*), 10, 11, 29, 87–100
Schoonover, Karl, 276–77, 278
Schuppli, Susan, 135
science fiction film, 10, 64–80
Andromeda Nebula (Sherstobitov), 65, 70–71, 73–74, 75
The End of August at the Hotel Ozone (Schmidt), 10, 11, 29, 87–100
The Moon Rainbow (Yermash), 65, 77–79
The Mysterious Wall (Povolotskaya), 65, 73–74, 75, 79
near-reach formula, 66–67
The Nexus (Antico), 278
Per Aspera Ad Astra (Viktorov), 65, 76–77, 79
Planet of the Storms (Klushantsev), 65, 72–73
space melodramas, 67

Toward a Dream (Karyukov), 65, 67–71, 80n2
  world-building, 65, 66, 69, 75, 79–80
Sembène, Ousmane: *The Cart Driver (Barom Sarret)*, 278
Sergienko, Rollan: *The Bell of Chernobyl (Kolokol Chernobylia)*, 125–30, 136
Shepitko, Larisa: *Heat (Znoi)*, 10, 51, 55–58
Sherstobitov, Yevgeni: *Andromeda Nebula (Tumannost' Andromedy)*, 65, 70–71, 73–74, 75
Shevchenko, Vladimir
  Chronicle of Difficult Weeks (Chernobyl: khronika trudnykh nedel'), 125–30, 132–37
  Kulunda: Hopes and Anxieties (Kulunda: trevogi i nadezhdy), 130
Shkliarevsky, Georgi: *Mi-cro-phone! (Mi-kro-fon!)*, 136, 141n48
Shpolberg, Masha, 11
Siberia, 6, 49–52, 178, 180, 186
Sinelnikov, Vladimir: *The Bell of Chernobyl (Kolokol Chernobylia)*, 125–27, 139–40n23
Skolimowski, Jerzy: *Essential Killing*, 248–50
Ślesicki, Władysław: *Summer of the Forest People (Lato leśnych ludzi)*, 239–41, 250n5
Slovakia, 5, 291–94, 297
Slovenia, 217–34
  democratization, 217, 219, 234
  independence, 217
  national film production, 219–20
  OHO Group, 12, 223–24
  sustainability and environmentalism, 217–18
  See also Prosenc, Sonja; Smrekar, Maja; Zdravič, Andrej
slow cinema, 7
Smrekar, Maja, 12, 235n21
  K-9_topology, 222, 226–28
  Survival Kit for the Anthropocene—Trailer, 222

Soderbergh, Steven: *Erin Brockovich*, 7
Sokurov, Alexander, 2, 6, 13, 255, 256–59, 264–65, 267–68, 289
  Days of the Eclipse (Dni zatmeniya), 258, 259
  Faust, 258
  Lonely Voice of Man (Odinokiy golos cheloveka), 257
  Moloch (Moloch), 258–59
  Mother and Son (Mat' i syn), 258
  Mournful Unconcern (Skorbnoye bezchustviye), 257
  Russian Ark (Russkiy kovcheg), 258, 259, 268
  Save and Protect (Spasi i sokhrani), 258
  The Second Circle (Krug vtoroi), 258
  The Stone (Kamen'), 258
  Taurus (Telets), 258, 259
Solntseva, Yulia: *Poem of the Sea (Poema o morye)*, 10, 45n47, 51, 54–55, 61
Sontag, Susan, 10, 160
Sophia, Zornitsa: *Forecast (Prognoza)*, 203
Soviet Union and Russia
  All-Union Institute of Cinematography (VGIK), 55, 129, 151
  collapse of the Soviet Union, 1, 2, 4, 170, 291
  first Soviet Five Year Plan, 3
  glasnost, 38, 124, 127, 131, 134, 137
  Lennauchfilm, 71, 75
  oil ontology and petro-cinema, 12, 177–89
  perestroika, 137, 257
  Soviet utopianism, 42n4, 67, 75–76, 188–89, 254–58, 261–64, 267–68
  Thaw era, 1, 10, 50–61, 67, 69, 129, 256
  Wismut (uranium mine in East Germany), 21–25, 33–35, 38–39, 42n1, 42n4
  See also Chernobyl Island nuclear accident; science fiction film

Spurný, Matěj, 27, 31–32
Spurný, Miloš, 43n17
Stalinism and Joseph Stalin, 25, 50, 70
  infrastructure under, 3, 254
  in *Khrustalyov, My Car!*, 265
  "near-reach" formula, 66–67
  post-Stalinist period, 53
  productivism, 32
  repression under, 255
  science fiction under, 66–67
  social realism, 66
  spaceflight as symbol of, 72
  vysotka (high-rise apartment building), 180
Stankov, Kiril: *Krapetz*, 212n10
Stanković, Peter, 220
Starosielski, Nicole, 288
Stefanov, Ljubomir: *Honeyland (Medena zemja)*, 213n20
Stöhr, Lóránt, 136
Stoyanov, Svetoslav: *The Last Black Sea Pirates (Poslednite Chernomorski pirati)*, 12, 196, 203, 204–8, 209, 210
Strugatsky, Arkady, 75
  Days of Eclipse (Dni zatmeniya), 257
  Stalker, 257
Strugatsky, Boris, 75
  Days of Eclipse (Dni zatmeniya), 257
  Stalker, 257
Sudek, Josef, 43n17
  Panoramic Prague (Praha Praha panoramatická), 26, 28–29
  Sad Landscape (Smutná krajina), 26, 27–28
Survila, Mindaugas: *The Ancient Woods (Sengirė)*, 148
Szaniawski, Jeremi, 2, 13
Szczepanik, Petr, 29
Szulkin, Piotr, 111
  Ga-ga: Glory to the Heroes (Ga, ga. Sława bohaterom), 108

Tanovic, Danis: *An Episode from the Life of an Iron Picker (Epizoda u životu berača željeza)*, 207
Tarkovsky, Andrei, 254, 256–58, 263, 265
  Mirror (Zerkalo), 261
  Solaris, 73–74, 75, 79
  Stalker, 3, 11, 75, 257, 261
Tarr, Béla
  The Turin Horse (A torinói ló), 158, 159, 160, 167–70, 171, 172
  Werckmeister Harmonies (Werckmeister harmóniák), 161, 170–72
Tetzlaff, Kurt
  The Garnison Church: Protocol of a Destruction (Die Garnisonkirche - Protokoll einer Zerstörung), 37–38
  Memories of a Landscape—For Manuela (Erinnerung an eine Landschaft – für Manuela), 36–37
Three Mile Island nuclear accident, 3–4
Three Worlds system, 14n7
Timoshenko, Semyon: *Napoleon Gas (Napoleon-gaz)*, 80n9
Todorov, Lyudmil: *The Summer Love of a Schlep (Lyubovnoto lyato na edin lyokhman)*, 203
trauma
  ecocinema and, 219
  forest as place of, 228, 231, 232, 244
  nuclear disasters and, 93, 132–33, 136
  of Petersburg, 253
  of the twentieth century, 25, 181
  of war, 262, 263
Trinity Test, 3
Trumpener, Katie, 6–7, 9–10
Tschirner, Joachim: *The Vanishing Villages of Wismut (Die verschwundene Dörfer der Wismut)*, 25, 38–39

Uexküll, Jakob Johann von, 65
Uhlig, Graig, 233
Ukraine, 5, 45n47, 54, 290. *See also* Chernobyl Island nuclear accident
Umwelt, 45n48, 65
Urusevsky, Sergei, 49–50, 51, 58, 62n9
utopianism
  climate change and, 190n9

Soviet utopianism, 42n4, 67, 75–76, 188–89, 254–58, 261–64, 267–68

Vančura, Vladislav: *Marketa Lazarová,* 28
Van Heuckelom, Kris, 12–13
Velvet Revolution, 26, 28
Verba, Robertas: *The Old Man and the Land* (*Senis ir žemė*), 152–53
Vertov, Dziga, 255
   Enthusiasm: Symphony of the Donbass (*Entuziazm: simfoniya donbassa*), 3
   "the interval" concept of, 133
   Man with a Movie Camera (*Chelovek s kinoapparatom*), 149
Vertov, Dziga: *Man with a Movie Camera* (*Chelovek s kino apparatom*), 149
Viktorov, Richard: *Per Aspera Ad Astra* (*Cherez ternii k zvezdam*), 65, 76–77, 79
Vivanco, Luis, 245
voice-overs, 34, 36, 68, 127, 129, 133–35, 137, 232, 247–48, 265, 294
Vulchanov, Rangel, 198–99, 202
   Aesop (*Ezop*), 202
   Escape to Ropotamo (*Byagstvo v Ropotamo*), 202–3
   The Sun and the Shadow (*Slantseto i syankata*), 202
   Where Are You Going? (*Za kade patuvate*), 199

Walker, Lucy: *Waste Land,* 276
Wanner, Catherine, 132
Waśko, Ryszard, 111
Weiss, Jiří: *Song of Subcarpathian Rus'* (*Píseň o Podkarpatské rusi*), 28
Wilbert, Chris, 163
Willoquet-Maricondi, Paula, 9, 12, 221, 224
Wolf, Korad: *Sun Seekers* (*Sonnensucher*), 22, 42n4

Wylie, Gillian, 277

Yanchev, Vladimir: *The Ancient Coin* (*Die antike Münze*), 202
Ybarra-Frausto, Tomás, 272, 279
Yeltsin, Boris, 178, 180, 259
Yermash, Andrei: *The Moon Rainbow* (*Lunnaya raduga*), 65, 77–79
Yurchak, Alexei, 108, 109, 120n4, 121n22

Zakhariev, Chris: *Getting Lost on Purpose* (*Da se izgubish narochno*), 199
Zchoche, Hermann: *Eolomea,* 202
Zdravič, Andrej, 12, 222
   experimental ecocinema of, 224–26, 228, 233
   Riverglass: A River Ballet in Four Seasons (*V steklu reke*), 7, 224–25
   Secrets of Soča (*Skrivnosti Soče*), 224–25
Žegulytė, Aistė: *Animus Animalis* (*A Story about People, Animals and Things*) (*Animus Animalis: istorij a apie žmones, žvėris ir daiktus*), 154–55, 171
Zhelyazkova, Binka: *The Big Night Bath* (*Golyamoto noshtno kupane*), 203, 212n14
Žilnik, Želimir: *Early Works* (*Rani radovi*), 281–82
Zubiaurre, Maite, 277
Zvyagintsev, Andrey, 13, 255, 259–61, 268
   Elena, 259, 260
   Leviathan (*Leviafan*), 259, 260
   Loveless (*Nelyubov*), 259, 261
   The Return (*Vozvrashcheniye*), 259–60, 261

Printed in the USA
CPSIA information can be obtained
at www.ICGtesting.com
LVHW012001160324
774517LV00004B/505